Y0-BNP-151

THE ORIGINS OF THE ENGLISH
MARRIAGE PLOT

Why did marriage become central to the English novel in the eighteenth century? Because as clandestine weddings and the unruly culture that surrounded them began to threaten power and property, questions about where and how to marry became urgent matters of public debate. In 1753, in an unprecedented and controversial use of state power, Lord Chancellor Hardwicke mandated Anglican Church weddings as marriage's only legal form. Resistance to his Marriage Act would fuel a new kind of realist marriage plot in England and help to produce political radicalism as we know it. Focussing on how major authors from Samuel Richardson to Jane Austen made church weddings a lynchpin of their fiction, *The Origins of the English Marriage Plot* offers a truly innovative account of the rise of the novel by telling the story of the English marriage plot's engagement with the most compelling political and social questions of its time.

LISA O'CONNELL is Senior Lecturer in the School of Communication and Arts at the University of Queensland. She is Vice-President of the Australia and New Zealand Society for Eighteenth-Century Studies and has authored numerous journal articles and book chapters on eighteenth-century literature and culture as well as co-edited *Libertine Enlightenment: Sex, Liberty and Licence in the Eighteenth Century* (2004).

THE ORIGINS OF THE
ENGLISH MARRIAGE PLOT

*Literature, Politics and Religion
in the Eighteenth Century*

LISA O'CONNELL

University of Queensland

CAMBRIDGE
UNIVERSITY PRESS

CAMBRIDGE
UNIVERSITY PRESS

University Printing House, Cambridge CB2 8BS, United Kingdom

One Liberty Plaza, 20th Floor, New York, NY 10006, USA

477 Williamstown Road, Port Melbourne, VIC 3207, Australia

314–321, 3rd Floor, Plot 3, Splendor Forum, Jasola District Centre,
New Delhi – 110025, India

79 Anson Road, #06–04/06, Singapore 079906

Cambridge University Press is part of the University of Cambridge.

It furthers the University's mission by disseminating knowledge in the pursuit of
education, learning, and research at the highest international levels of excellence.

www.cambridge.org
Information on this title: www.cambridge.org/9781108485685
DOI: 10.1017/9781108757706

First published 2019

Printed and bound in Great Britain by Clays Ltd, Elcograf S.p.A.

A catalogue record for this publication is available from the British Library.

Library of Congress Cataloging-in-Publication Data
Names: O'Connell, Lisa, 1965– author.
TITLE: The origins of the English marriage plot : literature, politics and religion in the
eighteenth century / Lisa O'Connell.
DESCRIPTION: Cambridge, United Kingdom ; New York, NY : Cambridge University
Press, 2019. | Includes bibliographical references and index.
IDENTIFIERS: LCCN 2019007065 | ISBN 9781108485685 (hardback)
SUBJECTS: LCSH: English fiction –18th century – History and criticism. | Marriage in literature.
| Marriage customs and rites in literature. | BISAC: LITERARY CRITICISM / European /
English, Irish, Scottish, Welsh.
CLASSIFICATION: LCC PR858.M36 036 2019 | DDC 823/.5093543–dc23
LC record available at https://lccn.loc.gov/2019007065

ISBN 978-1-108-48568-5 Hardback

Contents

Illustrations

Acknowledgements

This book was begun in Baltimore and completed in Brisbane and Berlin with the help of funding from Johns Hopkins University, the University of Queensland and the Australian Research Council. Because it has taken a longer time to write than I could have imagined, I have many friends and colleagues to thank. I am grateful to Marion Campbell, especially, who started it all, along with Terry Collits, Ken Ruthven, Bronwen Levy, David Bennett, Nancy Armstrong, Bill Keach and Len Tennenhouse, who were my teachers and advisors at Melbourne and Brown Universities; their examples were formative and their ongoing support more than I could have hoped for. Guy Rundle, Carolyn Stephens, Meredith Martin, David Herkt, Helene Nevola, Justin Clemens, Diana Barnes, Andrew McCann, Liz Day, Matthew Absalom, Kasturi Ray, Elizabeth McNulty, Gautam Premnath, Sadia Abbass and Annette Van have been good friends and fellow travellers. At Johns Hopkins University, Frances Ferguson, Neil Hertz, Amanda Anderson, Richard Halperin, Jennifer Culbert, Katrin Pahl, Irene Tucker, Mark Blyth and Claire Jarvis helped me to think harder. Peter Holbrook, Alison Scott, Brandon Chua, Eric Parisot, Kim Wilkins, Ross Knecht, Peter Cryle, Marina Bollinger, Gillian Whitlock, Nicholas Heron and Spencer Jackson have been among valued colleagues at the University of Queensland. Julie Park, Sophie Gee, Deidre Lynch, Jonathan Lamb, Bridget Orr, Peter Denney, Vanessa Agnew, Gordon Turnbull, Jennie Wawrzinek, Mirja Petri and Nick During have offered inspiration, guidance and good humour along the way. John Tinkler, Sharon Cameron and Ian Hunter made decisive comments on early drafts; Meegan Hasted, Lesa Scholl and Nicholas Lord helped to prepare my manuscript for press. At Cambridge University Press, my editors, Linda Bree and Bethany Thomas, offered sound advice and encouragement; Catherine Ingrassia and an anonymous reader made this an infinitely better book than it might have been. Dear friends – Karen Batson, Kate Chapple, Annabel Hickey, Heidi Gerton, Maggie Nolan and Amy Sepinwall – have always made a difference. My family made everything happen, of course, especially my mother, Margaret O'Connell, who told me I could do this, and my husband, Simon During, whose patience and support are endless. This book is dedicated to our daughter, Nell, who came along in the middle of it all, changed everything, and made me finish what I started.

Historicising the English Marriage Plot

Marriage, Religion and the State

Four city blocks south of where I write these sentences in Baltimore, a banner hangs on the façade of a famous Unitarian church. Taking a stand in the debate over same-sex marriage, it reads: 'Civil marriage is a civil right.' This redolent phrase is embedded in history. Two centuries ago, Mary Ann Thompson and William Coates, young English Unitarians about to marry, wrote a letter that made approximately the same point:

> The undersigned, being Unitarian Dissenters, present to you [the minister officiating their wedding] the following Protest against the Marriage Ceremony ... They lament that they are placed in a situation so unnatural, as that even forbearance to what they consider as established error would be a formal recantation of opinions which they have received, or convictions, and which they will renounce only on similar grounds. Against the Marriage Ceremony, then, they can but most solemnly protest, – Because it makes the marriage Ceremony a religious, rather than a civil, act; because as Christians and as Protestant Dissenters, it is impossible we can allow of the interference of any human institution with matters which concern our faith and consciences; – Because, as knowing nothing of a Priesthood in Christianity, the submission to a ceremony performed by a person in Holy Orders, or pretended Holy Orders is painful and humiliating to our feelings; – Because, as servants of Jesus, we worship the ONE LIVING AND TRUE GOD his God and our God, his Father and our Father, and disbelieve and abominate the Doctrine of the Trinity, in whose name the Marriage Ceremony is being performed. ((Signed) Wm. Coates, Mary Ann Thompson,)
>
> Members of the Church of God known as the Free-Thinking Christians. (London, 10 June 1814)[1]

This too is a protest against treating marriage as other than a civil union, and although it belongs to a different political order than the contemporary movement to legalise same-sex marriage, it is no less entwined with Christianity. Unitarians like Coates and Thompson did not accept the notion of the Trinity. In a rationalisation of Christian doctrine, they believed that only God the Father was divine. Such a belief had had serious implications: to declare it had been illegal in Britain until the year before their letter was written, when penal sanctions against anti-Trinitarianism, set in place by the 1698 Blasphemy Act, were at last lifted. Even so, Unitarians, like other English subjects, could only marry under the auspices of the Anglican Church. Almost all English marriages were solemnised in a church wedding presided over by an Anglican clergyman in an explicitly Trinitarian ceremony that called upon God to 'look mercifully' upon the marrying couple 'through Jesus Christ our Saviour, who lives and reigns with you in the unity of the Holy Spirit'.[2]

As far as Thompson and Coates are concerned, this ceremony was an abomination. It corrupted a privileged moment in their lives: the culmination of their personal marriage plot. That is why they addressed their letter of protest not to a civic authority but to an Anglican clergyman responsible for implementing the marriage law. And their letter was published in the newspapers, a sign that their questioning of the legitimacy of the church's role in weddings struck a chord. Such questioning animated religious nonconformists and secular-rationalists alike, and not just in Britain.

To take just one example, Immanuel Kant's famous essay, 'What Is Enlightenment?' (1784), had its origins in a newspaper dispute about marriage orchestrated by Johann Erich Biester, editor of the progressive *Berlinische Monatsschrift*. In 1783 Biester published his own rationalist 'Proposal, Not to Engage the Clergy Any Longer When Marriages Are Conducted', along with a rebuttal by clergyman Johann Friedrich Zöllner.[3] In that rebuttal, which defended sacramental marriage, Zöllner asked his adversaries: what is enlightenment? Kant's reply, a call to autonomous self-knowledge expressed as a critique of religion and paternalism, does not mention marriage. Yet its genesis in Biester and Zöllner's exchange reminds us that marriage was a touchstone of public discussion, helping to define a spectrum of opinion – conservative, oppositional, confessional, reformist, radical – across Europe.

Secular marriage reform of the kind that Biester envisaged was eventually to come to England, if under a different political franchise than that which regulated Coates and Thompson's involuntary Anglican wedding in 1814. Civil weddings were legally mandated in 1836, four years after the 1832 Reform Act which extended the franchise into the middle class and thus into English Dissent's heartlands. Thompson and Coates's letter makes clear, however, that in 1814 English marriage regulations enforced an alliance between the Established Church and the state's legal institutions, and thereby relayed a particular relation between government and faith into the lives of almost every citizen. In this sense, and against much received wisdom, English marriage in the Georgian period did not simply belong to civil society.[4] And it is no coincidence that the period in which such regulations were in place saw marriage become a subject of intense debate. It also saw the development of a new popular literary genre centred on courtship and marriage in the context of everyday life. That genre was the novel's marriage plot.

The English Marriage Plot

It is hard to dispute that the history of the early English novel turns on its use of the marriage plot, which is understood to occasion many of the genre's innovations, especially the development of literary realism in the hands of authors such as Samuel Richardson and Jane Austen.[5] Yet, despite the wealth of scholarly work on the novel's domestic themes, there exists no thorough investigation of the modern English marriage plot's political origins.[6] This book aims to make good that gap, not through a comprehensive account of the many fictions using the device, but by examining the political conditions under which the genre emerged and, more particularly, by placing it in a context that standard accounts of 'the rise of the novel' (as well as more narrowly defined genres like 'the court-ship novel' and 'domestic fiction') have tended to overlook.

I argue that English fiction turned to marriage between about 1740 and 1770 not so much out of an interest in the power dynamics of family life, or in the rise of individualism, or in the ethics of courtship, or even because of marriage's particular relationship to money and property. Rather, marriage moved to the centre of the English novel largely in response to changing relations between the Anglican Church, the English state and the commercial sphere. From the mid-eighteenth century, church and state played a joint role in the regulation of marriage, which was also an occasional topic of contestation between them. At the same time, the marriage ceremony itself was subject to the forces of money and commerce, most notably in so-called clandestine marriage markets where weddings could be bought for cash. Within these contexts, the minutiae of marriage and its ritual – when, where and how weddings were performed, as well as between whom and in whose presence – became matters of intense public interest. So much so, that when Samuel Richardson and his followers made marriage the telos of their fictions, they did so knowing that they were contributing not just to public debates about the state's role in the regulation of marriage but also to the wider political landscape within which those debates resonated.

Marriage's changing relation to church, state and commerce in eighteenth-century England has important consequences for the history of the novel form. Most obviously, it means the marriage plot needs to be understood as much in relation to political history as to the social, cultural or literary histories within which it has usually been considered. It also means that the marriage plot in its modern form did not emerge as an entirely secular phenomenon: it turns not just on familial struggles and contentions between husbands and wives or parents and children, as is often supposed, but also on alliances and tensions between vicars and squires in the context of the landed estate and the parish.

In this regard, the marriage plot's key context is *English*, not British: it presents not just oblique domestic allegories of political power and authority but also highly charged interventions in matters of church, state and community that shaped everyday life within a particular nation state. Indeed, the Englishness of the English marriage plot can hardly be too much emphasised even as the novel genre was formed within those currents of translation, internationalism and cross-cultural exchange that underpinned eighteenth-century writing more generally.[7] Its national specificity is twofold: it depends on the importance of Anglican ritual to English marriage, and on a quirk in the legislation controlling marriage after 1754 that made it easier to marry in Scotland than in England, a situation that tied marriage practices to national borders in a concrete way.

Yet even as the English marriage plot was anchored in public politics, this interest was expressed indirectly. Early realist novels do not so much reference debates over marriage (although these do feature in some fiction – Oliver Goldsmith's *The Vicar of Wakefield*, most famously) as develop key narrative features and structures that channel and respond to those debates in literary terms. Primary amongst these is the marriage plot's distinct characterology, as I call it. The genre develops an interest in particular offices – country vicars and squires – which accompanies, and on occasion rivals, its interest in marriageable young women, often of uncertain social status. Geography too, especially the distance between London and the country estate, and later the Scottish border, helps to structure the genre, as do the dangers of clandestine (or improper) marriage and a correspondent attention to proper wedding ceremony.

The term 'marriage plot', of course, is ambiguous. At one level it means any narrative that ends, or almost ends, in a marriage or marriages and that is largely concerned throughout with courtship. What I am calling the 'modern English marriage plot', however, cannot be reduced to these simple formal features, since narratives ending in happy marriages had been common across many languages for centuries. In prose, they reach back at least as far as Longus's *Daphnis and Chloe*.[8] The modern English marriage plot is not simply a mode of, for instance, Aristotelian comedy, or another of the various kinds of early modern prose fiction romance that often ended in marriage. Charlotte Morgan long ago listed seven such kinds, among which can be counted Eliza Haywood's bestseller, *Love in Excess* (1719), which concludes with no fewer than three marriages, a multiplication of the convention that suggests its purely formal function for amatory fiction of the period.[9]

The English marriage plot belongs, rather, to what was in effect a new genre of fiction, first developed by Samuel Richardson in *Pamela, or Virtue Rewarded*, published in 1740. In a now-famous letter to Aaron Hill, Richardson explained his intention 'to introduce a new species of writing that might possibly turn young people into a course of reading different from the pomp and parade of romance-writing'.[10] By 'dismissing the improbable and marvellous, with which novels generally abound', Richardson aimed to 'promote the cause of religion and virtue' (90). Yet his innovation has more readily been understood in literary-historical terms, as authoritatively summarised by Walter Scott in 1821:

> Hitherto, romances had been written, generally speaking in the old French taste, containing the protracted amours of princes and prin-cesses, told in language coldly extravagant, and metaphysically absurd. In these wearisome performances, there appeared not the most distant allusion to the ordinary tone of feeling, the slightest attempt to paint mankind as it exists in the ordinary walks of life – all was rant and bombast, stilt and buskin.[11]

Scott goes on to praise Richardson's representation of 'the natural linea-ments of the human countenance' in a manner characteristic of the nationalist, modernising lexicon in which *Pamela* was canonised. His assertion that earlier works were 'in the old French taste' is, of course, misguided. English novelists before Richardson, most notably Delarivier Manley and Daniel Defoe, often claimed to present faithful depictions of the world (or rather of 'History') in contradistinction to flights of heroic

'Fancy'.[12] Indeed, the decades before the publication of *Pamela* saw an extraordinary amount of prose fiction experimentation by women writers in particular – Aphra Behn, Delarivier Manley, Mary Davys, Penelope Aubin and Eliza Haywood – who are now regarded as pioneers of the modern novel, establishing many of the domestic concerns that are relayed into the marriage plot.[13]

Yet Scott's analysis is not wholly to be dismissed. Richardson's novels are in fact closer to the 'ordinary walks of life' than earlier fiction: they are written in the vernacular, they are more psychologically detailed and more able to excite readerly passion by empathetically engaging readers in characters' lives. The excitement, delight and controversy with which they were first received attests indubitably to that.[14] Precisely because Richardson was committed to a mode of Anglican moral reform that could reach new readers, his epistolary mode entails a particular form of immediacy; the sheer succession of letters expresses time as a succession of news, which allows a new sense of subjectivity, contingency and interest to enter the *récit*. These formal innovations are harnessed to a single thematic aim: narrative closure in marriage. Indeed, the features that mark Richardson's *Pamela*, in particular, as a 'true original', to use John Richetti's phrase, and as a founding text of what will come to be called 'realism', depend ultimately on that singularity of focus.[15]

It was in these complex terms, simultaneously moral, formal and historical, that *Pamela* presented a new kind of marriage plot. It tells the story of a rich, libertine squire, Mr B., who, after various attempts at seduction, marries his virtuous servant Pamela, and does so in a *proper* ceremony, that is, one that follows Anglican liturgy (albeit as revised by Pamela herself). This story allows the novel's action and characterology to be organised in the interests of a new social script which, as Ian Watt long ago noted, depends on its presentation of a marriage capable of transforming both its characters' social status and their inner selves.[16] Admittedly, in *Pamela* marriage enacts an interpretative rather than a narratological closure, since the story continues for many pages after its central characters wed, allowing Mr B. and Pamela to engage a number of post-marital challenges. This said, narratological and interpretative closure, marked in an Anglican proper wedding ceremony that legitimates simultaneously social status, states of feeling, Christian virtue and moral worth, will increasingly coalesce in realist novels written after 1740. More than anything, that coalescence defines the English marriage plot.

Eighteenth-Century Marriage and Post-Secularism

During the period in which Richardson wrote his novels, marriage's legal status and social function came under intense examination. In 1753 it was profoundly transformed when Lord Hardwicke's Marriage Act mandated Anglican weddings for all English marriages. It is certainly possible to exaggerate the Marriage Act's impact. After all, there was nothing new about the Anglican wedding ceremony in the eighteenth century; the Act simply gave statuary force to long-standing canon law requirements for Anglican weddings that were widely if not uniformly followed both before and after its introduction.[17] So while the Act changed some of the requirements for parish weddings and closed loopholes available to Dissenters, it did not substantively change the way that most English couples wed.

Yet, precisely as a statuary law mandating a religious rite, the Marriage Act realigned English marriage's relation to church and state, as well as to commerce, property, family and everyday life in England for more than a century. This is so even though – or perhaps because – the Act was introduced against a background of arguments over marriage's theological meaning, administration and liturgical status that reach back to the first days of the English Reformation and beyond.[18] And it is so even though the Act sparked virulent opposition and a long-lasting pamphlet war that I call the 'marriage debate'. That debate politicised marriage in new terms: now part of the apparatus of state, marriage became an important touchstone for emerging forms of political dissent, whether Tory, oppositional Whig, or, later, radical.

In the wake of the Marriage Act's reforms, marriage came to serve a double political function in the English context as both a religious rite *and* a vehicle for the state's administrative power. On one side, it was a performative vow sealed by a ceremony which had usually occurred as a witnessed religious rite (with minor exceptions) and was now legally mandated as an *Anglican* ceremony. At the same time, as regulated by statute, marriage channelled new forms of governmentality focussed on the population's security, health, prosperity and reproduction – what Michel Foucault famously called biopower.[19] Standing at an interface between confessional and secular culture, marriage belonged not to modern enlightened secularism, as has often been assumed, but to 'post-secularism'.

In the work of theorists such as Charles Taylor and Hans Blumenberg the term 'post-secular' refers to a cultural domain in which religious ideas and structures are not wholly superseded by civil-secular ones but rather are reoccupied or repurposed by them.[20] As Brent S. Sirota's recent work on the transformative effects of Anglican outreach in the period helps to demonstrate, English civil society itself was significantly shaped by Anglican revival efforts, which helped to install Christian social and philanthropic purposes at the heart of British identity.[21] Framed in these terms, and against Habermas's tacitly secularised concept of the emergent 'modern public sphere', the Marriage Act's purposes and effects can be re-described. It harnessed the sacred to the civic for new ends which included modern state- and nation-building.

If eighteenth-century English marriage was post-secular, then so too was the early novel, especially as envisioned by Richardson as a 'new species' of writing dedicated to Anglican outreach. Arguably too, post-secular continuities and disjunctions shaped the English marriage plot and enabled its remarkable versatility and longevity. Marriage's new double function gave it sufficient political energy and signifying force to form the crux of a new literary genre: the realist marriage plot. And by the same logic, the novel's realist marriage plot, for all its subsequent inventiveness, variety and refinement, is never fully secularised, even after the civil marriage provisions of 1836 and even in the hands of revisionary and secular writers later in the century. That is because the genre itself remained embedded in the narrative techniques, settings, characters and devices that underpinned its original missionary purpose.

Political Origins

This book traces the origins and early development of the English marriage plot through four main lines of argument. First, mid-century efforts to mandate *one* legal form for English marriage established the terms for a new prose fiction marriage plot that connected the sacred, the governmental and the civic. Second, distinctions between proper and improper marriage encoded different political understandings of the relations between church, state and population as sanctioned by natural law. Third, these politics shaped the attachment of the marriage plot in early English prose fiction to specific locations, character types and narrative forms as well as to descriptions of proper wedding ceremony. And, last, only after the growth of the commodity fiction market, especially from the 1770s, did the marriage plot (now largely divested of its *theo-political* interests) enable the realist novel to become precisely a *literary* genre, that is, a genre which positions itself within a literary tradition.

One further context is important to my case. Particularly in its early stages, the English marriage plot develops in the interface between the stage and print. This means that its history cannot simply be told through the English novel's 'rise' and formal development. It belongs, rather, to a set of recurring real-life questions about marriage regulation and proper wedding ceremony which helped to animate various literary genres and cultural forms, including the theatre. So, my account of the English marriage plot begins not with the novel, nor with proper church ceremony, but with the plebeian public sphere's lively tradition of mock marriages and clandestine weddings. This prehistory is important because it explains what is at stake in the division of 'proper' from 'improper' ceremony that will come to underpin the novel's marriage plot. London's unruly stage and street weddings are a neglected precedent for Richardson's and Fielding's prose fiction marriage plots, which pointedly overwrite them.

Yet even in the context of the novel alone, the English marriage plot is not a unified form. Its eighteenth-century development is discontinuous and uneven precisely because it drew energy and heterogeneity from the political sphere – from Anglican outreach projects, state-building, commercial innovation, radicalism and more. *Pamela*'s Anglican marriage plot is both consolidated and reversed in the gentlemanly 'patriot' theo-political fiction of Richardson's rivals and successors (Henry Fielding, John Shebbeare and Oliver Goldsmith), who anticipate and draw upon political opposition to the Marriage Act. Later in the century, as demands for the Marriage Act's repeal gained traction and drew on radical discourses often directed at women, the marriage plot was transformed again. At this point, a new generation of novelists, spearheaded by Frances Burney and indebted to a late strain of Haywood's fiction, developed courtship plots geared less to political than to moral and literary ends.

Finally, in Austen's fiction, the modern English marriage plot becomes the more narrowly literary form that historians and critics have long supposed it to be. Indeed, her default role as a touchstone for the formal achievements of the realist novel and its marriage plot barely papers over the diversity of the genre Austen mastered or its indebtedness to a century or more of political and religious contention. Austen's fiction exemplifies how the Englishness of the English marriage plot becomes implicit to the novel form after that plot congeals into literary convention and loses full connection to its political origins.

My argument is presented in five chapters. The first chapter, 'Church, State and the Public Politics of Marriage', is straightforwardly historiographical, examining the broad post-1688 theo-political settings in which marriage and prose fiction both changed their form. It outlines the situation in which the Marriage Act of 1753 was passed, paying attention first to the policies, natural law theories and state-building projects of the Court Whigs who enacted it, and then to the passionate arguments mounted against the Act by churchmen and others. The chapter contends that the tension between church and state that lay at the heart of England's mid-century marriage debate shaped not just the novel form but also politics more widely.

The second chapter, 'Clandestine Marriage, Commerce and the Theatre', examines the London-based trade in irregular marriages that the Marriage Act aimed to suppress and their entangled relation to the popular stage. In London's so-called clandestine marriage market – an unruly space where priests performed wedding ceremonies for cash – the marriage tie was exposed to deception and concealment while also responding to commercial demand. The chapter surveys the history of clandestine marriage and the stage device of 'mock marriage' with which it was twinned and which featured in the oppositional political comedy of John Gay and Henry Fielding. Those plays picture a world institutionally, politically and, indeed, ontologically very different from that of the post-Richardsonian novel. By mid-century, however, both the Marriage Act and the stage Licensing Act of 1737 had reformed the wedding trade and the theatre world, preparing the ground for a new mode of comedy allied to the Richardsonian marriage plot (and to proper ceremony) as spearheaded by David Garrick and George Colman's (ironically titled) Drury Lane hit *The Clandestine Marriage* (1766).

The third chapter, 'The New Fiction: Samuel Richardson and the Anglican Wedding', focusses on Richardson's formal innovations, which, I argue, depend upon his using novelistic fiction as a form of Anglican missionary outreach as well as on his own changing theo-political attachments. It illuminates various features of *Pamela*'s marriage plot: its spiritualisation of courtship; its emphasis on a triangular relation between a vicar, a squire and a literate servant; its setting in a rural parish and landed estate; its relocation of clandestine marriage's disorder; and, finally, its emphasis on proper Anglican wedding ceremony. To make its case, the chapter also offers a reading of *Sir Charles Grandison* (1753–4) and its central characters' carefully described public parish wedding. Richardson's weddings, I contend, are emblematic of a social order in which the novel comes to occupy a new and powerful position mediating religion and the state.

Chapter 4, 'The Patriot Marriage Plot: Fielding, Shebbeare and Goldsmith', explores a specific 'patriot' genealogy for the marriage plot. That genealogy begins in Henry Fielding's *Joseph Andrews* (1742) and continues in John Shebbeare's *The Marriage Act* (1754) and Oliver Goldsmith's *The Vicar of Wakefield* (1766). These novels respond to Richardson's innovations from a Tory perspective, jettisoning epistolary form, placing a naïve parson at the centre of their narratives and so masculinising the marriage plot. Each is set in a rural parish where tense relationships between squires and vicars reflect a corrupt governmental system, and in which the good parson emerges both as a figure of theo-political virtue and as a conduit for irony. To echo Patrick Parrinder, this is a literature of nation rather than of religion or of state.[22] Within this patriot lineage, however, the marriage plot's nostalgia and irony seem to concede that its values are realisable only imaginatively – that is, as fiction. By Goldsmith's time, when the politics of patriotism were all but defunct and when the Anglican Church was losing its social authority, the marriage plot can begin to be aestheticised, that is, treated primarily as a matter of form and style.

My final chapter, 'Literary Marriage Plots: Burney, Austen and Gretna Green', focusses on Frances Burney and Jane Austen's late-century rein-vention of the English marriage plot. Their courtship fiction subsumed the old church-state politics of the first-wave English marriage plot into literary and civil-secular values focussed on women. By the 1770s Gretna Green elopements were all that was left of the old clandestine marriage trade, and they now appealed to a radical politics of liberty associated with youth and autonomous desire, and thus with commercial romance. Burney waged war against romance of this kind by resituating Richardson's female-focussed deliberative marriage plot in London's polite marriage market. In doing so she established formal devices that repurposed the marriage plot to explicitly literary ends. Austen, absorbing Burney's innovations and writing in post-revolutionary times, returned the marriage plot to rural settings while further ironising and aestheticising it. In the process, how-ever, the English novel begins to shelter a *moral* realism, which removed the marriage plot from the church and state politics of its origins, aligning it instead with the gravitas and prestige of literary culture.

CHAPTER I

Church, State and the Public Politics of Marriage

This chapter outlines the theo-political conditions under which the English marriage plot was established. It shows how a particular party faction, the Court Whigs – which was committed both to a view of church-state relations that I call Erastian and to a particular understanding of natural law – reformed the regulation of marriage. Yet these efforts immediately met with contestation, much of which was based on alternative understandings of natural law and, implicitly, of church-state relations too. In the welter of debate triggered by the legislation, marriage was viewed as central not just to the polity but also to the divine order. The chapter is divided into two halves: the first sets the Marriage Act into the Court Whigs' larger political programme of Erastian state-building; the second shows how different concepts of natural law set the terms of the ongoing marriage debate that played a shaping role in the politics and literature of the second half of the century.

Imagining Marriage

We can begin with a marriage proposal. In 1769, the philandering Scottish Tory lawyer James Boswell wrote a letter of proposal to Margaret Montgomerie, his cousin, with whom he was deeply in love. Having suggested they live together in Europe since their marriage would not meet his father's approval, Boswell toyed with the idea of setting sail for America to 'become a wild Indian' should 'Peggy' refuse him. In his diary, he reported her acceptance of his offer like this:

> The important answer from M. was brought to me in the Parliament House: 'I accept of your terms'. For a minute or two my habits of terror for marriage returned. I found myself at last fixed for ever; my heart beat and my head was giddy. But I soon recovered and felt the highest admiration and gratitude on a conduct so generous ... I determined to make it my study to do all in my power to show my sense of her goodness. And I became calm

and easy, thinking that as I was now fixed in the most important concern, everything else was but secondary ... [That] night I was at the [debating] Society, and spoke against repealing the Marriage Act.[1]

This prenuptial exchange is revealing. Montgomerie's reply engages the language of diplomacy ('I accept your terms') while, as a long-time libertine, Boswell's immediate response to her acceptance is a resurgence of an old 'terror for marriage', a fear of being 'fixed for ever', which is only stifled by thoughts of his future wife's goodness. Those thoughts allow him more calmly to judge marriage as the 'most important concern', which in turn enables him later that night to attend a debating club where he will argue the case for Hardwicke's Marriage Act, still a topic of public debate sixteen years after its passage. (The first attempt at its repeal had narrowly failed in Parliament four years earlier.) Despite his sexual opportunism, Boswell has come to see marriage as an ethical telos in the formation of a life to which 'everything else was ... secondary', and more than that, one that requires state institutional support.

Montgomerie's reply imagines their bond differently: 'My heart determines my choice. May the Almighty grant His blessing and protection, and we need not be afraid; His providence extends over all the earth so that wherever you go I shall willingly accompany you and hope to be happy.'[2] Her Christian piety, blending romance with providentialism, imposes another layer of meaning upon their union, prompting Boswell to express a wish that they be 'truly happy together in devotion'.[3] Over the course of their subsequent correspondence, Boswell and Montgomerie assert their future union's significance in various terms – as an embodiment of natural law, as a Christian partnership, as a matter of state and as a bond of romantic companionship. Moreover, in place of his father's approval, Boswell had his patrons and heroes – Samuel Johnson, General Pasquale Paoli and Archibald Douglas – sign as witnesses to a mock legal marriage contract that he drafted himself.[4]

Not all of the Boswells' conceptions of marriage seem compatible with each other, but we can note that their sheer variety signals marriage's double (or indeed multiple) function as a key institution of public *and* private life, conceived in both civil-secular and religious terms. Samuel Richardson's *Sir Charles Grandison*, published the year that Hardwicke's legislation was passed, offers another such case, this time fictional. Early on in the story, Richardson's virtuous heroine, Harriet Byron, pursued by suitors none of whom she can even think of accepting, writes to her cousin, Lucy Selby:

> I have a very high notion of the marriage-state. I remember what my Uncle
> once averr'd; That a woman out of wedlock is half useless to the end of her
> being. How indeed do the duties of a good Wife, of a good Mother, and
> a worthy Matron, well performed, dignify a woman! ... My Grandfather
> used to say, that families are little communities; that there are but few solid
> friendships out of them; and that they help to make up worthily, and to
> secure, the great community, of which they are so many miniatures.[5]

It goes without saying that Harriet would not have accepted the promiscuous Boswell as a husband – 'Who can touch pitch and not be defiled?'
(1:26), she asks in reference to the folly of marrying a rake. But Harriet
and Boswell agree in assigning to marriage an elemental significance:
Harriet repeats her uncle's opinion that 'a woman out of wedlock is half
useless to the end of her being,' which is a version of Boswell's 'most
important concern'. For each, marriage is foundational to natural, civil
and Christian life.[6]

A married life, in both of these instances, is also an English one. For
Harriet and Boswell, marriage is associated not just with God or with nature
but also with English civil society. In Boswell's case, this 'Englishness' is
implicit in his public defence of the Marriage Act (statutory law which
applied only to England and Wales, not to his native Scotland) and in the
anglophile, Episcopalian sensibility he and Montgomerie shared.[7] Harriet's
'very high notion of the marriage-state', on the other hand, shared by
Richardson himself, is bound to a traditional Anglican invocation of
marriage as 'a little commonwealth' within the wider network of institutions
that constitute the great Christian commonwealth of England itself.[8]

For Harriet Byron and James Boswell, then, marriage is both a religious
rite and a central strut of the nation state. Their musings foreground the post-
secular contexts in which marriage was conceived and institutionalised in the
period. The crucial contemporary event that shaped their thinking was Lord
Hardwicke's Marriage Act, which established marriage simultaneously as an
institution of church and of state. But, as Byron and Boswell's comments also
begin to suggest, the Marriage Act was no isolated measure. It belonged to
a legislative programme put forward by Hardwicke's party – the Court
Whigs – aimed at extending governmental power into lived experience. It
did so via the church, on one hand, and literature, on the other.

Erastianism and the Court Whig State

The Marriage Act was passed in the last decade of a long period of Whig
hegemony. That hegemony began with the Hanoverian dynasty's

accession in 1714 and was consolidated by Robert Walpole's canny patronage politics. After 1742, it continued into administrations under the leadership of Henry Pelham, his brother Thomas Pelham-Holles, the Duke of Newcastle, and Lord Chancellor Hardwicke. In practical terms, especially under Walpole, Whig power was established and maintained through a system of influence that came to be known as 'Old Corruption', which created opportunities for revenue farming from state offices that were used to buy votes and loyalty.[9] In principle, it was legitimated by the Whigs' support of the 1688 constitutional settlement, which granted legislative power to the elected Parliament, secured the Protestant Succession and extended freedom of worship to all Christian confessions. As recent scholarship has also made clear, Whiggism was committed to a project of 'moral reformation' which aimed to establish and monitor social order while increasing benevolence and philanthropy.[10]

If Whig hegemony was underpinned by Old Corruption harnessed to constitutionalism and moral reformation, the Church of England functioned as its key enabler. The 1688 settlement had been a Protestant-inspired Erastian settlement insofar as it subordinated church to state. Yet its Erastianism was limited since the Church of England maintained unique privileges as an Established Church, if now under Parliament's effective control. Successive Whig states, therefore, supported the Anglican Church's central role in civil life while other Protestant denominations were merely tolerated. Most public offices, for instance, including university places, were officially closed to all but Anglicans. And moral reformation efforts largely proceeded through state support for civil associations in alliance with the churches, especially the Anglican Church. Indeed, as Tony Claydon argues, moral outreach of this type appealed to politicians not just because it was relatively non-partisan, but because its chief vehicle, the Church, 'offered many advantages as a carrier of state ideology in administration of all kinds'.[11]

For its part, the Anglican Church provided spiritual and moral legitimation for oligarchical state institutions. As E. P. Thompson caustically remarks: '[t]he limp magic of a sordidly-Erastian church ... supplemented the authority of the propertied over the people.'[12] In historical terms, this limited Erastian mode of governance brokered an uneasy compromise between the Lutheran view that the government of the church belonged to the civil magistrate and the High Church (quasi-Catholic) claim that the church possessed an apostolic authority independent of the state.[13] In this sense, eighteenth-century England straddled a post-secular divide: it was as much an 'ecclesiastical polity', in Richard Hooker's famous phrase, as an emerging nation state.[14] In practice, however, as Thompson suggests, the Erastian alliance amounted to a collusion of church and state in the interests of property, on one hand, and centralised administrative power, on the other.

Under this form of Erastianism, party divisions between Whigs and Tories were concentrated on religious issues as much as on questions of fiscal management or foreign policy (which themselves were not independent of religion). Thus, in Queen Anne's period, the Tory catch-cry against Whig state power and tolerance of Dissent was 'the Church is in danger.' That was a slogan whose appeal had diminished but by no means evaporated by mid-century. On the other side, 'Broad' churchmen like William Wake, Benjamin Hoadly and Francis Blackburne questioned the Anglican Church's independent power and insisted upon the secular magistrate's supreme authority.[15] Outside the Established Church, a latent Dissent-tinged republicanism, a distrust of 'priestcraft' and the church's secular power, along with ongoing fears of Jacobitism, variously fuelled parliamentary anticlericalism across the 1730s and early 1740s.[16] From within the Erastian alliance, then, Whig power could feel compromised and Anglican privilege imperilled.

The Court Whigs (aka the 'old Corps' or 'Establishment' Whigs) were most powerful between the end of the 1740s, when some important 'Patriots' (Chesterfield and Lyttelton) joined them, and 1760, when George III came to the throne. By this time, they had forged alliances with three important social blocs. Their first alliance was with the metropolitan financial and commercial sector whose interests could no longer be separated from the large landed estates (as opposed to the smaller gentry).[17] Their second alliance was with the Anglican episcopate, to which the Whig ministry, using its powers of ecclesiastical patronage, appointed loyal supporters. (Among the most powerful of these Erastian appointees was Edmund Gibson, Bishop of London, who had served as Walpole's 'Church Minister', organising the bishops in the House of Lords and acting as a broker between the ministry and the clergy.) Their third alliance was with Protestant dissenters who stood behind the Whigs' support for toleration and who feared the Jacobitism and 'Church is in danger' ideology among the Tory opposition.

Politically, the Court Whigs firmly rejected not just High Church Toryism but also the anti-centralising and governmental values of the so-called Country interest, which (confusingly) included many Tories and some Whigs.[18] Since 1689, the Country interest had been defined by its vigilance in locating threats to 'traditional' English liberties as mounted by oligarchic, commercial, Court or state interests.[19] In opposing Walpole, a Tory wing of the Country interest took shape as a 'Patriot' movement, whose chief ideologue was the charismatic Henry St John, Viscount Bolingbroke. From the 1750s on, anti-ministerial coalitions of Patriots, Tories and oppositional Whigs routinely championed the liberties of the 'people' against oligarchical interests, including the strictures of the Marriage Act.[20] Indeed, across the second half of the century, anti-Marriage Act polemic became a marker of political opposition.

On their side, the Court Whigs embraced so-called Ciceronian or (as their enemies put it) Venetian understandings of political institutions, namely the importance of maintaining government in the hands of an aristocratic oligarchy capable of sustaining security, order and justice. Resisting the temptation to accede to 'democratical' or 'seditious' movements such as those of the 1640s (which were still remembered), and fearing the political instability that marked Queen Anne's reign when Tory populism led to riots and disorder, the Court Whigs considered themselves not so much obliged to represent their electorate as to govern in the interests of a nation in which they, as large landowners, had the greatest stake.[21] Thus, for instance, Lord Hardwicke was disconcerted to find himself the object of significant popular support following his attacks on the Militia Act in 1757.[22] As Linda Colley has argued, it was as much Court Whig ruthlessness in using government and the law to maintain the rights of property as any consensus enabled by parliamentary rule that accounted for England's famous 'stability' over the period.[23]

Mid-century Court Whig state-building, however, was informed by a subtly different understanding of relations between the church, state and populace than earlier Whig administrations.[24] In particular, the Pelham regime (which passed the Marriage Act) departed from the narrow Erastianism of the Walpole-Gibson era. Following the failure of the 1745 rebellion, it put in place more fully developed measures to consolidate the state's role in the lives of the people often, but not always, by turning to the church. William Warburton, a literary-cum-ecclesiastical scholar and friend of Hardwicke, was a chief ideologue of this new twist in the Whig hegemony.[25] His *The Alliance between Church and State* (1736) defended the Established Church and the Test Acts by arguing that religion alone ensures the state's moral security. Against Hobbes's radically Erastian secularism on one side, and French Papist absolutism on the other, Warburton maintained 'that the Church should apply its best influence in the service of the state'.[26] To this end, its civil jurisdiction rightly concerned moral and religious outreach, and in particular, the 'reformation of manners' (176).

Warburton's *Alliance* heralded a synthesis of church and state focussed on lived relations, or what in his literary commentaries he called 'Life and Manners'.[27] It cannily aimed to harness Anglican pastoral practices and institutions (which, dating back to the post-revolution era, had been strongly Tory) to the Whig establishment by annexing the Church's philanthropic energy and achievements to a concept of an active state.[28] Partly under the influence of Warburton's Erastianism, conceived as a radical church-state continuity, local, parish-based matters of marriage, citizenship and population would be brought to the foreground of public policy, and simultaneously to the English novel's centre. Indeed, Richardson's new English marriage plot emerges under the auspices of the moral reform movement more generally.

As a prominent Court Whig churchman, Warburton enacted the principles of the *Alliance* on at least two occasions. In 1754, the same year that Hardwicke appointed him to the Prebend of Gloucester, he defended the Marriage Act from the pulpit in a sermon on marriage that used scripture to sanction state power. Even more striking, his famous preface to *Clarissa*'s second instalment (1748) praised Richardson's fiction less for its Anglicanism than for its moralism, as well as its immediacy and realism – its 'Faithful picture of Nature in *Private Life*' (my emphasis) – which, Warburton noted pointedly, could 'direct' readers' conduct and employ their pity.[29] Perhaps more than any other reader, he recognised what was at stake in Richardson's 'new species' of writing: a literary enactment of his own call for the cultivation of individual virtue as a guarantor of just and stable civil government.

Warburton's theological interventions underscore that the Court Whig hegemony was not focussed just on maintaining oligarchical power and property but also on tightening the church's connection to the state for the purposes of social control. Under the auspices of a loose alignment of propertied and ecclesiastical interests, the Court Whigs engaged increasingly confidently (if not without setbacks) in a form of state-building and rationalisation of the legal code that aimed to enhance sovereign power and to limit both private and collective non-participation in the state's legal apparatus. In this programme's interests, they also produced – or tried to produce – a more knowable and docile population. Where possible, such measures were sanctioned by a broad moral and social reform agenda, as would be the case for the Marriage Act. In this way, the modern administrable state emerged out of the intersection of Erastianism and Old

Corruption – a development that had important cultural and literary as well as social and political implications.

Philip Yorke, Earl of Hardwicke, was the Court Whigs' most prominent statesman and lawyer. He reached the height of his influence as part of the triumvirate that controlled the British government for a decade from 1744. Having been appointed by Walpole as Lord Chief Justice in 1733 and Lord Chancellor in 1737, he was granted a great deal of autonomy in the passage of legislation because, as Peter Brown puts it, the Chancellor's tenure on office 'did not depend on other cabinet changes'.[30] Of quite humble birth, he had quickly acquired solid Whig connections (he married the niece of another great Whig lawyer, Lord Somers). By the time he became Lord Chief Justice, he was managing a lucrative dual career as a lawyer and a politician. His influence was felt in other institutions too: he wielded considerable power in the Royal Society, for instance, partly via Reverend Thomas Birch, its secretary between 1752 and 1756, who was a Hardwicke family agent, spy and dependent.[31] As Thompson wryly observes, 'by the usual mysterious means', he acquired 'both a fortune and a reputation for probity'.[32] Perhaps the single most successful operator within the Old Corruption system, he bequeathed a mind-boggling million-pound estate to his heirs on his death in 1764.[33]

Hardwicke is remembered as a legal reformer and an influential proponent of natural law. Arguably, he was less an original legal thinker than the Whig administration's chief legal enabler. It is true that his 1743 ruling that only courts of equity could award plaintiffs costs helped to place equity at the centre of English law. But it is difficult to see how his storied commitment to justice – i.e. to the common law or to the jury system or even to the reform of equity – can be reconciled to his repeated willingness to legislate in the interests of property and the state.[34] Hardwicke's political career began, for instance, with a maiden speech arguing the case for treating the Irish Catholic peasantry as colonial subjects of the English Crown. In the early 1720s, he was a key figure behind the passage and prosecution of the notorious Waltham Black Acts, which in response to plebeian resistance to the game laws created about fifty new capital offences for poaching, initiating what is now understood as a systematic criminalisation of the poor.[35] And in 1729 and again in 1749, he ruled that, contrary to common belief, slaves were the property of their owners when in England as much as 'when they set foot in Jamaica, or any other English plantation', an opinion famously overturned by Lord Mansfield in *Somerset* v *Stewart* (1771–2).[36]

Even as Hardwicke consistently affirmed the rights of property against labour, including peasant and slave labour, he was also committed to the modern 'fiscal-military' economy.[37] In the 1740s and 1750s he supported the massive increase in taxation and public debt required for British military campaigns, as well as the Mutiny Bill of 1749 which helped to establish a modern peacetime standing army. He was responsible too for many of the twists and turns of Whig Erastian policy. His ruling in the 1736 *Middleton* v *Croft* case 'effectively exempted laymen from the jurisdiction of the Church', a decision that came to be seen as the definitive assertion of the supremacy of statute over canon law (and an important precedent for the Marriage Act).[38] He also, however, declared 'Christianity . . . part of the law of England', and tried to strengthen the Anglican Church's influence on society and manners (as per Warburton's *Alliance*) by discouraging pluralism and non-residential clergy.[39] In the same spirit, he was the main prosecutor of Catholic Jacobites after the rebellions of 1722 and 1745, when he formulated the various pieces of legislation that ended the old Highland clan culture, most famously by banning the tartan and eradicating the hereditary power of the Scottish chiefs. The latter measure was supported by a propaganda campaign authored by another prominent friend, Henry Fielding.[40]

Yet, unlike Fielding and other anti-Jacobites, Hardwicke was no English nationalist.[41] Rather, in the context of Britain and Ireland, he was a key proponent and enabler of a new form of internal colonialism by which English oligarchy came to dominate the old 'three kingdoms' by extending state power and rationality in terms that were not grounded in the various ideologies attached to English ethnicity, or English traditions of faith, or even common law.[42] In the end, Hardwicke stood not for English liberty, or even for Erastian state power, but for a monopoly of law and order grounded in constitutional monarchy. As Reed Browning puts it, for him, statute law was primary and it should 'run with its full force wherever the Georges were sovereign'.[43] It is perhaps an irony that (against his own intentions) the Marriage Act, Hardwicke's signature piece of legislation, applied only to England and Wales, since his own conception of the state was radically centralised and anti-nationalist.

Hardwicke's career demonstrates the Court Whigs' sweep and ambition at mid-century – their will to subordinate the church and to rationalise and extend the reach of the legal state and the modern commercial economy. Yet his Marriage Act belongs to a somewhat different order of government, one (as I have suggested) broadly concerned with the slow process of transforming the 'body politic' into an administered population. Two initiatives that came before Parliament in the same session as the Marriage Act offer fitting examples of Hardwicke's efforts to use legislation to extend the power of the state in this way. The first, the little-known National Registration Bill of 1753, passed the Commons but failed in the Lords, and so never became law.[44] The second, the Jewish Naturalisation Act, was passed successfully only to be quickly repealed after widespread protest.[45] Each illuminates the broader Court Whig legislative reform programme to which Hardwicke's Marriage Act belonged.

The National Registration Bill's full title was 'An Act for Taking and Registering an Annual Account of the Total Number of People and the Total Number of Marriages, Births and Deaths; and Also the Total Number of Poor Receiving Alms from Every Parish and Extraparochial Place in Great Britain'. It was designed to enforce what was in effect a census (it is sometimes known as the Census Bill) so as to provide the state with accurate information about the English population's size and nature. The debate it generated was a moment in what D. V. Glass has called the 'population controversy' which addressed the question of whether Britain was gaining or losing population, a topic of considerable political interest until the 1801 census.[46] The controversy had implications for what we would think of as political economy since, at this time, national 'prosperity' was understood in mercantilist terms as a loose summation of population and wealth. Depopulation fears were central to the Country opposition's anti-commerce and anti-luxury polemic, which held that excess wealth led to the over-refinement of the elite, an inflammatory argument used in John Brown's influential *Estimate of the Manners and Principles of the Time* (1757–8) and later by Wilkesite radicals.[47]

The Court Whigs, by contrast, sought to insert the bureaucratic state into the processes of belonging to, counting and reproducing the national body that had long been the domain of church and parish. Their National Registration Bill proposed a nationwide household census with mechanisms to record and report vital statistics to a central authority. Its figures would be based not on Christian rites of baptism and burial recorded in parish registers, but on actual numbers of births and deaths so as to account for the costs of parish-based poverty relief. Indeed, the Census Bill was an early, failed attempt to rationalise that system. Popular resistance to it, led by the Yorkshire Whig and Country interest pamphleteer William Thornton, took on Patriot tones. Leaving aside religious fears as to God's wrath if the population were to be numbered, and mercantilist fears about the consequences of disclosing the size of the nation's populace to its enemies, it was seen to endanger English liberty just by conceiving of the people as a serially countable population subject to rationalised administration.[48]

The Jewish Naturalisation Act (familiarly known as the Jew Bill) was debated and passed in Commons in April 1753 in the run-up to the Marriage Act's debate, before being swiftly repealed in November. Introduced as a private member's Bill and lobbied for by London's Jewish community, it permitted a small proportion of Jews (an affluent minority of Sephardic descent) to become naturalised subjects of the British Crown. By its provisions, Parliament could consider naturalisation requests from Jews on an individual basis, a prohibitively expensive business, particularly for the impoverished Ashkenazi community.[49] In the xenophobic wording of *The Gentleman's Magazine*, it aimed to augment national wealth by welcoming 'rich foreign Jews'.[50] The Jew Bill's real aim, however, was to enable the British state's improved access to European-based transnational finance capital, a significant proportion of which lay in Sephardic hands.[51]

Despite finding sufficient support among the Tories and the Ministry to be passed, the Jew Bill sparked wide-scale vituperation. It revealed, as Robert Harris argues, 'sentiments and views which had long remained hidden or suppressed at a national level', making apparent the breadth and depth of resistance to the Court Whig programme not just by politicians jockeying for places but also by large groups within the population as a whole.[52] The popular protest drew on old Christian anti-Semitic traditions and was especially virulent because it expressed fears that English subjects were no longer to be defined by their Christian Protestant identities, and that the 'national body' would be open to Jewish miscegenation.[53] One Tory banner read simply, 'No Jews: Christianity and the Constitution'.[54]

The Jewish naturalisation protests were also motivated by fears of commercialism and, more particularly, of the increasing influence of fluid capital as against the landed estates. Concerns that the Jew Bill would give rise to a new 'Jewish landed interest' were misplaced: as Hardwicke indicated privately to Thomas Secker, Bishop of Oxford, when Secker enquired whether the Jew Bill granted Jews the legal right to acquire British estates, it did not give Jews such a right which however, according to most lawyers, they already possessed.[55] Nonetheless, the protests, whose fury surprised both the Whig and Tory parliamentary elite, seem to have been directed at exactly the kind of citizenship the Jew Bill envisaged, one in which individuals could join the nation state on legal terms that took no account of ethnic or religious self-recognition and that were established in the interests of capital. Despite attempts to close down on the opposition, including buying the silence of the Tory-Patriot newspaper *The Protestor*, edited by one-time Fielding associate James Ralph, the government realised that the legislation jeopardised its chances in the 1754 election and repealed it that year, with Hardwicke's own encouragement.[56]

The failures of the Jewish Naturalisation Act and the National Registration Bill reveal a pattern of state intervention and popular response that will be repeated and more fully sustained in the context of the Marriage Act's successful passage. Each measure underscores the controversy surrounding the Court Whig conception of the nation state as composed of citizens detached from native English identities and traditions. Each was consistent with Court Whig Erastianism, introducing rational centralising procedures to existing church- and parish-based practices, partly in the service of political economy. Each provoked a nativist backlash on the basis of its threat to traditional (Christian) understandings of belonging and identity. Indeed, the new forms of opposition created and channelled by these measures are as historically significant as the form of governmentality they represent. Together they mark an early moment in the formal politicisation of English ethnicity and, at the same stroke, in the new politicisation of disenfranchised groups in response to statist attempts to reconfigure the social body. These groups – namely the poor, women, children and labouring classes – would soon be championed under the banner of English liberty as the Marriage Act's signal victims.

Proper Ceremony

The Marriage Act was formally titled 'An Act for the Better Preventing of Clandestine Marriages'.[57] Initiated in the House of Lords in response to *Cochran* v *Campbell*, a Scottish appeal case involving a bigamous marriage, it was designed to end so-called clandestine marriages which were performed privately by clergymen often for commercial rather than for pastoral reasons. It was felt to be an urgent measure because such irregular marriages could elude parental control and threaten ordered property succession.[58] When Attorney General Dudley Ryder introduced the Marriage Act to Parliament, he did so specifically on the grounds that it would protect rich families from 'infamous sharpers' intent on abducting heiresses, as well as helping to prevent bigamy.[59] Hardwicke worked to secure its passage in the face of vigorous debate in both Houses, as well as an avalanche of opposition in print. Arguably the most significant of all his legal reforms, it was consistent with the Court Whig legislative programme since, in effect, it annexed Christian married relations to the business of an administered state.

The Marriage Act decreed that the only valid form of English marriage was that performed by an ordained priest according to the Anglican liturgy in an Established Church within appointed hours. This meant that the state now regulated the form of weddings and marriages. On one hand, the Marriage Act merely consolidated canon law and continued a long-standing tradition of church-celebrated weddings in England. On the other hand, it established a single form of 'proper ceremony' for English marriages, mandated by both church and state. Here the administrative rationalism that drove the Jewish Naturalisation Act and the National Registration Bill operates through the Anglican Church.

The Marriage Act allowed some exceptions to its provisions, most of which were negotiated during its passage through Parliament. Quakers and Jews were exempt, and the legislation itself did not apply in Scotland (on the grounds of the religious independence guaranteed upon Union in 1707) or to members of the royal family, or to colonial marriages 'beyond the Seas' (XVIII). Importantly, it did require the conformity of England's Dissenters and Catholics, thus subjecting them to the Church of England's authority. And while it aimed to make the celebration of marriages public (and thus accountable) by requiring that weddings be conducted according to the Canons of 1607 (i.e. in a church or chapel in the couple's parish of residence, between the hours of eight in the morning and noon, after banns had been announced there three Sundays in advance), it nonetheless remained possible for the rich to avoid scrutiny. They could do so either by purchasing a license from a bishop to wed without banns or by procuring a special license from the Archbishop of Canterbury to marry 'at any convenient time and place' (VI). Trade in such licences was restricted by the Marriage Act, but remained a lucrative clerical perquisite: indeed Laurence Sterne's literary career began as a side effect of a controversy surrounding this issue, when in 1759 he wrote *A Political Romance*, a satire against Francis Topham, a York-based ecclesiastical lawyer who was making serious money in just such an enterprise.

These concessions aside, the Marriage Act mandated the Anglican Church wedding as a universal and public form of English marriage. It was able to do so effectively when earlier attempts to close down on clandestine weddings had failed because – in true Court Whig style – it joined centralising bureaucratic procedures to existing parish practices and structures, and used the magistracy and capital code to enforce them. First, to prevent the secret marriages of minors (especially those whose unions might jeopardise large estates or fortunes), the Marriage Act made the written consent of parents or guardians mandatory for those under twenty-one marrying by licence (XI). And, second, all marriages were to be recorded in parish registers now numbered and ruled so as to prevent fraud (XIV). Echoing the rationalising spirit of the National Registration Bill, the Marriage Act specified the precise form of register entries, requiring the signatures of the contracting parties and the minister and two 'credible' witnesses.[60]

Most importantly, the Marriage Act made provision for the nullification of any marriage performed in violation of its requirements (VII, XI).[61] Although their application was uneven, these so-called nullity clauses lay at the crux of the Marriage Act's will to suborn the Church. They gave the state the power to dissolve a religious ceremony if it was not accompanied by specified legal forms; as such they were to become the focus of particularly intense opposition. Punishments for errant clergymen were also severe: they were subject to a felony charge and fourteen years' transportation for conducting irregular weddings, and to the death penalty for fraud upon a marriage register or license – the latter *without Benefit of Clergy* (XVI). The Marriage Act's final clause, an Erastian coup de grâce added at Hardwicke's suggestion, required the Marriage Act itself to be publicly read from the pulpit four times each year (XIX).

Historians have long debated the Marriage Act's impact. Some have viewed it as a modernising force through which marriage and family entered the enlightened civil sphere; others as a regressive measure whereby the state reinforced the position of the propertied and patriarchal elite.[62] More recent discussion has eschewed grand narratives: Rebecca Probert, for instance, takes the minimalist view that the Marriage Act's provisions represent a 'gradual progression towards regularity and formality' which for the most part operated in continuity with the Canons and allowed the ecclesiastical courts to maintain their jurisdiction over marriage (although, as she concedes, they were now constrained by statute in determining whether a marriage was valid).[63] R. B. Outhwaite, on the other hand, views the Marriage Act's repudiation of the long-standing church principles of consent and indissolubility as a radical shift that enhanced secular-civil authority.[64]

Most striking for our purposes, however, is the degree to which the Marriage Act accommodated both church *and* state, harnessing old ecclesiastical practices to the machinery of the modern state to create a code that heightened the stakes of marriage for couples, parents, witnesses and celebrants alike, as attested by the remarks of Boswell and Harriet Byron discussed at the beginning of this chapter. On one hand, the Marriage Act's strict provisions for public weddings, parental consent, witnesses and registration rendered English marriage a civil-secular institution of a kind consistent with Protestant Europe's reformed marriage codes.[65] On the other hand, by mandating the Anglican wedding service as the only legal form of matrimony, it perpetuated the sui generis status of the Anglican establishment even as it reformed the regulation of marriage.[66]

In practical political terms, the Marriage Act's synthetic approach made it workable, unlike the Jewish Naturalisation Act and the National Registration Bill. The Marriage Act escaped their fate because it attached traditional Tory interests to Whig ones, drawing the rituals and ceremonies of Anglican faith, and the primacy of parish life, into the broader flows of capital and biopower. The Country opposition, based in the rural clergy and small squirearchy, barely objected because the measure increased the church's social power even as it rendered it a servant of state. And from the Court Whig point of view, the acquiescence of the bishops in the House of Lords under Thomas Secker exemplified the values of an enlightened church that, in the words of Attorney General Dudley Ryder, threw aside 'superstitious opinion' to render 'Christianity consistent with common sense'.[67]

Yet the coalitions and compromises that enabled the Marriage Act's success also meant that it sparked widespread and prolonged protest. The first wave of attacks on the Marriage Act emphasised its effects on plebeian welfare. They expressed fears that its barriers to easy weddings would limit marriage opportunities among the poor, increase the number of illegitimate children, encourage 'vice and immorality' among young women unable readily to marry their seducers, and hence lead to new divisions between rich and poor.[68] However, unlike the resistance to the Jewish Naturalisation Act, which was primarily popular, the resistance to Hardwicke's Marriage Act was barely accompanied by violence or ritual protest.[69] While some opponents did link the Marriage Act to the reviled 'Jew Bill', their protests were for the most part polite, proceeding through literate channels of political, religious, intellectual – and, indeed, literary – debate.[70]

The immediate opposition to the Marriage Act was organised within two main vectors: one associated with High Church Tories who believed that the state had no business controlling a sacred Christian rite; the other associated with Patriots, disaffiliated Whigs and radicals who argued that the Marriage Act shored up oligarchy by creating barriers to marriages between rich and poor. Yet, even as opponents of the Marriage Act roughly divided in this way, its politics are difficult to map. Outhwaite cautions that the Marriage Act's opponents cannot be regarded as offering a principled repudiation of 'the landed wing of the ruling class' (as represented by the Court Whigs). They contributed, rather, to an internecine and 'complicated mix of ideology, connection and faction that defy clear-cut analysis'.[71] Certainly, the Marriage Act was a focal point for factional manoeuvring. Because the old-style Tories, closely connected to the rural clergy and small squirearchy, barely objected to it, its parliamentary opposition was led by the Duke of Bedford and Henry Fox, out-of-office Whigs who sought payback for Hardwicke's prevention of the Duke of Cumberland (Fox's patron) from succeeding George II as regent in the case that George III came to the throne while under age. At this level, opportunism reigned.

Nonetheless, the resistance to the Marriage Act shaped oppositional alliances and new forms of culture, especially literary culture, for decades to come. This was not least because it connected those forms of ordinary life that were traditionally of interest to theatre and fiction – namely, love and marriage – to the business of government. In a letter to Elizabeth Carter, Richardson himself claimed to have influenced its passage by circulating his correspondence on *Clarissa* with the young Hester Mulso.[72] In that exchange, Mulso disputed Richardson's endorsement of parents' authority in marriage (memorably insisting that 'inhuman parents' like the Harlowes who 'treat their children as chattels' test the very limits of filial piety).[73] For his part, Richardson rallied old Tory and conduct book theories of filial duty against Mulso's Lockean case for children's rights, including the right to 'shake off that unnatural yoke' of parental tyranny.[74]

Of course, we can't know what kind of influence, if any, Richardson and Mulso's correspondence had on the parliamentary debate of the Marriage Act. Richardson clearly felt vindicated by the Marriage Act's parent consent requirements for minors, but his intervention may also have backfired since in speaking against it in Commons, the young Charles Townshend appears to have channelled Mulso's critique when he presented a harrowing quasi-fictional account of a younger son prevented from marrying an heiress by her dictatorial and unfeeling parents.[75] The speech was landmark in its own right, initiating a long-lasting representation of the Marriage Act as a form of tyranny over minor children that would weave itself into the sentimental novel's conventions.[76] From the beginning, then, the Marriage Act and its critique were implicated in fictional worlds.

Indeed, the concern that the Marriage Act augmented the state's power over private lives and, in particular, the private lives of minors united all protests against it. In general terms, its critics regarded it as another move to establish a new kind of governmentality over the population at large, extending what Fox himself memorably termed the 'Great Spider of the Law' into wholly new territory.[77] This objection energised anti-ministerial forces in Parliament and beyond, and was also to have an important afterlife in literary fiction. It was expressed, however, not through a defence of individual liberties in the style of Mulso and Townshend, nor by appeals to freedom of conscience and toleration (despite the fact that the Marriage Act's provisions signally disadvantaged Dissenters). In its conceptually most powerful form, early critique of the Marriage Act's statism was made from a High Church, anti-Erastian point of view, which contested the secular state's right to intervene on the church's domain.

Marriage and Natural Law

The Marriage Act redrew the boundary between church and state in terms that were not just Erastian but also post-secular. In historical terms, this meant that the Marriage Act was an important test case for conceptualising the boundary between the divine and the secular according to natural law. Theories of natural law were central to the legitimation of the Court Whig project itself, which held that the English constitution, in offering all subjects liberty, was grounded in the laws of nature, namely the principles of right and justice that God had embedded in his creatures and the nature of things.[78] Principles of natural law also grounded Court Whig concepts of security and order. Thus, for instance, Lord Hardwicke believed that natural law as distilled in common law and the constitution provided sufficient liberties for the state and the oligarchy to act in the interest of strict subordination and control.[79] As Samuel Richardson put this idea in his edition of Sir Thomas Roe's papers, '[w]e are by nature prone enough to liberty.'[80]

Natural law was central to the debate about marriage regulation because, for the Marriage Act's opponents and advocates alike, marriage belonged to universal laws of nature and thus could not be sanctioned by statute, or positive law, alone. This meant that the pamphlet literature around the Marriage Act often called upon competing theories of natural justice, variously conceived as the will of God, the dictates of nature or as ancient tradition.[81] In this context, the marriage debate unfolded in two stages: the first was the initial Court Whig case for marriage reform, which made direct appeal to the famous German secular legal theorist, Samuel

Pufendorf, in asserting the state's sovereign right to regulate marriage. The second – which gained momentum after the Marriage Act's passage – involved an extended pamphlet war that pitted High Church views on divine natural law against Whig Erastianism, and which established a matrix for later developments, both political and literary.

The Court Whig case for marriage reform was argued most forcefully in 1750 by the king's chaplain, Henry Gally, in *Some Considerations on Clandestine Marriages*.[82] Unlike previous polemical writing against clandestine marriages which had mostly focussed on their corrupting effects on the Anglican clergy, Gally made a signature Whig appeal to good government, security and prosperity, declaring that the 'Business of Society' is 'not only to promote the Encrease of its Members, but also to provide for their Happiness'.[83] Taking aim at the ecclesiastical code's permissiveness, he pointed to the 'bad Consequences of a public Nature' caused by clandestine marriages, which 'disturb the Peace and good Order of Society, and interrupt that due Course of Justice, by which Liberty and Property can only be preserv'd'.[84]

Amongst the more egregious cases of such disturbance Gally noted were those of Mary Redding, an heiress ruined after being forced into a clandestine marriage, and more notoriously the courtesan Con Phillips, who confessed in her memoir to having secretly married a bigamist in order to screen herself from debt before going on to remarry several times.[85] For Gally, cases like these showed that irregular marriages thrive in the corruption they also foster. His concerns echoed Hardwicke's own when, in his legal practice, he encountered instances of fraud and deception enabled by the old ecclesiastical marriage regime. The case of *Bennet and Spencer* v *Wade* (1742), in which a senile man had been 'imposed upon' by an apothecary who married Wade's sixteen-year-old daughter, made a particular impression on Hardwicke, as did the landmark (Scottish) suit *Cochran* v *Campbell*, occasioned by a bigamous wife's claim to a captain's widow pension.[86]

All these cases involved marriage's monetarisation in the face of church inertia. As such, clandestine marriage was for Gally in particular a symptom of a deeper malaise that threatened the social order upon which the cohesion of the state depended. It was in response to this threat that Gally turned to Pufendorf's secular natural law theories which had indeed helped to legitimate civil marriage regimes across Protestant Europe.[87] In his treatise on the *Law of Nature and Nations* (1672) Pufendorf had extended Locke's theorisation of marriage as the 'first society' to argue that, because marriage is 'the main foundation of a social life', it is also a vital domain of civil government.[88] Such claims were embedded in the larger intellectual endeavour to shift natural law's authority from the church to the state in order to protect Protestant sovereignty against papal claims. For Roman Catholicism, God's natural law was morally superior to local civil law: in Thomist terms it was 'the form in which human reason has access to God's imprinting of purposive nature'.[89] Against this scholastic tradition Pufendorf posited an immanent law of nature as the foundation of all human societies. Natural law thus precedes and enables 'the laws of nations', but with important qualifications. On one side, it stands as the source of sovereign power, and thereby guarantees sovereignty's reasonable and just intent. (Indeed, it does so because Pufendorf understood natural law to confer rights only insofar as it also conferred obligations.) On the other side, natural law is not continuous with sovereign legislation since it could not, under all circumstances, determine and express the interests of particular national communities. Those considerations required positive law.

As the institution that most firmly connects human society to nature, marriage holds a central place in Pufendorf's social theory. 'Who is there', he asked, 'that can pretend to be insensible how little Difference would be left between Beasts and Men, should the Ordinances of Marriage be universally cancelled and repealed?'[90] Marriage is not just a 'general Ordinance of Nature', it is nothing less than 'the Source of private Families' which 'by consequence, suppl[ies] Matter for the composing of all Sovereignties and States'.[91] By this logic, the regulation of marriage is where civil authority can best lay claim to benevolent and morally sanctioned sovereign power. Yet it followed too that 'though Persons are naturally free to marry whom they please, yet a Government, if it seem for the Interest of the State, may, in some Cases, restrain and limit this Privilege.'[92] Here lay a strong theoretical rationale for state-imposed marriage restrictions of the kind the Marriage Act introduced to England.

More particularly, Pufendorf offered Gally a powerful counter-argument to High Church objections to state-mandated legal weddings, and in particular to provisions for the state to annul marriages that had been improperly celebrated. From the ecclesiastical point of view, such measures undermined the scriptural doctrines of consent and indissolubility (Matthew 5:19), by permitting positive law to override religious ritual forms. Against this kind of orthodoxy, Gally unleashes Pufendorf's secularism:

> The Force of civil Laws is ultimately founded in the Obligations of the Law of Nature. And there the only Point to be considered is, whether the civil

Power can put such Restraints and Limitations upon the Law of Nature, as
are for the common Good of Society. But this must be allowed. For Society
is essentially founded on such a Power. It cannot subsist without it. And all
civil Laws are, in some Respect or other, Abridgements of natural Rights.[93]

'[T]he common Good of Society', as Gally goes on to make clear, consists
primarily in the security of property rights, as protected in this instance by
the legal curtailment of clandestine unions otherwise tolerated by the
Church.

Pufendorf's secular theory of natural law was also central to Gally's
defence of another controversial aspect of the Marriage Act legislation:
the restrictions on the marriages of minor children. Following Pufendorf,
Gally held that the 'magistrates' have the same power over the community
as fathers over their families. But this power takes a different form in the
case of state officials because it needs to consider precisely that 'common
Good of Society' which individuals themselves cannot grasp from their
limited perspective. From this point of view, the natural right of minors to
marry must indeed be 'abridged' since the social contract can only be
honoured in the form of public legislation – i.e. statute law requiring
parental consent for the marriages of minor children – that can be applied
universally to private lives.[94]

In using Pufendorf's theory of natural law to sanction placing marriage
(and marriage restrictions) at the heart of an administered state, Gally's
Considerations set the theoretical terms for Hardwicke's Marriage Act. Yet
in the hurly-burly of public debate surrounding the Marriage Act, Gally's
objections to the scandals caused by clandestine marriages carried more
weight than his erudite arguments about civil sovereignty and natural law.
Somewhat paradoxically, in the parliamentary debate it was the Marriage
Act's opponents who first made natural law arguments to discredit it.
Oppositional Whigs Robert Nugent and Henry Fox initiated a chorus of
complaint that the Marriage Act improperly infringed upon the laws of
God and nature (which until now, as Fox wryly remarked, even the High
Church had seen fit to leave well alone).[95] And this line of attack shaped the
subsequent pamphlet debate between divines on both sides, which came to
turn on disagreements about secular natural law's place in the English/
Anglican polity.

Henry Stebbing, an established High Church controversialist, was one
of the Marriage Act's most formidable Tory critics.[96] Stebbing had made
his name in the 1740s by joining a pamphlet war against William
Warburton's *The Divine Legation of Moses Demonstrated* (1738–41),

a monument of anti-deist scholarship. Now, a decade later, he contested the Marriage Act on grounds that would have seemed odd to the Anglican Jacobite faction whose descendent he was.[97] In a series of pamphlets, he argued that the right of contracting marriage cannot be granted by society but is rather a natural right: 'no Man, by entering into Society, can be presumed to have yielded up into the Hands of Society, his natural Right to contract Marriage ... It is a Right *unalienable*.'[98]

Like Gally, Stebbing uses Grotius and Pufendorf to make his point.[99] Crucially for him, however, the natural right to marry is not secular: it is bequeathed to humans by God in order to prevent fornication while preserving the species according to the divine injunction to 'go forth and multiply.'[100] Here the Lutheran account of marriage as earlier outlined by Martin Buce and John Milton, for which marriage primarily satisfied the fundamental human need for companionship and sociability, is rejected in favour of a more orthodox understanding of marriage as a social remedy allowing for humanity's need to reproduce itself while curbing the sinful desires of the flesh. Thus, for Stebbing, the state has no role in managing marriage because marriage is not an expression of that essential sociability which grounds natural law. In particular, the state did not have a right to deny the legitimacy of consensual marriages, nor to place arbitrary restrictions on the biblical injunction to increase and multiply.

Stebbing's natural law argument found its most practical application against the Marriage Act's nullity clauses and was most strikingly deployed in his second anti-Marriage Act pamphlet, *A Dissertation on the Power of States to Deny Civil Protection to the Marriage of Minors* (1755). Here he argued that the state possesses no right to prevent minors from marrying in obedience to God's will. Invoking the ideas (and intensity) of young love, Stebbing reanimated the old Tory interest in cases where human law contradicts divine law, this time, however, in the name of eros and liberty. Surprisingly, in *A Dissertation* Stebbing's defence of divinely inspired natural law becomes consonant with secular conceptions of individual freedom, also based in 'natural rights', and parsed as the capacity to fulfil private desires, much as Hester Mulso had argued in her correspondence with Richardson. Here Tory polemic begins to converge with radicalism in a manner that anticipates later developments in the marriage debate.

The most sustained Erastian response to Stebbing and other Tory critics came from none other than William Warburton, who publicly defended the Marriage Act's strictures in his 1754 sermon 'On the Nature of the Marriage Union'.[101] Drawing on his own theorisation of 'mixed' government in *The Alliance between Church and State* (1736), Warburton sidelined

Gally's secularism on one hand and Stebbing's orthodoxy on the other, in order to conceive of marriage precisely as a (post-secular) institution where God's authority and governmental power fold into one another.

Warburton's sermon begins by reminding his audience that the Old Testament Mosaic laws permitted polygamy and divorce only as concessions to the Jews' 'hardness of heart'. Once these dispensations were overturned by Christ, however, any attempt by 'human Authority' to 'put Man and Wife ... asunder' is 'highly criminal'.[102] The divine contravention of divorce nonetheless allows us to have a clearer notion of what the marriage union itself properly consists of, both in relation to 'Revealed Religion' and to 'Civil Government' since marriage is 'of a MIXED nature; in part a sacred ordinance, in part a human institution'.[103] On this basis, Warburton goes on to argue that while God has made marriage an 'indissolvable tie' and civil authorities are required to insist on his will, it is nonetheless also true that neither God nor Moses nor Jesus prescribed particular forms for the celebration of marriage. These forms are therefore a matter for the 'civil Magistrate' to determine in precisely the manner of Hardwicke's legislation:[104]

> From these clear *principles*, and this certain *deduction*, we collect the *justice* and Religion, as well as *expedience* and true Policy of a late salutary Law solely calculated for the support and ornament of Society: by which the just rights and Authority of Parents are vindicated; the peace and harmony of families preserved; the irregular appetites of Youth restrained; and the worst and basest kind of seduction encountered and defeated. I mean, that sage provision, whereby all pretended Marriages, not solemnized as the WISDOM OF OUR ANCIENT CONSTITUTION directs, are rendered null and void.[105]

Warburton's defence of the Marriage Act and its nullity clauses is strikingly original. Unlike Gally, he has no truck with Pufendorf's balancing of universal natural law and the positive laws of sovereign states. He appeals, rather, to an 'ancient constitution' in which God's will and the magistrate's authority are joined. In effect, he gives Hardwicke's legislation divine sanction, but in Erastian terms that echo theories of absolutist sovereignty rather than the Pufendorfian natural law tradition.

Indeed, Warburton's seemingly ad hoc Erastian absolutism introduced an unexpected turn into the marriage debate, especially in light of his own (and Hardwicke's) adhesion to the Whig principles of 1688. It did, however, address the Court Whigs' urgent need to sanction the state's administrative reach and power in relation to marriage in a situation in which only the Established Church possessed sufficient geographical coverage and powers of legitimation to implement their policy.

The same ad hoc logic may also explain why Warburton saw fit to include in his sermon on the nature of the marriage union the strongest possible censure of clandestine marriage:

> For the dissolution of a mock-marriage not entered into with the previous qualifications the Law of Nature enjoins, nor executed by the public forms which the Laws of Society require, is so far from *putting asunder those whom God hath joined together*, that it is only breaking an insolent and disorderly confederacy in licentiousness, where God's Sanction and the Magistrate's Authority are equally insulted: and by a crime too which indeed savours the most of that very impiety we are so commendably anxious to avoid: there being nothing which God hath more inseparably united than the *obedience* of Children to the *care and protection* of Parents.[106]

Clandestine marriage harnesses sin and crime in a 'confederacy' of licentiousness. As such, it 'insults' both 'God's Sanction and the Magistrate's Authority' and doubly violates natural law (as divine will and social contract). Warburton's unmitigated censure of clandestine marriage thereby justifies the Marriage Act's strict nullity clauses. It also hints, however, at the important role such censure will play in efforts to define and inculcate proper marriage ceremony in the context of the English marriage plot.

The first wave of the marriage debate among Anglican divines brought about an unexpected set of positions on the relationship between church and state. Whig apologists like Gally used concepts of natural law to posit a secular theory of sovereignty while sanctioning the role of the state in private or civil life and condemning commerce's encroachment on married relations. Tory thinkers like Stebbing used the discourse of natural rights – the right of all to marry in the eyes of God – to rebut state power and assert a sovereign and divinely sanctioned individualism emblematised by young love and clandestine marriage. Finally, in Warburton, Whig Erastianism moved towards an unorthodox concept of constitutionalism that located civil power's authority in the divine as mediated by the Church, endorsing marriage reform and censuring clandestine marriage for religious and secular reasons.

Collectively these arguments underscore the Marriage Act's post-secularism. They set the terms for its lively public and literary reception in ways that underscore not just marriage's theo-political charge but also a consensus about its centrality. As the divines who quarrelled about Hardwicke's Marriage Act agreed, marriage lay at the heart of English social and religious relations, as the Boswells and Harriet Byron affirmed (and as presumably most English subjects would). Marriage's controversial new function after 1754 – as an administratively engaged institution of church and state grounded in nature – only served to emphasise this the more by making marriage a crux of the period's governmental, political and social transformations. The Marriage Act helped to enable a new kind of state to emerge, one concerned with the population's moral welfare as well as its security and stability. It also lay at the heart of an ongoing debate about the relation between divine and secular natural law within the polity. And, as we see in the next chapter, it played a central role in what we might call, after Foucault, the disciplining of English society by repressing a complex and vital clandestine culture.

CHAPTER 2

Clandestine Marriage, Commerce and the Theatre

Clandestine marriage played a significant role in the English marriage plot's development. Before being suppressed by the Marriage Act, it had spawned its own popular culture, whose history helps to explain what was at stake in the division of 'proper' from 'improper' ceremony that was so important to the new genre. This chapter outlines the conditions for the rise of clandestine marriage before taking account of its cultural profile centred on London's so-called Fleet marriage market, a hub of the city's boisterous commercial street life and tavern culture and a focus of its stage entertainments. If the marriage debate appealed to erudite theories in the halls of power, clandestine marriage and its representations belonged to more unruly and demotic spaces. In a remarkable feat of reconfiguration, however, by the century's second half clandestine marriage had become an element of respectable (and sentimental) culture.

Improper Precedent

Clandestine marriages were weddings *not* conducted in a church or chapel in the bride's parish in accordance with the Canons. Performed by clergymen out of hours, outside a consecrated church or chapel, or without notice of intent (i.e. the calling of banns or an application for a license to marry), they were 'clandestine' because they were not subject to the public scrutiny that the church required.[1] The practice dated back to the eleventh century, when the Church established its authority over marriage through the doctrine of consent and, historically at least, it catered largely to itinerant populations, such as soldiers and sailors, who needed to wed outside the confines of a parish.[2] In the wake of early modern England's successive confessional regimes, clandestine weddings emerged as an increasingly popular alternative to regular parish weddings because, although technically 'irregular', they were valid and binding at ecclesiastical law. Essentially, a clandestine union could ensure couples a degree of convenience or privacy, even respectability. The same logic sustained an illicit trade in marriage licenses for those able to pay for a dispensation to wed at a time or place of their own choosing. As *The Craftsman* noted, 'the profitable Trade of *Licences* ... is chiefly supported by the natural Bashfulness of People ... who don't care to have their *Amours* exposed in a full Congregation.'[3]

Clandestine marriage in England flourished especially between the Restoration and the mid-eighteenth century. By the time it was outlawed in 1754, it accounted for between half and three-quarters of London's weddings and, in Lawrence Stone's estimation, some 15 to 20 per cent of the marriage trade in England.[4] Estimates vary, however: Donald Spaeth notes that as many as one in four English unions may have been clandestine in the late seventeenth century; Rebecca Probert tempers Jeremy Boulton's earlier claims about its metropolitan dominance.[5] Most recently, Gill Newton's inclusion of fresh figures for two large and rapidly growing suburban parishes (Clerkenwell in the north-west and Aldgate in the east) confirms that it was, indeed, the 'commonest means of marrying' in greater London, where, as she puts it, 'clandestine marriage became not so much the exception as the rule.'[6]

The demographics of clandestine marriage tell a plain enough story about its growing importance in the first half of the eighteenth century, yet its cultural profile remains largely unexplored. Indeed, by regarding clandestine marriage in narrowly quantitative terms – that is as an exception to, or latterly as a variation on, established patterns of regular clerical marriage – historiography has left untold the story of its broader impact. That story is threefold. First, as a form of church matrimony unattached to the parish, clandestine marriage brought marriage and church ritual into a new connection with secular culture, and in particular with the forces of commercial capital that fuelled London's growth in the period. Second, it played a sustained and prominent role in the emergent media and entertainment sphere, both on the licensed and unlicensed stage and in the rapidly expanding print market. Indeed, by the 1730s, London's freewheeling clandestine marriage market was one of the Georgian era's signature cultural novelties and was widely featured in plays, prints, newspaper reportage and fiction of the period. And, third, in the lead-up to the Marriage Act, clandestine marriage was targeted by the forces of moral reform as a mode of *improper* marriage against which new regimes of politeness, gender and proper ceremony defined themselves. These factors constitute the backstory through which clandestine marriage played a shaping role in the novel's emerging English marriage plot.

The clandestine marriage phenomenon in England was sui generis. Perhaps most fundamentally, the practice was based on a widely held perception that priests were necessary to weddings, as Donald Spaeth observes.[7] Although not strictly speaking true, this belief had taken hold in England by 1640, and flourished in the wake of the confusion caused by shifts in marriage protocols during the Interregnum and the Restoration.[8] Some specialist knowledge of ecclesiastical law is required here.

In canon law consent, not ceremony, was the basis of marriage, which meant that the crucial distinction for ecclesiastical courts was not whether a priest was present at a union but whether marriage vows were uttered in the present or future tense. Furthermore, verbal spousals in the present tense (*per verba de praesenti*) made before witnesses constituted an irrevocable marriage contract, while an oral promise to marry in the future (*per verba de futuro*) had the status of an engagement that could be broken legally by mutual consent, and only amounted to a binding union if followed by consummation.[9] The consensual essence of the ecclesiastical code meant that *any* exchange of vows in the present tense made before witnesses was valid as a marriage contract, whatever its circumstances. As the ecclesiastical lawyer Henry Swinburne put it in his *Treatise of Spousals* (1686), spousals *de praesenti* are 'in truth and substance very Matrimony, and therefore perpetually indissoluble, except for Adultery'.[10]

Ecclesiastical marriage nonetheless made a functional distinction between a verbal contract of consent and a clerical marriage formally celebrated in a church. In doctrinal terms, the 'essence' of marriage turned on witnessed consent, but in practice a consensual contract was 'both binding *and* incomplete' until it was solemnised by church ceremony.[11] Marriage in early modern England, Probert notes, 'may well have been a process rather than an event, but the final stage – that of solemnisation – cannot be assumed to be optional' (46). The distinction was routinely parsed in terms of natural law theory in much the same way as Warburton reasoned in his sermon on marriage. A consenting couple might be married according to conscience or in the eyes of God (i.e. natural law), but their union was not complete until it underwent the 'public forms' mandated by the 'Laws of Society'.[12] Proper ceremony was in this manner a necessary supplement to consent. It took the form of a public Anglican wedding ceremony as prescribed by the Canons (which ruled when and where it could happen) and by the Book of Common Prayer (which mandated its liturgy).

From the late seventeenth century, however, clandestine marriage came to occupy a new place in the interstices of English law. At that time, the common law courts began to supplement the Church's doctrine of consent with a doctrine of 'ministerial intervention' so as to enable reliable material evidence of marriage to be secured for property settlements.[13] This meant that clerical marriage, which remained inessential to the marriage bond according to the Church, was necessary for securing spousal property rights at common law. Clandestine marriage could accommodate this contradiction since, unlike simple verbal spousals, it offered a valid, if irregular, union at ecclesiastical *and* common law while also avoiding the strictures of regular parish weddings. In this context, clandestine marriage became a fully functional alternative to regular marriage (although it did expose couples to some risk of punishment as well as to a heavier burden of proof should their union be contested).[14]

While the equivalence of regular and clandestine marriage at secular law helps to explain the rising popularity of clandestine marriage, it also explains why recent specialist historians have come to view that popularity as evidence of 'the success of clerical marriage as the mark of binding matrimony' rather than as a rejection of the Church or the norms of Anglican marriage, as an earlier generation of historians had supposed.[15] Indeed, clandestine weddings allowed the Church to meet real community needs for quick and easy marriage. On the demand side, there were many reasons to marry without publicity or communal approval, most obviously for religious non-conformists, pregnant women and minors.[16] On the supply side, illicit weddings offered an informal source of income for a large sector of the Anglican vicarate at a time when many clergymen struggled to make a respectable living.[17] Curates were particularly active in this regard, but incumbents also performed irregular marriages to supplement their income.[18]

Yet in doctrinal terms clandestine marriage remained anathema to the Reformed church on two counts. First, it undermined the primary purpose of public weddings, which was to mark marriage's status as a foundational social institution (and thereby wholly to reject Roman Catholic models of celibacy and sacramental marriage).[19] Second, clandestine marriage exposed clergymen to the dangers of worldly vice and corruption. On these grounds the ecclesiastical courts punished clergy for performing irregular weddings (subjecting them to three years' suspension), and occasionally excommunicated couples for undergoing them.[20] In practice, however, clandestine marriage had long been tolerated because it catered to people outside local parish communities who were relatively unfixed in the social hierarchy. Arguably, these conditions fuelled the ongoing development of clandestine marriage markets.

In rural areas, for instance, clergymen routinely performed clandestine weddings for couples travelling from other parishes (which in itself was technically illegal), as did clergy in so-called peculiar parishes, also known as 'lawless churches', who for one reason or another claimed exemption from episcopal authority. Among the most notorious offenders were those known as 'strolling clergy' – unbeneficed clergymen who wandered from parish to parish picking up what fees they could for performing ad hoc ecclesiastical rituals. One divine complained of 'a parcel of strolling curates in South Wales, and some . . . in North Wales, who for a crown or at most for a guinea, would marry anybody under a hedge'.[21] These non-resident clergy themselves operated on the peripheries of the parish system and at the lowest end of the church hierarchy. They catered largely to itinerants, particularly soldiers and sailors, whose own patterns of migration from country to city (and thence into imperial service) helped to fuel the clandestine marriage boom. Military and imperial labourers were especially prominent among those who took advantage of extemporary wedding services before 1754.[22]

It was in London, however, that clandestine marriage flourished as a fully fledged 'trade' or 'market'. By the late seventeenth century the city had developed an extensive network of lawless churches where large numbers of couples married outside their home parishes. These attracted intense public scrutiny, not least from the wits of Grub Street and the Restoration stage. For example, in 1700 William Congreve's *The Way of the World* made topical reference to two of London's most prolific lawless churches: St Pancras in the Fields and St James Duke's Place (both in the vicinity of suburban Clerkenwell).[23] At Duke's Place, which provided the earliest recorded systematic clandestine service, Reverend Adam Elliott performed as many as forty weddings in a day, and clocked more than 40,000 marriages in the period between 1664 and 1691.[24] Congreve's play opens with an ironic comparison of the Duke's Place wedding service with that of its closest rival, St Pancras:

> Sir, there's such Coupling at *Pancras*, that they stand behind one another, as 'twere in a Country Dance. Ours was the last couple to lead up; and no Hopes appearing of Dispatch. Besides, the Parson growing hoarse, we were afraid his Lungs wou'd have fail'd before it came to our Turn; so we drove round to *Duke's-Place*; and there they were rivetted in a trice.[25]

Here the clandestine wedding trade is the stuff of pure farce, its rough and ready plebeian simplicity and anonymity contrasting with the delicate negotiations required for the union of the play's genteel characters (which it nonetheless enables).

In a similar spirit, the periodical press treated clandestine marriage as a low-life suburban parody of pastoral ideals. In 1709 *The Tatler* took a polite and comic view of them, finely attuned to the class calibrations of London's commercial community:

> Colonel *Ramble* and my self went early this Morning into the Fields, which were strew'd with Shepherds and Shepherdesses, but indeed of a different Turn from the Simplicity of those of *Arcadia* ... we saw at a Distance a Company coming towards *Pancras*-Church ... [W]ho should it be but Mons. *Guardeloop*, mine and *Ramble's French* Taylor, attended by others, leading one of Madam *Depingle's* Maids to the Church, in order to their Espousals ... [T]he Morning being rainy, methought the March to the Wedding was but too lively a Picture of Wedlock itself. They seem'd both to have a Month's Mind to make the best of their Way single; yet both tugg'd Arm in Arm ... [T]hey were in a dirty Way ... The Bridegroom's Feathers in his Hat all droop'd, one of his Shoes had lost an Heel. In short, he was in his whole Person and Dress so extremely sous'd, that there did not appear one Inch or single Thread about him unmarried.[26]

Here a mock-heroic mode of double address serves to mark out 'the Colonel' and his interlocutor Isaac Bickerstaff from the sorry spectacle they meet, and by implication *The Tatler's* own readership from the tailors, seamstresses and other wage earners who (apparently) participated in the illicit marriage market.

I say 'apparently' because, although skilled labourers and artisans constituted a significant proportion of London's clandestine wedding market, its class composition was more mixed than early accounts suggest.[27] By the late seventeenth century the clandestine system catered not just to a growing demographic of urban-based artisan and commercial classes but also to the wider population. Probert offers evidence of this shift in her 'reassessment' of marriage law and practice in the period.[28] Drawing on comparative data (which traces the trajectory of 'test groups' of English couples across selected parish registers, baptismal registers and settlement examinations), she notes in particular that the bulk of clandestine marriages were 'regular' except that they were performed in a church outside of the bride's native parish.[29] More generally, her demographic work, along with Newton's, confirms not just the ubiquity but also the ordinariness of clandestine marriage in the period.[30]

Congreve seems intent on dramatising this very point: London's thriving clandestine wedding trade drew the church and marriage itself into 'the ways of the world' – that is, into the dynamic flows of labour and capital that connected the metropolis to an expanding world of commerce and empire. At St Pancras, the demand for instant weddings is such that couples 'stand behind one another'; while at Duke's Place, they are 'rivetted in a trice'. Together, these two lawless churches resemble nothing so much as a marriage machine, offering the sacred bond of matrimony instantly and in regular repetition. Indeed, from this satiric point of view, clandestine marriage was nothing less than an adaptation of clerical marriage to the rapidly growing metropolis and the emergent secular modernity it represented.

If Congreve satirises the commercial *scale* of London's clandestine wedding trade and the highly mimetic sociability of its mass marriages, *The Tatler* gently mocks another of the trade's modern novelties, namely its predisposition to spectacle and entertainment. Indeed, as Bickerstaff remarks, far from being hidden or obscure the clandestine wedding presents 'too lively a *Picture* of Wedlock itself' (italics mine). His eyewitness account belongs to a new literature of London that embedded the polite male spectator in the cityscape so as to present plebeian street life from his bemused and ambulatory point of view.[31] This ironic perspective, which makes a spectacle of (supposedly) demotic public life, became the hallmark of urban verse satire after John Gay's *Trivia* (1716), and played an important role in shaping clandestine marriage's popular representation. Indeed, Bickerstaff's testimony shows the degree to which the term 'clandestine' was already a misnomer by the early eighteenth century since Mons. Guardeloop and Madam Depingle's clandestine nuptials do not take place in secret. They belong, rather, to a new and highly visible mode of conjugality that was part of the metropolitan streetscape, and indeed of day-to-day commerce.

Fleet Wedding Commerce

Nowhere was the spectacle of clandestine marriage more fully displayed than at London's so-called Fleet marriage market. Here clerical marriage was reinvented as commerce: part street market, part criminal subculture, part shopping experience. Fleet marriages began in the Fleet debtors' gaol in the 1670s when imprisoned clergymen conducted irregular weddings in the prison chapel, St Bride's, and occasionally in their prison chambers.[32] They did so on the basis of a claim that the prison lay outside the Bishop of London's authority. Fleet weddings soon developed a reputation as the cheapest and easiest marriages in London: they involved just a few words and could be performed at any time. From the beginning, simulation and mimicry reigned there. It was said, for instance, that in false deference to the Canons Fleet parsons stopped their clocks between the hours of eight and twelve, the legal hours for church weddings.[33] On the back of efforts to control the clandestine marriage trade, the wider area around the prison became a wedding hub. When Parliament legislated against church-based clandestine marriage services at St James Duke's Place and Holy Trinity Minories in 1695 and 1696, Fleet parsons began to cater to the increased demand for their services by performing ad hoc weddings in the taverns and shops adjacent to the prison, in the precinct known as 'the Rules' or 'Liberties'.[34]

In 1712 Parliament moved again to stop the growing illegal wedding trade, this time targeting the Fleet itself with an act that threatened to imprison offending ministers in Newgate and to impose hefty fines on prison keepers who allowed marriages in their gaols.[35] In response, Fleet turnkey John Lilley established a wedding 'chapel' nearby at the Bull and Garter alehouse, where Fleet parsons could continue to perform weddings with impunity. It was a pioneering move: Lilley's was the first quasi-commercial clerical marriage service in London that was not church-based and that therefore made no claim to immunity from ecclesiastical authority. However, it did assume a secular mantel of legitimacy for its weddings: clients were issued bogus marriage documents imprinted with the city arms and passed off as 'my Lord Mayor's certificates'. Following Lilley's example, some twenty or so marriage 'chapels' or shops sprang up in the Rules, forming a network or 'market' of competitive clandestine wedding services not wholly disconnected from the Church but distinctly extramural to it. Here couples sought quick and easy unions, and needy parsons from all over England readily joined the trade.[36]

At the Fleet, clandestine marriage became entangled with crime and commerce because the area itself contained both a prison and a marketplace. Of course, the Fleet prison was not an apparatus for producing discipline and remorse in the contemporary sense: prisoners paid a boarding fee to the warden and had free access to the Rules, an area outside the prison walls abutting the commercial district of New Market. To mitigate overcrowding, many were even allowed to live in the Rules, also in exchange for a fee. As Miles Ogborn notes, like the old debtors' sanctuaries of London which shielded debtors from arrest, the Rules were a liminal zone: 'in effect a prison outside the prison walls, but . . . also part of the city's streets and buildings'.[37] Yet the Fleet was not just a place where crime and penality merged with street commerce. The clandestine wedding market added a certain *frisson* to the area's reputation for law-lessness, rendering it a distinctly sexualised node of London's cultural geography.[38] As one popular compendium remarked, the Fleet was 'the common place for joining all rogues and whores together'.[39] There newly married couples were indistinguishable from 'rogues and whores', while priests themselves doubled as wedding pimps and hustlers.

As a new urban habitus where the mercantile-commercial economy intersected with – and morphed into – a criminal 'underworld,' the Fleet was a domain of the 'picaresque proletariat', to use Peter Linebaugh's evocative term for the mobile mass labour force that developed in Britain in the period.[40] These were the wage earners of maritime capitalism – especially the Atlantic's seafarers, sailors, soldiers and itinerant labourers – many of whom, having been untethered from commons and parish and (very often) pressed into active service, lived deracinated, intermittently urban lives which routinely included clandestine marriages. Beneath the often glib association of Fleet marriages with crime, scandal and disorder lay deeper structures of social division. As Linebaugh notes, the Newgate Ordinary's records show that many condemned men were seafarers in the navy or the merchant marine. Fleet unions, often bigamous, were common in this milieu, as they were for the women hanged at Tyburn.[41] Indeed, as a strut of a black economy that drew plebeian women into petty theft and sex work, the Fleet was heavily implicated in what Defoe termed 'Conjugal Lewdness or, Matrimonial Whoredom', in his 1727 polemic on the topic. The phenomenon, whereby individuals notched up a slew of casual, extemporary unions, is exemplified by the five marriages (two legal, three bigamous) that serve as a prelude to Moll's life of crime in *Moll Flanders* (1722).

The Fleet's convergence of sex, crime and commerce attracted significant literary commentary. Sterile 'mercantile' or 'commercial' marriages, driven by financial interest alone, had long been a rich vein of satire, on the Restoration stage, for instance. The Scriblerians, however, made clandestine marriages their own, milking them as tropes of human commerce. Alexander Pope, John Gay and John Arbuthnot's inaugural collaborative project, a satirical farce entitled *Three Hours after Marriage* (1717), took a bigamous city marriage of doubtful – likely clandestine – origins as its point of departure for an excoriating critique of corrupt, money-driven, urban values. Gay's later stage hit, *The Beggar's Opera* (1728), famously transposed the joke into lowlife, using Jonathan Swift's clever suggestion for a 'Newgate pastoral' to figure London's rogues, whores, thief-takers and highwaymen as a microcosm of Walpole's England.

Less often noticed, however, is *The Beggar's Opera*'s extended and topical treatment of marriage: the Beggar introduces his play as an ironic epithalamion, celebrating the marriage of two fictional ballad singers, 'James Chanter and Moll Lay', the latter clearly also a prostitute.[42] Its setting – the Newgate and St Giles areas of London – borders the Fleet; its (highly convoluted) domestic subplot is premised on the proximity of the clandestine marriage market. Indeed, Macheath's world is one in which secret unions – of the kind he contracts with Polly – proliferate, creating a shadow world of bigamous, indeed polygamous, relations. His rakish charm enables him to collect wives; he is surrounded by no fewer than five at the play's end when, in a dark libertine joke, he struggles to choose between married life and the gallows. After all, for Macheath (as for Moll Flanders), the slippage between the marriage knot and the hangman's noose was more than metaphorical. Gay's earlier play *The What D'ye Call It* (1715) joked about the dizzying complexities of staging marriage vows (of which more in what follows). *The Beggar's Opera*, by contrast, offered a blunt Fleet-inspired satire of comic closure per se. In a world upended by Court Whig misrule, the highwayman cheats the hangman, husbands and wives cheat each other, and London's underworld mimics Whig hegemony.

While the Fleet marriage market belonged to London's storied criminal subculture, its growth was sustained within regular forms of business and street commerce. Couples could be wed at a barber, coffee house, alehouse, inn or chapel, in addition to the prison itself. The 'marriage shops' that sprang up in the Rules refashioned the Anglican wedding as a commodity, diligently reformatting all of its features for the world of consumerism. They marshalled available commercial infrastructure to attract custom: cluttering the streets with banners and signs; sending pliers touting for business over all Ludgate Hill; and advertising their services in broadsheets and penny newspapers. 'Bride cakes', wedding paraphernalia, feasts, lodgings for consummation or even a temporary spouse were among the variety of goods and services on offer.[43] At taverns like Lilley's, which kept a small room available as a 'chapel' and a parson on call, weddings were conducted as a profitable aside to the sale of alcohol. The average price of a Fleet wedding was 7s. 6d., the equivalent of a week's wages for a working man, although it could go as low as 2s. 6d., if one were willing to forego a certificate. The fee was usually paid in advance of the ceremony, the convention being to lay the agreed sum of cash on the Bible together with a wedding ring.[44] Perhaps no more compelling symbol exists of the Fleet's mix of commercial, civil and sacral culture.

The Fleet's unseemly convergence of work-a-day commerce, irregularity and Christian ritual set the tone for public censure of its renegade priests. Thomas Pennant, a late eighteenth-century Whig naturalist and traveller, recollected the Fleet of his childhood like this:

> In walking along the street, in my youth, on the side next to this prison, I have often been tempted by the question, 'sir, will you be pleased to walk in and be married?' Along this most lawless space was hung up the frequent sign of a male and female hand conjoined, with, 'Marriages performed within', written beneath. A dirty fellow invited you in. The parson was seen walking before his shop; a squalid profligate figure, clad in a tattered plaid night-gown, with a fiery face, and ready to couple you for a dram of gin, or roll of tobacco.[45]

Here the Fleet parson boldly fronts the street tableau. 'Squalid', 'profligate' and 'fiery face[d]', he is unquestionably an object of disgust, a 'dirty fellow' who embodies the fraud and insobriety associated with Fleet marriages. He also channels a long tradition of fraudulent priestly characters dating back to the 'phony parsons' who personified the Restoration stage's anticleric-alism. As a caricature of clerical venality, Pennant's Fleet parson belongs to the gallery of gentleman rogues who, after Gay, populate the satiric London underworld. He channels living referents too, such as Reverend Alexander Keith, who styled himself a Tory popular hero and led a public crusade against the Marriage Act, or the notorious Dr Gaynam, a watchmaker turned 'priest', whose unscrupulous early dominance of the Fleet trade earned him the nickname 'The Bishop of Hell'. One satirist figured him in Miltonic terms as having 'reign'd' over the illegal marriage trade in 'bloated, reeling majesty'.[46]

The Fleet registers themselves, however, offer an arresting counterpoint to the emerging media stereotype of the Fleet parson as worldly rogue. They include evidence of the real-life struggles of parsons like Walter Wyatt, who performed weddings at Fleet from 1713 to 1750 and who noted in his private pocketbook of 1736: 'ye Priest can do ye thing y^t is just and right [at the Fleet], unless he designs to starve. For by lying, bullying, and swearing, to exhort money from the silly and unwary people, you advance your business and gets ye pelf, which always wastes like snow in sun-shiney day.'[47] Underscoring the gap between his Fleet 'business' and his clerical vocation, Wyatt engages in a revealing mock-theological dialo-gue between his 'interest' and his 'conscience': "'Give every man his due, and learn the way of Truth", says Conscience. Reply: "This advice cannot be taken by those that are concerned in the Fleet Marriages."'[48]

Nonetheless, it was as a satanic, ungodly priest that the Fleet parson emerged as a minor character in novels of the period. Harriet Byron memorably describes the 'vile' clandestine priest – half 'wretch', half 'sycophant' – whom her abductor, Sir Hargrave Pollexfen, hires to perform a chamber wedding against her will in *Sir Charles Grandison*'s first volume (1:154). Noting that the priest is unmoved by Harriet's plight because he is beholden to the squire's money and influence, Richardson associates him, in broad terms, with Whig Erastianism. Harriet's natural piety, on the other hand, is signalled by the fact that she is offended less by the parson's 'frightful visage' than by the truly 'horrid sight' of the Book of Common Prayer nestled in his filthy hands. For Richardson, the liturgical text – which, Harriet notes, 'once had been gilt', but is now 'dog's-ear'd' and 'open'd . . . at the page of matrimony!' – is a metonymy for the debasement of the Anglican Church and its rituals at the Fleet. Its perfunctory approach to nuptials contrasts with the elaborate ceremonials of the 'proper' wedding by which Harriet and Sir Charles will eventually be united.

Moral outrage quickly became the lingua franca of anti-Fleet discourse, yet its politics was complicated. As Richardson demonstrates, it could borrow from old Tory Christian polemic to push a Whig reformist agenda. In this way, Fleet weddings were routinely associated with London's gin craze, which itself was targeted by yet more Court Whig legislation aimed at social control: namely, the Gin Acts of 1736 and 1751.[49] Charles Knight records that coach loads of sailors on shore leave headed to the Fleet for group weddings during which 'the drink is passed to and fro; winks, nods, whispers, and roars of laughter form a running accompaniment to the ceremony [and] practical jokes are played on the reverend functionary.'[50] Knight's anecdote relays a host of anxieties concerning the ease of Fleet weddings, their 'improper' flouting of ritual and protocol, and not least, like gin itself, their deleterious and contagious social effects. And once again the clandestine wedding – like those at St Pancras and Duke's Place – is presented as a mode of mass marriage-cum-public spectacle by way of the crude comic objectification of its participants.

This is not to say that moral outrage against clandestine marriage belonged to reformist efforts alone. Plays, poems, prints and satires from both sides of the political divide routinely figured clandestine marriage as a low-life spectacle with a cast of subaltern characters (the renegade parson, the sailor groom, the prostitute bride and a crowd of gaping onlookers) set in London's plebeian streetscape presented as a space of disorder, deception and lawlessness. Such caricatures served Tory anti-Erastian and anti-commercial satire, on one hand, and Whig anticlericalism as well as high-minded Court Whig reformist moral polemic, on the other. Increasingly too, as that reformism took hold, the Fleet became a metonymy for the whole clandestine marriage market. Fierce moral censure of its excesses was channelled into the Marriage Act debates, so that, as Miles Ogburn has argued, the sheer volume of anti-Fleet rhetoric helped the Court Whigs to secure bipartisan parliamentary support for clandestine marriage's eradication.[51]

Improper Femininity

Censure of the Fleet reserved its most damning invective not for its priests or drunkards, but for its women. In this spirit, William H. Draper's pro-Whig reform poem *The Morning Walk, or, City Encompassed* (1751), a conventional (male) ambulatory satire, offered the following Fleet wedding tableau as a pointed indictment of London's street culture and the modes of public femininity it fostered:

> Behold! what shocks the eye, intoxicate,
> A tatter'd female drunk, with sulph'rous GIN,
> In high procession born, and wicker pride,
> Her legs wide-sprawling, portrait true of shame,
> To durance she is carried with huzza's
> Of a broad-staring, gaping, lew'd-mouth'd crowd.
> All conqu'ring GIN, how great thy triumphs here![52]

Debauched, inebriated and carried aloft through London's streets, Draper's Fleet bride is a spectacle of improper femininity. Her wanton self-display before a 'lew'd-mouth'd crowd' underscores, once again, the social divisions enacted by Fleet satire. This time, however, sex itself – 'Her legs wide-sprawling, portrait true of shame' – lies at the heart of the 'shock' scripted for polite readers.

The visual template for such representations, I'd argue, was John June's influential pair of mid-century engravings: 'A Fleet Wedding. Between a Brisk Young Sailor & His Landlady's Daughter at Rederiff' and 'The Sailor's Fleet Wedding Entertainment'. Published in 1747 at the high point of the Fleet trade, they literalised earlier figurations of clandestine marriage as spectacle, presenting the Fleet wedding as part of an unruly plebeian public sphere as evoked in William Hogarth's street-life prints and in a way that cemented the social divisions they encoded.

Tellingly, June's iconography of the Fleet wedding developed in comic dialogue with Hogarth's own visual commentary on elite marriage

Illustration 1 John June, 'A Fleet Wedding. Between a Brisk Young Sailor & His Landlady's Daughter at Rederiff', 1747.

Illustration 2 John June, 'The Sailor's Fleet Wedding Entertainment', 1747.

practices, *Marriage A-la-mode* (1745).[53] Hogarth had depicted a fashionable alliance of landed and commercial wealth so as to satirise Court Whig greed and folly, presenting across six engravings a moral tale of the 'appalling retribution' following from an arranged marriage of the foppish son of the impoverished Earl of 'Squander' to the daughter of a rich city merchant. June's diptych poses a blunt plebeian counterpoint: the rise and fall of a Fleet union between a sailor and a prostitute. The first plate depicts a wedding party – Jack the tar, a symbol of imperial Englishness, his bride, Molly, and her mother (his Rederiff landlady soon to be revealed as a bawd) – alighting from a coach at the Fleet market and greeted by rival parsons as well as by a requisite 'gaping crowd' of onlookers. The second plate transitions abruptly to the wedding feast – a tavern scene of drunken revelry – where the celebrations are interrupted by a bailiff arriving to arrest the groom for his new wife's debts and to inter him in the nearby Fleet prison.

Viewed as a companion piece to *Marriage A-la-mode*, June's Fleet wedding is a masterpiece of comic reversal.[54] It contrasts the Fleet's brisk cash economy with the protracted financial negotiations of elite espousals, and it reduces the disastrous chain of events leading to the wealthy couple's demise (adulterous affairs, a fatal dual, a Tyburn execution, a suicide) to the bathos of a soon-to-be-spoiled wedding breakfast. More subtly, its black humour extends and deepens *Marriage A-la-mode*'s critique of the elite marriage market's cynical manipulation of the legal principle of coverture whereby a husband assumed legal and financial responsibility for his wife upon marriage. Hogarth's fashionable bride, by virtue of her fortune, is figured conventionally enough as an object of exchange, who facilitates a transfer of assets between men on the society marriage market. June's Fleet bride, by contrast, duns the hapless sailor, and the law itself, by marrying so as to screen herself from debt. Anecdotal evidence suggests that this practice, a kind of coverture in reverse, was common enough at the Fleet, as was bridal pregnancy.[55] For this reason the area developed a reputation as a haven for predatory women understood to engage in a debasement of marriage that June's prints literalise as prostitution.

Descriptions of the Fleet neatly discriminated between kinds – and classes – of women. Plebeian women were routinely understood to be complicit in the marriage market's quasi-criminal culture of deception, while elite women were usually figured as its innocent victims. Forced weddings, in particular, were publicly denounced in such a way as to make the trope of imperilled female virtue – like the prostitute bride – a set piece of Fleet reportage and caricature. The following letter, printed in Richard

Russel's staunchly Tory *Grub-Street Journal* in 1735 and signed by a woman, is characteristic:[56]

> There is a very great evil in this town, and of dangerous consequence to our sex, that has never been suppressed, to the great prejudice and ruin of many hundreds of young people every year ... Since midsummer last, a young lady of birth and fortune was deluded and forced from her friends, and by the assistance of a wry-necked swearing parson, married to an atheistical wretch, whose life is a continual practice of all manner of vice and debauchery ... Sir,
>
> > your constant reader and admirer,
> > Virtuous.[57]

Virtuous's objection to the Fleet's predatory and 'atheistical' culture seems to be turned to High Church ends. Here the 'evil' of clandestine marriage inheres primarily in its association with urban public space, that is, with the 'town' and its ambient sexual threat to women. Indeed, as an agent of 'vice and debauchery' that takes the form of marriage, clandestine marriage endangers female propriety precisely by failing to distinguish between the public commerce of sex work and the rituals of church ceremony.

Virtuous's censure signals a broader anxiety still. As a mechanism for the abduction of young women 'of birth and fortune', clandestine marriage raises the spectre of *mésalliance* on a grand scale. By claiming that clandestine unions cause the ruin of 'many hundreds of young people every year', Virtuous applies the scale and disorder of London's plebeian clandestine wedding trade to the elite. Yet, while secret unions posed a challenge to elite marriage, their numbers were in fact negligible, at least within the Fleet. As John Southerden Burn's mid-nineteenth-century study of the Fleet registers established, the area attracted very few wealthy or aristocratic patrons. Entries are scattered for propertied men marrying lowborn women, possibly to avoid scandal and public disapproval, while Burn finds fewer instances of elite women marrying commoners, noting isolated cases such as a pocketbook entry for 'William Phipps, St Andrew's Holborn, Esq. & Lady Catherine Annisley, of Stoke Pogis, Buckinghamshire. B.&S'.[58]

Yet even as cross-class clandestine marriages were isolated events, a stream of alarmist rhetoric emphasised their threat precisely as an affront to the modes of parental authority that regulated the polite marriage market. That 'market', in a metaphorical use of the term, was based on long-established practices whereby elite young women circulated in public and semi-public places under the sanction of their parents or guardians in order to secure suitable marriage partners. Superficially, it was a protected market quite distinct from the open human commerce of the Fleet. Yet as

June's prints and many other (usually Tory-inflected) Fleet satires implied, elite and plebeian marriage markets alike treated women as property, exposing them to a perilous slippage between agency and coercion. The freedoms and dangers of that elision for elite young women were power-fully fictionalised in Richardson's *Clarissa* (1747). For non-elite women, however, its stakes concerned not just moral virtue or social standing but also economic survival, and on this basis the Fleet marked a boundary between proper and improper femininity.

Clandestine marriage itself, however, did seep into genteel marriage practices. From the 1730s on, it found a home in the recently developed and fashionable West End. This shift happened primarily under the influence of Reverend Alexander Keith, a fractious public figure in mid-eighteenth-century London who played a maverick role in clandestine marriage's history. Keith established a genteel clandestine marriage service at St George's Chapel, Hyde Park Corner, soon after it was built in the 1730s in order to cater to the growing population in the recently created parish of St George's, Hanover Square. From at least 1735 he performed weddings there at premium rates (a guinea until four in the afternoon, more thereafter, which included a license on a five-shilling stamp and a certificate) and at any hour, employing a staff of 'regular clergymen' (i.e. fully credentialed curates) and advertising his service in the daily newspapers.[59] His was a 'very bishopric of revenue', as Horace Walpole remarked, clocking 723 weddings in 1742, for instance, compared to just 40 at the neighbouring parish church, St George's, Hanover Square.[60]

Keith soon ran afoul of the establishment. His story demonstrates how church politics and new print readerships helped to reshape the mid-century clandestine marriage business in specifically post-secular terms. Edmund Gibson, the Whig Bishop of London, excommunicated Keith in 1742 after Dr Trebeck, the rector of the neighbouring church, successfully sued him at ecclesiastical court for lost revenue, arguing that all marriages in the parish ought to be celebrated in the parish church. Refusing to accept the ruling, Keith took his grievances directly to the public, using press advertisements to defend his right to celebrate marriages while reassuring readers that he remained open for business despite being excommunicated:

> This is to acquaint the Publick,
>   That Mr. Keith, the Minister of May-Fair Chapel, not being under the Authority or Jurisdiction of the Bishop or his Court, these 21 Months past, looks upon himself to be no ways affected by any thing they can do: And therefore the Marriage-Fees, Licence on a Five-Shilling Stamp, together

with the Certificate, amount but to a Guinea on Sundays till Six at Night, except the Time of Divine Service, which is from half an Hour after Eleven till One, and from Four till Five o'Clock; but on the Week-Days it is a Guinea till Four, a Guinea and a Half till Seven, and two Guineas after Seven at Night.

The Way to the Chapel from the City is thro' Piccadilly, by the upper End of St. James's Street, and down Clarges-Street [*sic*]. It is adjoining to the new Market near Hyde-Park-Corner.[61]

When Keith was further charged with contempt of the Church and imprisoned at the Fleet, his career took an unexpected turn. He served his sentence in open defiance of Gibson and the Whig authorities, living in high style on the profits of two marriage chapels: one in the Rules of the Fleet prison, to which he remained closely confined, the other, a new 'Little Chapel in May-Fair' which he established 'within 10 yards' of his original business and operated through curates.[62]

Once again, Keith used the newspapers to campaign against the Church hierarchy while extending his business's profile. Regular advertisements pointing out the advantages of a Mayfair wedding directed couples to the 'Little Chapel in May-Fair, near Hyde-Park-Corner, opposite the great Chapel, and within Ten Yards of it. ——— There is a Porch at the Door, like a Country Church Porch'.[63] Increasing the stakes, they also offered readers a spirited account of Keith's grievances. When his wife died unexpectedly in 1749, the event was instantly leveraged into the Little Chapel's media campaign, with advertisements over several years informing the public that her body had been 'embalm'd and wrapt up in Lead' before being transported to 'an Apothecary's in South-Audley-Street, where she lies in a Room hung with Mourning, and is to continue there 'till Mr. Keith can attend her Funeral'.[64] Indeed, Keith's provision of commercial information about his chapel (the price schedule for weddings and so on) was habitually embedded in personal detail of a kind that created a dynamic narrative context for his business.

Walpole's commentary on Keith points to the disquiet he caused the Whig establishment. In a 1754 letter to George Montagu, Walpole remarks satirically that, in the wake of the Marriage Act, Keith might venture to establish a 'Grand mart for marriages' with a 'Catalogue of Males and Females to be disposed of in marriage to the best bidder'.[65] Off-hand ridicule of clandestine marriage 'commerce' was common enough, as we know, yet Walpole also concedes that Keith's business acumen, not to say his mastery of the media, had changed the social profile of clandestine nuptials, making them 'fashionable' if not entirely respectable among the young elite whose marriages were ordinarily subject to strict parental control.[66] By his report, in the months before the introduction of the Marriage Act, the Duchess of Argyll fretted openly 'that all the girls will go off before next Lady-day' (i.e. 25 March 1754, when the Marriage Act came into effect).[67] Keith's Little Chapel recorded no fewer than sixty-one weddings on that day and more than 6,000 in the decade preceding it.[68]

Walpole and Argyll were reckoning with the mimetic effects of a new, print-mediated version of the elite clandestine marriage story that featured neither seedy Fleet abductions nor forced marriages, but rather the elopement of rich young couples evading parental control. Amongst the most famous of these cases was James, Sixth Duke of Hamilton, and Elizabeth Gunning, a society beauty, who married at Keith's Mayfair Little Chapel on St Valentine's Day 1752. Walpole's commentary on the 'noise' surrounding that event was typical of the reportage-cum-gossip that elite clandestine weddings in general produced: Hamilton and Gunning met at a party at Bedford House, Walpole tells us, and when the local parson refused to marry them without a license, they headed to Keith's chapel for a midnight wedding ceremony using an ad hoc ring taken from a bed curtain.[69] In the circulation of this narrative and others like it, we can recognise amatory fiction topoi specifically addressed to female readers who were understood to be susceptible both to the contagions of novel reading and to the temptations of elopement and unregulated marriage – just as the Duchess of Argyll feared.

Keith's chapel was instrumental in adapting what had been the plebeian, street-based marriage market to the tastes of London's polite consumers, especially women, and thence to the expansion of new commodity markets geared to romance, novelty and fashion. But Keith himself was not simply an opportunist: he was an outspoken Tory populist and churchman who martyred himself to the anti-Marriage Act cause (his livelihood was compromised by the Marriage Act and he died in penury in 1758). The contradictions that marked his career are writ large in his *Observations on the Act for Preventing Clandestine Marriages* (1753), which defends easy marriage and propagation on biblical grounds while also arguing in mercantilist terms that the Marriage Act's strictures endangered the 'welfare and prosperity of Britain'.[70] Indeed, Keith saw no disconnect between Tory populism and modern commerce. 'One native', he opined, 'is far more valuable both to King and government, than ten, yea, I might say twenty, naturalised foreigners, whether they be Germans, or of that favourite race of mortals who are the seed of Jacob' (4). It followed that English couples ought to be free to marry within a week's acquaintanceship (18) and instant wedding services ought to thrive under the old motto 'happy is the wooing that is not long a-doing' (18). For Keith, this heady mix of love, commerce and nativism reflected the true merits of a humble 'love of . . . king and country' (4), rooted in 'the peasantry and lowest class of people' (17).

For Keith, then, marriage belonged neither to the Erastian church nor to the state, but to the demands of the market as it catered to nation-building and trade:

> [W]hat I have offered is for the good of my country . . . I have learnt from experience, that in a state, the youth cannot be too much encouraged to marry, nor opportunity and means leading thereto too frequent, nor too often set before them, when they have once agreed no law should procrastinate them, for the stock of people are the riches and strength of the nation.

Keith's ensuing critique of the Marriage Act was prescient. Take this droll aside on its betrayal of the Whig principle of toleration:

> It is [a] great pity, the compliers [sic] did not add, that no papist, or enemy of the present government should be married, because this would be an effectual method to put an end to popery and jacobitism in this kingdom, and be a surer and shorter way with them than Daniel de Foe's shortest way with the Dissenters, when he proposed to hang the then living ones. (5–6)

Or, in the pamphlet's conclusion, this curiously hedged effort to adopt the stance of oppositional patriotism:

> Now, if the present Act, in the form it now stands, should, which I am sure is impossible, be of service to my country, I shall then have the satisfaction of having been the occasion of it, because the compilers thereof have done it with a pure design of suppressing my CHAPEL, which makes me the most celebrated man in this kingdom, tho' not the greatest. (32)

It is not hard to see why Keith was often dismissed as an eccentric. Yet even this final, oddly calibrated flourish of self-importance is not entirely misguided, since Keith's legacy is significant for the developing English marriage plot. By embedding clandestine marriage practices into polite commercialism directed at women, by taking seriously the modes of mimetic desire clandestine marriage called forth, and by doing so inside Tory populism, Keith helped to create the conditions for a powerful set of counter tropes – of liberty, young love and secret romance – that came to attach to genteel clandestine marriage and elopement. His Mayfair chapel was in this sense a London-based prefiguration of the Gretna Green romance, an important late-century variation of the marriage plot addressed in my final chapter.

Staging Mock Marriage

I have shown how the intimate connection between theatrical comedy and clandestine marriage is telegraphed in the opening scene of Congreve's *The Way of the World*. It is apparent too in William Warburton's memorable remark in his 1755 sermon in support of the Marriage Act that the practice of verbal spousals was a mere instrument of 'mock marriage'. In this critique, he echoed Solicitor General Lord Barrington, who, in the parliamentary debate of Hardwicke's Marriage Act, described the whole apparatus of the Fleet and its weddings as a 'burlesque upon the marriage ceremony'.[71] The tenor of these remarks is familiar enough; they belong to the moral-reformist attack on the old marriage code's capacity for fraud and deception, which took the Fleet wedding, in particular, to be a grotesque inversion of the regular parish ceremony. Striking about them too is their clear allusion to the popular theatre: as if clandestine marriage itself belonged to those modes of mockery and burlesque that had been staple entertainments on the stage in the lead-up to the 1737 Licensing Act, and that, after its passage, nominally at least became the province of London's unlicensed theatres.

The historical links between clandestine marriage and the theatre were indeed well established, originating in the stage device of mock marriage. Mock marriages, as such, were common enough in the eighteenth century, both on the stage and in everyday life. Schoolboys, for instance, could be ritually declared 'married' to the rod that beat them, and in so-called molly houses, where men met for sex with one another, sometimes paid, sometimes not, mock marriages were sometimes performed as a prelude to the act itself.[72] As a comic stage convention, however, mock marriage lay at the heart of the English theatre's presentation of the wedding ceremony and, according to some commentators, at the heart of popular (mis)understandings of the ecclesiastical marriage code.

The device dates back at least as far as Ben Jonson's city comedy, *Epicoene, or The Silent Woman* (1609). There the main character, Morose, a wealthy gentleman who 'loves no noise', weds Epicoene, a boy disguised as a silent, biddable woman.[73] The marriage has been arranged by Morose's nephew Dauphine, in an effort to protect himself from his uncle's plans to disinherit him in favour of a son. When Morose discovers Epicoene's apparently adulterous habits, Dauphine offers to save him from the marriage on the condition that his own inheritance is secured. After exposing Epicoene as a boy and voiding the marriage, Dauphine also reveals that the two learned churchmen who have advised Morose of the impossibility of divorce from Epicoene are fakes, a further element in the elaborate fraud through which the old man has been outwitted.[74]

The Jonsonian mock marriage is produced within a web of deception and reversal involving both gender and ordination fraud. Strictly speaking, Epicoene's gender, as an *error personae*, invalidates the marriage at canon law. Yet as Restoration dramatists drew upon and developed the mock marriage motif, very often as a tool for libertine satire and anticlericalism, the phony priest became a standard device for manipulating marriage plots. Acts of priestly masquerade at a wedding ceremony served as a popular farce effect in comedies such as Wycherley's *The Country Wife* (1675), Shadwell's *A True Widow* (1679), Aphra Behn's *The False Count* (1681), Thomas Scott's *The Mock Marriage* (1696) and Susanna Centlivre's *The Beau's Duel* (1702).[75] Yet all those rakes, gallants, fops, ladies and servants performing mock wedding ceremonies on stage in the guise of priests were not simply comic. They helped to foster the more general belief that doubts about a clergyman's authenticity might render any marriage 'mock' or void and served to strengthen an assumption that drove clandestine marriage markets: that the presence of a clergyman, rather than simple consent with witnesses, was necessary to marriage.[76]

In his path-breaking book *Matrimonial Law and the Materials of Restoration Comedy* (1942), Gellert Spencer Alleman goes so far as to suggest that the representation of marriage on stage – especially the mock marriage farce so popular in Restoration comedy – was in part responsible for a widely held assumption that a false clergyman automatically invalidated a marriage.[77] Yet as Alleman also notes, for all the Restoration fascination with marriage, on only two occasions in the period was the 'act' itself ever represented on stage under the guise of fiction. The first was John Dryden's *Wild Gallant* (1662–3), the only late seventeenth-century play to simulate a wedding ceremony on the boards. Significantly, however, the ceremony is not staged as the central action, but occurs to the side of the stage as a pantomime or dumb show in which the crucial utterances – the vows – are reduced to an inaudible murmur.[78] The play's text, printed in 1669, provided stage directions noting: '*The Parson takes them to the side of the stage: they turn their backs to the Audience, while he mumbles to them.*'[79] Only one play, Behn's *The Younger Brother* (1696), stages a conventional contract *de praesenti*.[80]

Almost uniformly the marriage action that floods the Restoration stage occurs off stage because the words and rituals of marriage were off limits to theatrical representation. As such, they marked the limits of mimesis itself. Why did marriage mark this threshold? Most obviously, as Alleman suggests, comic playwrights sacrificed the spectacle of matrimony (so heavily emphasised in Fleet satire, for instance) in deference to the theatre's powerful Christian critics, for whom weddings were sacred rituals. Although those critics lost the struggle against dramatic representation and imitation per se with the restoration of the theatres in 1660, they nonetheless mounted a systematic attack against the stage's irreverence for Christian values. As early as the 1670s, the moral reformation movement targeted the culture of libertine wit and satire in the king's playhouses as an enemy of married virtue. Most famously, non-juror Jeremy Collier's *A Short View of the Immorality, and Profaneness of the English Stage* (1698) targeted the comic representation of mock marriages as an abuse of clergy.[81] Yet, while it was certainly the case, as the anonymous author of *An Account of Marriage* (1672) asserted, that 'holy wedlock' had become a subject of satire and diversion for theatre audiences, in one fundamental respect – the refusal to feign marriage vows – the stage maintained an adamantine respect for matrimony.[82]

But this demurral did not hinge upon piety alone. As part of his attempt to explain the reluctance of comic dramatists to stage the marriage service, Alleman concedes: 'the actors may have believed that the performance of such a ceremony would have bound them in a valid if involuntary irregular marriage.'[83] Yet such a concern rests upon a very different understanding than the one that supposed that if a clergyman weren't properly ordained any marriages he officiated were not valid. Indeed, it seems to contradict that view by suggesting that the radical force of mock marriage lay in the understanding, shared by players, audiences and playwrights alike, that there was no essential difference between a theatrical simulation and a real marriage tie.[84] The consensual definition of marriage allowed no scope for mock, blank or fictional utterances of the vow because, for the ecclesiastical code, the speech act itself was the essence of the marriage bond. This performative – or magical – aspect of marriage, which based a sacral, lifelong tie on the momentary utterance of a phrase in any context at all, was a literary commonplace. It prompted Aphra Behn to call the wedding ceremony 'the conjuring knot'[85] – her pun on 'knot' and 'not' emphasising both the vow's power *and* fragility, just as later in the century Richardson's Lovelace figures the fine line between Clarissa's ruin and her nuptial salvation as a mere sleight-of-hand, a piece of 'for-better and for-worse Legerdemain'.[86]

The theatre's obsession with fake marriages and phony priests can be understood in these terms. They are motifs that in various ways momentarily diffused or disarmed marriage's performative power, enabling the presentation of the marriage vow without evoking its irreversible effects. The mock marriage was quite literally a 'mock up', an exploratory space that rendered marriage's representational opacity momentarily transparent, its non-referentiality temporarily contained. At the same time, it foregrounded a radical undecidability between phony marriages and real ones. Indeed, the tantalising possibility that the theatrical and the real could fuse even – or particularly – in a staged marriage act may help to explain clandestine marriage's insertion into the heart of theatrical culture.

The Restoration theatre's reluctance to stage the marriage ceremony (other than as a dumb show or as an implied action), therefore, rests on a sense of that ceremony's volatile properties, and upon the further knowledge that just as the 'mock' or fictional performance of the 'conjuring knot' could not ultimately be disentangled from its real effects, its 'real' performance was also troublingly unstable. As J. L. Austin has famously pointed out, the performative speech act has the power to bring about what it names, but it is just as likely to miscarry or to 'misfire'.[87] That is to say, it might be rendered invalid by a myriad of unforeseen events, which in the case of eighteenth-century marriage could include unknown acts of bigamy, doctored registers and records and contestations produced by the conflicting requirements at common and ecclesiastical law. Theatrical mock marriages pointed to this uncertainty. They turned upon the slippage between phony marriages and real ones and thus foregrounded the ways in which the marriage vow was open to improper or unlicensed expropriation, especially in the context of London's thriving clandestine marriage market.

By allowing playwrights to toy with the hermeneutics of marriage on the London stage, mock marriages became theatrical cognates for clandestine marriages, helping to fuel the ongoing clandestine marriage trade even as they also worked to inoculate players against the effects of a marriage code that did not distinguish between the wedding ceremony and its simulation. As a motif that marked the limits of theatrical mimesis like no other, mock marriage would go on to play an important role in the comic theatre's transformation across the eighteenth century. It was reinvented and to some extent repurposed in the context of the new wave of commercial entertainment that reshaped the London stage for growing audiences in the century's first decades. Indeed, it stands not just at the epicentre of a remarkable burst of experimentation and entrepreneurship that marked the theatre in this period but also at the heart of the political controversies that culminated in the stage Licensing Act's censorship of the theatre.

The Licensing Act of 1737 marks the moment at which the stage itself was corralled into regularity. In this regard it was analogous to the Marriage Act: both were Court Whig measures aimed at policing the excesses of London's expanding commercial public sphere on moral grounds. Like the Fleet marriage market, the unlicensed theatres were unruly spaces of performance, mimicry and profit, catering largely to London's expanding suburban population. Indeed, the two were bound together as such: the insobriety, prostitution and petty crime long associated with the theatre merged seamlessly with the Fleet's rogue wedding culture, which not coincidentally was geographically close to Drury Lane.

Although they belong to different ministries (Walpole's and Pelham's, respectively) and to different moments of Whig hegemony, the Licensing Act and the Marriage Act each extended the state's power into new domains of governmentality. Indeed, there is evidence to suggest that Hardwicke himself played a role in drafting Walpole's Licensing Act in the spring of 1737.[88] Just as the Marriage Act used the authority of the state to close down illicit weddings in the Fleet by mandating proper church ceremonies, the Licensing Act closed down the unlicensed playhouses that had proliferated in the wake of the 1729 opening of Thomas Odell's theatre in Ayliffe Street, Goodman's Fields, in defiance of the royal patents.[89] It did so by reinforcing the patent theatres' exclusive rights under royal license and by subjecting scripts to censorship by the Lord Chamberlain. Each act worked hand in glove with existing institutions to insinuate the modernising state into their monopolies: the Licensing Act strengthened the patent theatres while the Marriage Act worked through the agency of the Established Church.

In this light, the Licensing Act was not just a form of political censorship aimed at the theatres, or even another alignment of state power with moral reform. Like the Marriage Act, it was arguably a piece of economic legislation, and perhaps once again of biopower, since it enabled the state to increase its regulation of audiences and popular entertainment.[90] While the Marriage Act closed down clandestine marriage as a threat to propertied social order, the Licensing Act was touted as nothing less than a matter of national security.[91] *The Daily Gazetteer*, a Court Whig mouthpiece, made the moral case against the theatres in precisely these terms:

[T]he *Personal* Abuse of *Majesty* itself, as well as encouraging and promoting all manner of Vice and Immorality, is carried to such a Length, that if some speedy and effectual Stop be not put to such daring Licentiousness, we can expect nothing less than to fall a Sacrifice to *Those*, who lie in wait to destroy us.[92]

The argument for the regulation of the theatres was also posed as a *business* case. Samuel Richardson's anonymously published *A Seasonable Examination of the Pleas and Pretensions of the Proprietors of, and Subscribers to, Play-Houses, Erected in Defiance of the Royal Licence* (1735) called for an end to the encroachment of unlicensed commercial theatres on mercantile districts at the edges of the city where patent requirements were not enforced.[93] Speaking in the persona of a master tradesman and citizen in defence of 'Honest Tradesmen', Richardson rounds on the 'shameful Depravity' of current stage entertainments which 'invite and catch ... the City-Youth' to follow 'licentious Example':[94]

To see the vile Rogueries of an Harlequin *Shepherd*, the Villanies of *Newgate* and *Bridewell*, a detestable *Mackheath* [*sic*], and all the miserable Farcical Trumpery that is so often acted on the Stage! These are delicate Amusements for the Minds of working Tradesmen: Fine Relaxations from Business: Great Encouragements for them to return with Ardour to it again: Noble Subjects for *Conversation* with their Wives and Families upon what they have seen and heard: Proper Equivalents for the Money it costs them, and for the Time which they might so much better and more comfortably employ, for their Families [*sic*] Benefit (73).

Richardson goes on to explain that these plays, many of which begin before the working day has ended, 'by Degrees unhinge [the tradesman's] Mind from Business, make his Trade undelightful to him, and allow at most but a second Place to his first Duties' (75).

Here the old High Church religious critique of the theatre is recalibrated for a new set of moral and commercial interests. The problem is no longer the high-minded atheism, libertinism or wit of the two court theatres, but low-life entertainments (harlequinades, ballad operas and the like) as they help the commercial stage to expand and unleash a wave of wasteful amusements on city workers and apprentices. Unlicensed playhouses threaten to compromise not just piety or morality but also business and work. Richardson's emphasis on labour and production is new, as is his implicit suggestion that the theatre *ought* to model exemplary scenes of family and civic life so as to offer 'Proper Equivalents for the Money it costs [its audience], and for the Time which they might so much better ... employ' (73).

Arguably, *A Seasonable Examination*'s mercantile-commercial twist on Anglican reformism is the 'seasonable' moment out of which a new post-secular case for the regulation of the stage emerges from the older Christian polemic against the theatres. Importantly, that case turned on a moral distinction between 'improper' and 'proper' 'diversion'. To use Richardson's words, the 'vile Rogueries', 'Villanies' and 'Farcical Trumpery' of the illegitimate stage ought to be replaced by the 'Fine Relaxations', 'Great Encouragements' and 'Noble Subjects' to which the theatre could aspire (73).[95] Richardson recycled this argument from his own earlier conduct book for young urban workers, *The Apprentice's Vade Mecum* (1733), where he had opined that 'under proper Regulations, the Stage may be made subservient to excellent Purposes, and be an useful Second to the *Pulpit*.'[96] Pamela herself would soon again ventriloquise it in the context of a new species of moral reformist fiction.[97]

'Proper Regulation' as Richardson saw it was proposed in part by oppositional Whig Sir John Barnard's private bill to suppress unlicensed theatres, then before Parliament (though soon to be withdrawn). Barnard's bill marked the beginning of Walpole's campaign to regulate the theatre by calling for limits to the increasing number of 'Diversions and Entertainments exhibited on the Stage' (65).[98] Yet for Richardson and indeed Walpole (although for very different reasons) that bill did not go far enough, since it did not aim to regulate the *content* of plays, as the later Licensing Act would.[99] Richardson's concern with content as it shaped the 'minds' of young audiences, in particular, resonates with Warburton's developing interest in an alliance between literature, religion and the state that could reach into lived relations. He was an early advocate of stage censorship, not as conceived of by Walpole as a means of silencing political dissent, but rather as a means of harnessing mimesis for new modes of 'rational and instructing Entertainment' which he would soon himself pioneer in his prose fiction marriage plots.

Tellingly, *A Seasonable Examination* casts its nascent distinction between proper and improper entertainment in terms of the same social divisions that drove the representation of clandestine marriage:

> [T]he Diversions of the Stage have taken no small Hold of the Minds of the lower Class of People in those Parts: And tho' the Stage, under a proper Regulation, might be made a rational and instructing Entertainment, yet, as it is *now* manag'd, and generally *has been* order'd, we cannot help thinking it a very improper Diversion to be planted among the Working Class of People. (74)

The phrase 'working class' would of course go on to become one of the most resonant in the language, but here in an early usage, Richardson describes not class in the modern sense but a wage-earning section of the population that has increasing access to commercial leisure and services (including clandestine marriage) and for whom new forms of exemplary, 'proper' entertainment need urgently to be created. [100]

Improper Diversions: *The What D'ye Call It* and *Pasquin*

Mock marriage energised the very kinds of 'Diversion and Entertainment' that Richardson abhorred. Indeed, it thrived within the modes of 'irregular drama' that characterised the comic stage's initial response to the commercial cultural sector's expansion.[101] As theatre historians have noted, the success of spectacular entertainments in the first three decades of the eighteenth century triggered a flurry of comic experimentation in the patent theatres. On one side, the moral reform movement influenced a wave of reform comedies inspired by Colley Cibber's penitent rake narrative, *Love's Last Shift* (1697).[102] On the other side, as the stage of the pre-Licensing Act era was flooded with pantomimes, dances, operas and the like, a strand of legitimate drama departed from classical norms to blend self-reflexive comic experimentation with topical satire.[103] With striking regularity, these playful, often incendiary, theatrical satires featured mock marriages.

Two examples will suffice. The first is John Gay's *The What D'ye Call It*, a country farce in two acts, first performed at Drury Lane in 1715. One of Gay's earliest stage experiments, it inaugurated the anti-Court Whig lineage of theatrical parody and experimentation that led to Gay's invention of the 'ballad opera' form in *The Beggar's Opera*.[104] Importantly, *The What D'ye Call It*'s Tory politicisation of the comic marriage plot in a country estate anticipates *Pamela* too, and in unexpected ways. The second – very different – example is Henry Fielding's *Pasquin: A Dramatick Satire on the Times*, a topical burlesque that was the stage and media sensation of the 1736/7 season. Now largely forgotten, *Pasquin* was performed sixty times between March and May 1736, nearly topping *The Beggar's Opera*'s first season run and enabling Fielding's ad hoc theatre troupe – the 'Great Mogul Company' at the Little Theatre, Haymarket – to outperform the patent theatres and other unlicensed rivals on the Licensing Act's eve.[105]

The What D'ye Call It and *Pasquin* stand at either end of a short era of irregular eighteenth-century stage comedy in which formal experiment was bound to cultural critique and political satire. Both are rehearsal plays by playwrights with anti-Court Whig sympathies (Tory in Gay's case, and at the time oppositional Whig in Fielding's). The rehearsal play itself was not a new form in this period; it dated back to the Restoration, having been established by George Villiers in his comedy *The Rehearsal* (1671). Its revival in the early eighteenth century, however, joined efforts to police popular entertainment, since it brought a mordant critical irony to the enactment (or re-enactment) of the breakdown of traditional stage genres and hierarchies.

The crusade against generic unorthodoxy was paradoxical. Playwrights like Gay and Fielding, in particular, inevitably mimicked and drew energy from the very forms of popular culture they satirised (this was the basis of Richardson's objection to *The Beggar's Opera*, for instance).[106] Certainly the clandestine marriage phenomenon counted among these popular formations and helped to serve the equivocal demands of cultural critique, in part by referencing the indeterminacies of the old marriage code, and in part by drawing on the Fleet's scandalous and populist energy. Mock marriage interested Gay and Fielding both as a topical motif and as a tool for formal experimentation with the comic marriage plot. Perhaps most importantly, by pushing the boundaries of dramatic representation it laid claim to new audiences and larger market share.

The What D'ye Call It is a highly self-conscious 'metatheatrical burlesque on genre' (as Lisa Freeman calls it), in which a country gentleman puts on a play acted by his tenants whose fictional roles ghost their real-life situations.[107] The joke of its title – its 'doubtful Appellation'[108] to use Gay's own words – is further extended by its hyphenated subtitle: a 'tragic-comi-pastoral farce' (preface, 137–8). As Gay remarked in the play's preface, 'I am the first who have introduced this Kind of Dramatick Entertainment upon the Stage' wherein 'several Kinds of the Drama' are 'interweav[ed] so that they cannot be distinguish'd or separated' (preface, 1–2, 9–10). Accordingly, the play and inset play alike unfold in non-sequiturs that culminate not in a wedding but in a mock wedding that unexpectedly turns out to be real and that, in the context of the frame narrative, unites a pair of unlikely stage lovers as a proper married couple. With considerable irony, Gay terms this resolution a 'happy Catastrophe' (preface, 27–8).

The play's rehearsal plot involves Sir Roger, an ambitious country squire, who stages private theatricals as a means of enhancing his status amongst the local gentry whom he assumes have never before seen a play. Under his direction, his steward arranges an 'entertainment' (the play within the play) that presents 'all sorts of Plays under one' (introductory scene, 58) and ends in a mock wedding that becomes an opportunity for a real marriage between the amateur players, Sir Roger's son Thomas and his steward's daughter Kitty, who has been seduced by the young squire and has fallen pregnant to him. It is tempting to describe this marriage, anachronistically, as *Pamela*-esque since it unites a young 'Booby Squire' (introductory scene, 44), as he's called, with a labouring-class woman in the context of a country estate. Yet it does so not in Richardsonian terms (i.e. by mustering moral sentiment) but merely through the steward's wily manipulation of the theatre's old mock marriage tradition.

Gay himself is alive to the wedding's literary and social *frisson*, but he also trades on its singularity as a theatrical performance. Sir Roger, in his role of quasi-stage manager, echoes Gay's own earlier facetious trumpeting of the frame play's innovations, this time seriously when, with great fanfare, he announces the performance of the wedding finale and explicitly refers to its novelty as a staged event:

> Ay, now for the Wedding. Where's he that plays the Parson. Now, Neighbors, you shall see what was never shewn upon the *London* stage. (final scene [fs], 1–3)

Significantly, however, the performance of the wedding is waylaid. A squabble breaks out between the squire and his vicar, who is in fact a curate and has resolutely refused to lend his gown for the amateur theatricals (which he terms 'a Profanation' [fs, 7]). In what seems a reference to Collier's objection to the stage's anticlericalism, the dispute escalates when the curate announces himself ready to present the squire with 'two and twenty good Reasons against it from the [church] Fathers' (fs, 10–11). Enraged by the curate's scruples, Sir Roger reminds the assembled players and audience that he holds 'the Presentation' (fs, 20) and goes on to order the curate to join the theatricals by performing the play's marriage himself. The parish clerk and the steward step in to negotiate an apparent compromise whereby the curate agrees to perform the wedding privately 'in the Parlour within' (fs, 24), since:

> he saith he will not and cannot in Conscience consent to expose his Character before neighboring Gentlemen; neither will he enter into your Worship's Hall for he calleth it a Stage *pro tempore*. (fs, 24–7)

It is hard not to notice an emergent theo-politics here, a whiff of critique concerning the squire's high-handed, ungodly ways that would have resonated with contemporary audiences as a pro-Tory line, especially since much of the inset play narrative turns upon the injustices and indignities inflicted on the tenant class by the recent Game and Recruiting Acts.[109]

The curate, who does not appear on stage until the ceremony itself, stands for modest piety and High Anglican values against the squire's emphatically Whiggish tolerance for worldly ways and libertinism. This is subtly confirmed when the steward later reveals that Sir Roger has been tricked: a reverse mock marriage has occurred, whereby the curate performed a real wedding between Kitty and Thomas under cover of the squire's play. Justice is done for Kitty, and a proper union is sealed between the two young lovers. As the steward explains to Squire Roger: 'I had no way but this to repair the Injury your Son had done my Child – She shall study to deserve your Favour' (fs, 43–5). Finally – and as if to channel decades of anxiety surrounding the performance of marriage on the English stage – the unwitting groom, Squire Thomas, remarks to the steward: 'these Stage Plays are plaguy dangerous Things – but I am no Such fool neither, but I know this one was all your Contrivance' (fs, 54–6). Here what will become a stock type – the young libertine booby – is exposed in terms that seem to anticipate his later centrality to the novel's marriage plot.

As a witty dénouement, the 'happy Catastrophe' of Kitty and Thomas's union might have been the end of the matter. After all, wrongs have been righted and the clever novelty of an inset mock marriage-turned-real restores, or redistributes, popular justice in the frame narrative's world. At an extra-diegetic level, however, Gay's relation to the mock marriage turned real is more like Sir Roger's than the steward's: that is to say, it is a distinctly guarded one. Indeed, Gay's *The What D'ye Call It* repeats the demurral at the heart of Sir Roger's 'entertainment'. It too pushes the limits of experimentation and representation – by touting the staging of a real wedding – only to retreat into pantomime.

The history of mock marriage helps to make sense of Gay's demurral. In a move familiar from Restoration precedents, when the curate refuses to perform a public wedding in the squire's hall (i.e. as an on-stage ceremony in the inset narrative) the event occurs instead as a dumb show in a parlour (i.e. off-stage space). However, Sir Roger, keen to let his audience *see* the wedding action as promised, allows them to spy with him on the ceremony, which proceeds in silence:

> Why, what's a Play without a Marriage? And what is a Marriage, if one sees nothing of it? Let [the curate] have his Humour – but set the Doors wide open, that we may see how all goes on.

[. . . *Sir* Roger *at the Door pointing*]
So natural! d'ye see now, Neighbours? the Ring, i'faith. To have and to hold! right again – well play'd, Doctor; well play'd, Son *Thomas*. Come, come, I'm satisfy'd – now for the Fiddles and Dances. (fs, 32–39)

Gay's stage directions indicate clearly enough that Sir Roger's commentary on the wedding has the status of an aside, one that plays up the comedy of his own deception, to be sure, but that also functions prophylactically to install him as a buffer between the performance of this marriage act and the two audiences witnessing it: Sir Roger's fictional onlookers and the Drury Lane audience.

Double-framed in this manner, *The What D'ye Call It*'s mock marriage foregrounds the interchangeability of the mock and the real like no other. It presents a stage marriage that is all at once real *and* fake: mock for the inset play, real for the frame play, and mock again for Gay's audience. It is important to notice too that this back and forth involves a switching of sight and sound: the spectacle of the ceremony and Sir Roger's insistence upon its visibility is substituted for the sound of the liturgy and the verbal utterances (the exchange of vows) that are essential to the marriage bond according to the old ecclesiastical code.

It would seem then that Gay has it both ways. The mock marriage device is inserted into the heart of his comedy as a crowd pleaser, which spills out into the real, *and* as a gesture of pure form, a mise-en-abyme effect, which signals for a coterie of knowing viewers that this is theatre about the theatre, reflecting on its own position in London's entertainment world. Of course, it is also true to say that Gay's politicisation of the marriage motif in an extended comic to-and-fro between vicar and squire – it is not yet a 'plot' – is, or seems to be, undercut by the uncertainty of the marriage rite's status – its flipping from pretend to real, mock to serious, so invisibly and speedily. But in the end, that is the point of *The What D'ye Call It*'s burlesque on genre. Here the play of connections and oppositions – Sir Roger as the bad Whiggish squire versus his curate and his steward as plebeian patriots, on one hand, and the unlikely alliance between the gulled Sir Roger and the playwright, Gay himself, on the other – constitutes an unstable field upon which the theatre's uneasy cultural status, its uncertain location in the commercial sphere at this time, joins political topicality.

Fielding's *Pasquin* is set in a London playhouse where rival productions are under rehearsal: 'a comedy call'd The Election', and an 'emblematical Tragedy' titled 'The Life and Death of Common Sense'. Subtitled

A Dramatic Satire on the Times, the play was also nothing if not topical: it is largely remembered as a proximate cause for the 1737 stage Licensing Act; it broke new ground in theatrical marketing by mixing the worlds of advertising and entertainment; and it put the Haymarket on the map as a niche playhouse between the patent and unlicensed theatres.[110] Certainly *Pasquin* belonged to a lineage of anti-ministerial satire that reached back to *The What D'ye Call It* and included *The Beggar's Opera* and some of Fielding's own earlier plays. At this stage of his theatrical career (and after a period of writing both regular five-act comedies and irregular satirical farces for various theatres), Fielding had established his 'Great Mogul' company at the Haymarket so as to engage in open mockery of the establishment and patent house managers alike.[111] With characteristic verve, he made a virtue of his company's relative obscurity, using mock-heroic jokes to promote the play, listing the names of characters rather than actors on the advertising bill, and uniquely holding benefit nights for his lead actresses in character.[112]

Pasquin's real novelty for London audiences, however, was its double rehearsal plot. As Fielding acknowledged in his dedication to Rich, this was borrowed from *The Contrast*, a burlesque by the Hoadly brothers that ran for just three nights at Covent Garden, in April–May 1731. That play had been hastily withdrawn at the request of their father, Whig Latitudinarian churchman Benjamin Hoadly, then Bishop of Winchester, who was anxious to avoid the controversy that might attend a close association with the theatre world.[113] For Fielding, however, the complexities of the double rehearsal plot spoke eloquently to the mixed purposes and motivations that had brought him to that world's margins as a non-patent entrepreneur. It paired two plays – comic and tragic – in rehearsal and framed them with interspersed commentary from their authors (Trapwit and Fustian, respectively) who pass criticism on each other's work while parrying the satirical remarks of a phlegmatic critic (Sneerwell).

So *Pasquin* was meta-metatheatre. Its novelty and humour lay in a dizzying set of alignments and disconnections between the frame play's in-house literary-commercial references (which worked as a kind of backstage drama) and the farcical content of its inset rehearsal narratives. And for Fielding, that content was not merely an occasion for the extension of playhouse themes (as it had been for the Hoadlys) but for highly topical excursions into party politics, on one hand, and London's culture wars, on the other.[114] *Pasquin*'s rehearsal comedy was a satire of borough electioneering and petticoat government, while its rehearsal tragedy was an allegorical story of England's cultural decline rendered as a mock-epic battle at Covent

Garden. There, Queen Common Sense is vanquished by the forces of Ignorance, which include the learned professions of law, 'physick' and – most notably – the Anglican clergy, alongside irrational entertainments.[115]

Fielding's inflammatory appropriation of the double rehearsal plot served two purposes. Most obviously, its novelty enabled him to market *Pasquin* in eye-catching terms to London audiences by telegraphing its assemblage of oppositional topoi in mock-heroic playbills for benefit nights and extended performances. It also accommodated a serious purpose by providing a template of the structures that joined the theatre (and culture more generally) to politics and religion. The latter marks *Pasquin* out among the period's experimental comedies and possibly explains why the play served as the trigger for Walpole's Licensing Act. Beyond the noise and humour of the play's own meta-commentary and insider playhouse jokes, its two (otherwise disparate) inset plays functioned as components of a holistic allegory of opposition.

The rehearsal comedy readily lends itself to oppositional themes. It is titled 'The Election' and set on the hustings where the Court Whig candidates – Lord *Place* and Colonel *Promise* – resort to bribery, while their Tory opponents – Sir *Henry Fox-chace* and Squire *Tankard* – rely on populist sloganeering.[116] Recent critics have insisted that its political satire is multidirectional, in tune with the aleatory, self-reflexive humour of Fielding's irregular plays.[117] Certainly, this is an attack not on one or other party but on both indifferently, but it is also grounded in a critique of corruption in the political system as such. In this sense, I would agree with Martin Battestin that Fielding's critique of the connection between money and party links the rehearsal comedy to the politics of the Patriot movement in its Bolingbrokean guise, despite much scholarly scepticism about this connection.[118]

Pasquin's rehearsal tragedy – 'The Life and Death of Queen Common Sense' – was also Bolingbrokean. Drawing on Pope and Swift, it mounted a hard-hitting critique of ignorance and superstition as enemies of a generalised right reason, here personified as 'Queen Common Sense'. To be sure, much of this critique was quasi-Scriblerian (for a time Fielding adopted the pseudonym Scriblerius Secondus), echoing *The Dunciad*'s satire on the encroachment of nonsense.[119] But a key target of *Pasquin*'s satire in the rehearsal tragedy was the Established Church, as allegorised by the charlatan 'Firebrand Tartuffe, Priest of the Sun', Queen Common Sense's chief adviser who treacherously murders her. Importantly, the flagrant anticlericalism that underpinned Firebrand's characterisation marked a departure from its Scriblerian precedents, as well as from the broader Tory/rustic populism that had shaped Gay's *The What D'ye Call It.* It was nonetheless consistent both with Bolingbroke's attempt to create a political system with minimal ecclesiastical agency and with Fielding's own flirtation with deism and freethinking in this period.[120]

Arguably, then, *Pasquin's* double plot seeks critically to connect the various elements of the Hanoverian settlement – religious, commercial, cultural or political – so as to present them as a conjoint structure that threatens enlightened practical reason, or common sense. From this viewpoint, W. B. Coley is almost certainly correct in his recent assumption that it was the rehearsal tragedy's anticlericalism more than the rehearsal comedy's attack on political corruption that emboldened Walpole to close down the theatres.[121] After all, generalised political satires – attacking the 'Great Man', harlequinades, Grub Street hacks etc. – were commonplace enough in the 1730s, but the flagrant irreligion of the season's most successful comedy was a fresh provocation. When Fielding sought to cash in on audience demand for *Pasquin* by continuing performances on prohibited Lent days, he found himself attacked from both sides of politics, giving Walpole safe grounds to act against the unlicensed theatres in such a way as to appease those most suspicious of his administration – the High Church party and the moral reform movement – without affronting his Dissenting support.

This brings us to *Pasquin's* marriage plot, which belongs to the rehearsal comedy but is significantly shaped by the play's broader irreligion. Fielding's experimentation with marriage takes a very different direction from Gay's reverse mock marriage in *The What D'ye Call It.* In that play, Kitty and Thomas's marriage is fully motivated, and the ruse arranged by Kitty's father, the steward, retrospectively legitimates the couple's sexual consummation. By contrast, *Pasquin's* rehearsal comedy closes with the union of two 'lovers' – Miss Mayoress and Colonel Promise – who have never before spoken to each other, and who have nothing except party political interest to connect them. This is a joke on contemporary comedy's supposedly loose ways with narration and its dependence on the marriage plot in particular, as well as, once again, on the mercenary nature of party politics. In a final twist, their expeditious courtship ends in a flash wedding performed 'behind the Scenes' (283) by a parson who has 'ply'd several Years at the Fleet' (283).

While Gay's mock marriage was significantly overdetermined, albeit ironically, as his play's telos and closure – subsuming and resolving both frame and inset plots – Fielding's marriage turns upon a comedy of nothingness, or almost nothingness. Miss Mayoress and Colonel

Promise's union is a *reductio ad absurdum*, which plays on marriage as 'the usual Reconciler at the End of a Comedy' (284), as Trapwit puts it, in such a way as to mock narrative closure. By the same stroke, it evacuates love and sacredness from marriage. Consecrated in a spirit of fraud, the marriage connects the groom's political mendacity to the bride's insatiable taste for low entertainment. Like the election result where bribery ensures the return of the defeated Court candidates, it is a sign of a corrupted society.

Yet, even as it reduces comic marriage to a zero point – a blip – *Pasquin* nonetheless evokes marriage's affective power in a highly unusual silent betrothal scene. Trapwit, the author and director of the rehearsal comedy, touts the penultimate scene of his play as 'the best Scene of Silence that ever was pen'd by Man' (281). This is partly, no doubt, a satirical reference to the speechless pantomimes that were the period's most popular theatrical attractions. Yet because Trapwit's silent scene is, paradoxically, the occasion of Colonel Promise and Miss Mayoress's first acquaintance with each other *and* of his marriage proposal to her *and* her acceptance of him, its commentary reaches much deeper. Trapwit intends for the scene of silence to be broken by an explosion of noise. Like Sir Roger's hopes for his wedding scene in *The What D'ye Call It*, he expects the silent betrothal to be a show stopper: 'to catch the Admiration of every one like a Trap, and raise an Applause like Thunder, till it makes the whole House like a Hurricane' (281). The silent betrothal of course implicitly refers to the reason why theatrical weddings were silent or off stage – namely, because they marked mimesis's theatrical limits. Yet, for all its irony and self-conscious awareness of marriage as the comic stage's most hackneyed trope, for all its ludic disturbance of generic sequence (the silent betrothal precedes and upstages the off-stage Fleet wedding, after all), the scene nonetheless allows Fielding to channel marriage's performative energy and audience appeal into *Pasquin*'s comic experiment.

Following Gay, neither Trapwit nor Fielding takes the risk of letting the couple exchange vows audibly. Instead, after Miss Mayoress promises to marry the Colonel and in addition to make a 'good wife', Trapwit remarks to Sneerwell:

> That single Promise, Sir, is more than any of my Brother Authors had ever the Grace to put into the Mouth of any of their fine Ladies yet; so that the Heroe of a Comedy is left in a much worse Condition than the Villain of a Tragedy, and I would chuse rather to be hang'd with the one, than married with the other. (282)

This is where Fielding's irony cuts deepest, both as a commentary and as a meta-commentary on the comic marriage plot. Most obviously Trapwit's celebration of Miss Mayoress's mere promise to be a 'good wife' is a joke on the genre's neglect of domestic virtue. But it is a joke that speaks back to the theatre's moral reformist critics by wittily alluding to the mise-en-abyme effects of critique itself. Essentially, Fielding places domestic virtue into a feedback loop, bringing the Richardsonian critique of Gay into dangerous proximity with Gay's own ironic mingling of comedy and tragedy, marriage and the gallows in *The Beggar's Opera*'s final scene.

Unlike *The What D'ye Call It*'s reverse mock marriage (which flipped from fake to real before safely becoming fake again), Fielding's comic experiment with *Pasquin* ultimately backfired. In triggering the Licensing Act, it had real-life effects. But there is an echo of *The What D'ye Call It*'s caution here too. *Pasquin*'s betrothal can be thought of not as a reverse mock marriage but as a mock marriage once removed. The lovers' exchange of promises does indeed break the 'scene of silence' with a performative, quasi-liturgical act that anticipates marriage (but that does not seal the act itself). In doing so it draws attention to how, in almost voicing the unvoicable, Trapwit himself enacts Fielding's project as a whole. He signals the way that *Pasquin* visibly and audibly presents hegemony's structures.

Together, Gay and Fielding's plays demonstrate that by the early eighteenth century mock marriage was less a motif of anticlerical or libertine satire than a vehicle of a new kind of comic meta-theatre given over to political critique. Each used the mock marriage device to critique traditional comedy's formal constraints by playing with the ontological boundaries of mimesis. Gay's meta-theatre served a volatile Tory politics; Fielding's engaged a less partisan, more opportunistic, provocative topicality. In each case, theatrical mock marriage's dangerous proximity to real marriage intensified that political charge: this was not just theatre about theatre, it was theatre about the theatre that had also to be careful not to become real.

Experimentation with mock marriage on the London stage at this time knowingly alluded to and exploited the connections between the theatre world and the clandestine marriage market. Indeed, Gay and Fielding's marriage plots openly relied on the unreformed marriage code's indeterminacies, on one hand, and the liberties of the unlicensed stage, on the other. Unregulated marriage and unlicensed theatre were soon to be subsumed by the Whig state, however, under the auspices of the Marriage and Licensing Acts. In mandating distinctions between proper and improper modes of marriage on one side and theatre on the other, these Acts would create a new set of parameters for comic narrative and performance on the stage.

Marriage on the Licensed Stage

When the Licensing Act reorganised the relations between the legitimate and illegitimate stage, it imposed a censorship regime that marginalised the irregular and unlicensed theatres, along with their attachment to mock marriage. As theatre historians agree, the patent theatres engaged in a broad reconstruction of theatrical comedy for respectable audiences in the post-Licensing Act period. In line with the Licensing Act, they abandoned political satire, embracing instead comedies of manners and intrigue, on one hand, and sentimental romance – including a string of popular adaptations of *Pamela* – on the other.[122] At the same time, however, the unlicensed stage continued, but now with non-spoken entertainments only (also in line with the Licensing Act). It developed into the lively, even anarchic sphere that Jane Moody called 'illegitimate theatre', where popular spectacles, grotesqueries, simulacra, novelty acts and musical entertainments were staged well into the nineteenth century, mostly at minor theatres and for heterogeneous audiences.[123]

To grasp more precisely how the Licensing Act's partitioning of the theatre affected the representation of clandestine marriage on the eighteenth-century stage, we can take as an example the 1748/9 season. Its interest as a mid-century moment falling between the Licensing and Marriage Acts also coincides with David Garrick's ascendancy in the London theatre world, itself shaped by his allegiance to the Court Whig regime and its stage licensing and marriage reforms.

The 1748/9 season was the second year of Garrick's proprietorship of Drury Lane, but he had already begun to consolidate his authority at that playhouse in part by bringing Shakespeare's romance-tragedy *Romeo and Juliet* to mainstream London audiences. Just a few months later and in the same season, the so-called Bottle Conjuror failed to appear at the Little Theatre in the Haymarket, in a famous hoax perpetrated by two noblemen intent on demonstrating 'the credulity of the English nation'.[124] These two events alone tell us a great deal about the London stage's social bifurcation in the wake of the Licensing Act. On one hand, Garrick's star was rising at Drury Lane; he would go on to reshape stage culture, enhancing the theatre's cultural prestige by harnessing moral reform to new illusionistic stage practices as well as to the Shakespearean roles that were his specialty.

On the other hand, the Bottle Conjuror's notorious no-show at the Haymarket channelled a countervailing history of theatrical illegitimacy and disorder, triggering a playhouse riot that came close to destroying the Little Theatre, thus demonstrating the stage's continued volatility and agency.[125]

Richardson's *Pamela* arguably counts as a third term in the history of the comic stage in this period, one also harnessed to the Anglican reform of manners movement, as I argue in more detail in the next chapter. The novel was published late in 1740, triggering a flurry of imitations, parodies, refutations and adaptations constituting what William B. Warner terms 'the *Pamela* media event'.[126] The *Pamela* vogue quickly spilled into stage entertainment, inspiring Henry Giffard – who incidentally had been a target of Richardson's *A Seasonable Examination* – to produce a 'salacious' adaptation of the novel for his unlicensed Goodman's Fields theatre.[127] Despite these beginnings, by the 1748/9 season *Pamela* was on its way to becoming ubiquitous in the patent repertoire, both as a template for the narratives of sentimental domesticity that shaped new forms of comedy in the Licensing Act's wake, and in a string of plays and comic opera adaptations. The latter included most notably Isaac Bickerstaff's 1765 sentimental comic opera *The Maid of the Mill*, which immediately became almost as popular as *Pamela* itself. Another comic opera, William Shield's *Rosina* with a libretto by Frances Brooke, was performed first at Covent Garden in December 1782 and more than 200 times before 1800.[128]

Let us turn to the London theatre listings in *The General Advertiser* for just one evening's entertainment on Monday, 12 December 1748 (see Illustration 3). At a glance, the entries clearly show how central marriage and romance tropes were to the mid-century stage, comic and otherwise. The fare at the five biggest venues – licensed and unlicensed – was as follows:

The King's Theatre Haymarket (a fashionable company specialising in Italian opera and concerts) offered a recently introduced comic variant of opera titled *Orazio*, as well as 'dancing between the Acts' for the price of half a guinea. The two royal patent houses presented spoken theatre (as was their exclusive right under the Licensing Act), namely, at Drury Lane a revised production of Shakespeare's *Romeo and Juliet* (its eleventh night) and a (rather pantomimic) adaptation of Milton's *Comus* at Covent Garden. Notwithstanding its tragic themes, *Romeo and Juliet* is promoted with 'new costumes' and the addition of a 'new masquerade dance proper to the play', and staged alongside a farce afterpiece, *The Devil to Pay*, a crowd favourite. Both plays feature the stars of the day (Spranger Barry as Romeo and Susannah Cibber as Juliet, while Peg Woffington

Illustration 3 Theatre listings. *The General Advertiser*, 12 December 1748.

appeared as *Comus*'s heroine, The Lady). At both houses admission was set at standard patent prices (boxes 5s, pit 3s, gallery 2s).

At the (unlicensed) New Wells Theatre at Goodman's Fields in Whitechapel, at this time under the management of the Hallams, 'a pint of wine' bought entry to an extended programme of musical entertainment – all non-spoken and spectacle-driven – which included rope dancing, tumbling, singing, comic dancing and pantomime performed by a company of fifty or more actors and dancers.[129] The main piece on 12 December is a plebeian marriage tableau, listed as 'The Sailor's Progress, with the Humours of the Fleet Marriage' and described as a performance of 'several scenes in Grotesque Characters'. It possibly involved a combination of spoken and musical performance and was almost certainly based on June's print, published just the year before. It was staged alongside dance and pantomime pieces: 'The Quaker's Wedding' preceded it and the highly popular *Harlequin Statue*, once a mainstay at Jonathan Rich's Covent Garden, followed as an afterpiece.[130]

Finally, at his so-called Auction Room, the erstwhile New Theatre (aka the summer or 'little theatre') in Haymarket, Samuel Foote lists 'by Desire' 'the forty-second Day's Sale' of his exhibit of 'a Choice Collection of Pictures; all warranted Originals, with some entire New Lots'. This, as everyone knew, was Foote's latest one-man show of improvised 'character' performances – earlier called 'Diversions' or 'encounters' – at which he mimicked celebrities of the day, establishing a genre loathed by many of his peers. Arguably Foote's take-offs channelled the old Haymarket spirit of irreverent topical satire and as such paid minimalist homage to Gay and Fielding's earlier burlesque experiments (without their sustained political or critical purpose or any noticeable anxiety about the problems of repeating and re-enacting low cultural forms). Certainly, Foote operated at the very limits of the Licensing Act: to avoid its constraints his take-offs were unscripted, usually advertised as 'morning shows' or matinees and performed with musical accompaniment. As at Goodman's Fields, audiences paid admittance under the pretext of taking a beverage, in this case a 'Dish of Tea' or 'Chocolate'.

It seems clear enough that the Licensing Act organised the distribution of marriage tropes across the mid-century stage. In broad terms, *The General Advertiser*'s listings suggest that marriage narratives per se belonged to the sphere of spoken drama (to traditional forms such as tragedy, and most of all to comedy), while the Fleet wedding tableau found a natural home in the sphere of illegitimate theatre, that is, amongst the assemblage of non-spoken entertainments that graced the unlicensed stage.[131] Certainly, the low comedic presentation of clandestine marriage 'in several scenes' at the New Wells contrasts tellingly with the extended narratives of Shakespearean tragic romance and Miltonic chastity performed on the patent stages, confirming a cultural divide between the world of low entertainment as it spilled into mimicry, farce and disorder, and spoken repertory theatre's aspiration to a new kind of moral respectability and cultural authority based at least to a certain extent on an established literary canon. Insofar as clandestine marriage belonged to the theatre's own clandestine sector – that is, to the sphere of the minor unlicensed theatres that sought to evade the licensing laws – there was a resonance across one clandestine institution to another. In this way, the Licensing Act's partitioning of the theatre prepared the ground for a reconfiguration of comic tastes, plots and conventions in line with the Marriage Act's later reforms as they distinguished between legitimate and clandestine marriage.

Yet this account is too simple. As *Pamela*'s own theatrical adaptations show, and as Moody and others have argued, there was considerable slippage between licensed and unlicensed entertainments.[132] Indeed, the permeability of that boundary is nowhere more apparent than in the patent theatres' repurposing of the unruly trope of clandestine marriage after the Marriage Act's passage. Garrick himself was instrumental in establishing the terms upon which clandestine marriage was reabsorbed by mainstream theatre in the second half of the century, as a staple of main-piece theatre at Drury Lane *and* as a mode of spectacular entertainment on the licensed and unlicensed stage. It is to this final chapter of the history of clandestine marriage in the theatre that we now turn.

Garrick and the Vernon Affair

David Garrick played a forgotten off-stage role in the enforcement of the Marriage Act. Indeed, the circumstances of his involvement in the fatal punishment of two clandestine priests in the aftermath of the Marriage Act are worth recounting because they demonstrate (once again) the remarkable web of connections between the worlds of clandestine marriage and the theatre. The priest most directly concerned was Reverend John Wilkinson, father of the actor Tate Wilkinson, who started out as a mimic in London in the 1750s under Garrick's patronage and later became a successful manager on the northern provincial circuit, where he earned a lifelong reputation as 'the wandering patentee'. Wilkinson senior was the clergyman in residence at London's Savoy Chapel where, alongside his regular parish duties, he developed a lucrative sideline in clandestine weddings, which turned out to be the very last such business in London.

Wilkinson's rationale for his enterprise was familiar enough. He claimed that the Savoy Chapel was 'peculiar', and hence exempt from the Marriage Act's requirements. In his memoir, Tate Wilkinson recalls the situation like this:

> [M]y father began the dreadful experiment of exerting his supposed rights as minister of the Savoy [he] judged he had a right to grant licences as usual; and that it was a privilege annexed to the Savoy, as being extra-parochial . . . The famous Doctor Killigrew, who had been many years minister of the Savoy, and all my father's predecessors had ever retained the power and right of granting licences for marrying from their own authority; and being extra-parochial, my father judged himself secure, and not within the reach of that severe act.[133]

Wilkinson was a latecomer to the marriage business who set out to exploit an opportunity created by the Marriage Act. In the months after the Marriage Act closed down lawless churches and marriage shops, he promoted Savoy weddings with a marketing campaign that informed Londoners of the chapel's convenience, namely its 'five private ways by land . . . and two by water'.[134] He was soon capitalising on a new and short-lived irregular marriage monopoly, celebrating 1,190 weddings in 1755 alone.[135]

Among the hundreds of couples scrambling to get married at the Savoy were two junior members of Garrick's Drury Lane Theatre Company – Master Joseph Vernon, a singing star, and Jenny Poitier, a 'girl dancer'. They were married by John Wilkinson's curate, Dr Grierson, without the consent of the bride's parents.[136] Sadly for them, Garrick had become an enforcer of new standards of sexual morality at Drury Lane in keeping with his strong connections to the Whig regime and to cultural authority in general. He and his wife, Eva Maria, were exemplars of married virtue and he had come to view his managerial role as paternalist, particularly in the case of a young star like Vernon who had joined the company as a child.[137] So when news of Vernon's clandestine wedding (and subsequent infidelities) reached George Garrick, David's brother and Drury Lane's manager of day-to-day affairs, he told David about the breach of sexual etiquette.

Coincidently, George himself had been married at the Savoy, three years earlier, to Catherine Carrington, the daughter of a king's messenger – this, however, had been a regular ceremony, contracted with the full knowledge and approval of Catherine's father.[138] David had been instrumental in bringing about that match, drafting his brother's formal letter of address to Mr Carrington and dispensing to him the best of conduct book advice: 'You cannot be too circumspect in the grand affair of your life.'[139] George's marriage to Catherine helped to solidify institutional links between Drury Lane and the Whig administration, while the rival company at Covent Garden sought political influence with the oppositional circles surrounding the Prince of Wales (at one point Garrick's rival for the affections of his future wife).[140] Faced with Vernon's flagrant contravention of the Pelham ministry's new Marriage Act and an opportunity to prove their loyalty to the king's cause, the Garrick brothers called the errant newlyweds to account. This is how Tate Wilkinson recounts their 'fateful' interview with Vernon:

> [T]hey summoned Mr. Vernon to appear, and to give King David a satisfactory account of his marriage, as to the where and the when … Infidelity was so demonstrative on both sides, that the archbishop's licence would have had very little force in tying faster the marriage noose. – The lady liked a variety of husbands, and the gentleman a plurality of wives … Mr. Vernon's assertion as to his being really married at the Savoy to Miss Poitier, Mr. David Garrick affected not to believe; but asked, who married them – if it was Doctor Wilkinson? Mr. Vernon, replied, 'No, – the clergyman's name was Grierson'. – Mr. David Garrick still seemed not convinced, but insisted on seeing the certificate, which Mr. Vernon immediately obtained from Mr. Grierson, and gave it to Mr. David Garrick, who delivered it to Mr. Carrington; and Mr. Grierson was, in consequence … committed to Newgate, tried, and condemned to transportation for fourteen years. (79–80)

The Vernon affair, courtesy of Garrick's intervention, put an end to the clandestine trade at the Savoy. Grierson, Wilkinson's unlucky deputy, didn't survive his sentence, and Wilkinson, who was also charged, died of 'sorrow, sea-sickness and gout' before his ship had left Plymouth for the trans-Atlantic crossing.[141] Seventeen-year-old Tate found favour where his father faced ruin: some two months after Dr Wilkinson's tragic demise, he obtained an interview with Garrick and entertained the manager and his wife with a take-off of none other than Samuel Foote (126). On the strength of this performance Garrick hired the younger Wilkinson and soon granted him leave to accompany Foote on a provincial tour. However, the fallout from the affair did not stop there. Vernon himself suffered a career setback when he discovered that his testimony against

Grierson had made him unpopular with audiences. He was booed off stage in the part of Palemon in *The Chaplet* and Garrick had to protect him until the controversy had died down and audiences again accepted him.[142]

Garrick found the means to convert his crusade against clandestine marriage – his 'meddling', as Wilkinson put it (78) – into further commercial success. With George Colman, he went on to write one of the era's most successful comedies, straightforwardly titled *The Clandestine Marriage* (1766). As if to harness some of the popular energy of the anti-Marriage Act cause, the play's advertisements cited William Hogarth's *Marriage A-la-mode* and John Shebbeare's novel *The Marriage Act* (1754) as its precursors. Shebbeare was a Tory propagandist, committed to anti-Hardwicke protest. Hogarth had painted a well-known portrait of Mr and Mrs Garrick's conjugal felicity (*David Garrick and His Wife*, 1752), but his work, including *Marriage A-la-mode*, was habitually in the spirit of a populist satire whose purposes were very different from Garrick and Colman's here. Indeed, the first painting of Hogarth's recent *Election* series (1754) had included the epithet 'Marry and Multiply in spite of the Devil and the ——[Court]', a critical reference to the Marriage Act and its supposed depopulating effects.[143]

The play's title, *The Clandestine Marriage*, did its popularity no harm at all. Originally called 'The Sisters' (probably in homage to the parallel sisterly marriage plots in Shebbeare's novel), the change capitalised on memories of London's only recently defunct illicit marriage trade. Yet the play itself suggests that Garrick had come to take a rather sober view of the Marriage Act controversy, or at least of his own role as a suppressor of clandestine marriage at Drury Lane. By far the play's most popular and sympathetic character was the old rake Lord Ogleby, a 'superannuated juvenile in spirit' who falls in love with the heroine, Fanny, a city heiress, not knowing that she has secretly married her father's shop boy, Lovewell.[144] The role was played by Thomas King – and it made him famous – but it was Garrick himself who had created and played its prototype, Lord Chalkestone, in *Lethe, or Esop in the Shades*, a Drury Lane favourite first performed in 1740.[145] The character had been a late addition to *Lethe* in 1756, the year that the Vernon affair had broken, and it proved so popular that Garrick was asked to present a command performance of the role for the king. The resurrection of the Chalkestone role in *The Clandestine Marriage* carried with it the conspicuous mark of Garrick auteurship, one that spectators like Frances Burney appreciated.[146]

Given these connections, it is no surprise that *The Clandestine Marriage* uses the persona of the genial, ageing rake to stage a benevolent reworking of Garrick's role in the Vernon affair. In a comic moment that uncannily echoes the interrogation of Vernon by 'King David', Lord Ogleby, upon learning of Fanny's previous attachment, demands to know 'the how, the when, and the where' of the affair, hoping to elicit a declaration of love for himself.[147] When he finally discovers the secret of her marriage to Lovewell, however, Lord Ogleby makes every effort to convince her father of the worthiness of their love match against the claims of the moneyed and titled suitors that have been chosen for her. In the end it is Lord Ogleby's generosity that facilitates general acceptance of Fanny and Lovewell's secret union. In an astounding act of revision, the play drops all question about the circumstances of their illicit vows, remaining conspicuously silent on the very point of matrimonial detail that had so concerned Garrick himself a decade earlier, and that, in a different spirit, had haunted the Restoration and eighteenth-century stage before him.

The Clandestine Marriage became standard repertory at Drury Lane and a formidable rival to Bickerstaff's hit Pamela play, The Maid of the Mill, at Covent Garden. The two comedies regularly faced off across the late 1760s and 1770s, demonstrating not just the lockdown of Richardson-inspired marriage plots on the post-Hardwicke patent stage but also the broad sentimental reconstruction of comedy in the post-Licensing Act period.[148] Certainly Garrick and Colman's play resolves the competing claims of money, social status and love within the standard plotlines of domestic romance (as opposed to libertine or political satire). Yet it also privileged illicit (if not mock) marriage. This suggests that Garrick's role in accommodating theatrical culture to proper ceremony came to involve the subtle alignment of clandestine marriage acts with Richardsonian values of moral reform and sentimental affect. It involved rewriting the relations between legitimate marriage and the clandestine modes of matrimony that the Marriage Act had rendered socially obsolete (or, in the case of Scotch elopements, marginal and remote).

Indeed, the play's most radical act of revision is not its flattering view of Garrick's role in the Vernon affair, but its reconstruction of the social profile of clandestine marriage itself. The secret marriage between Fanny and Lovewell bears little or no resemblance to the boisterous, public modes of clandestine marriage that were integral to London life and culture up to 1754 (or 1755, if we count Savoy weddings). Fanny is no Fleet bride, and even her pregnancy, hinted at in the first scene of the play, is a departure from the conspicuous prenuptial fecundity of many women who married at the Fleet. Like her marriage, Fanny's pregnancy is a secret – one that Lovewell himself is unaware of – and it stands as a sign of their clandestine union's impending legitimacy. The play represents its namesake only insofar as it transfigures the unruly clandestine marriage tradition into a simple, secret marriage act, one that has occurred in the play's past and around which no uncertainty exists, apart from the means of its disclosure and acceptance. In this way Garrick and Colman reduce clandestine marriage's social and historical meanings to themes of romance, secret love and most of all to a *Pamela*-inspired ideal of domestic conjugality.

In recasting clandestine marriage as a form of domestic romance, Garrick and Colman paradoxically invested it with an intensity that regular marriages lacked. Indeed, Fanny and Lovewell's clandestine union is a mode of what we might call hyper-nuptiality, more legitimate, because more ethically grounded in love and consent, than the bartering and alliance-making that pass for marriage with Fanny's father (who tells Lovewell: '[I] can't think of you for a son-in-law. – There's no *Stuff* in the case, no money, Lovewell')[149] and her sister Miss Sterling ('Love and a cottage! – Eh, Fanny! ... give me indifference and a coach and six!').[150] Within the crude opposition between love and money that *The Clandestine Marriage* stages, the performative aspect of clandestine marriage culture – which foregrounds the fine line between a marriage act and its miscarriage and which sets marriage into the structures of contingent urban encounters – falls out of view entirely. The mechanics of marriage – 'the how, the when, and the where' of Fanny and Lovewell's wedding – become irrelevant within the overwhelming moral force attributed to the couple's love, which more than any ritual or bureaucratic requirement is what makes their marriage a 'proper' one. Here clandestinity is occluded – but not actually displaced – by romance.

Garrick and Colman's play forged a new connection between clandestine marriage and popular stage entertainment that helped to naturalise post-Hardwicke matrimonial culture in part by repressing the residual modes of imitation and performativity upon which that culture depended. Certainly, the Marriage Act was enforced less by the policing of the boundary between legitimate and illegitimate marriage acts (its nullity clauses were rarely enforced legally, as we know) than by the normalisation of distinctions between proper marriage and its others as reinforced by literary marriage plots. This situation helps to make sense of Garrick's dual role as a crusader against clandestine marriage in the Vernon affair and as a promoter of its stage afterlife.

For it was under Garrick's stewardship too that illicit matrimony and elopement became staple comic themes for Drury Lane afterpieces which presented music, dancing, mimicry, burlesque, performing animals and special effects to supplement main pieces like *The Clandestine Marriage*. Because afterpieces competed most directly with the pleasures of the illegitimate stage, their genealogy on the patent stage is revealing. The year after *The Clandestine Marriage*'s premiere, Garrick introduced *The Elopement* (1767), a pantomime that played thirty-five times in the 1767/8 season, culminating in a Royal Command performance with *The Clandestine Marriage* on 11 January 1768.[151] The piece was soon staged in heavy rotation with *A Trip to Scotland* (1770), a farce interlude by Garrick's friend, poet laureate William Whitehead, which satirised the fashion for Scotch elopement in the wake of the Marriage Act.

The Elopement's mise-en-scène included a spectacular 'night' scene, depicting St Paul's cathedral and the old Fleet marriage precinct, Ludgate Hill, under lights as if to celebrate the demise of London's old plebeian public sphere and its clandestine marriage market.[152] Yet both afterpieces, along with *The Clandestine Marriage*, kept the theme of secret marriage central to the Drury Lane repertoire well into the 1780s.[153] By that time, it was also a crowd pleaser at the Little Theatre, Haymarket, now under the management of George Colman, Garrick's erstwhile partner and co-author of *The Clandestine Marriage*. Colman produced Charles Stuart's comic operetta *Gretna Green*, which premiered in 1783 to a remarkable thirteen-year run of success.[154] It dissolved the stage's earlier fascination with mock marriage and the clandestine wedding market in a new kind of sentimental romance, examined more closely in our final chapter.

Garrick is rightly regarded as the figure who did most to modernise the theatre in the eighteenth century by adapting the 'rakish' world of the royalist theatre to a new commercial and respectable urban culture. It is also clear that he played a role in the history of the English marriage plot, not least by overwriting the old connection between matrimony and mimicry which stretched back to Restoration comedy and which continued to survive in the world of unreconstructed 'low' comedy favoured in the illegitimate theatre. Garrick's romantic reinvention of clandestine marriage for the patent stage was a clever commercial decision which helped to rewrite the terms in which clandestine marriage was remembered, erasing much of its unruly history. Nonetheless, it owed everything to Richardson and the new novel form for which marriage is truly 'the grand affair of ... life', and for which moral worth is measured by the presence or absence of proper marriage acts. The next chapter develops these claims more fully as it turns to *Pamela*'s influential treatment of clandestine marriage and proper ceremony.

CHAPTER 3

The New Fiction
Samuel Richardson and the Anglican Wedding

In the summer of 1753, while controversy over the Marriage Act and the Jewish Naturalisation Act was in full flow, Richardson, by then a successful London printer and a famous author, wrote to Elizabeth Carter in support of both bills.[1] The letter has been understood to indicate that he was a proponent of the Court Whig programme.[2] But that is not quite so. On the marriage question in particular, Richardson's opinions differed from those which motivated Hardwicke's legislation, even though his novels also rejected the modes of clandestine marriage that the legislation abolished.

This chapter explores the precise nature of Richardson's affinities and differences with the Hardwicke legislation in the context of his two marriage-focussed novels, *Pamela* and *The History of Sir Charles Grandison*. In *Pamela*, published well before that legislation was passed, he transformed marriage into the narratological and characterological crux of his fiction by posing it as the moment at which Christian virtue most immediately meets worldly interests, especially for women. Richardson was more concerned than the Court Whigs with marriage as a key element in a Christian life and, arguably, more concerned than any prose fiction writer before him with describing the wedding ceremony. He also granted ideal typicality to the Anglican landed estate in which his married couple will live, paying especial attention to the two offices – those of the vicar and the squire – that controlled the parishes to which estates were attached.

Each of these innovations aligned *Pamela* with oppositional Tory-Country interests. In *Sir Charles Grandison*, however, the first volumes of which were published in the year Hardwicke's Marriage Act was passed, Richardson came closer to the Whig regime's representation of marriage. Indeed, certain of its conceptual and narratological structures embodied principles underpinning the Court Whigs' agenda, while the characterisation of Sir Charles as a landed gentleman with more or less unlimited access to capital figures the alliance between landed and moneyed interests that effectively undid the Bolingbrokean Country interest. Yet Sir Charles also takes an ethical stance against what are seen as the dominant tendencies of the age and quite consciously removes himself from the public world of Parliament and civil debate, only minimally participating in a social order deemed less than ethically fit. Here Richardson revealed himself as supporting the increase of state power and structure required by Hardwicke's reforms but from a position that was less at home with the post-1688 Erastian settlement than were the Court Whigs. He was more fearful than they of modern degeneration and vice and more committed to pious, virtuous, private living. In this sense, his writing continued to resonate with the Country imaginary.

The tensions and accommodations between Court and Country that shaped *Pamela* and *Sir Charles Grandison* laid the foundations for Richardson's influential Anglican marriage plot. They also opened a new space for the novel form to function both as a tool of Christian outreach and as a commodity for the book trade, of which Richardson was an innovative and successful member. That double purpose sets the terms for my broader argument that Richardson's 'new species of writing' transformed the relationship between literature and marriage on two fronts: it invented a new kind of distinctly English marriage plot which attached moral, political and religious importance to proper church ceremony; and it set the novel genre on a new path of moral-literary realism for which literature itself was a relay point between the claims of spiritual orthodoxy and the worldly purposes of the marketplace and the nation state.

High Church Toryism and the 'New Fiction'

Current scholarship links Richardson to High Church Toryism early in his career before a later accommodation to the Court Whigs.[3] We know, for instance, that in 1722, the year that the one-time leader of the Anglican Lower House of Convocation, Francis Atterbury, was arrested for fomenting the Jacobite plot that would lead to his banishment from Britain, Samuel Negus, a printer and informant for the Whig ministry, prepared for the government a list of the political affiliations of London's printers. Negus classified the young Richardson among the 'High Fliers', that is, among the Tories with High Church or nonjuring (and almost certainly Jacobite) attachments whom Atterbury led.[4] However, by 1733, when Richardson became an author, his Tory affiliations were more muted. At that time he published his earliest known work, *The Apprentice's Vade Mecum*, exhorting London apprentices to pious living and advising them against participating in urban vice, including commercial entertainment. The pamphlet articulated his animus against disorder and clandestine culture, and was a key source for his polemic against unlicensed theatres in *A Seasonable Examination*.

Certainly at this point Richardson's Toryism did not prevent his successful contracting for print jobs from the Whig administration, nor his embracing of many of its policies.[5] But his Tory affiliations had not disappeared.[6] At least while he was writing *Clarissa*, he remained an associate of opponents of the regime such as his medical advisor, the Scottish Jacobite George Cheyne; and his friends John Freke, the surgeon, electrician and mystic; and John Heylin, the so-called Mystic Doctor who had once employed William Law, the widely read nonjuring theologian, as his curate.[7] Freke and Heylin were among the select group to read *Clarissa* in manuscript. And in the late 1730s he engaged with the Jacobite Tory historian Thomas Carte in compiling, editing and printing the papers of the seventeenth-century Royalist diplomat and colonial entrepreneur Sir Thomas Roe (whose efforts helped to establish the trading power of the East India Company), a labour of love which positioned Richardson against at least the truest of true Whigs.[8]

Yet even as Richardson's political sympathies shifted (or were hedged for practical purposes), his commitment to religion – and specifically to High Church Anglicanism – remained constant. The older scholarship that views him as some kind of 'puritan' is mistaken – there is no room even for Dissent in his fiction.[9] Nor was he an ambiently 'Protestant' author but precisely an Anglican one: Richardson's High Church proclivities are plainly evidenced in his early pamphlet writing. *The Apprentice's Vade Mecum* and *A Seasonable Examination* were both written in the wake of Collier's *A Short View of the Immorality and Profaneness of the English Stage* (1698) and Law's *The Absolute Unlawfulness of Stage Entertainments* (1726).[10] Collier and Law were not writing against the London theatre as puritans or as Dissenters interested in resisting licentiousness on hard Calvinist ascetic grounds, nor as proponents of that mode of Court Whig law and order aimed at securing state control over society in the interests of economic production and capital accumulation. Rather they were nonjurors – Anglican divines who refused allegiance to the post-Stuart monarchs.[11] (Collier was to become the pre-eminent nonjuring bishop.) The nonjurors also rejected urban dissoluteness and entertainment – especially the theatre – from a perspective that wished to retain Anglican absolutism's theo-political order against its undoing by court license, urban commercialisation and religious backsliding.

As a pamphleteer, Richardson inherited precisely this High Church polemic, while as an active tradesman and printer he modified it. His *Vade Mecum* cites Collier against unbelievers at some length and, in its dedication, declares itself a riposte to the 'Degeneracy of the Times, and the Profaneness and Immorality, and even the open Infidelity that is everywhere propagated with Impunity'.[12] Its third part, dedicated to religion, repudiates atheism and Lockean deism, arguing that the mystery of Christianity can neither be reduced to nor understood through reason. Richardson here defends miracles and appeals to the pure morality of 'primitive' Christianity in terms that echo Law among others.[13] Yet the *Vade Mecum* does not just sermonise its audience; importantly, it fashions itself as a new kind of literary product which seeks to connect with young readers in an 'easy and pleasant Manner' (6). As Louise Curran has argued, the pamphlet, with its moral intent, lays a foundation for the plain, familiar style that *Pamela* will later bring to epistolary fiction.[14] Its second part, for instance, presents the 'Rules and Directions for the Behavior of Young Men' (tp) in a strikingly direct second-person mode 'address'd to the Youth himself' (6):

> [Y]ou are more *interested* to perform well, than even your Master is; for he can be only benefitted for a *Time* by your good Service; whereas you will reap the Benefit of it to the End of your Life, and, in all Probability, to the End of Time, and for ever: for ... to do your Duty to Man is a first Step in the Way of doing what is required of you by God Almighty. (27)

The *Vade Mecum* flatly insists that an ethic of piety (doing what God requires) is at one with being a good employee (doing your duty to man). The pamphlet's Anglicanism routinely takes the pragmatic turn that we saw in *A Seasonable Examination*'s embrace of commercial values, declaring, for instance, that dissipation among apprentices not only destroys their personal prospects for success and salvation but also damages national productivity (24). Some commentators have noted a contradiction here: Richardson opposes the Whiggish market economy and its dire religious-moral consequences while blithely promoting the prudential virtues required to be a successful tradesman within it.[15] Yet such an objection misses the sheer novelty of his intervention, since for him living as a good Christian, being obedient to one's master and being prosperous as a master are all purposes that work to God's end. This insistence makes space for a new kind of literary purpose, hinting strongly at the broad outreach that Richardson (as a printer-author) had begun to envisage for a familiar writing practice addressed to youthful readers as Christian souls and as members of a widening prosperity-oriented reading public.

Viewed in this way, the *Vade Mecum* offered itself to readers not just as a tradesman's conduct book but as a very contemporary mode of Anglican missionary address, one that takes its place among an array of similar Tory-inflected efforts. Jeremy Gregory has argued that the Church's civil outreach efforts in the eighteenth century were a continuation of the Reformation project of 'spreading Christianity and Anglicanism to "the dark corners of the land"'. They can also be understood as arising from the Tory-Anglican concerns that animated Richardson and other Anglican reformers to counteract the Church's perceived loss of socio-political authority.[16]

Those concerns motivated various forms of enterprise and activity including the initiatives of the energetic Thomas Bray, particularly the Society for Promoting Christian Knowledge (SPCK) and the Society for the Propagation of the Gospel in Foreign Parts (SPG), and also Bray's earlier schemes for establishing libraries for poor Anglican clergy unable to afford books themselves. They also include the Society for the Reformation of Manners (SRM) which, although by no means just a Tory association, was, in the words of a recent church historian, established 'by the reactionary and authoritarian demands of the fractious lower house of Convocation'.[17] They cover too the setting up of the Foundling Hospital (Thomas Coram, the leading figure here, was an associate of Bray and the Jacobite General James Oglethorpe and, like them, a pioneer in Anglican moral colonialism). They further include the Anglican movement to make the use of the catechism more universal and effective; they even encompass Oglethorpe's colonisation of Georgia as part of an emigration scheme for the unemployed and those at risk of penality. Indeed (and to go no further) such efforts share much with Wesleyanism itself, which emerged in the 1730s among young Oxford-based Tory Anglicans (the 'Holy Club') primarily concerned to restore Christian values across society as a riposte to free living and the church's loss of social power.[18]

The point of citing the *Vade Mecum* among these outreach initiatives is to insist that, with Richardson, prose fiction itself joins the Tory-Anglican current of moral reform. Arguably, *Pamela*'s singularity is defined precisely by its missionary effort which, as much as anything else, marked it off from earlier fictional genres and modes. Literary critical orthodoxy tends to obscure this point by presenting Richardson as a moderniser: as an apostle of individualism, of paternalism, of companionate marriage, of moral virtue (rather than religion per se), and of what is in effect a 'Puritan' pre-formation of secular, liberal family values.[19] These values are of course consistent with the social stratum to which Richardson himself belonged – the middling sort – and with the commercial values that shaped the literary marketplace within which he forged his career as a printer and a writer; they are also consistent with Richardson's commitment to address a widening audience, his desire to develop a plain style by which he could 'writ[e]to the multitude'.[20] But Richardson's religious purposes, which work towards specific – and rather different – ends, need to be part of this picture too.

If nothing else, his ongoing refusal to allow religion to accede to the oligarchy reminds us that Tory-Anglican religious politics drove his fiction. The instructive coda of *Pamela*'s first edition signalled as much with this exhortation:

> Let good CLERGYMEN, in Mr. WILLIAMS, see that whatever Displeasure the doing of their Duty may give, for a Time, to their proud patrons, Providence will, at last, reward their Piety, and turn their Distresses to Triumph; and make them even more valued for a Conduct that gave Offence while the Violence of Passion lasted, than if they had meanly stoop'd to flatter or sooth the Vices of the Great. (500–1)

Richardson's appeal to the autonomy of clerical conscience is pointedly anti-Erastian, suggesting that shifting relations between the Church and the Court Whig state were indeed a key context for *Pamela*'s marriage plot (as will become clear later in what follows). It also reminds us that his commitment to solicit the wider population into an Anglican moral and spiritual order meant that his novels addressed not a particular literary readership (as did the amatory fiction of the 1720s), or even a specifiable market sector, but the polity at large envisaged as constituted by Christian subjects open to Anglican spiritual and moral reformation.

That such a religious community is Richardson's ultimate object of address has important literary consequences. The first is that he is not just interested in the reader *qua* reader but in the reader *qua* soul. At the level of content, this is one reason why, for instance, vicars figure quite largely in his fiction (as characters and as readers), especially in his marriage plots.[21] It is also why religious reflection and ritual – acts of prayer, psalm-singing and the wedding ceremony itself, for example – are so important to it. But Richardson's religious mission also means that an alternative mode of address, one that is overtly self-reflexive or concerned about reader response, often in relation to traditional learning, is inappropriate. We can find one version of such a mode of address in Fielding and another in Eliza Haywood's *The History of Miss Betsy Thoughtless* (1751) where a typical chapter heading runs: 'Is the recital of some accidents, as little possible to be foreseen by the reader as they were by the persons to whom they happened'.[22] But such self-reflexivity would damage Richardson's missionary aims.

Because Richardson's object of address is ultimately the Christian soul rather than the polite reader, he crafts a new narrative structure from which the extra-diegetic narrative voice has been almost wholly removed to be replaced by sermonic/didactic prefaces and codas, on occasions written by clergymen such as William Warburton. Tellingly, *Pamela* was introduced in the Tory magazine the *Weekly Miscellany*, edited by Richardson's friend the High Churchman William Webster, who almost certainly wrote the pre-publication puff too. It announces that the book is especially (but not only) aimed at women; that its appeal lies in its narrative interest and capacity to solicit readerly identification ('there is no reading it without uncommon Concern and Emotion'), which echoes its 'spirit of Truth and agreeable Simplicity'.[23]

Webster claims too that *Pamela*'s value lies in its capacity to 'form the tender Minds of Youth for the Reception and Practice of Virtue and Honour; confirm and establish those of maturer Age on good and steady Principles; reclaim the Vicious, and mend the Age in general'. The sheer lexical variety and boldness of his panegyric is striking: *Pamela* engages reflection *and* emotion *and* naturalness *and* substance *and* simplicity *and* principle; while addressing young *and* old, virtuous *and* vicious. This is a set of qualifiers that no polemical or even sermonic discourse could easily bear. But Webster's capacious description catches those qualities of the text that would prompt Aaron Hill, for instance, to recommend it as nothing less than 'the *Soul* of Religion'.[24] These comments hint at why Richardson's religious outreach project ultimately found expression not in advice book exhortation but in *literature*: not the traditional conception of literature connected to learned, classical, courtly or simply pleasure-orientated interests and attainments, but rather literature as a mode of recasting a well-known product of the book trade (the letter collection) as a tool of moral missionary endeavour. This is the context in which Richardson harnessed his new fictional mode to private religious, moral and spiritual ends.

The Invention of the Anglican Marriage Plot

Richardson came to epistolary fiction by accident (although he seems to have composed letters for illiterate neighbours in his youth). He agreed to write a collection of 'familiar letters on the useful concerns of common life' on the invitation of the Anglican bookseller Charles Rivington and his associate John Osborn.[25] In the process, he experimented with tailoring his model letters to provide moral lessons in 'how to think and act justly and prudently' in commonly encountered situations. About half of the letters published in *Letters Written to and for Particular Friends* (1741), also known as *Familiar Letters*, concerned courtship and marriage. These include instructions to 'orphan ladies' about how to judge proposals of marriage and to rebut clandestine addresses;[26] advice to widows and widowers against remarriage;[27] a letter from a mother to her daughter, jealous of her husband;[28] a young gentlewoman writing to her aunt about the merits of her competing suitors;[29] and – most notably – a maidservant seeking her father's advice about how to resist her master's sexual importunities.[30] This last became the basis of a further project, the two-volume romance written between November 1739 and January 1740 also published by Rivington and Osborn as *Pamela, or Virtue Rewarded*.

While there was nothing new about epistolary fiction as such, Richardson's adaptation of the mode was unique.[31] Pamela's letters were not just written in a plain first-person style (without 'Froth and Whip-syllabub', as Webster put it) but at especially dramatic moments (and at whatever cost to verisimilitude) they were written at the very time of action – a technique Richardson famously called 'writing to the moment'.[32] By turning the situations in which the letters themselves were composed and transmitted into elements of plot and characterisation, Richardson injected a new level of immediacy into his fiction. New too was the letters' range of tones. Characteristically, they offer reports of events by one character to another while also recording the writer's subjective responses to those events, whether Christian and virtuous, or libertine and freethinking, or witty and rebellious.

By working simultaneously on two levels – plot and character – and by enabling a dialogue between different points of view to take on a dramatic narrative form, Richardson developed a style which could render interiority with unprecedented solidity. Pamela's startling story of upward mobility is told from her singular perspective while being embedded in real-time accounts of the ethically challenging and ambiguous situations out of which it proceeded. In this way, Richardson fused characters' subjectivity, the onward movement of plot and the reflective unfolding of moral truth. And by the same stroke, he freed his fiction from those modes of extra-diegetic address that risk breaking the mimetic illusion, thereby enabling his readers to 'slip invisible, into the domestic privacy of characters, and hear and see everything that is said and done', as Francis

Jeffrey remarked.[33] This was the crux of Richardson's new style: writing itself seems to dissolve into unmediated personhood and presence. Inside *Pamela*'s immersive fictional structure, the heroine's courtship and eventual marriage expresses and legitimates her moral character and spiritual worth, which constitutes her claim on salvation. For readers, her slow, fraught and discursive progress towards securing a spouse acquires something like the quality of lived experience.

Richardson's second important prose innovation was his narrative focus on marriage. Literary historians from Ian Watt to Thomas Pavel view Richardson's marriage plot as his signature legacy: in formal terms, it enabled him to focus on a single dramatic situation rather than on the diffuse adventures that had sustained the episodic structure of earlier prose narrative genres.[34] As Watt long ago claimed, Richardson's representation of a new and unusual kind of situation – a maidservant's resistance to the sexual advances of a country squire culminating in their marriage – had the effect of pulling together various pre-existing fictional modes (the romance, the picaresque, the 'low-life' novel) into the discrete and dilated form of the modern novel.[35] Feminist scholars have since noted that the love-courtship-marriage topos was not new; it had been a particular staple of amatory fiction – whether on stage or in print – since at least the last two decades of the seventeenth century when women began to be courted as a market sector.[36] Nonetheless, Richardson's moral realism is widely regarded as a departure from the modes of romance, idealism, allegory, scandal and gossip that marked the amatory mode – one signalled in *Pamela*'s bold replacement of seduction with marriage.

While marriage is unquestionably *Pamela*'s primary focus, it is neither a unitary theme nor a merely literary-formal trope: Richardson's treatment of marriage is highly topical. As we see in more detail in what follows, for Pamela marriage becomes singular (or 'proper') only by virtue of her pointed rejection of alternative marriage modes belonging to libertinism and clandestinity. Her trials take form not just as resistance to seduction per se but also as resistance to the wrong kind of nuptial arrangements – sham marriages, clandestine marriages, contract marriages, common law marriages – which constitute an archaeology of those marriage forms that the Hardwicke Marriage Act will prohibit. Most pointedly, Pamela's reward is not simply marriage, but a carefully described *Anglican* marriage which represents the full legitimation of her orthodox Christian piety.

Arguably, then, Richardson reset the traditional marriage plot as part of an Anglican-Tory response to the Hardwicke era's church-state politics. At the same time, in distinguishing and ranking particular kinds of marriage practices, his marriage plots, for all their grounding in a High Church mission, narrativise Court Whig reformism. For him (again, somewhat paradoxically) the Anglican wedding revealed its full spiritual and social authority, and indeed its charisma, only when opposed to rivals and alternatives. Crucially, Richardson's marriage plot depends on a distinction between *proper* marriage and its 'others', one that rejects clandestine marriage culture and its fictional and theatrical analogues as *improper*. That binary structure lies at the heart of his fiction and continues the anti-stage programme of his earlier pamphlets by injecting ethico-political force into the distance between 'new fiction', on one hand, and popular modes of scandal and theatricality, on the other. Indeed, after *Pamela*, the prose fiction marriage plot becomes invested in narrating the wedding ritual itself, a feature which marks it out from the eighteenth-century stage which continued assiduously to avoid the mimetic performance of marriage.

The previous chapter showed how the literary-satiric representation of mock marriage (and its social cognate, clandestine marriage) was organised around a binary of polite and impolite culture that reinforced social division. As Richardson carried that tradition from the stage and newsprint spheres into the novel, it underpinned a baseline distinction between proper and improper marriage that became central to the ongoing development of the English marriage plot. 'Improper' marriage, as exemplified by a welter of anti-Fleet discourse, remained associated with the chaos, energy and contingency of the plebeian/urban public sphere as well as with other forms of alterity. By contrast, 'proper' marriage, as fictionalised by Richardson and later reinforced by the Marriage Act, comes to be defined by an alliance of church and state articulated in the context of the English country parish and the landed estate. It achieves this in part by aligning itself to a domesticity and soulful interiority whose other was the idle theatre-goer or bad apprentice as seen from the perspective of the Anglican moral mission.

The following sections make good on these claims by examining first, *Pamela*'s extensive use of the clandestine (or 'sham') marriage motif; and second, its presentation of a romantic triangle between a squire, a clergyman and a virtuous young woman (which I call its 'clerical subplot'). The first returns us to the unruly culture of clandestine marriage; the second to the Erastian politics of church and state. These contexts shaped Richardson's marriage plot as it presented Pamela's highly subjectivised and spiritualised courtship, on one hand, and her proper Anglican wedding ceremony, on the other.

The 'Sham Marriage'

At its most basic level, Pamela and Mr B.'s courtship begins as a struggle between Anglican virtue and libertine, aristocratic desire.[37] Pamela's virtue is tested by a battery of contrivances by which Mr B. attempts to seduce her, all of which belong to traditional scripts for exogamous sexual relations. These fall into three categories: the coercive threat of rape, consensual models of contract (which may or may not end in common law marriage), and a variety of mock marriage plots, none designed to end in a proper church ceremony. Pamela's resistance to each of these scripts underpins her self-formation as the deep and soulful subject of a new kind of Anglican marriage plot.

Mr B. attempts rape in two much-discussed scenes which establish the highly literate – indeed, discursive – nature of Pamela's identity.[38] During the second and more threatening of these, he is smuggled into Pamela's bedroom disguised as Nan, a servant woman. Pamela at this time is particularly bereft of support. Defending herself against Mr B.'s threats of violence, she tells him plainly enough: 'Words are all that are left me.'[39] Indeed, Pamela employs an impressive range of rhetoric to deflect Mr B.'s desire, ranging from terse moral argument ('should not a Gentleman prefer an honest Servant to a guilty Harlot?' [121]), to elaborate sophistry ('Sir . . . I am of no Consequence equal to this, sure, in your Honour's Family, that such a great Gentlemen as you . . . should need to justify yourself about me' [73]) – this from a woman who has privately vowed that 'VIRTUE *is the only nobility*.'[40]

Pamela becomes especially eloquent (or, as Armstrong puts it, 'metaphysical') when Mr B. changes tack from physical coercion to a consensual approach, which he terms 'honourable' (187).[41] Of course, it is only after Mr B. has had Pamela imprisoned at his Lincolnshire estate under the watchful eye of his housekeeper Mrs Jewkes that he assures her that 'I will not approach you without your Leave' (117). When he does indeed forego physical force, he presents Pamela with a seven-point plan to formalise relations between them, offering her 500 guineas to become 'Mistress of my Person and Fortune, as much as if the foolish [marriage] Ceremony had passed' (191). Pamela's written responses to the plan – point for point – constitute the lexicon of her moral and religious beliefs. Mr B.'s offer of '500 Guineas' for her favour, for instance, provokes a particularly telling rebuff: 'I reject it *with all my Soul*. Money, Sir, is not my chief Good' (189, my emphasis).

Precisely because Pamela perceives herself as a fully formed 'soul' – formed in the practices of Christian obedience and devotion – she refuses

to be the subject of a non-religiously endorsed contract of domestic
cohabitation. After all, that contract requires a body alienable from the
moral self, while a soul cannot be alienated from bodily acts. Pamela
cannot make her own body an object of exchange, to become, as she
puts it, 'a vile kept Mistress' (187). And, as she explains to Mr B., the
grounds of her refusal extend beyond her own free will:

> I know, Sir, by woful Experience, that I am in your Power . . . Yet, Sir, will
> I dare to tell you, that I will make no Free-will Offering of my Virtue. All
> that I can do, poor as it is, I will do, to convince you, that your Offers shall
> have no Part in my Choice; and if I cannot escape the Violence of Man,
> I hope, by God's Grace, I shall have nothing to reproach myself, for not
> doing all in my Power to avoid my Disgrace; and then I can safely appeal to
> the great God, my only Refuge and Protector, with this Consolation, That
> my Will bore no Part in my Violation. (190–1)

It is clear enough that Pamela's refusal of Mr B.'s threats and offers allows
her to fashion (or at least to reconfirm) an identity 'deeper' than her body
but indivisible from it; and that her 'Virtue' and 'Dignity' are finally
contingent upon God's grace.

Pamela's self-formation, however, is rather differently engaged and
exercised by another series of challenges to her virtue, this time involving
clandestine marriage. During her 'days of bondage' at Lincolnshire, Pamela
learns of the strategies by which Mr B. hopes to claim a husband's sexual
rights to her body without violence and without incurring the responsibility of coverture. He plans to use loopholes in the marriage code to
subject her to husbands who will, however, remain under his control. His
first move is to try to arrange a match between Pamela and his dependent,
the parson Mr Williams, in a deal whereby Pamela's body would be
available to Mr B. as the price for Williams succeeding to the clerical living
in his gift. A little later, a still more unpleasant marriage scheme eventuates.
Mrs Jewkes secretly informs Pamela that Mr B. intends to punish Mr
Williams by forcing him to marry her off to his sinister crony, Mr
Colbrand. Once that wedding had been performed, Mr B. would 'buy
[her] of him on the Wedding-day, for a Sum of Money' (179) before
Colbrand returned to his original wife and family.

The medley of English marriage law anomalies invoked here – clandestine marriage, wife sale and bigamy – provokes a noteworthy response from
Pamela:

> But this, to be sure, is horrid romancing! but abominable as it is, it may
> possibly serve to introduce some Plot now hatching! – With what strange

> Perplexities is my poor Mind agitated! Perchance, some Sham-marriage may be design'd, on purpose to ruin me: But can a Husband sell his Wife against her own Consent? – And will such a Bargain stand good in Law? (179–80)

Pamela associates Mr B.'s designs with 'romance', by which she means the plays and prose fictions in which such ruses were commonplace. More importantly, for the first time Pamela is here forced to reflect upon her dilemma in terms of the larger public sphere – in terms of law and equity, not ethics. Yet, in the revised edition of the text, she considers the question of her legal rights and status only to dismiss it, concluding that in regard to feminine virtue, the reach and authority of the law cannot combat the 'lawless' oligarchy and marketplace: 'But what is law, what is any thing with the lawless? And if I am bought and sold, and taken away by the vile purchaser, what will a legal punishment for wickedness committed, avail the irretrievable injured!'[42]

Once again Pamela confirms herself to be *all* soul, which she conceives of as a space of legal nothingness, because 'nothingness' represents an absolute rejection of the 'vile' values of commerce and material exchange, in a social setting in which the law alone cannot order or even provide compensation for wrongs. Pamela will no more be 'bought and sold' as a 'wife' than she will be a 'kept Mistress, or kept Slave' (137), even if this refusal involves, as it does, a surrender of civil rights and legal status. In this sense too Pamela's spiritual-moral self has oppositional political resonance in the context of Whig hegemony since it is gained and preserved through a rejection of the legal power of a state whose sovereignty is, by implication, not just limited but questionable.[43]

If B.'s threats of clandestine marriage help to trigger Pamela's 'deep' and soulful resistance to him in the early stages of their courtship, they also underpin her reversal of feeling in the novel's second volume, her falling in love with Mr B. *Pamela*, after all, is a story of double reformation: Mr B.'s conversion from rake to willing husband turns upon his reading Pamela's letters (as Michael McKeon has influentially argued, Mr B. undergoes a shift from adversarial to ideal reading positions through which he imbibes domestic virtue by identifying with Pamela's text).[44] Pamela's change of heart, however, occurs rather differently, via Richardson's remobilisation of the old theatrical trope of mock or 'sham' marriage, as he terms it. Deployed across an extended section of the middle of the text, it provides the conditions for Pamela's piety, virtue and self-understanding to detach from chastity per se so as to become meaningfully reconceived around proper marriage.

This is not to forget that Richardson's sham marriage has long been read in very different terms. Most famously, Henry Fielding instantly recognised its comedic potential, forever redefining Pamela herself by means of a clever synecdoche linking her with the mooted 'sham marriage' by which Mr B. plans to ruin her. Fielding's rhyming pun – 'Shamela' or more pointedly 'Miss Sham' – ridiculed Pamela's 'vartue' and exposed the cant of her name itself, since 'Pamela' is derived from the literary-romance tradition rather than from ordinary usage. In shaming Pamela as a slut and a hypocrite, *Shamela* belongs to a long line of 'anti-Pamelaist' polemic that has foreclosed critical interest in her change of heart.[45] Arguably, Fielding himself nonetheless grasped something of the (perverse) gravity of mock marriage for Richardson since Mr B.'s decision to abandon the 'sham' wedding and to take Pamela as his legitimate wife prompts his burlesque moniker, 'Booby'. With this joke, *Shamela* recalls with some precision a Tory-Scriblerian literary precedent for Richardson's marriage plot: Gay's comic trope of the young libertine-cum-'Booby Squire' in *The What D'ye Call It* who is gulled into marrying a plebeian woman by means of a mock marriage which turns real.

While *Pamela*'s sham marriage (like her name) is indeed borrowed from romance and theatrical repertoire, it is put to extended and pointedly non-comedic use in Richardson's novel. To begin with, *Pamela*'s sham marriage is not a complete fraud; and for reasons bound to clandestine marriage's social functionality for cross-class couples, it is not merely a comic simulation of the marriage ceremony for effects of farce or meta-theatre. Rather it is a narrative device through which Pamela comes to reckon with her whole 'self' (i.e. both her faith and her feelings) and through which a new kind of proper marriage between social un-equals can come into view. Commentators have rightly noted that Pamela and Mr B.'s exogamous union openly rejects the endogamous logic of aristocratic marriage codes (in the text, given rather shrill articulation by Mr B.'s sister, Lady Davers), proffering instead Pamela's moral authority as the basis of a new kind of bourgeois companionate marriage ethic anchored in modern regimes of gender and domestic femininity rather than social status per se.[46] Arguably, however, Pamela's subjectivity (and indeed, the novel's embrace of companionate marriage) rests upon a more fundamental precondition: the rejection of clandestine marriage itself and the ambivalence and uncertainty it represented. In crafting a credible fictional union between a squire and a maidservant, Richardson must all at once evoke and dismiss its theatrical-clandestine precursors.

Structurally, the sham marriage is crucial to *Pamela*'s courtship plot since it resolves an otherwise intractable narrative impasse for the unlikely couple. When, towards the end of the first volume of the novel, Mr B. first confesses his love to Pamela in earnest, he despairs of marriage: 'I cannot endure the Thought of Marriage, even with a Person of equal or superior Degree to myself . . . How, then, with the Distance between us, and in the World's Judgement, can I think of making you my Wife?' (213). How indeed? The volume closes with Pamela's report of Mr B.'s insistence on the rake's creed – 'Indeed, I cannot marry!' (218). But this turns out to be a moment of brinksmanship not unlike Boswell's momentary 'terror for marriage' in the face of his cousin Peggy's acceptance of his marriage proposal, for in the early stages of volume two, Mr B. does indeed begin to broach marriage in earnest. At the same moment, however, the spectre of sham marriage enters the text. In what can only be read as a proto-Gothic moment (laden as it is with the full freight of anti-Fleet discourse), Pamela is visited by a Romany fortune-teller who leaves a note to warn her that Mr B.'s new, loving demeanour is his most wicked trick:

> The 'Squire is absolutely determin'd to ruin you. And because he despairs of any other way, he will pretend great Love and Kindness to you, and that he will marry you. You may expect a Parson for this Purpose, in a few Days; but it is a sly artful Fellow of a broken Attorney, that he has hir'd to personate a Minister. The Man has a broad Face, pitted much with the Small-pox, and is a very good Companion . . . Doubt not this Advice. Perhaps you'll have but too much Reason already to confirm you in the Truth of it. From your zealous Well-wisher,
>
> '*Somebody.*' (225)

Pamela quickly realises that a sham marriage to Mr B. – designed to satisfy her scruples and give the semblance of legitimacy to his desire – is the most pernicious of all the threats to her virtue. Unlike rape, contract, or even arranged marriage, all of which she might resist, the sham marriage upsets the terms upon which she defines and understands her own virtue. At this moment, those terms are legalistic: 'how dreadful must have been my lot, when I had found myself . . . a guilty harlot, instead of a lawful wife!' (224). The real horror for Pamela is that as a 'sham' wife she would be – like the prostitute bride of Fleet caricature – adrift in a libertine netherworld, all at once neither harlot nor wife but both harlot and wife, as Mr B.'s confession of the details of his plan later reveals:

> I had thought [the phony parson] should have read some Part of the Ceremony (as little as was possible, to deceive you) in my Chamber; and

so I hop'd to have you mine upon Terms that then would have been much more agreeable to me than real Matrimony. And I did not in Haste intend you the Mortification of being undeceiv'd; so that we might have liv'd for Years, perhaps, very lovingly together; and I had, at the same time been at Liberty to confirm or abrogate it, as I pleas'd. (268–9)

From the moment that Pamela learns of the 'sham marriage' plot, she is haunted by it precisely as the shadowy and deceptive double of the real – the legal, the religious – thing. To be sure, Pamela's fear of sham marriage is animated by Fleet caricature, but it also needs to be understood in the context in which clandestine marriages were the most common means through which gentlemen married women of lower social station, and where the distinction between such clandestine marriages and sham marriages was particularly fine.

Up to this point in the story, Pamela's identity has been shaped agonistically by a commitment to Christian virtue expressed against Mr B.'s worldliness, desire and money. In the face of his impending reformation, however, she becomes a divided, doubting, 'tremulous' self, as if to internalise an ontological uncertainty attached to marriage itself. What follows for Pamela is an extended process of self-scrutiny mixed with Anglican self-abasement which unfolds across distinct stages of fear, confusion, self-questioning and finally self-mortification. Each occurs in response to Mr B.'s earnest and repeated attempts to press his suit. Together they showcase the full subjective range of Richardson's immersive epistolary mode as well as the component parts of what will become Pamela's new married identity.

The first such moment occurs when Mr B., having read Pamela's 'suicide' letters, is finally moved to make an 'honourable address': 'I will endeavour to defy the World, and the World's Censures, and, make my Pamela Amends, if it be in the Power of my whole Life, for all the Hardships I have inflicted upon her' (241). Pamela's conflicted response, noticeably drained of her former gusto, takes the form of a polite demurral edged with fear:

> All this look'd well; but you shall see how strangely it was all turn'd. For this Sham-marriage then came into my Mind again; and I said, Your poor Servant is far unworthy of this great Honour; for what will it be, but to create Envy to herself, and Discredit to you? Therefore, Sir, permit me to return to my poor Parents, and that is all I have to ask. (241)

Strikingly, both Mr B.'s defiant proposal and Pamela's faltering reply are addressed towards, although not directly about, marriage. The sham marriage dangerously promises what is a so far undefined alternative for

Pamela. As she remarks in the revised edition of the text, 'fears will ever mingle with one's hopes, where a great and unexpected, yet uncertain good opens to one's view.'[47] In this context, a marriage with Mr B. crystallises or 'opens to . . . view' as, precisely, *not* a sham wedding. After Mr B. takes umbrage at Pamela's cold reply and bids her leave his house immediately, she is thrown into turmoil. At this point her 'spontaneous writing' transmutes into a dialogic mode of self-address through which she can question her own motives:

> I think I was loth to leave the House. Can you believe it? – What could be the matter with me, I wonder! – I felt something so strange, and my heart was so lumpish! – I wonder what ail'd me! – But this was so *unexpected!* – I believe that was all! – Yet I am very strange still. Surely, surely, I cannot be like the old murmuring *Israelites*, to long after the Onions and Garlick of *Egypt*, when they had suffer'd there such a heavy Bondage? – I'll take thee, O lumpish, contradictory, ungovernable Heart, to severe Task for this thy strange Impulse, when I get to my Father's and Mother's; and if I find any thing in thee that should not be, depend upon it, thou shalt be humbled, if strict Abstinence, Prayer, and Mortification, will do it! (244–5)

In her state of self-division (both 'I' and 'thee'), Pamela equates Mr B. with Egyptian 'Onions and Garlic', remembered comically but tellingly from her biblical reading. The disquiet caused by her own 'lumpish, contradictory, ungovernable Heart' is speedily resolved into the promise of a specifically High Church Anglican programme of 'Abstinence, Prayer and Mortification'.

At this point Pamela receives a letter from Mr B. disavowing the sham marriage plot and assuring her that his offer had been genuine. It is now that the capacity for humility and self-mortification that she knows in herself (and is confident that she can bring to bear upon herself if needs be) provides her with the assurance that the 'strange' new emotion she feels – love – is not just real but also consonant with her spiritual life. Her faith, or better, her religious practice, is, in effect, her love's precondition. The coincidence of her own penitential intentions and Mr B.'s commitment to proper ceremony allows her at last to acknowledge her love for Mr B., if only in the context of self-mortification and loss:

> And all this wicked Gypsey-Story is, as it seems, a Forgery upon us both, and has quite ruin'd me! . . . This was a Happiness, however, I had no Reason to expect. But to be sure, I must own to you, that I shall never be able to think of any body in the World but him! Presumption! you will say; and so it is: But Love is not a voluntier Thing – *Love*, did I say! – But come, I hope not! – At least it is not, I hope, gone so far, as to make me *very* uneasy: for I know

not *how* it came, nor when it began; but creep, creep it has, like a Thief, upon me; and before I knew what was the Matter, it looked like Love. (248)

The sham marriage scenario is indeed a sham, but it has nonetheless revealed to Pamela that she did not know herself (or her own heart, at least). In light of this recognition, the terms of her own virtue can be revised:

> I should have bless'd myself, in having escap'd so happily his designing Arts upon my virtue; but *now*, my poor Mind is all topsy-turvy'd, and I have made an Escape to be more a Prisoner! . . . – O my treacherous, treacherous Heart! to serve me thus! And give no notice to me of the mischiefs thou wast about to bring upon me! But thus foolishly to give thyself up to the proud Invader, without ever consulting thy poor Mistress in the least! . . . O perfidious Traitor, for giving up so weakly, thy *whole Self*, before a Summons came, and to one too, who had us'd me so hardly! (248–9)

Pamela's ungovernable heart can now be retrospectively reclaimed by her 'whole Self' – her soul – so that her virtue is no longer defined around her virginity and her resistance to Mr B.'s desire, but rather is envisaged as a lost horizon ('a whole Life of faithful Love, and chearful Obedience' [248]) compromised not by Mr B.'s imprisonment of her but by her imprisonment of herself (i.e. by her own heart's 'treachery').

Finally, Mr B.'s second letter, begging Pamela to return, triggers her capitulation to a love now strengthened by religious faith and self-doubt: 'I resolved to obey him; and if he uses me ill afterwards, double will be his ungenerous Guilt!' (252). On this understanding, Pamela returns to Mr B. at her 'liberty', able to replace one 'whole [resisting] Self' (249) with another loving self: 'yet all the time this heart is *Pamela*' (251). We know, however, that the lengthy narrative process of self-reckoning-cum-spiritual reflection by which she chooses to accept – and indeed to 'obey' – him involves the re-appropriation of her heart by her soul as triggered precisely by the slippage between mock marriage and an as-yet-undefined proper alternative.

In addition to enabling Pamela's self-reckoning, the sham marriage serves two further functions in Richardson's marriage plot. It underpins the semi-formal declarations of love which cement the religious-moral terms of Pamela and Mr B.'s union (via a mutual disavowal of their worldly interests) and it later serves to set their marriage apart from Mr B.'s libertine sexual history. In each case, the sham marriage – once again by virtue of its ontological uncertainty – troubles the very categories of companionate love, marriage and property which it helps to construct and which will become the hallmarks of Richardson's marriage plot and its new regime of domestic moral virtue.

Mr B. makes his most powerful declaration of love to Pamela after renouncing the sham marriage through which he had planned to ruin her: 'tho' I doubted not effecting this my last Plot, [I] resolv'd to overcome myself . . . rather than to betray you under so black a Veil' (269). Soliciting Pamela's affirmation of a heartfelt return of the 'true Love' (270) he bears her, he disclaims any material motive for marriage in what amounts to a ritual disavowal of his own 'Interest':

> [C]an you return me sincerely the honest Compliment I now make you, that as in the Act that I hope shall soon unite us together, it is impossible I should have any View to my Interest; and, that Love, *true* Love, is the *only* motive by which I am directed; that, were I not what I am, as to fortune, you could give me the Preference to any other Person in the World that you know, notwithstanding all that has pass'd between us? (270)

Richardson signalled the importance of this moment by later terming it (somewhat pompously) a 'declaration of reciprocal love'.[48] Yet it is anything but reciprocal and Mr B. manifestly fails his own test. '[T]he Act' by which he evinces his own disinterestedness – a marriage tie with Pamela based upon 'voluntier Love' (270) – can be self-certifying only insofar as it rests upon the earlier distinction he has drawn between sham marriage ('treading in a Path that another had mark'd out for me' [269]) and an 'Original' marriage tie, as he puts it (269).[49] Indeed, Mr B. sabotages his own claim that his love is guaranteed by the absence of material motive or 'interest', by conceding that a consideration of property law has prompted him to propose a real marriage ahead of a sham: 'if I should have a dear little one, it would be out of my own power to legitimate it, if I should wish it to inherit my Estate' (269).

On Pamela's side, the ultimate declaration of love – against interest – works differently. Mr B. asks her to express her 'Preference' for him against all other men in terms other than his fortune. First, she must deny desire for men closer to her class or type (namely, Mr Williams), but then she must also prove that her attraction to Mr B. does not issue from his rank and fortune. Pamela's motive, then, can be nothing but love, understood as an affective bond untainted by sex or money. She begins with characteristic humility:

> 'Why . . . should your so much obliged *Pamela* refuse to answer to this kind Question? . . . You, Sir, are the only Person living that ever was more than indifferent to me; and before I knew this was what I now blush to call

it, I could not hate you . . . tho' from my Soul, the Attempts you made were shocking and most distasteful to me. (270)

The revised 1801 edition of the text included the following addendum:

Yet allow me to add, that not having the presumption to raise my eyes to you, I knew not myself the state of my own heart, till your kindness to me melted away, as I may say, the chilling frost that prudence and love of virtue had cast about the buds of – What shall I say? Excuse, sir – '[50]

It is reasonable to conclude that Pamela's addition of an avowal of love stands as an answer not just to Mr B.'s 'kind' question but also to *Pamela*'s critics who, along with Fielding, were convinced that her love was indeed motivated by social ambition.[51] Tellingly, it is in herself that Pamela finds her answer: 'I knew not myself the state of my own heart.' For her love to be 'true' – that is, motiveless – it must happen not just outside her interest but outside her conscious will and bodily passion precisely as revealed during her period of penitential self-reflection.

Pamela's fully convincing denial of motive is consistent with a deep and divided self, a self that can accommodate and be guided by a love that works beneath awareness, interest, will, virtue itself. A love that seems to be a kind of grace, indeed. Privately Pamela reflects that 'Love is not a voluntier Thing . . . I know not *how* it came, nor when it began' (248). Arguably, however, in light of our analysis of the sham marriage trope, we can now pose a more accurate formulation of the text's workings. Pamela's primitive 'unconscious' modulates into (loving) consciousness through the penitential process by which she rejects all alternatives to her legitimate union with Mr B. and which can only unite with virtue through the Anglican wedding ceremony – a ceremony which (through secular love's grace) will join soul to soul more than body to body or citizen to citizen. Yet as such, of course, and in the context of the Court Whig state's impending marriage reforms, it will also align strict religious piety with secular power.

Pamela's wedding, however, does not draw the novel to a close, nor does her marriage put an end to the text's persistent allusions to mock marriage and the dark libertinism for which it comes to function as a synecdoche. Shortly after her wedding, Pamela discovers that Mr B. had already formed a union of sorts with another woman, Miss Sally Godfrey, a 'Lady . . . of . . . good Family' (480) with whom he has a young daughter. Sally's mother hoped to arrange a sanctioned alliance with Mr B. in the conventional elite manner, but finding him 'too unsettled and wild' (480) for such a plan, she laid a plot to entrap him into marriage with her daughter. That plot comes out of the repertoire of theatrical narrative: they arranged for Mr B. to be caught in a compromising position with Sally and forced to 'promise Marriage on the Spot [having] a Parson ready' for the purpose (480). Mr B. narrowly escaped the ruse while Sally found herself pregnant and without a respectable spouse.

Sally Godfrey's fall stands as a counter-narrative to Pamela's spectacular social ascent;[52] yet while she is a seduced sister whose story evokes Pamela's pity, both women have sham marriage to thank for their fates. Sally's reckless pursuit of her own 'interest' recalls the grasping, improper and soulless femininity understood to be harboured in the chaos of the clandestine marriage market. Richardson adds an inventive (Anglican reformative) twist to that narrative, however, by having Sally not simply break with Mr B. but ship herself off to Jamaica where she eventually marries in the corrective spirit that inspired Oglethorpe to establish Georgia to begin with. Pamela contrasts with Sally not just in her chaste virtue but also in being placed in a set of conditions, both narratological and social, that allow her to discover her love for Mr B. while remaining true to her piety and Christian ethos (which are realised in her wedding ceremony, as we see later). Sally's remorse and exile, on the other hand, allow us to surmise that these conditions do not quite hold on the far side of the colonial border, which is here figured as the natural extension of clandestine culture.

We can now recognise that Richardson is developing a marriage plot related to those issues which would later motivate the Marriage Act. On one hand, he introduces a catalogue of sham marriages as a series of obstacles that must be rejected on the way to a true marriage; this is a pattern that might serve as an allegory of the Marriage Act's exclusion of alternatives to church marriage. But his rejection of sham marriages does not just serve the purpose of creating administrative order, which was the Court Whigs' goal. Instead, Pamela's path towards rejecting sham marriage becomes an exercise in orthodox spiritual development of a kind that is more akin to the Tory project of moral outreach than to the Whigs' will to control the populace. We might say that Richardson and Hardwicke agree in their rejection of alternatives to the proper Anglican marriage, but they do so on different grounds. Hardwicke is concerned with public administrative order, while Richardson is concerned with private moral development. This distinction returns us to the politics of church and state that divided Whigs from Tories. In *Pamela*, Richardson addresses this issue most directly in what might be called the clerical subplot.

The Clerical Subplot

We have been examining *Pamela*'s spiritualised courtship in relation to the archaeology of nuptial practices prohibited by Hardwicke's legislation, but an account of the novel's clerical subplot will help further to clarify both Richardson's relationship to the Whig programme and the foundations of a distinctly Anglican marriage plot. Some further contextualisation is helpful here. In Chapter 1, we saw that the Erastianism that underpinned Whig administrations (and Hardwicke's marriage reforms) assumed that church, state and civil society were interdependent. Yet, as Richardson's own coda urging clerical autonomy (quoted earlier) makes clear, this model faced special challenges in the context of country estate and parish life, where tensions threatened between the clergy's formal responsibilities to God and Christian doctrine on one side, and on the other, the land-owner's unprecedented legal, economic and social power.

By the time Richardson wrote *Pamela*, Whig Erastian policies had begun to shape and divide the Anglican clergy. Because church places were largely controlled by patronage, vicars became increasingly connected by family to the landowning gentry and increasingly self-reproducing (by the century's end about half of all clergymen were sons of clergymen).[53] As G. F. A. Best has argued, by 1740 squire and parson were allied in a situation that generated 'a new version of establishment theory' which underscored 'the social affinities between clergy and laity, tending to glorify their interconnections and mutual dependence'.[54] At the same time, however, among the less well-connected ranks of the clergy poverty and difficulties in finding preferment contributed to the formation of what Joseph Addison in *The Spectator* famously called the 'subaltern' clerical class.[55] We have already encountered this subaltern class in the previous chapter – it was largely they who engaged in the clandestine marriage trade – and we return to them in the next chapter.

Pamela's clerical subplot directly engages this history. Its storyline can be easily summarised: Mr Williams, whom Mr B. had known at university, has taken clerical orders but has not yet been granted a parish living. He is waiting for the death of the elderly parson whose living Mr B. controls, and in the meantime has charge of a school in the neighbouring village where he teaches Latin. He also serves as a curate for both the incumbent and the village parson, giving occasional sermons for each. He belongs, in short, to that class of clerical subalterns who will become important to the senti-mental novel (and not just courtship fiction) as it develops through Parson Adams, Sterne's Yorick and even Goldsmith's Dr Primrose.

Williams makes his appearance once Pamela has been abducted by Mr B. and imprisoned at his Lincolnshire estate. She turns to Williams as the person who might best help her: as she puts it, 'I thought his cloth would set him above assisting in my ruin' (111). All at once he becomes central to the plot. At first Pamela hopes to attend church with him but is prevented by Mrs Jewkes. Encouraged by Pamela, he then enters into a clandestine correspondence with her in which he reveals an unclerical disposition for what Mr B. will later call 'intrigue' (282). Once it is clear that the local gentry have no interest in rescuing Pamela, Williams, inspired by love (or at least what he will announce as love) goes so far as to suggest that Pamela would best escape Mr B.'s clutches were he himself to marry her. He writes to her: 'My whole Dependence is upon the 'Squire; and I have a near View of being provided for by his Goodness to me. But yet, I would sooner forfeit all my Hopes upon him, and trust in God for the rest, than not assist you, if possible' (128).

It turns out, however, that Pamela is not interested in marrying Williams, remarking that 'of all things, I did not love a parson' (143). This under-motivated comment seems less to express Pamela's personal lack of romantic attachment to the cloth than to indicate the discrepancy between her Christian virtue and that of the Established Church. It may even suggest that she is one of those Anglicans who (like Law and John Wesley) were distanced from the visible church to which they nonetheless belonged.

There are political nuances here too: Pamela's quick rejection of Williams is in the spirit of her rejection of the law as described earlier. Her rather unecclesiastical Anglicanism becomes more explicit when Mr B. later contrasts the lessons offered by the clergymen of his acquaintance with the lessons which he has learnt from her 'good example' and which she in turn has learnt from her own 'dear Father' (308). The vicar of the parish, Mr Peters, more worldly-wise than Williams and a representative of the compromised Anglican clergy, refuses to come to Pamela's aid in these highly charged words as reported by Williams:

> He [i.e. Mr Peters] imputed selfish Views to me [i.e. Mr Williams] ... And when I represented the Duties of our Function, &c, and protested my Disinterestedness, he coldly said, I was very good; but was a young Man, and knew little of the World. And tho' 'twas a Thing to be lamented, yet when he and I set about to reform the World in this respect, we should have enough upon our Hands; for, he said, it was too common and fashionable a Case to be withstood by a private Clergyman or two; And then he utter'd some Reflections upon the Conduct of the Fathers of the Church, in regard

to the first Personages of the Realm, as a Justification of his Coldness on this
score. (134–5)

Mr Peters seems to appeal to Tory doctrines of passive obedience and non-
resistance which direct Christians to accept forms of secular authority in
place. But he does so in a moral rather than in a political spirit, as if
principled non-resistance meant non-resistance to sin itself. Mr Peters's
indifference to Pamela's plight is in keeping with the Whiggish clergy's
corrupt acquiescence to the squirearchy and its Erastian defalcation of its
social and ethical duties. Pamela's disgust with Mr Peters's indifference
leads her to shun public attendance at church and incline instead to what
she calls 'private devotions' (140), there to sustain the piety which will allow
her to declare in a letter to Mr Williams that her soul is 'of equal
importance with the soul of a princess' (158), which (as we have seen) is
the Christian claim on which her right to marry Mr B. will rest.

When the clergyman whose living Williams expects to receive from Mr
B. fortuitously dies, Pamela piously writes: 'What the World is! One Man's
death's another Man's Joy!' (143). At this point the full force of Williams's
dependency on Mr B. becomes apparent in terms that implicitly lament the
Church's loss of wealth and status. By now Mr B. is suspicious of Williams,
leading him to test the curate's involvement with Pamela by pretending to
offer him not only the promised living but also Pamela's hand in marriage.
Williams falls into the trap by embracing Mr B.'s plan and confessing his
love for Pamela, at which point the increasingly savvy Pamela realises that he
has 'no discretion in the World' (149); later she complains of his 'fatal
openness' (158). The parson is revealed as impossibly unworldly, an important moment for the post-Richardsonian novel as we come to appreciate
more fully in the next chapter.[56] And then, in a brutally effective display of
secular power, Mr B. promptly has Williams imprisoned on charges of debt
by falsely claiming that Williams's salary is owed to him.

When Mr B. and Pamela at last come to an understanding and begin to
plan their wedding, Williams is restored to favour in an elaborate reconciliation process orchestrated by the squire. Williams is first required to
disclaim his romantic interest in Pamela by undertaking a friendship
ceremony with the future couple at which Mr B. declares: 'I give you
Pamela's Hand in Token of her Friendship and Esteem for you; and I give
you mine, that I will not be your Enemy' (306). The ritual gestures towards
the wedding to come and importantly reconfigures Williams's status in
relation to his patron, if only by allowing him to attain a degree of
autonomy from within his dependency. As Pamela writes:

For it must be always a Sign of a poor Condition [Richardson was to revise this to 'dependent Condition'] to receive Obligations one cannot repay; as it is of a rich Mind, when it can confer them, without expecting or *needing* a Return. It is, on one side, the State of the human Creature compar'd, on the other, to the Creator; and so, with due Deference, may be said to be God-like, and that is the highest that can be said. (273)

Under that understanding between Williams and Mr B., which Keymer astutely terms a 'studied reconciliation', a church-state relation at some remove from Whiggish Erastianism is being figured, precisely because a reformed Mr B. expects no 'Return'.[57] If Mr B. figuratively invokes secular power and interest and Mr Williams the church, the church is being allowed freedom just because, in worldly terms, it has so little power. (It's worth noting as an aside that Mr B. and Williams's reconciliation begins its final stage after Mr B. and Pamela encounter Williams reading Boileau's *Lutrin*, a mock epic which pokes fun at the Church through an argument about the disposition of church furniture.) This understanding will also allow Mr Williams to preside over the couple's wedding ceremony on legitimate Anglican terms before finally succeeding to the living in Mr B.'s gift.

The material details of that ceremony receive a great deal of narrative attention. In strictly formal terms, of course, the epistolary mode (unlike the theatrical performance) can narrativise every point of the wedding ceremony without risk of enacting it. And in choosing to do this, it is as if Richardson puts to rest finally not just Pamela's fears of a sham but also the *frisson* and ambiguity of clandestine marriage and theatrical mock marriages per se, the complexity and indeterminacy of which is now internalised in Pamela herself as a character.

Mr B. proposes that the wedding be privately performed in 'your own Chamber, or mine' (277), remarking meaningfully: 'I hope you are not afraid of a Sham-marriage . . . pray get the Service by Heart, that you may see nothing is omitted' (276). Pamela, however, insists upon a church wedding, telling Mr B. that the 'Holy Rite' ought to be performed in a 'Holy Place' (276).[58] But she too is disinclined to a public wedding in the parish church in part because this would expose her to general curiosity. Her choice of a private wedding requires the rehabilitation of the estate's private chapel which, having fallen into two generations of disuse, has become a lumber room. As Bonnie Latimer observes, this is an index of Mr B.'s (inherited) neglect of his religious duty to his household, just as the chapel's refurbishment for the wedding – 'all new white-wash'd, and painted, and lin'd' and fitted with a 'new Pulpit-cloth, Cushion, [and]

Desk' (304) – symbolises the Brandon estate's High Church Anglican renewal encouraged by Pamela.[59]

In its restored glory, the chapel will become the estate's spiritual centre, a private sanctified space served by its own private chaplain (a position that will go to Williams) who will regularly perform the 'Divine Service' there, in a move that precisely marks Pamela (and Richardson) as High Church supporters of the extension of Eucharist into ordinary churchgoing. The first Sunday after the restoration of the chapel, and after a careful discussion about which Scripture text the sermon should use, Mr B. and Pamela attend not one but two services there in company with other members of the household and the local community. At the first service, Mr Williams preaches and Pamela's devout father stands in as clerk, leading the singing of the 23rd and 67th Psalms, the first of which is cited in its entirety. Pamela notes with High Church unctuousness, 'I never saw Divine Service perform'd with more Solemnity, nor assisted at with greater Devotion and Decency' (313). The second service largely consists of a reading of the 87th Psalm, partly in its orthodox form and partly in a revised version that Pamela herself had written while imprisoned and had applied to her own situation: again the whole text is cited.

The wedding ceremony itself is performed privately, by license and with considerable effort to prevent news of it reaching Mr B.'s family. At first Pamela resists being rushed towards the day, remarking that such 'thoughtless Precipitancy' (327) is only too common (a precipitancy which, of course, Hardwicke's legislation was to end). After Mr B. sends Mr Colbrand to fetch the marriage licence '[so] that [she] may have no Scruple unanswer'd' (302), Pamela responds with joy: 'O how my Heart flutter'd at the Sight of it!' (325). There is further protracted discussion about the day for the event: Mr B. wants it sooner, Pamela later, and on a Thursday, to satisfy a 'superstitious Folly' (326). Again they compromise, deciding upon the nearest Thursday yet announcing a bogus later date to fool Lady Davers. Pamela reads the service in advance to prepare herself for the occasion, which she understands as 'awful' in the sense of Christian sublimity (340). She dresses in white (a satin nightgown bequeathed her by Mr B.'s late mother) and is given a plain ring by Mr B. (the wedding ring had been a topic of intense debate in early Reformation Protestantism, and the ring's plainness seems to be a reminiscence of that controversy).[60] The wedding is performed by Mr Williams, witnessed by Mrs Jewkes, Mr Peters and Nan, who guards the chapel door against intruders. Oddly enough, in many of these carefully narrated details, Pamela's wedding acquires some of the very qualities of the clandestine unions that it is set against. For that reason too it eschews the merely secular display and grandeur of conventional elite weddings.

Pamela is attentive to every liturgical detail of the ceremony, which she conventionally calls 'the Solemnity' (341). Her narration of the service follows the forms mandated by the Book of Common Prayer, punctuating each step of the ritual – the declarations, the pledge, the ring ceremony, the joining of hands, the pronouncement, the blessing, the psalm, the prayers and the final exhortation – with a report on her feelings in a manner that flirts with, but never quite lapses into, evangelical affect: 'I trembled so, I could hardly stand, betwixt Fear and Delight' (345). The ceremony pauses just after Mr Williams repeats the traditional Anglican legitimations for holy matrimony, according to which marriage is a symbol of the 'mystical union' between Christ and his church, ordained for purposes of procreation and a remedy against sin for 'the mutual society, help and comfort' of couples. The Book of Common Prayer charges the couple to imagine themselves as 'at the dreadful day of judgement when the secrets of all hearts shall be disclosed' and to answer from that imagined position whether there are any impediments to its proceeding. In this instance, Pamela improvises her reply, 'None, Sir, but my great Unworthiness' (344).

Pamela's response represents the culmination of an extended set of internal and external struggles and negotiations over mock marriage, proper marriage and wedding protocols. Uttered at this point in the narrative and from this place, within this ceremony, Pamela's exclamation of 'Unworthiness' is able to refer not just to the conventional Christian abasement of a sinner in relation to God's awful Majesty, but also to her genius for humility and penitence as well as to her social status as a servant – and in such a way that each of these significations implies the others. But it is also, as it were, a democratic abasement – it is shared by all Christians. Pamela's 'Unworthiness' is a condition both of the Christian soul as such and of her social/gender station in particular. In these terms, it allows her to function as a base for that image of a hierarchical society that the High Church Tories and the Court Whigs shared, but as one who is, at the same time, spiritually anyone's equal.

Pamela lies at the novel's heart too as the supremely articulate letter writer, narrator extraordinaire and main agent of both the plot and its Christian purpose. As such she is not wholly to be read as a figure of abstracted social and political history because, as critics generally agree, she also represents a new social force.[61] At one level, she takes concrete shape as a character on a terrain where social/professional groups like the clergy and the squirearchy are organised into precise political typologies incorporating personality and ethical disposition, and she herself is positioned among them as the reward in an uneven struggle between vicar and squire – that is, as the object of government itself and the reproductive body of the nation. But more importantly as it will turn out, she also represents a feminised, highly literate, spiritualising force, capable of disseminating moral reformation which cannot be quite contained within the bounds of either church or state, even though it is connected to and connects both. In these terms, the social and cultural force that Pamela signifies and expresses is the institution of literature itself. My last chapter shows how Haywood, Burney and Austen will expand that self-referential space in their development of what I term the 'literary marriage plot'.

Sir Charles Grandison

Each of Richardson's novels is an experiment in moral outreach and each attempts to overcome difficulties encountered in its predecessors. But all are exposed to a problem to which I have already gestured: how may a pious Christian negotiate between Christian virtue and secular actuality (and in particular libertine desire) so as to make a successful marriage in both religious and social terms? In *Pamela*, a virtuous and independently minded servant reforms a rich rake and marries him. *Clarissa* spells out the costs of a young woman finding herself in a situation where the possibility of a successful marriage disappears. There, a freethinking aristocratic libertine, Lovelace, rapes a virtuous young woman who has fled from her family on the grounds that they have jettisoned their moral authority over her. She is left to Christian perfection and death. *Sir Charles Grandison* is different again: here another virtuous and independent young woman, Harriet Byron, meets a benevolent landed gentleman, Sir Charles. They wish to marry but must first overcome his prior engagement to an Italian Catholic noblewoman, Clementina della Porretta. This commitment prevents Sir Charles from immediately declaring his love for Harriet, a concealment that establishes the novel's narrative mode and tone as it proceeds towards their wedding.

As a marriage plot, *Sir Charles Grandison* departs from *Pamela* in three important ways. First, it is much less concerned with social mobility: in particular, none of its main characters belongs to the labouring class, as Pamela does; the earlier novel's whiff of destratification has now disappeared. Instead, a polite, leisured and virtuous couple negotiates obstacles and opacities on their path towards marriage (a set-up which owes much to Eliza Haywood's *The History of Miss Betsy Thoughtless*, published two years earlier). Second, the clerical subplot so important to *Pamela* (as well as to subsequent marriage plots) is here downgraded. It is not required because Sir Charles is not a rakish squire but a Christian gentleman who draws spiritual sustenance and support from his wise clergyman mentor, Dr Bartlett. Indeed, Sir Charles and Bartlett's firm alliance, grounded in faith, clearly signals that the novel is not finally engaged in a Tory-Country critique of landed oligarchy. Third, while *Pamela* relied on a seduction narrative in which marriage acquires its full significance only after Pamela resists a series of illegitimate unions, *Grandison* pre-emptively renders such a plot void simply because its virtuous central characters have no need to undergo moral reform or to experience religious inspiration.

It is true, however, that Harriet (like Pamela) must resist abduction and a forced clandestine wedding at the hands of a rake, Sir Hargrave Pollexfen. That these perils are again presented in the spirit of the Hardwicke reforms is telegraphed most clearly by Harriet's lurid description of the 'vile' Fleet parson and his 'dog's-ear'd' Book of Common Prayer (1:154), as well as by Sir Charles and Dr Bartlett's insistent denunciations of 'chamber marriages' (2:328, 3:193).[62] The attempted forced wedding, which occurs in the novel's first volume, is the means by which Harriet and Sir Charles meet in a situation that allows them to display the virtue and courage that mark them as worthy of each other. Sir Charles heroically rescues Harriet, to be sure, but not before she even more heroically withstands a battery of harassment and assault from Sir Hargrave. Harriet does not just resist or dodge clandestine marriage, as Pamela does: she actively and piously defies it by striking the Book of Common Prayer from the Fleet parson's hands (1:155), in an incident which featured in Thomas Stothard's illustrated 1783 plates and which arguably marks an important moment for the English marriage plot's development (see Illustration 4).

Harriet's defiance dramatises a momentary convergence of two strains of Richardson's Anglican marriage plot – one residual, the other emergent. As Toni Bowers has observed, *Sir Charles Grandison* commences with a literal interruption of the seduction narrative, which it subsequently marginalises.[63] It thereby heralds a generic shift for the novel form towards a mode of 'manners fiction' confined to the world of polite, endogamous courtships. Here, rival suitors proliferate; misunderstandings, delays and uncertainty abound; and – most importantly – desire, seduction and clandestine marriage are relegated to a libertine netherworld. Manners fiction, then, is a fictional corollary of the moral reform movement as it reshapes the elite marriage market (which Burney, Austen and others will further explore). In *Grandison*'s early stages, it eclipses the old demotic

Illustration 4 Thomas Stothard, 'Grandison, Plate XIIII', 1783.

world of the clandestine marriage. Harriet's remarkable gesture of defiance marks the collision of those two worlds, illustrating what happens when proper femininity encounters improper ceremony so as spectacularly to discountenance it.

Harriet's close encounter with clandestine marriage accrues none of the haunting liminality of Pamela's mooted sham marriage; it functions as the crisp point of departure for *Grandison*'s revision of *Pamela*'s marriage plot. That revision culminates in a joyous *public* wedding which occupies much of the novel's sixth volume and which is quite unlike Pamela's private wedding or indeed any earlier fictional presentation of marriage. In thematic terms, it follows from the larger social setting in which Sir Charles and Harriet's union is placed (whereas Pamela's marriage was the climax of her private spiritual development and courtship). In political terms, it signals Richardson's accommodation with the Court Whigs: marriage becomes a carefully described social event as much as an Anglican ritual, confirming the couple's worldly standing and Christian virtue. As such, it functions both as a sanction of character and as a capstone of a peaceful and hierarchical social order.

Yet, *Sir Charles Grandison* does not end with a wedding.[64] Once again, proper ceremony is carefully described and strategically positioned (in this case, in the novel's penultimate volume) so as to mark interpretative rather than merely formal closure. In the spirit of Anglican moral outreach, the novel's final, post-nuptial volume details the couple's early married life at Grandison Hall and spells out the terms for a resolution of Clementina's story under the aegis of what Sir Charles describes as a 'triple friendship' among the protagonists (which echoes the earlier friendship ceremony between Pamela, Mr B. and Mr Williams).[65] Such framing suggests that *Grandison*'s public wedding carries so much gravitas not just because it culminates a prolonged, triangulated courtship, nor because it sets the couple in a larger social context of 'manners' fiction, nor even in an imagined 'affective community', but because it stands as the ultimate sanction of the novel's central experiment: its presentation of Sir Charles himself as an almost perfect character.[66]

Richardson famously advertised *Sir Charles Grandison* as presenting 'the Example of a Man acting uniformly well thro' a Variety of trying Scenes, because all his Actions are regulated by one steady Principle: A Man of Religion and Virtue; of Liveliness and Spirit; accomplished and agreeable; happy in himself, and a Blessing to others' (1:4). The novel's eponymous hero embodies a synthesis of divine law, secular authority and human sympathy as a gentlemanly ideal, enabling Richardson once again to bind his marriage plot to character and virtue (as was the case in *Pamela*), but now cast in freshly topical terms. Indeed, the traits which constitute Sir Charles's near perfection mobilise the very natural law concepts through which English marriage was redefined and debated in the context of the Marriage Act. The following sections offer an analysis, first, of Sir Charles as an agent of natural justice (which leads, not coincidentally, to his role as a 'marriage-promoter' [2:323]) and, second, of Richardson's fulsome description of Sir Charles and Harriet's public wedding which pioneered the presentation of proper ceremony for a generation of literary courtship narratives to come.

Sir Charles and Natural Law

As a rich, cosmopolitan English squire, a magistrate and a public figure, Sir Charles seems to represent a new alignment of landed and moneyed interests that unsettles Bolingbrokean 'Country' ideals. Yet Richardson's High Church oppositionalism has not wholly disappeared, since Sir Charles consciously removes himself from the public and parliamentary world, only minimally participating in a social order considered less than legitimate; he can contemplate living in Italy because he is in retreat from English politics and administration. As a result, the novel mainly consists of incidents in which Sir Charles performs his benevolence, rationality and virtue by *private* acts of judgement and negotiation.[67] While secular juridical theorists such as Pufendorf argued that the state rather than the church was the proper instrument of natural law, and Court Whig divines like Gally (following Grotius) presupposed natural law as the arbiter of human sociability, Richardson here seems to suggest that its principles can be enacted situationally in everyday life. In this way, I'd argue, *Grandison* fictionalises an alternative conception of natural law which casts Sir Charles as an Anglican landed gentleman doing the paternalist state's work from a position of independence outside the state itself.[68]

As a man of religion, Sir Charles proves himself 'the very Christian in practice that [the gospels] teach a man to be' (1:440).[69] Harriet, who writes this quite early in her acquaintance with him, continues, 'Must not then the doctrines introduce the mention of a man who endeavors humbly to imitate the Divine example?' Such a measure of character helps to account for Sir Charles's much noted lack of subjectivity, since he is after all an iteration of Christian perfection rather than a developing self in the style of Pamela or even Harriet.[70] Even more importantly, however, in him the secular and the religious are not disentangled; by functioning simultaneously as an exemplar of Christian perfection *and* a worldly agent, Sir Charles expands practical Christianity's domain. His imitation of Christ takes the form of a series of actions and ethical choices befitting a philosophical Anglican gentleman whose active virtues reach beyond the old Catholic intellectual, cardinal and theological virtues to include tolerance, non-violence, filial obedience and chastity.

So, in effect, Sir Charles practices a form of theosis precisely in his role as an uncannily effective negotiator in the difficult, secular situations with which the novel's first two volumes are concerned. What, then, are the Christian principles and acts of practical benevolence that enable him both to embody virtue and to enhance his enormous prestige in this way? First, in his private life, his ethical principles mark him out from his peers (although he feels no compunction to justify them publicly). He refuses to fight in duels, for instance, in a gesture that follows Pufendorf's explicit exclusion of duelling from the realm of natural justice.[71] Much of the novel's first volume involves him in displaying courage precisely by that refusal as well as in decrying the principles of honour that sanction duelling. He actively objects to libertinism as well, and of course his brave rescue of Harriet from Sir Hargrave Pollexfen's attempt to abduct her begins their attachment. Yet, presumably out of filial piety, he does not cross his selfish, weak, libertine father but rather placates him, waiting until his death to free his sisters from paternal tyranny. He also abjures the culture of commercialism and fashionable self-display, subtly inoculating his ward, Emily Jervois, against it too.

Later in the novel, Sir Charles's support for a hierarchical and re-feudalised social imaginary becomes clear, one which includes a revival of sumptuary laws (3:124) while also being tempered by a tolerance for those whom he calls, in the Tory fashion and in a rare overtly political declaration, 'Schismatics' (3:141). He chooses as his spiritual advisor the good Anglican clergyman Dr Bartlett, who is described in terms similar to those that denote Sir Charles himself as both a 'Saint' (1:275) and a 'fine gentleman' (1:226). Sir Charles also renovates his landed estate's chapel, taking care not to distinguish his own pew, a 'beautification' that symbolises his care for the estate's spiritual welfare and that implicitly places him in the Laudian Anglican lineage (2:7).[72] He proves himself capable not only of sympathetic identification with others but also of considerable tolerance and moral generosity, as exemplified by his kind and non-judgemental treatment of his father's mistress (or common law wife), Mrs Oldham, after his father's death (1:370). Finally, Sir Charles is unremittingly humble, discounting his own agency for his acts of goodness in order not 'to depreciate the First Cause' and to give God 'his due' (2:615).

If Sir Charles's judgements and values present a dizzying mixture of the arcane and the prescient, that is because from his own point of view (and Richardson's) they are an expression not of partisan politics but of God's and nature's legislation of the world. From this perspective, he consistently acts on principle while also reliably conforming to his denominational creed. Indeed, Richardson's description of him as a 'Man of Religion and Virtue' is insufficient to capture his spiritual-moral superiority. On the basis not only of his social status as a rich landed gentleman but also of his attempt to act charitably by aligning himself to God's all-embracing vision, he positions himself as an impartial judge in relation to the difficult situations that he faces, many of which involve issues concerning natural and distributive justice. He is also able to reflect semi-philosophically on the grounds of his actions. In the spirit of Grotius and Pufendorf, his secular principles are a mixture of the juridical and the sentimental. Arguably, it is his juridical tact even more than his benevolence that aligns him to natural law.

Thus, for instance, when Sir Charles is required to persuade a fortune-hunting military man, Captain Anderson, to release his sister Charlotte from a betrothal, he does so not by committing himself to using his interest on Anderson's behalf, which he cannot do in good conscience since he has no faith in Anderson, but by acting generously to him privately, that is, by buying him off – which, as it turns out, is one of Sir Charles's characteristic moves. Since he is not interested in money for its own sake or in social display, his fortune is routinely available for his benevolence. In such situations, however, he insists that he listens to all sides of the case, goes 'to the bottom' of affairs and confronts contingencies by appropriately changing 'his method of proceeding' (1:361–2). At the same time, he treats others with trust and respect rather than with suspicion and reserve, even where, like Sir Hargrave Pollexfen, they threaten violence. This permits him to appeal to others to act in conformity with his own best opinion of them and not to jeopardise the moral reputation that he grants them, so as to give them, as he puts it, the opportunity to present themselves as they are. Sir Charles is a man of principle, then, in the sense that he is concerned to examine and to spell out general laws. And as such, his actions and thoughts are of public interest despite his persistent renunciation of the public sphere.

Sir Charles's commitment to a post-secular mix of principle and creed is nowhere more apparent than in his marriage brokering (where, coincidentally, his juridical skills and his benevolence also neatly converge). As he forthrightly declares: 'I am for having every-body marry' (1:428).[73] This position lies somewhere between a conventional Protestant/ Lutheran endorsement of marriage as a Christian's social or earthly duty and a Pufendorfian understanding of marriage as a core business of the administered state. Pufendorf, we will recall, believed that marriage was universal in all societies and as such was a primary instance of natural law. Arguably, here Richardson transposes secular natural law's intellectual and juridical framework from the state to the domain of a private landed gentleman in order to strike a balance between Court Whig statecraft and Bolingbrokean Country party ideology for which the landed estate is a basic unit of order and government.

Certainly, it is by enabling marriages that Sir Charles enacts the principles of natural justice most clearly.[74] In addition to believing that marriage is a duty (2:429), he spends a great deal of time arranging, mending and monitoring matches among his circle of acquaintance. He works for Clementina's marriage with the Count of Belvedere when she would prefer to join a convent after she has rejected Sir Charles himself, firmly insisting against Roman Catholic ideals of celibacy that 'you may live to your God in the world . . . and wants not the world . . . such an example as you can give it?' (3:429). Indeed, he encourages the most unlikely characters to marry, including his uncle the aged Lord W., whom he rescues from a common law relationship with a servant, Mrs Giffard, by matching him with Miss Mansfield, a younger woman who has been overlooked in the society marriage market. Characteristically, Richardson conveys Sir Charles's skilful negotiations in this case by providing the reader with considerable financial detail, since Sir Charles has to overcome Lord W.'s miserliness by helping to pay Mrs Giffard a proper annuity (£250 as against £150). However, the real point is that Lord W. will be reformed (and Miss Mansfield socially redeemed) just by marrying, and thus returning simultaneously to the Christian community and the elite public sphere. Because marriage is a natural law imperative for Richardson in *Grandison*, marriage choice falls more under the sway of mature prudence than of love. Indeed the novel mounts a quasi-philosophical critique of love as the primary ground for marriage choice. In this it differs from *Pamela*, in particular, where, as we know, marriage among principals rests on a love that combines grace with Christian virtue. One of *Grandison*'s distinctive narrative features is that almost all its characters marry partners who are not their heartfelt first choice.[75] Clementina would rather marry Sir Charles than Count Belvedere, whom she is set to espouse as the novel ends; Sir

Charles would rather marry Clementina than Harriet if only to meet his prior obligations to her; Emily would rather marry Sir Charles than Sir Edward Beauchamp. Charlotte Grandison has been betrothed to the opportunistic Captain Anderson from whom she has to be detached before she can marry more prudently. And so on. Even a character who does marry her first choice – Harriet herself – is placed in a situation where she is forced to come to terms with the possibility of not being able to marry for love.

In a letter written when she believes that Sir Charles will marry Clementina, Harriet articulates the distance between love and marriage, writing to her cousin:

> What think you, my dear, is the Love which we vow at the altar? Surely, not adoration: Not a preference of that object *absolutely*, as in excellence super-ior to every other imaginable being. No more, surely, in most cases, than such a *preferable choice* (all circumstances considered) as shall make us with satisfaction of mind, and with an affectionate and faithful heart, unite ourselves for life with a man whom we esteem; who we think is no disagreeable companion, but deserves our grateful regard; that his interest from henceforth should be our own, and his happiness our study. (2:547)

The language of prudence could not be more insisted upon. Here the self who decides to marry settles upon a 'preferable choice' rather than an absolute preference. It is as if the novel's many checks to love and first choice become the condition required to make a good marriage.

Indeed, Harriet's understanding of the spousal ethos, that it requires a husband's 'interest [to] be our own', is wholly consonant with the elite marriage market: if one exchanges 'interest' with one's spouse, then it is wholly appropriate to marry not out of one's own interest or one's passionate commitment to another but on the basis of a rational choice made in the context of one's social circle. Here Harriet mounts a critique of the very modes of love and *first* attachment celebrated by the Marriage Act's High Church opponents, such as Henry Stebbing, for whom young love and liberty were in continuity with God's will, and for whom the Marriage Act's legal strictures were in violation of divinely inspired natural law. By contrast, Harriet and the novel itself see no tension between marrying for prudential, rational reasons and marrying as an Anglican Christian. After all, that is one of the reconciliations that the novel is working to achieve within an understanding of natural law that aligns piety with state power as modelled by Sir Charles himself. Love is not the driving force of marriage except insofar as it consecrates a larger rational sense of civil and religious responsibility, that is, of natural law.

Importantly, however, marriage also reveals the limits of natural law in *Sir Charles Grandison*: Harriet asks rhetorically, 'is not human nature the same in every country, allowing only for different customs?' (1:184–5). This is a vernacular statement of another fundamental presupposition of natural law: the principle of uniformity that allows Sir Charles readily to join the community of Italian Catholics around Clementina without a trace of xenophobia. Many of Richardson's readers were shocked by his embrace of toleration in this regard.[76] Yet the practical uniformity of human nature is tested by the breakdown of Sir Charles's betrothal to Clementina. Marriage may still belong to natural law in Pufendorf's terms to the extent that Sir Charles, and by implication Richardson, is able to countenance marriage across confessions. But in the end that marriage cannot happen because, in Clementina's view, the religious barriers are indeed too strong.

At this point Richardson's marriage plot transforms the uniformity of human nature posited by natural law into a roaming sympathetic imagination, the terms of which are suggested by Clementina, when having decided that she cannot marry Sir Charles because he refuses to convert to Catholicism, she makes an appeal for his friendship instead:

> Tell me, then, my brother, my friend, my faithful, my *disinterested* friend, what I shall do . . . to be able to look upon you *only* as my brother and friend? – Can you not tell Me? Will you not? Will not your Love of Clementina permit you to . . . [s]ay, 'you are the friend of her *Soul*.' If you cannot be a Catholic *always*, be a Catholic when you *advise* her. And then, from your love of her Soul, you will be able to say, 'Persevere, Clementina! and I will not account you ungrateful.' (2:612)

Here Clementina asks Sir Charles to become Catholic, not in fact but out of a disinterested sympathetic imagination which allows him to identify with many positions.[77] Alternatively but simultaneously, she also invites him to love her *soul*, not as a corporeal man or out of rational objectivity but as an orthodox Christian who recognises the soul as a shared gift from God, created in love and reason.

Whichever description we prefer, Sir Charles's ability to remain Clementina's mentor after their engagement collapses marks his full achievement as an English gentleman. On the basis of a shared humanity, he has remained true to his identity as an Anglican while retaining his enlightened capacity to communicate across a divide which is less natural or cultural than confessional. Sir Charles's refusal to convert to Catholicism marks the novel's primary affirmation of Anglicanism's definitive place in the English constitution. Indeed the Anglican ideal that he embodies is characterised by its openness to the commerce of the wider world ('[h]is heart ... generously open and benevolent to people of all countries' [3:263]), whereas Clementina and her family (and by implication Italian Catholics *en bloc*) cannot transcend creedal limits.[78] In this way, Sir Charles's sympathetic Anglicanism provides the grounds for his benevolence and allows the novel to figure his union with Harriet as an expression of their shared humanity *and* their Englishness via his incarnation, we might say, both of human sympathy and, no less importantly, of natural justice.

The Public Wedding

After reading *Sir Charles Grandison*, Mary Wortley Montagu famously remarked that 'Richardson is so eager for the multiplication of [marriages] I suppose he is some parish curate, whose chief profit depends on weddings and christenings.'[79] Her mock complaint – steeped in Whiggish anti-clericalism – obliquely points towards one of *Grandison*'s less noticed innovations: its extended presentation of a parish wedding in the context of a country estate. In the novel's sixth volume, after a prolonged courtship overshadowed by Clementina's prior claim on Sir Charles and punctuated by numerous other weddings (including Harriet's botched forced wedding to Sir Hargrave), Sir Charles and Harriet marry at last. Theirs is a public ceremony performed in the local church in accordance with the Canons, followed by communal celebrations at her Uncle's Selby's home. In this regard, it differs from Pamela's private wedding, conforming instead to the spirit of Protestant reform which viewed the marriage ceremony as a public witnessing, and to the Marriage Act's reiteration of long-standing ecclesiastical requirements that (with minor exceptions) marriages be celebrated publicly during canonical hours in the bride's parish of residence. Tellingly, the event is described at great length and in a heightened epistolary mode. Indeed, it is described by two narrators – Harriet's cousin Lucy Selby and Sir Charles's rebellious sister, Charlotte, now Lady G. – who, unusually, take turns writing a single letter between them, reporting in both present and past tense and, alternately, in their characteristically ardent (unmarried) and arch (married) tones.[80]

For Montagu, Richardson's 'multiplication' of weddings signalled his latent Toryism (and indeed his parochialism and venality: uncannily she assigns him the priestly persona not of a clerical missionary but of a subaltern cleric spruiking for business). Arguably, however, the singularity with which Richardson treats Sir Charles and Harriet's public wedding can be understood as an endorsement of Court Whig marriage reform in the context of *Grandison*'s particular literary experiment: its presentation of a near perfect man. Sir Charles's public wedding is represented so fully because, given marriage's topicality in 1753, it is an ideal whose ritual arrangements have communal and political meanings. Otherwise put: the detail with which Richardson describes the ceremony expresses the importance of presenting an Anglican wedding, which unlike Catholic weddings is not a sacrament but rather a visible sign of a secure theo-politically legitimated social order. The care and complexity with which the marriage is represented reflects Sir Charles's status as a gentlemanly ideal whose every action, and in particular whose arrangements for this public ritual, has wider social implications. In these terms, the wedding itself stands as a public and ritualistic enactment simultaneously of the couple's faith, their distanced submission to Hardwicke's Erastian settlement and their secure reputation for virtue and benevolence.

It follows that while *Grandison*'s wedding is richly described as an Anglican liturgical and ceremonial event in *Pamela*'s style, it is not soulfully narrated by the bride herself. Indeed, despite Harriet's status as the emotional and epistolary centre of the novel, her accustomed voice of frankness is set aside in this instance because, as a public event of familial and communal gravitas, indeed, as a literary-missionary moment, the wedding is best described not subjectively by one of its participants but infectiously and enthusiastically by third-party witnesses who can model and attest to its broader exemplary force.[81] Lucy and Charlotte's jointly authored wedding letter is couched precisely in these terms. Its mode of address – elite and female, doubly so – is particularly significant since social status and gender (as opposed to Pamela-esque subjectivity and soul) turn out to be the central markers of the public wedding and its representation.

For Richardson, this double mode of address seems to serve at least two purposes: as part of a missionary effort to endorse public weddings in a manner that mitigated polite concerns about female modesty (exemplified by Harriet's very real and ongoing discomfort with being improperly exposed on 'so public a Day' [3:199]) and, more instrumentally again, as a means of crafting a new literary-commercial twist on his marriage plot aimed at further expanding his female readership. As Lady G. reminds Lucy, their shared description of the wedding:

cannot . . . after so many wishes, so many suspenses, so much expectation,
before it came to this, be too minute. Every woman's heart leaps . . . when
a Wedding is described; and wishes to know all, *how and about it.* (3:223)

Every woman's heart leaps when a wedding is described – except Mary
Wortley Montagu's, or perhaps even Lady G.'s, since her own commentary
shades into irony. But that is just the point. Wedding talk, whatever its
tone, is women's business, as Richardson knows and as a generation of his
followers was to acknowledge (including Maria Edgeworth in *Belinda*, as
we see in the Afterword). Yet while such talk played to (apparently)
gendered readerly appetites as Lady G. suggests, it also engaged marriage's
public and political meanings, as Montagu insists. Indeed, this conjunction meant that in bringing Richardson's Anglican marriage plot to
a climax by aligning Sir Charles's gentlemanly exemplarity with the public
wedding, *Grandison* also underscored the manner in which public weddings brought an emergent female public sphere into view.

At the request of Harriet's grandmother, Mrs Shirley, the wedding takes
place on a Thursday in November, which, given the restrictions of the
Anglican nuptial calendar, was a preferred season for marriage.[82] It happens under the stewardship of Harriet's substitute father, her Uncle Selby,
and on his landed estate, although it would appear that Sir Charles helps to
pay for it. Uncle Selby wishes for a public celebration so '[t]hat we may
have a joyful Day of it; and that all our neighbours and tenants may rejoice
with us' (3:193). Harriet demurs, expressing her preference for a 'private'
exchange of vows in a 'sacred place', but her grandmother nonetheless
insists (somewhat tautologically and on different grounds from Uncle
Selby's) that the ceremony *'cannot* be a private one . . . Every-body's eyes
are upon us. It would be an affectation in us, that would rather raise, than
allay curiosity' (3:193). A little later, the Selby/Shirley preference for
a public marriage is carefully re-described not as a reflection of the families'
public standing or reputation, nor as an occasion to advertise Harriet's
triumph in marrying a rich man, but as a celebration of Sir Charles's
'transcendent merit' (3:217).

Even recalibrated in these terms, the event's public nature causes both
Sir Charles and Harriet difficulty since, as we have seen, both are committed to the private world as against the public one. As Sir Charles rather
convolutedly tells his sister, Lady G., although he looks upon marriage in
an 'awful light' (3:217) and joins Uncle Selby's censure of 'chamber weddings' (3:193) as he calls them, a 'public ceremony is not what he would
have proposed' out of concern for Harriet's proper disinclination to enter

the public sphere. Nevertheless, it 'being proposed [by her family], he would not, by any means, decline it' (3:217). The residue of High Toryism that remains in him conforms to the status (or statist) quo as he becomes, conventionally enough, 'absolutely passive as to the oeconomy of the approaching solemnity' (3:214), which is ceded to Harriet's female family members under Uncle Selby's stewardship. Here 'oeconomy' means not just the ceremony's financing but also its organisation, hinting at what Alison Conway describes as a disjunction between Sir Charles's ability to wield power 'absolutely . . . as a civil authority' and, precisely, his passivity 'in the empire of love' where 'he proves curiously incapable of lifting a sceptre.'[83] He 'acquiesce[s]' completely, for instance, when Mrs Shirley politely refuses his request that his own 'dear' chaplain Dr Bartlett perform the ceremony instead of the local incumbent Dr Curtis, who as Mrs Shirley assures him, is also 'a very worthy man' (3:194).

For Harriet, like Pamela, the wedding is a 'very solemn event', not just as a Christian ritual but also because the 'married state' carries with it an awareness of the more 'perfect state' beyond, that is, of the afterlife (3:18–19, 221).[84] While she is not haunted by thoughts of sham marriage as such, she is oppressed – aggrieved even – by the 'arduous task' (3:217) of submitting to the exposure of a public wedding:

> My spirits sink at the thoughts of so public a Day . . . Sir Charles is tenderly concerned for me. It would be impossible, he says, that the Day could be private, unless I were to go to London, and the very proposing of that would put my uncle out of all patience, who prides himself on the thought of having his Harriet married from his own house: Nor could I expect my grandmamma's presence. (3:199)

Another alternative lurks beneath Harriet's conflicted desire to avoid the exposure of a public wedding while pleasing her family: the clandestine marriage as it was associated with spectacular modes of public and improper femininity, on one hand, and, on the other, with a new-fashioned mode of avoiding the expectations and duties of the elite marriage. Partly to discountenance any such associations while also eschewing an appearance of show or extravagance, the couple departs from traditional form: they do not wear 'full [wedding] dresses' with Harriet in particular appearing in a mere 'Morning dress' of 'Virgin white' (3:219). (Full wedding dress here means a bespoke wedding garment, usually lavishly trimmed with ribbons, buttons, flowers and so on, and even adorned with fertility symbols such as ears of corn. Such dresses were usually but not always white.)[85]

Harriet's refusal of conspicuous finery signals both her preference for modest privacy and her insistence on the ceremony's religio-spiritual force. Indeed, her reserve towards traditional festivities and folk-cultural motifs recalls Puritan objections to 'heathen' popular customs on the grounds that they mix sacred rites with secular amusement.[86] Yet Harriet's retreat from the public gaze is simultaneously a retreat into a spectacular virginity which allows her to look '*so* lovely! *so* silly! and *so* full of unmeaning meaningness', as Lady G. puts it (3:214). This intensification of her role as virgin bride is itself highly ritualised and gendered: she is provided with a train of seven virgins for the festivities who are matched by Sir Charles's seven gentlemen (and accompanied by four 'bride-maids' at the church itself).

While the wedding may be public, it is planned and celebrated in a highly stratified manner. Uncle Selby (presumably with Sir Charles's sanction) does not invite his tenant farmers to the celebrations in the 'Great Hall' at Selby House, allowing them, with their wives and children older than twelve, to celebrate instead in his 'Great Barn' (3:200). This building is fully heated and lit for the occasion, but the farmers are served only cold food and are entertained separately from the gentry. Another group – the 'poor' and 'the populace' (3:201) – are further removed from the action: they are expressly 'not to be admitted' to the Selby House celebrations in order to avoid 'the confusion' attendant on the presence of what Lucy terms the 'promiscuous multitude' (3:201). Instead, two tenant farmer houses in the neighbouring village are kept open on the day (along with another near Shirley Manor) for 'all who choose to go thither'. In a characteristic example of Sir Charles's strategic charity, a selection of paupers receive a payment of ten shillings, conditional on them not being 'troublesome' (3:201).

In this way, the wedding arrangements (or 'managements' [3:204] as Lady G. terms them) reflect a vertically organised local community while endorsing an elite point of view that is distant and fearful of the lower ranks. Social relations on the Selby estate are experienced not through shared festive traditions or carnivalesque mixings but through managed hierarchies and the 'charitable' use of money. Such an approach belongs more nearly to a Court Whig than to a Tory or Country party social imaginary, in particular because it does not assume that the poor have a natural deference, let alone respect, for the squirearchy. Importantly, there is no hint here of an organic parish community (as there will be for Fielding, Goldsmith and other authors who will engage Richardson's marriage plot). Rather, economic interests and continually negotiated stratification prevail.

The wedding day begins with the singing of an Epithalamion to the bride (one of the few folk customs to be included). As the couple meet before setting off to church, Sir Charles delivers this characteristic speech to Harriet:

> This Day, my dearest Love, we call upon the world to witness to our mutual vows. Let us shew that world, that our Hearts are one; and that the Ceremony, sacred as it is, cannot make them more so. The engagement is a holy one: Let us shew the Multitude, as well as our surrounding Friends, that we think it a laudable one. Once more I call upon you, my dearest Life, to justify my joy by your *apparent* approbation. The world around you, loveliest of women, has been accustomed to see your *Lovers*; shew them now the Husband of your choice. (3:222)

Sir Charles insists that their wedding has a missionary exemplarity: 'the Multitude' should witness it not just to understand its holiness but also to perceive that the ritual does not add to the sacredness of his and Harriet's 'Hearts'. Harriet's reply combines admiration and reproach. It understands Sir Charles's bathetic move from 'sacred' to 'laudable' as referring to the secular aspects of a religious occasion: 'O Sir! you have given me a motive! I will think of it throughout the whole Sacred Transaction' (3:222). This exchange is part of Sir Charles's efforts to reconcile Harriet to the ceremony's communal aspects and, more especially, to adjust those aspects to its sacredness, which requires no publicity at all. The secular motive he adduces returns to Richardson's use of competition among suitors as a narrative device. Like Mr B., who insisted upon Pamela's ritual disavowal of rival suitors and of any 'interest' in marrying him, Sir Charles needs Harriet's 'apparent approbation' because she has been pursued by so many. All the while, Harriet herself seeks no such approbation in return, finding security instead in the ceremony's sacral status.

The wedding party proceeds from Selby House to the parish church in eight coaches in an order prescribed by Uncle Selby. Sir Charles's 'state coach' is not used, being reserved for a later public appearance. The half-mile procession to the church, mostly narrated by Lucy, is witnessed by lines of 'spectators' (3:223), but by the time the party reach the churchyard, the onlookers have become a 'mob', if calmed at least temporarily by an almost mesmerised respect:

> The whole Church-yard seemed one mass . . . of living matter, distinguished only by separate heads; not a hat on the mens; pulled off, perhaps, by general consent, for the convenience of seeing, more than from designed regard in *that* particular. But, in the main, never was there such silent respect shewn,

on the like occasion, by mortal mob. We all of us, Lady L. have the
happiness of being beloved by high and low. (3:224)

It's a curiously hedged description: the crowd, a 'mortal mob' rather than
any kind of community, take their hats off not out of deference but in
order to see better; they are silently respectful but only 'in the main'. And
yet Lucy can declare that the group has the happiness of being beloved by
high and low, a sentiment which if not exactly ironical in the context, is
using 'beloved' in its weakest sense. The 'respect' which unites this assem-
bly implicitly stands against the noisy spectacularised spaces of the distant
clandestine marriage markets. But perhaps a little ominously, the wedding's spectators seem less spiritually or religiously engaged than Sir
Charles himself had hoped. The mere 'respect' they feel seems ideologically
to place them as ripe for administration of the kind that Hardwicke's
Marriage Act was pioneering.

Next, as the couple alight from their carriage to approach the church,
four tenant farmers' daughters wearing traditional wedding clothing strew
flowers along their path, 'much pleas[ing]' Sir Charles and leaving Harriet,
once again, 'affected' (3:224–5). Lady G. resumes her narration 'from
within the Church' (3:225) which is 'full of people', 'all the pews near the
Altar' filled with 'Ladies and well-dressed women of the neighbourhood'
(3:225), a detail which once again underscores the presence of a significantly
female public. As Uncle Selby, Harriet's 'Nuptial Father' (3:225), gives the
bride away, she is hardly able to approach the altar for trembling, while her
bridesmaids begin to cry. Upon a signal from Sir Charles the minister
begins the service, while Lady G. both faithfully narrates the singularity of
the event and, at key moments, ironically contrasts it with the interrupted
clandestine ceremony that Harriet was forced to undergo by Sir Hargrave
and with her own wedding: 'The Doctor began – "*Dearly Beloved*" – Ah,
Harriet! thought I: thou art much quieter now, than once thou wert at
these words' (3:225).

With '[n]o *impediments* . . . confessed by either of the parties' (3:225), the
ceremony proceeds smoothly enough: 'Charles [having] the office *by* heart;
Harriet *in* her heart' (3:226), which is presumably why she does not
'hesitate at the little piddling word *obey*', as Lady G. remembers quibbling
during her own service (3:226). The exchange of vows, the presentation of
the ring, the minister's declaration 'pronouncing them Man and Wife in
the name of the Holy Trinity' (3:226) and his final blessing are all duly
noted. The service ends, however, with a notable off-script addendum: Sir
Charles performs an impromptu act of obeisance to his bride, 'bending his

knee . . . taking her Hand, and saluting her' (3:226) while Harriet responds with a low courtesy. As a ritual of polite sensibility, it complements the religious ceremony just performed: 'her the loveliest of women, and him the most graceful and polite of men' (3:226), as Lady G. puts it. It is also more than a little theatrical, however, as signalled by the warm response of the congregation now figured, less conventionally, as an 'applauding multitude' (3:226). Faintly echoing the public street and stage spectacles associated with clandestine weddings, it marks the occasion's transition from solemnity to celebration.

The ceremony over, the company proceeds once more through the churchyard where joyous parish-wide celebrations begin to unfold:

> The Bells were set a ringing . . . and Sir Charles Grandison, the Son of our venerable Mrs. Shirley, the Nephew of my uncle and aunt Selby, Husband of my dear and ever-dear Harriet, and the Esteemed of every heart, led his graceful Bride through a lane of applauding and decent-behaving spectators, down through the Church – and still more thronging multitudes in the Church-yard; the four little Flora's again strewing flowers at their feet, as they passed. (3:229)

Amidst bells, flowers, crowds, blessings, tributes and other nuptial blandishments, Sir Charles's new married status is celebrated in ever-expanding familial and communal terms as 'Son . . . Nephew . . . Husband . . . Esteemed of every heart'. Strikingly, however, Lady G.'s narration of the commencement of festivities is focussed less on the newlyweds than on crowd behaviour as it reflects the virtue and benevolence of the 'Happy Pair' (3:227). As they leave the church, we are told, they are feted by '[still] applauding and *decent-behaving* spectators' (my italics) before being greeted by 'thronging multitudes in Church Yard' and still more '[c]rouds' (3:230) lining their return passage to Selby House.

That *Grandison*'s public wedding models a top-down, Whig-oriented model of social relations becomes clearest, however, when Lady G. accounts for the 'Joy' that suffuses itself amongst the wedding party and their gentry guests at the 'Great Hall' reception:

> There was among us the height of Joy; Joy becoming the awful Solemnity; and every one was full of the decency and delight which were given and shewn by the crouds of spectators of all ranks and both Sexes; a delight and decency worthy of the characters of the admirable Pair. And Miss Nedham declared, and all the young Ladies joined with her, that if she could be secure of the like good behavior and encouragement, she would never think of a Private Wedding for herself. (3:230)

The modes of polite behaviour, social discipline and limited community proper to a public wedding could hardly be more emphasised: the '[c]rouds of ... all ranks and both Sexes' are commended on their 'decency and delight' – and then, additionally, on their 'delight and decency' – as inculcated by the union of the 'admirable Pair'. Yet all the while the wedding's most immediate exemplary effect is understood in plainly gendered terms when Miss Nedham and 'all the young Ladies' voice a newfound collective motive to disclaim private weddings and, indeed we might add, the rival appeal of fashionable clandestine weddings more generally. (Surely this is one moment of the text that prompted Mary Wortley Montagu to call out what she perceived as Richardson's vulgar endorsement of parish weddings.)

The polite celebrations in the Great Hall at Selby House are mirrored by those in the Great Barn where the tenant farmers also assemble for feasting and dancing, although a 'formal supper' has not been supplied. At this point the event's political implications are even more clearly spelled out. After dinner, Sir Charles 'and the men' leave the polite group to sit with the farmers for a moment. The farmers treat the nuptials as one in a line of similar events available to local memory, recalling earlier gentry and Selby family weddings. But limits to this sense of collectivity are quickly imposed when Sir Charles refuses the farmers' particular request (termed 'an *hugeous* favour') to be allowed to toast the bride 'tho' at ever so great a *distance*' (3:233). He promises instead another celebratory dinner (presumably not to be attended by Harriet) before the couple leave for his estate in Northamptonshire. Then the talk turns to electoral politics:

> They all got up to bow and courtesy, and looked upon each other; and the men, who are most of them freeholders, wished to the Lord for a new election, and that he would come among them. They had no great matter of fault to find, they said, with their present representatives; but any-body who would oppose Sir Charles Grandison, would stand no chance. The women joined in the declaration, as if they thought highly, as Sir Charles pleasantly observed, of their own influence over their husbands. They all wondered that he was not in Parliament, till they heard how little a while he had been in England. (3:234)

It is a suggestive moment in demonstrating the farmers' passivity and powerlessness. Sir Charles's wedding has prompted their political support of him despite his being relatively unknown to them, a support that therefore seems to belong to traditions of deference rather than to political principle or policy.

It may be, however, that the sudden support for Sir Charles by the Selby estate's tenant farmers – their desire for him to 'come among them' – reflects a Bolingbrokean and patriot civic republican longing for political leaders who are not aligned to party as such but who govern just in the public interest. Interestingly enough, this longing combined with powerlessness also erodes gender hierarchies. The women express opinions as freely (if as powerlessly) as their husbands. (And this suggests too that Harriet's shrinking from public attention is a function of the elite menfolk's power and public responsibilities.) When, in the end, Sir Charles remains silent about his political intentions, it is not clear whether this is because the farmers' sentiments are just conventional, or more likely because he has no interest in joining Parliament and the divisions and groupings of the formal political world.

In the polite sphere itself, gender differences intensify as the evening wears on. Emily Jervois, despite herself, begins to feel pity for Harriet: the immensity of change in Harriet's life after the marriage, which will oblige her to live in a new house, to join a new family and 'leave her own, who so dearly love her', is figured as an '*irrevocable* destiny' which terrifies her (3:215). Emily's sympathetic fear segues into Harriet's own increasing anxiety about the night ahead, which leads her to 'give up form' (3:236) and request to leave the party early, unattended. At this, Lady G. remarks: 'After all ... we women, dressed out in ribbands, and gaudy trappings, and in Virgin-white, on our Wedding days, seem like milk-white heifers led to sacrifice' (3:236). This is a bracing depiction of the public wedding, although it is less than a serious critique of married gender relations. Rather, Lady G.'s remark once again attests to the 'solemnity' and 'awfulness' of marriage, especially for women whose fears and criticisms reflect its simultaneously sacred, sexual, social and economic impact. At the same time, it is yet another instance of the text's Whiggish tolerance, its capacity to voice esoteric views (here that of Lady G. herself) and as such is in line with its attitude to Catholics and Schismatics. In the end, these tolerated differences of gender and creed belong to the margins of an event – and indeed a text – that insistently points towards the figure of the good man.

Sir Charles's 'transcendent merit' (3:217) is made most apparent in an event that takes place early in the morning after the wedding when, in a meeting of women only, Harriet's grandmother Mrs Shirley offers a benediction which becomes another celebration of Sir Charles's character, this time in a fairly secular key:

> The Bride threw herself at her grandmamma's feet, for her blessing. It was
> given in such a tender and pious manner, that we were all affected by it. The
> best of Sons, of Men, said she, afterwards, has but just left me. What
> a blessing to all around him, is a good man! Sir Charles Grandison is
> every thing. But, my dear Loves, to the younger Ladies, Let a good man,
> let life, let manners, be the principal motive of your choice: In *goodness* will
> you have every sanction; and your Fathers, Mothers, Relations, Friends,
> every joy! My dearest Love, my Harriet . . . there was a time that I thought
> no man on earth could deserve you: Now it is my prayer, and will be, that
> you may deserve this man. But let us join the gentlemen. Fear not, my
> Harriet – Sir Charles's character will preserve with every one its dignity, and
> give a sanction to the solemnity that has united you to him. My dearest
> Love! be proud, and look assured: You may, or who can? Yesterday's
> transaction is your Glory; glory in it, my Harriet! (3:239)

What is remarkable (and indeed revolutionary) about this passage is the
inversion through which Sir Charles's character sanctions the solemnity
rather than vice versa. And here Richardson's larger project reaches
a climax.

Marriage's legitimation lies in the moral character of those who marry,
a moral character that is divided between Christian devotion (or virtue)
and social elevation (or dignity). As such, marriage is neither simply civil
nor sacramental. Rather it is – or should be – the outcome of individuals'
successful negotiation between the sacred and the secular, as proved precisely in character. Sir Charles achieves an all but Christological charisma
('The best of Sons, of Men') whose goodness provides 'every sanction'. It
can do so because Sir Charles is not simply supremely virtuous but because
his character is itself an embodiment of natural law as 'the form in which
human reason has access to God's imprinting of purposive nature' – or, as
Lady Beauchamp, one of the many recipients of Sir Charles's kindness,
puts it: 'Justice and He are one' (3:294).[87] The question of whether
a particular state can or cannot fine-tune divine law in relation to marriage,
debated by Hardwicke's Marriage Act, is beside the point for someone who
is both an English landed gentleman and an embodiment of that law.
Whereas Pamela had a soul, upon which her revolutionary democratic
claims were mounted, Sir Charles himself exemplifies a meeting of divine
and secular law.

How does this difference affect *Sir Charles Grandison*'s capacity to
contribute to literature as an institution? *Pamela* had already, in effect,
positioned character as marriage's sanction (although the principle was not
there clearly stated), but of course Sir Charles's character differs significantly from Pamela's. He is primarily a practical Christian gentleman; she

is a servant and a Christian soul, writing her way to moral grandeur and social elevation and creating literature as a new kind of religio-moral social force as she does so. *Grandison* assumes rather than recreates that force: it is as if, in accommodating Hardwicke's Erastian and oligarchic reform of marriage culture and thereby further improving the marriage plot, Richardson did indeed lose touch with the specifically writerly and thence literary energy of Pamela's devout Tory animus against social participation. In his embodiment of natural law, in his commitment to public wedding as an endorsement of social hierarchy and order, in his fluent, exemplary, always-already-perfect integration of the sacred and the secular, Sir Charles himself represents a hiatus in the novel form's oppositional energies.

Ironically, we must turn to a different strain of fiction – Henry Fielding's satirical engagement with Richardson, no less – for the vital development of Richardson's Anglican marriage plot. The next chapter explores how Fielding deployed and extended key Richardsonian nuptial tropes, including the clerical subplot and the parish wedding, precisely as a means to harness oppositional political energy.

CHAPTER 4

The Patriot Marriage Plot
Fielding, Shebbeare and Goldsmith

The previous chapter showed that in mid-century England, where marriage loomed large as a political and moral topic, Richardson's Anglican
marriage plot elevated the novel form by figuring marriage as an institution
joining the church and the state, and then by imagining characters like
Pamela and Sir Charles Grandison who enact and embody that nexus. In
the end, Richardson's novels authorise their own imaginative – that is to
say, literary – power by mediating between faith and citizenship (or better,
by relaying faith into conjugality) inside the Erastian nation state.

It turns out, however, that the latent nation-building tendencies of
Richardson's marriage plots are more fully realised in a different programme: in a series of mid-century oppositional and satiric-sentimental
novels that respond to *Pamela*. Of these, the most important are Fielding's
Joseph Andrews (1742), John Shebbeare's *The Marriage Act* (1754) and
Oliver Goldsmith's *Vicar of Wakefield* (1766). Each places marriage at the
front and centre of a 'Patriot' vision of the English landed estate and does
so by masculinising *Pamela*'s plot, and more particularly, by foregrounding
its clerical subplot. The good Tory vicar (who stands in contrast to the
libertine squire) emerges as a key protagonist. Like Mr Williams, he
eventually comes to officiate the central characters' weddings and to
share in the largesse of an ending where injustices are put right and virtue
rewarded. Importantly, this settlement is embedded in an imagined community that is once again Anglican but now explicitly based in an idealised
rural English parish. Unlike Mr Williams, however, Patriot fiction's good
Tory vicar is also figured ironically. Richardson's missionary seriousness
gives way to a lighter, less calculable tone, as the England represented by
the rural parish is revealed as nostalgic and utopian.

The Patriot marriage plot, as I call it, typically merges the Anglican
country parish wedding (as pioneered by *Sir Charles Grandison*) with
traditional comic-romance closure (as reinstated by *Joseph Andrews*). It
thereby produces a specifically English nuptial-pastoral ideal, albeit one

subject to irony. Furthermore, in transforming and consolidating Richardson's Anglican marriage plot, it will have a decisive effect on the history of the English novel, enabling later writers – Frances Burney and Jane Austen in particular – to treat marriage itself as the genre's pivotal convention.

Fielding and the New Fiction

When *Pamela* was published in 1740, Henry Fielding was no longer involved in the theatre; the 1737 Licencing Act had been successful in that at least. For two years after being excluded from the stage, Fielding published nothing under his own name although he continued to write surreptitiously while consolidating his relationship with his fellow ex-Etonian George Lyttelton, who became his patron. In making this move, Fielding became attached to the 'boy Patriots' (nurtured by the out-of-favour Court Whig Lord Cobham) who were under the sway of Bolingbroke's defence of liberty and advocacy of non-partisanship. Alongside Lord Chesterfield, Lyttelton was a leading light for this generation of the Patriot opposition. For the next five years, until the publication of *Joseph Andrews*, Fielding wrote in their interest.

Like Bolingbroke, the boy Patriots were distinguished from the mainstream Tory opposition by their efforts to forge a connection between the state and the people which was independent not just of the party system but also of the Established Church, and indeed of instituted religion.[1] Fielding's own flirtation with irreligion, already apparent in *Pasquin*, aligned him with this experimental strain of the oppositional programme, which in Bolingbroke's writings of the time (notably *The Idea of a Patriot King*) took a secularising and utopian turn. On the basis of Thomas Lockwood's findings, scholars are now sceptical that Fielding contributed to Bolingbroke's *The Craftsman*, the most substantial of the period's anti-Walpolean periodicals.[2] He did, however, write a short squib, known as the 'Mum Budget' letter, published in May 1738 in *The Craftsman's* successor, *Common Sense*, sponsored by Lyttelton and Lord Chesterfield. It celebrated – ironically, of course – the advantages of remaining silent in Walpole's Britain. He also served as writer for and shareholder in another oppositional paper, *The Champion*, where he undertook what Bertrand Goldgar has described as his 'first serious venture into journalism', writing demotic essays on various topics under the pseudonym 'Captain Hercules Vinegar', an ex-prize fighter at Hockley-at-the-Hole Bear Garden, a monument of 'low' or irregular London entertainment.[3]

After Fielding ended his involvement with *The Champion* in 1740, he took up literary rather than political projects, including the magazine *The History of Our Own Times*, which he may have edited alongside the Anglican clergyman William Young, who, as tradition has it, was the model for the hero of his next major literary work, *Joseph Andrews*.[4] His first prose fiction, *An Apology for the Life of Mrs Shamela Andrews*, published on 4 April 1741 (again anonymously), pointedly ridiculed Richardson's missionary purpose. Framed by a gushing epistolary exchange between two parsons, it zeroed in on *Pamela*'s clerical subplot, satirising its vicar-squire themes. Shamela, a sometime Methodist, carries on an adulterous affair with Parson Williams, now robustly reinvented as a charlatan priest, while Mr B. is reduced to a mere citation of Gay's booby-squire from *The What D'ye Call It*.[5]

If *Shamela*'s politics were broadly oppositional, echoing *Pasquin*'s anticlericalism while weaponising anew old tropes of Tory satire, *Joseph Andrews* took a different path. It is, after all, a vicar-centred marriage plot, and one which arguably seeks less to satirise than to engage and redirect Richardson's missionary purpose. Certainly, *Joseph Andrews* was a political novel which brought oppositional Patriot themes to the novel form, as J. A. Downie has recently emphasised.[6] Yet by the time it was published in 1742, Fielding's own allegiances had shifted. He was paid off by Walpole, who resigned in that year, an act which caused disarray among the opposition, some of whom now joined the reconstituted Court Whig administration. This switch was an early sign that Country–Court/Tory–Whig divisions would be reconfigured in the century's second half, providing the ground for the later stages of Fielding's career, when, rather than being attached loosely to the opposition, he was firmly in the administration, in receipt of important places by virtue of that change.[7] It suggests too that *Joseph Andrews* straddles a political *volte face*: when Fielding wrote the novel in 1741, he was still attached to the boy Patriots, but that was no longer so by the time it was published, just three weeks before Walpole's resignation.

The complexity of Fielding's career in the post-Licensing Act years suggests that *Joseph Andrews* was more than an opportunistic intervention in *Pamela*'s remarkable success. It was a daring literary experiment in the spirit of Fielding's earlier theatrical experiments with genre, topicality and metanarrative. Fielding is widely understood to have set new parameters for the English novel and to have done so not just by experimenting with prose form but by also reflecting on how the new fictional realism itself might be situated within established genre theory. As a 'Species of writing' concerned with the everyday life of common people, it lent itself to a hybrid mode of 'comic epic', as *Joseph Andrews*'s preface famously argued.[8] If Richardson wrote inside converging currents of contemporary Anglican moral reform and print commerce, Fielding's rebuke of him would reinvent classical protocols – both comic and epic – for a modern readership.[9]

In following *Pamela*, however, *Joseph Andrews* also intervened in a particular political – or theo-political – debate about marriage protocols, the minutiae of which, as Fielding knew, rightly belonged to comedy. By dint of its singular convergence of tradition and topicality, *Joseph Andrews* went on to reorder marriage's relation to narrative form in ways that substantively shaped the modern English marriage plot. This claim is more usually made about Richardson, but it is no less true of Fielding.

Joseph Andrews

Joseph Andrews's transposition of Richardson's marriage plot proceeds, in the first instance, from a comic gender inversion. *Pamela* recounts the story of a servant girl who, against all odds, marries her master after resisting his advances. *Joseph Andrews* tells the story of her brother, Joseph, a footman who is also 'virtuous' in the sense that he too remains chaste until marriage. Where Pamela resists her master, Joseph resists the persistent sexual approaches of Lady Booby, his mistress (who is Mr B.'s recently widowed aunt). He also resists Lady Booby's servant, Mrs Slipslop, whose sexual advances are more open still. The satiric humour of these inversions works by suggesting that the plot is less probable even than *Pamela*'s since, as far as the eighteenth-century reader was concerned, it is simply unbelievable that a young man like Joseph should resist sexual opportunity. All the more so because Joseph's virtue is less motivated than Pamela's: he is not guided by Christian principle, neither is he rewarded with social elevation. Rather, he is in love with his (equally virtuous) sweetheart, Fanny Goodwill, who is also a servant, and whom, we are to assume, he would have married had neither been virtuous at all. Indeed, theirs is a heartfelt, mutual attraction which faces no immediate social obstacles.

Simply by casting Joseph and Fanny as members of the lower classes, Fielding severed the links between marriage, literacy, religion and social mobility that underpinned *Pamela*'s narrative. In Richardson, a servant girl improves her status by spiritually and morally converting her master, largely through letter writing. In Fielding, by a series of contrivances, a servant is revealed as a member by birth of the respectable classes. He turns out to be a changeling, as does Fanny, so their attachment remains endogamous. By a logic of equivalence, his good nature and her beauty are ultimately filial, a matter of blood. As McKeon and others note, this revision does not just resist the levelling possibilities that inform Richardson's narrative, it also hints at a providential sanction for the received social filiations and hierarchies affirmed by Joseph and Fanny's union.[10] Moreover, as Paula McDowell argues, Fielding's attachment to received hierarchies renders him sceptical of the culture of education and 'improvement' that underpinned the moral reform movement.[11] Nowhere does he suggest that reading and writing teach virtue (or lead to 'progress'), and that is why his couple is uneducated – Joseph has received minimal schooling and Fanny is illiterate – as indeed was most of the English population in the mid-eighteenth century.

The novel's second major transposition of *Pamela* concerns narration. Introducing his trademark discursive narrator, Fielding replaced Richardson's first-person epistolary form (i.e. Pamela's subjective voice) with a third-person mode which brought a new extra-diegetic authority into the novel form. As an experiment in genre, *Joseph Andrews* is persuasive in large part because of the authority and the charisma of its learned narrator, who is gentlemanly, classically educated and witty (qualities he shares with the novel's author). His strikingly fresh tone blended existing modes: the essayistic tradition of Addison and Steele with the Shaftesbury of *Characteristics*, on one hand, and, on the other, Fielding's own demotic persona of Captain Vinegar in *The Champion*. Crucially, Fielding's narrator does not belong to the fictional world of his characters: they belong to one (imaginary) civil sphere while he, along with his implied readers, belongs to another. (One minor character does bridge this divide: Mr Wilson, who turns out to be Joseph's biological father, and whose career, not coincidentally, has included a period as a London hack writer.) No such disjunction exists in *Pamela*, of course: Fielding's narrator is indebted to the default 'mock-heroic' mode of satiric writing which structured Gay and Fielding's own meta-theatre, for instance, and clandestine marriage satire more generally.

Joseph Andrews's revision of *Pamela* also works by invoking a non-Richardsonian literary filiation. The first edition's title page informs readers that the novel is 'Written in Imitation of the Manner of CERVANTES Author of *Don Quixote*'. The story is a Quixote narrative turning upon clashes between a subjective, idealised order – the world as Parson Adams sees it – and the 'real' world, where the 'real' aligns with the point of view of pragmatic 'common sense' (a highly charged term which was brought into prominence by Shaftesbury, adopted by Bolingbroke and the 'boy Patriots' and played a central role in *Pasquin*). The 'real' here also means a debased version of epic qualities and actions, that is to say a masculine world of adventuring, fighting and feasting as distinct from *Pamela*'s cloistered, domestic sphere. In these terms, the 'comic epic' mode lays claim to a fictional realism conceived as a recasting of the heroic from everyday material, on one hand, and, on the other, as a rejection of 'romance', or the idealism of *Pamela*'s Christian mission.

In a further debt to Cervantes, *Joseph Andrews*'s plot is episodic and peripatetic in the mode of the picaresque. After being dismissed from Lady Booby's household, Joseph sets off for London in search of employment, joined by Parson Adams, who naïvely hopes to sell his sermons to a bookseller in the city. Much of the action consists of their chance encounters on the road, even if the road here is not very long, with most scenes taking place no more than a few miles beyond their parish. The novel's humour, then, largely consists of a series of (mis)adventures and pratfalls in which Joseph's good nature and Adams's unworldliness encounter a materialistic, competitive, snobbish society. These encounters are described with an emphasis on sociability and physicality (once again in contrast to the intense carceralism and interiority of Pamela's narrative).[12] As was the case for Cervantes, they are double-edged – comic *and* epic – because Joseph and Adams are definitively good-natured, as well as being unlikely heroes: strong, agile and brave.

In keeping with comic protocol, questions of marriage and itinerancy structure the picaresque plot. Indeed, the central characters – Parson Adams, Joseph and Fanny – are on the road and have no accommodation in society because Adams forbids Joseph and Fanny to marry immediately, as they wish to do. Theirs is a courtship narrative that ends in happy marriage, but (as was the case in *Sir Charles Grandison*) not before being prolonged by delays to that ending, here as ordered by Adams himself. In the first instance Adams advises Joseph and Fanny to delay their marriage 'till a few Years' Service and Thrift had a little improved their Experience, and enabled them to live comfortably together', presumably to avoid their dependence upon the parish.[13] While on the road, Joseph and Fanny are strictly speaking extra-parochial and hence unable to marry other than clandestinely; later, after their return to the parish, Adams insists upon further delay to comply with church rules for the calling of banns three successive weeks before the wedding.

Arguably, Adams's insistence on proper ceremony (and procedure) functions as a structuring device in *Joseph Andrews*, much as the sham marriage motif did for *Pamela*. Mock weddings, clandestine marriages and phoney priests do not appear in Fielding's novel, neither do the modes of soul-making and character interiority that turn upon sham marriage in *Pamela*. Indeed, the old, unruly performative marriage tradition which haunts Richardson's heroine, and which featured in many of Fielding's own plays, is conspicuously absent here. Instead, the novel embraces proper ceremony as an uncontested element of comic-epic form, for which it functions, conventionally enough, as closure. That the wedding ceremony itself is an object of solemnity – as it was for Richardson – becomes clear in the novel's closing scene when Parson Adams rebukes Pamela and Mr Booby for laughing during Joseph and Fanny's wedding (342), as if it were merely an occasion for festive merriment, or worse, an entertainment or comic spectacle (precisely as theatrical mock marriages and plebeian Fleet weddings were understood from an elite viewpoint). It turns out that earnest compliance with ecclesiastical protocol grounds the comic-epic marriage plot, even if that plot is also shaped by narratorial distance and irony. In this regard Fielding is Richardson's unlikely disciple.

This insight takes us to the heart of the last (and for our purposes most important) of Fielding's revisions of *Pamela*: his recasting of *Pamela*'s clerical subplot as a main plot. It is clear enough that Pamela's brother, Joseph, is not the novel's central character. That role is taken by Reverend Abraham Adams, Parson Adams. Indeed, Adams is the only character mentioned in the novel's preface, which claims him as a true original:

> As to the Character of *Adams*, as it is the most glaring in the whole, so I conceive it is not to be found in any Book now extant. It is designed a Character of perfect Simplicity; and as the Goodness of his Heart will recommend him to the Good-natur'd; so I hope it will excuse me to the Gentlemen of his Cloth; for whom, while they are worthy of their sacred Order, no Man can possibly have a greater Respect. They will therefore excuse me, notwithstanding the low Adventures in which he is engaged, that I have made him a Clergyman; since no other Office could have given him so many Opportunities of displaying his worthy Inclinations. (10–11)

In this light, *Joseph Andrews*'s key transposition is less the comic substitution of Joseph for Pamela as a love object than the replacement of Pamela the servant with Parson Adams the good-hearted country cleric as an embodiment of virtue. By placing Adams at his novel's centre, Fielding retains a focus on religion, if in a manner that makes fun of – satirises – *Pamela*'s Christian mission, just as *Shamela* did. This time, however, Richardson's commitment to Christian virtue is not so much ridiculed as recalibrated: Fielding insists on the importance of Adams's office because it enables him to chronicle the good clergyman's 'Opportunities' to enact practical virtue in the context of ordinary English country life.

Fielding's decision to foreground Richardson's clerical subplot needs to be viewed in light of his own shifting allegiances. Certainly, his turn to clerical themes is consistent with that strain of Tory-Patriot ideology which emphasised popular community, but it also suggests a departure from the modes of freethinking that marked his earlier work and attached him to the boy Patriots (even if he had already written 'An Apology for the Clergy' for *The Champion*). In this light too his claim for Adams's sui generis status (as 'a Character of perfect Simplicity') prepares the ground for another significant revision of *Pamela*: the transposition of charity for (Richardsonian) chastity as his novel's key virtue. Chastity is a source of the moral authority that Pamela enacts both in her world and in those letters through which she acquires her remarkable influence over others (including, finally, Mr Williams and Mr B.). Yet Pamela becomes an independent letter writer because she has so little concrete social context. Unlike Adams, she does not hold office or circulate in a wider community. Her social world barely extends beyond the squire's household, and the two Brandon family estates at Lincolnshire and Bedfordshire are, for her, all but interchangeable.

Richardson's elision of public space (which reaches its apex in Pamela's insistence on a private wedding) has a missionary purpose: it reflects *Pamela*'s injunction to live as a devout and moral self rather than as a civic and worldly self. *Joseph Andrews*, by contrast, rejects the separation of self and world that underpins Pamela's chaste soul-making. The novel focusses, rather, on the social networks and connections within which Adams's charitable acts unfold.[14] This emphasis drives the novel's relocation of *Pamela*'s setting from the domestic sphere of a vaguely identified country estate to the concrete locale of a contemporary Somersetshire parish and its surrounds. With this change, Fielding makes two major revisions to the architecture of the novel form: he embeds it in the specificities of English rural parish life and foregrounds the centrality of vicar-squire relations in that context. Together, these revisions increase the stakes of the contest for authority between church and state that animated *Pamela*'s clerical subplot. I address each in turn before examining how they reshape the novel's marriage plot.

The Parish

Joseph Andrews's primary setting is an English parish because the parish was, as W. M. Jacob notes, 'the basic unit of local government' in eighteenth-century England.[15] As such, it was the key institution in the lives of ordinary people like Joseph and Fanny and thus part of Fielding's realism. All of England was divided into parish districts, which were primarily administered by the Anglican Church. Parish membership was, in the first instance, nativist: one belonged to a parish by virtue of being born there. This meant that English subjects were English on the basis of being born into a parish and that they were Anglican by default. It also meant that at the level of ideology, the local parish community could function (or be exploited) as a signifier of Protestantism and/or Englishness itself, as indeed it did for the Tory imagination in particular.

Parish life and governance were based on communal participation. Householders were obliged to pay annual tithes for clerical services, for instance, even if they had opted for Catholicism or Dissent (although, after 1736, Quakers were an exception). Formal decisions were made by the vestry which was usually elected by ratepayers. The vestry levied fees, kept records of births, deaths and marriages, provided local services (including credit, roads and church repair) and administered relief to the poor.[16] The local squire, however, very often controlled the vestry because of his position as primary landowner. As the 'impropriator' of church tithes, he owned the rights to them and he appointed the clergyman to the parish living. His ability to exercise lay patronage over Church benefices was politically valuable, not least because parsons could in turn ensure that eligible parishioners voted according to the squire's will.[17]

The parson's duties were primarily devotional and pastoral, although he attended to some secular matters in his role as the vestry chairman.[18] Many parishes were served not by beneficed vicars but by 'curates', who had been ordained but had not acquired their own living (and who often worked for an absentee priest in that practice of clerical outsourcing known as pluralism). Curates and incumbents performed mostly the same tasks, if at rather different levels of remuneration. Typically, they celebrated at least one service on Sunday at which they gave a sermon. In a few instances they also offered a service on weekdays (Parson Adams does so but usually only his wife and clerk attend) (287–8).[19] The priest catechised parish children and provided lay services such as transcribing wills and letters. He also visited, and often tended, the sick in lieu of professional medical aid. For a fee, he churched, baptised and buried parishioners and, after 1754, he, and only he, married them.

In rural parishes particularly, the church itself was the centre of local communal life. It functioned, minimally, as the regular meeting point for villagers for whom neither a modern print public sphere nor a modern leisure culture existed. In such cases the weekly sermon was the main source of news and commentary on the larger world for many parishioners, bridging local and national circuits of information. The church building itself was also a source of community pride, and through its burial ground and parish records a repository of local memory. All of these functions and meanings allowed the parish to accrue considerable ideological significance. In particular, because rural collective life was primarily organised around the parish and so many country clergy remained Tory in the years following the constitutional settlement, the country parish and parson became key tropes for the oppositional imaginary. High Church Tories emphasised not just clerical independence and orthodoxy but also the spiritual and pastoral vitality of a church life based in rural rather than urban England. In this way, as Linda Colley has helped us to realise, the matrix of rural parish life was seen to form the basis of Englishness itself.[20]

Yet even as the eighteenth-century rural parish functioned as a site of imaginary power, it was also a space of social division. As rural clergy were exposed to the ongoing effects of Whig hegemony, they increasingly became objects of religious and social critique. To begin with, the period saw a narrowing of the clergy's class base: vicars joined the civil magistracy next to secular landowners, and they became increasingly self-reproducing and professionalised and thus detached from their parishioners.[21] Church taxes – tithes – were widely resented, not least because some clergymen used their office for personal enrichment. Some also came under attack for neglecting their duties: Parson Trulliber in *Joseph Andrews*, who is more farmer than priest, is a well-known fictional example of this kind of 'bad parson'. And finally, tensions between the interests of the parish as an administrative unit and the parson's spiritual and pastoral vocation were exacerbated by measures like the Marriage Act, which used parish and priest as instruments of state.

Polemical attacks on the problems and failings of the parochial clergy became the basis of a literary-rhetorical genre of its own in this context. John Eachard's influential satire, *The Grounds and Occasions of the Contempt of the Clergy and Religion Enquired Into* (1670), attributed the lessening of the quality of 'our Clergy' to 'ignorance' and 'poverty' among them.[22] By Walpole's time, the genre included anti-Erastian attacks on the corruption and privileges of Whig churchmen – Richard Savage's 'The Progress of a Divine' (1735), a swipe at Walpole's ally Bishop Gibson, may stand as an example. Contempt of the clergy, as it was called, was strongly tied to the continued growth of Addison's 'subaltern' clerical class, many of whom turned to the disreputable irregular wedding trade. This underclass was symptomatic of an oversupply of clerical labour that persisted across the century. According to Geoffrey Holmes, at any one time about two-thirds of all clergy belonged to the subaltern class (i.e. were curates or vicars of indigent parishes and thereby condemned to more or less genteel poverty). A proportion of these remained unbeneficed throughout their career.[23]

Because the Church was not sufficiently wealthy to provide pastoral coverage across the nation, infrastructure was often in disrepair in poor parishes, with many not able to provide housing for a vicar. Many clergy were badly paid: average wages were about £30 p.a. (less than a moderately successful London tradesman), but starvation salaries of less than £10 p.a. were not unknown among curates in Wales, for instance.[24] Poorer parsons were often conspicuous by their threadbare clothing (like Parson Adams, they might wear a cassock, gown and three-cornered hat – the oddity of his dress is a running joke in the novel).[25] In order to make ends meet, they taught in schools, set up shop, farmed and provided practical legal services.[26] While such activities connected them more closely to the local community, their poverty meant that they struggled to secure basic respectability, so exposing them to scorn in a society in which 'politeness' was so powerful a criterion of full social personhood.

Parson Adams is a curate in just such a rural parish. As a member of the clerical subaltern class he is paid the princely sum of £23 p.a., endlessly scrambling to increase his income in order to support his wife and six children (23); on one occasion he describes living 'a full Month on one Funeral sermon' (133). The novel is interested in how his career has unfolded. In a passage that underscores the importance of parish politics to Fielding's realism, Adams provides a fulsome account of how he managed to secure his curacy:

> [T]he Rector, whose Curate I formerly was, sen[t] ... for me on the Approach of an Election, and [told] me if I expected to continue in his Cure, that I must bring my Nephew [a shopkeeper and an alderman of a corporation] to vote for one Colonel *Courtly*, a Gentleman whom I had never heard Tidings of 'till that Instant. I told the Rector, I had no power over my Nephew's Vote ... That I supposed he would give it according to his Conscience, that I would by no means endeavour to influence him to give it otherwise. He told me it was in vain to equivocate: that he knew I had already spoke to him in favour of Esquire *Fickle* my neighbour, and indeed it was true I had: for it was at a Season when the *Church was in Danger*, and when all good Men expected they knew not what would happen to us all ... I persevered, and so did my Nephew, in the Esquire's Interest, who was chose chiefly through his Means, and so I lost my Curacy. (132–3)

Adams describes a parish – and indeed a social order – in which politics and Church preferment are entirely interdependent, where claims to faith and affiliation are staked for worldly reasons and where irreligion is a default position. As was to be expected of a country parson, his loyalties are with the Church-supporting Tory faction – this much is clear from his citation of the well-worn catch-cry, 'the Church [is] in danger.' The parish's rector, however, supports Colonel Courtly (whose name gives his politics away) and operates in a (supposedly) Walpolean fashion by threatening to evict Adams from his cure if Adams does not secure his nephew's influence for Courtly. Naturally, Courtly's Tory opponent, Esquire Fickle, lives up to *his* name, 'never so much as go[ing] to Church' (133) after securing election.

Adams's backstory repeats much of *Pasquin*'s critique of party politics. Once again, the implications of Fielding's satire would appear to be Bolingbrokean, especially when we learn that a Patriot King figure, Sir Oliver Hearty, a huntin', fishin' country squire with no real interest in politics, restored Adams to his place in the parish (such as it is). '[B]y his Interest with a Bishop', Adams explains, 'he got me replaced into my Curacy, and gave me eight Pounds out of his own Pocket to buy me a Gown and Cassock, and furnish my House' (134). After Adams's influential nephew dies, however, Adams himself is of so little consequence that Sir Oliver's successor, Sir Thomas Booby, does not even bother to meet with him.

In this parish, then, relations between squire and curate are easy to describe. They barely exist, as the narrator makes clear: '*Adams* had no nearer Access to Sir *Thomas*, or my Lady, than through the Waiting-Gentlewoman' (25). Sir Thomas and Lady Booby belong to a Whig squirarchy that is oriented towards London's world of consumption, fashion and entertainment, and which regards its country tenants as 'Brutes' (25). Even more tellingly, Sir Thomas and his parson are in a 'constant State of Civil War' over tithe litigation. Yet while Adams is regarded as a lowly 'Domestic', he feels no resentment at his ill treatment (25). As he explains to a fellow traveller:

> Sir *Thomas*, poor Man, had always so much Business, that he never could find Leisure to see me ... However, on all proper Seasons, such as the Approach of an Election, I throw a suitable Dash or two into my Sermons; which I have the pleasure to hear is not disagreeable to Sir *Thomas*, and the other honest Gentlemen my Neighbours, who have all promised me these five Years, to procure an Ordination for a Son of mine ... tho', as he was never at an University, the Bishop refuses to ordain him. (134–5)

Once again, Adams offers a grim picture of rural parochial life, this time as it is stifled by ecclesiastical patronage and indifference to merit – a little world where 'consequence' is measured politically and economically. At the very least his account reveals deep flaws in the Erastian state and with the Whig-Church alliance forged by Walpole and Gibson under strain. His own pragmatic response to the situation (supporting the Tories while spruiking for his 'honourable' Whig overlords at his sermons) would seem to confirm both Whig complaints about Church self-interest and High Church critiques of collusion with Walpole (here scaled down to the level of the parish where Sir Thomas trades on empty promises to 'procure' an ordination for Adams's son).[27]

Yet, importantly, Adams himself draws no such conclusions from his situation. He accepts the abuses of which he is an innocent victim, thus demonstrating his commitment to the (increasingly obsolete) doctrine of passive obedience. The disjunction between Adams's subaltern position and its fulsome representation presents a paradox. It is as if the text mounts a Patriot/anticlerical critique of High Church orthodoxy while appealing to one of its core principles. Yet, for Fielding, Adams's passive obedience is a definitive mark of office and hence of character. He is precisely a good parson, as long constructed and imagined by a lineage of writers, including Fielding himself in *The Champion*. This lineage provided Fielding both with the terms of his characterisation of Adams and with the ironical distance through which Adams's goodness and the politics of rural parish life are presented.

Vicars and Squires

John Dryden and Joseph Addison's contributions to the good parson tradition are especially important to *Joseph Andrews*. Each wrote in the wake of the 1688 settlement, although from different sides of the political spectrum: Dryden in support of church autonomy, Addison in support of a church-state accommodation. In loose informal terms, their dialogue shaped an ongoing eighteenth-century literary conversation about vicars and squires. Dryden's much-admired 'The Character of a Good Parson', published posthumously in *Fables, Ancient and Modern* (1700), was a Tory appropriation of Chaucer's 'The Parson's Tale', written during the 1690s, when Dryden, a Catholic, had retreated from public life.[28] Its model of clerical virtue was the nonjuring Anglican bishop Thomas Ken, who gave up his office in 1691 in loyalty to the Stuarts. Ken remained an exemplary figure for Tories until well into the nineteenth century, partly on the basis of Dryden's panegyric.[29]

Written in heroic couplets and harnessing the nativist appeal of Chaucer's England, Dryden's poem styles Ken as a humble parish priest and High Church hero:

> A Parish-Priest was of the Pilgrim-Train;
> An awful, reverend, and religious Man.
> His Eyes diffus'd a venerable Grace,
> And Charity itself was in his Face.
> Rich was his Soul, though his Attire was poor;
> (As God had cloath'd his own Embassador). (320)

In this opening stanza, Ken appears as a clerical subaltern, a poorly attired figure of Christ-like humility. Charity is the byword of his churchmanship: his parish is 'Wide' (322) and his duties ceaseless; he serves the 'Sick' and succours 'the Distress'd' (322). A holy life of pastoral care and spiritual vitality forms the basis of his clerical independence and authority. He tames 'the proud', cheers 'the penitent' and rebukes 'rich Offenders[s]' (323). For Dryden, what matters most is that Ken practises what he preaches:

> His Preaching much, but more his Practice wrought;
> (A living Sermon of the Truths he taught;)
> For this by Rules severe his Life he squar'd:
> That all might see the Doctrin which they heard.
> For Priests, he said, are Patterns for the rest:
> (The Gold of Heav'n, who bear the God Impress'd). (322)

Ken, '[a] living Sermon of the Truths he taught', is a good parson not on the basis of his words or 'Signs of earthly Pow'r' (323), but on the basis of his commitment to his parish in the form of practical divinity. His actions, as they imitate Christ, serve as a 'Pattern' for the community at large, including his social superiors.

Just eleven years after the publication of Dryden's poem, Joseph Addison presented a rather more equivocal picture of parish life, focussed less on the character of the good parson than on lived relations between the vicar, the squire and their parishioners. Addison wrote a series of essays for *The Spectator* in July 1711, in which Mr Spectator, the periodical's personification of its Whiggish metropolitan values, visits his friend Sir Roger de Coverley, a guileless Tory squire, in the country.[30] Mr Spectator reports on aspects of country life, including relations between Sir Roger and the parson of the local parish whose living he controls. Sir Roger is described as a 'good Churchman' who 'has beautified the Inside of his Church with several Texts of his own chusing: He has likewise given a handsome Pulpit-Cloth, and railed in the Communion-Table at his own Expence' (460). He is thereby placed among those landed gentry who, like Sir Charles Grandison and Mr B. (under Pamela's influence) but unlike Fielding's Sir Thomas Booby, are engaged in restoring sacral aura to church interiors after the period of Calvinist iconoclasm and de-ritualisation of religious worship.[31]

In addition to beatifying the parish church, however, Sir Roger has chosen a particular kind of parson for the benefice in his gift, an action that subtly ironises his good churchmanship. His candidate (who, tell-ingly, is never given a name) is described as a 'Clergyman rather of plain Sense than much learning, of good Aspect, a clear Voice, a sociable Temper, and, if possible, a Man that understood a little of Back-Gammon' (440–1). The incongruity of the skills listed here is character-istic of the soft irony (as I call it) with which Sir Roger and his affairs are treated. Harsh critique of Sir Roger's criteria for selecting a parson is avoided because, from Addison's perspective, a certain diminution of the parson's spiritual vocation and responsibilities – even his familiarity with backgammon – is what enables an effective relation between him and the patron who supervises, and in this case carefully controls, his pastoral duties. For Addison, as a Whig, the squire's control of the vicar reflects proper limits to the Church's autonomy. Thus, for instance, Sir Roger provides the parson with copies of 'all the good Sermons which have been printed in *English*' (441) (with John Tillotson's Whiggish sermons lead-ing the list), one of which the parson is required to read to his parishi-oners each Sunday so as to offer 'a continued System of practical Divinity' (441).

The clergyman's value to Sir Roger, however, is more functional and secular still: Sir Roger tells Mr Spectator that '[t]here has not been a Law-Suit in the Parish' since the clergyman arrived (441). Indeed, by means of his weekly services, the parson orchestrates a local civilising (as against a spiritualising) mission:

> It is certain the Country people would soon degenerate into a kind of Savages and Barbarians, were there not such frequent Returns of a stated Time, in which the whole Village meet together with their best Faces, and in their cleanliest Habits, to converse with one another upon indifferent Subjects, hear their Duties explained to them, and join together in Adoration of the supreme Being. *Sunday* clears away the Rust of the whole Week, not only as it refreshes in their Minds the Notions of Religion, but as it puts both the Sexes upon appearing in their most agreeable Forms, and exerting all such Qualities as are apt to give them a Figure in the Eye of the Village. A Country-Fellow distinguishes himself as much in the *Church-yard*,

as a Citizen does upon the *Change*; the whole Parish-Politicks being generally discuss'd in that Place either after the Sermon or before the Bell rings. (460)

Addison's account of the Sunday service's function in the community is multilayered. Primarily, the service creates civility by enforcing physical hygiene and mutual self-display, its religious aspects reduced to a deistical 'Adoration of the supreme Being'. But it also grounds a rural and local public sphere where civil and rational discussion of parish politics replaces legal wrangling. On the occasions when Sir Roger's choice of a sermon fails to inspire the parishioners, he takes charge by waking parishioners who fall asleep during the service (while nonetheless prone to napping himself). Indeed, nobody dares stir until he is 'gone out of the Church', and his departure down the aisle is a ceremony of collective deference, his tenants serially bowing as he passes by (461).

The Spectator's attitude towards Sir Roger and his parish organisation is a complex mixture of affection and distance. Certainly, Mr Spectator himself (and the periodical's implied reader) is more intellectually sophisticated than Sir Roger and his parishioners. Furthermore, Mr Spectator's relation to the countryside is wholly different from that of its rustic inhabitants since it demands of him no responsibility or attachment. For him, the rural setting is an object of study and reportage as well as an occasion for proto-romantic inspiration. In one walk through the woods, he sublimely loses himself and is inspired to embark on an extraordinary and barely Christian theological meditation in which the afterlife becomes a proving ground for the progressive quest of perfection, with which, on this enlightened account, we are all already engaged in the mortal world (456–9).

Yet, despite Mr Spectator's own advanced theological metaphysics, the curious blend of Tory re-sacralisation and Whig Erastianism that characterises Sir Roger's leadership of his parish is by no means under critique. Indeed, Mr Spectator's endorsement of Sir Roger is confirmed when he compares relations in his parish to a neighbouring one, where (like Sir Thomas Booby and his vicar in *Joseph Andrews*) 'the Parson and the 'Squire . . . live in a perpetual State of War'; where the Squire does not attend Church, and where, therefore, the Tenants are 'Atheists and Tithe-Stealers' (462). Mr Spectator goes on to reflect philosophically on the need for the Squire to play a central role in parish affairs because, as he observes, these days 'ordinary People'

> pay as much Deference to the Understanding of a Man of an Estate, as of a Man of Learning; and are very hardly brought to regard any Truth, how important soever it may be, that is preached to them, when they know there are several Men of five hundred a Year who do not believe it. (462)

In England now, Addison concedes, authority derives from wealth and property – including money made from commerce – rather than from learning or religion. This recognition is true even in rural parishes, where, as a consequence, 'Adoration of the supreme Being' primarily serves the purposes of a Whig-endorsed social order in which squires, not vicars, run things.

Dryden and Addison's vastly different accounts of the good vicar under-score what was at stake politically in the representation of the English country parish. Dryden's parson hero is granted considerable autonomy and spiritual ambition; his kingdom is not that of this 'world below' (323) and he is committed to poverty and charity in emulation of 'primitive' (324) Christianity. More pointedly, he asserts '[t]he People's Right' (323) where that right is thought of, in an emerging oppositional spirit, as the cornerstone of a traditional social order comprised of monarch, church and people (323). In the poem's final stanzas, after he has relinquished his benefice, Ken's parish becomes the nation at large, a 'Cure of Souls' united in love and passive obedience:

> Now, through the Land, his Cure of Souls he stretch'd,
> And like a Primitive Apostle preach'd.
> Still Chearful; ever Constant to his Call;
> By many follow'd; Lov'd by most, Admir'd by All. (324)

Of course, Addison cannot endorse Dryden's notion of a good parson because it is rooted in a Tory theo-politics based upon divine right that, as far as the Whigs were concerned, had been displaced. Yet Addison also recognises that much of the country remained under the sway of Tory views and interests, and this is why he describes the ideal-typical English rural parish as one in which Tory squire and vicar alike accommodate to a Whiggish reality in which social deference to wealth and property trumps older modes of sovereignty and organic community. (Indeed, *Pamela*'s story of a Whiggish squire undergoing a Tory-Anglican-inspired moral reformation reverses the terms of Addison's move to similar effect although in a limited country-house domestic context.)

Importantly, this political accommodation lies behind the rhetorical tone of *The Spectator*'s parish-based essays, namely a tone of soft irony. It is ironic because at the level of theology and philosophy, Addison and his implied readers inhabit a different world than that of Sir Roger, his parson and their parishioners; it is 'soft' irony, however, because Mr Spectator and the villagers share a social order dominated by money and its privileges, and Sir Roger's lordship of his parish is attuned to the structure of subordination and deference required by the civil society that Addison and his readers inhabit too. This double relation between narrator and reader on one side and the rural parish on the other is not to be found in Richardson, but it is repeated (if in a somewhat different modality) by Fielding, where it helps to shape his treatment of the marriage plot.

Fielding made his own contribution to the 'good parson' question in four essays published in *The Champion* in March and April 1740 and entitled 'An Apology for the Clergy'.[32] He begins by claiming in earnest that the legitimation of the Anglican priest's office depends on '[t]he Awe which the wiser and better Part of Mankind have of the Supreme Being, and consequently of every thing which seems more immediately to belong to his Service' (256–7). He goes on to argue, like Dryden before him, that the clergy are primarily judged by their practical divinity, that is, by their actions as they imitate Christ's 'Humility' in relation to the community at large and as promulgated in the Gospels (259–60). Yet the 'Supreme Being' evoked here, like Addison's, has none of the qualities of the orthodox Trinitarian God.[33] Fielding's practical Christianity as a criterion for clerical office concedes nothing to sacral powers; rather, for him a good clergyman enacts 'an Idea of all the *moral* Virtues' (283; italics mine). Most of all, he performs charity and humility, which means that in practice he sanctifies his office by resisting envy and self-interest and by refusing to 'think evil' (269).

In the last essay of the series, however, Fielding takes the invocation of practical Christianity further. He insists that the Church itself invites contempt of the clergy through its pursuit of wealth and autonomy. While such an argument merely repeats a critique of the Church shared by many Whigs and Bolingbrokeans, it leads Fielding to assert that church reform is not primarily a matter of ecclesiastical governance. It must be enacted, rather, in the lives of individual vicars:

> [A]s nothing can hurt Religion so much as a Contempt of the Clergy, so nothing can justify or indeed cause any such Contempt but their own bad Lives. If there are any therefore among them who want Reformation in this Particular, it would be a truly Episcopal Office to attempt it. (286)

Fielding's intervention in the contempt of the clergy debate culminates in a singular kind of anti-Erastianism. He wishes to detach the church from the state, but insists that what matters most is not the inculcation of religion as such, but the moral character and action of individual priests as measured by their contributions to a parish community.

The Champion essays offer an emergent rationale for Fielding's characterisation of Parson Adams, not simply as a 'good clergyman' but as a 'good-natur'd' clergyman, whose 'good nature' and 'office' by definition connect him to the people and set him at odds with worldly interest per se. Indeed, Fielding's description of the office of the rural clergyman in the essayistic context of his 'Apology' shares much with Addison's emphasis on the moral influence of the Church, yet it lacks *The Spectator*'s complementary type of the 'good' or 'worthy' squire – a Sir Roger figure – who stands for the secular oligarchical wealth and power under whose patronage a good vicar (and vibrant Church) can flourish. This omission of the good squire is significant: it can be understood as pointing to the absence of goodwill for the church among the ruling oligarchy, a line of critique that need not imply any substantive Christian faith on Fielding's part, of course, and that is consistent with his ridicule of the affectations of Whig oligarchs and Booby squires alike in his plays and squibs. Most importantly, however, it is an omission that prepares the ground for Fielding's new iteration of the vicar-squire trope as it returns to Dryden's good parson now laced with Addison's irony.

Parson Adams and the Patriot Wedding

Joseph Andrews describes a good parson in the tradition just outlined, and as Fielding had invoked him in *The Champion*.[34] Most crucially, Parson Adams is a 'good parson' under irony: 'part clergyman, part Quixote', as Judith Hawley has remarked.[35] Adams is naïve and unworldly and no less importantly he is also in constant contradiction with himself. He abhors vanity and believes himself free of it – after all, he is deeply committed to the virtue of humility – yet he is prodigiously vain about the quality of his sermons. He is gentle and pacific, but also violent. He believes that knowledge is best when it derives from books but in fact his authority arises out of his spontaneous generosity and respect for others, from his good nature in other words. He is learned but at the same time as superstitious as a child, believing in ghosts. He is a firm observer of High Church forms yet praises anticlerical thinking.[36] His favourite reading is Aeschylus in the original Greek, yet Aeschylus' tragedies – and the *Prometheia* was at this time widely attributed to Aeschylus – stand at a distance from the Christian purpose which defines the good parson.[37] Then too Adams becomes an object of fun by preaching providentialism to others, as he does to Joseph, who falls into despair believing Fanny may be raped, only to be himself extravagantly gripped by despair on hearing that his own child may have been killed in an accident (309–10).

These contradictions do not just help ground Fielding's irony, they are immanent to Adams's characterisation. They allow Fielding to insist, more powerfully than in his *Champion* essays, that what matters is not what Adams preaches, or believes, or even thinks, but what he *does*. In practical terms, what counts is not knowledge or faith or representations but in particular charity, where that virtue involves not just benevolence but practical love for others. As Adams himself tells the coarse and avaricious parson Reverend Trulliber, whoever 'is void of Charity, I make no scruple of pronouncing that he is no Christian' (167). This insistence on charity requires soft irony to be fully pictured and is finally exhortatory; it puts pressure on the reader to emulate it. It also has an indirect, literary-satirical resonance since, as noted earlier, Adams's charity stands against Pamela's primary virtue – her chastity (and the evangelical soul-making and faith it entails) – which, by contrast, is made to appear egocentric and manipulative.

Adams's charity, however, presents a problem – one he shares with *Pamela*'s Mr Williams and which belongs to the general situation of country clergy subject to the squire's control of parish affairs. His office places him between the divine and the worldly, and most pressingly between his pastoral duty to his parishioners and the demands of his secular overlords, the Booby family. Adams does not enjoy the support of a 'good squire' for his churchmanship, and what replaces support from above is support from below, from the people of the parish, presented as a Christian community. Like Bishop Ken, Adams is loved and revered: 'his Word was little less than a Law in his Parish: for as he had shewn his Parishioners by a uniform Behaviour of thirty-five Years duration, that he had their Good entirely at heart; so they consulted him on every Occasion, and very seldom acted contrary to his Opinion' (49).

Towards the beginning of the novel's last book, a scene unfolds which clearly reveals the competing axes of worldly patronage and charitable pastoral care underpinning parish governance. When Lady Booby, Adams, Joseph and Fanny return home from their travels, the narrator contrasts the people's reception of Lady Booby and Adams, squire and vicar, respectively. Lady Booby enters the parish in a 'Coach and Six':

> amidst the ringing of Bells, and the Acclamations of the Poor, who were rejoiced to see their Patroness returned after so long an Absence, during which time all her Rents had been drafted to *London*, without a Shilling

being spent among them, which tended not a little to their utter impover-
ishing; for if the Court would be severely missed in such a City as *London*,
how much more must the Absence of a Person of great Fortune be felt in
a little Country Village, for whose Inhabitants such a Family finds
a constant Employment and Supply. (277)

The 'Acclamations of the Poor', Fielding's irony suggests, anticipate little
more than a temporary stay of the effects of Lady Booby's absentee land-
lordism. Her patronage, such as it is, diminishes the parish's prosperity and
inspires no genuine attachment.[38]

By contrast, we are told, 'if [the villagers'] Interest inspired so public
a Joy into every Countenance, how much more forcibly did the Affection
which they bore Parson *Adams* operate upon all who beheld his Return':

They flocked about him like dutiful Children round an indulgent Parent,
and vyed with each other in Demonstrations of Duty and Love. The Parson
on his side shook every one by the Hand, enquiring heartily after the
Healths of all that were absent, of their Children and Relations, and exprest
a Satisfaction in his Face, which nothing but Benevolence made happy by its
Objects could infuse. (277–8)

Adams's virtue is a matter not only of pastoral benevolence and charity but
also of 'Duty and Love', as if the social hierarchy ('Duty') has combined
with familial affection and been sanctioned by collective Christian feeling
('Love'). Nonetheless, a vicar-squire alliance of sorts remains intact here,
since Adams's place in the parish supplements Lady Booby's presence (or,
indeed, her absence) rather than opposes it. Lady Booby's status is able to
inspire the people's *public* affirmation, while Adams's care and guidance
form the basis of genuine authority and collectivity.

The homecoming scene crystallises a connection between Fielding's
parish-orientated   populism   and   Bolingbroke's   Patriot   politics.
Bolingbroke, especially in *The Idea of a Patriot King*, hoped to reform
English politics and government by sealing a more immediate bond between
the monarch and the people based on the good nature of both.[39] For
Bolingbroke such a bond obeyed natural law as well as an ancient constitution that warranted the 1688 settlement and its core values of Protestantism
and liberty, but (more or less implicitly) it did so in a way that underpinned
the filiative hierarchy of estates, castes and offices. The purpose of drawing
attention to Bolingbroke's political theory is not to argue that Fielding was
influenced by *The Idea of a Patriot King* (he may or may not have read it), or
even to argue that the novel adheres to Bolingbroke's theo-political imaginary (since no benevolent squire or monarch appears in *Joseph Andrews*).

Rather it is to suggest that the characterisation of Parson Adams in terms of his thoroughgoing charity and humility and the love and trust that bind him to his parishioners can be understood, in broad terms, to bring Bolingbrokean desires and fantasies into alignment with Tory ideas of the good parson and of the good social order grounded in primitive Christianity, parish paternalism and submission in adversity. Certainly, Tory and Patriot critiques of Walpolean oligarchy routinely overlapped in their appeal to king and country, even as their different relations to the Church separated them. Adams was a fictional device for bridging that difference.

Parish politics and vicar-squire relations are directly addressed in *Joseph Andrews*'s marriage plot. The novel culminates in the presentation of Joseph and Fanny's long-delayed wedding, officiated by Parson Adams. As noted earlier, Fanny and Joseph want to marry but can't afford to live together independently, so it is only when their true parentage is revealed that their wishes can be fulfilled. Even at this point, however, Parson Adams insists that they not take the quickest passage to marriage, which would be the purchase of a licence for a private wedding after permission from his Church superiors. (Another, more humble, alternative, a mere exchange of vows and consummation, is not mentioned here, although the novel soon addresses it.) Adams insists, rather, on a 'regular' parish marriage, which as we know required the publication of banns from the pulpit on three successive Holy Days. Presumably he does so because he wants to respect the Church's full forms, but other motivations may also come into play. The calling of banns enables Fanny and Joseph's intentions to be publicly announced to the parish, while allowing Adams to pre-empt any impediments to their marriage raised by Lady Booby (since banns required objections to be made publicly too).[40]

In support of the delay required by banns, Adams takes the opportunity to deliver a characteristic, if rather self-conscious, 'Sermon' against Joseph's unseemly 'Haste' in wanting to marry:

> Now, Child, I must inform you, that if in your purposed Marriage with this young Woman, you have no Intention but the Indulgence of carnal Appetites, you are guilty of a very heinous Sin. Marriage was ordained for nobler Purposes, as you will learn when you hear the Service provided on that Occasion read to you ... To marry with a View of gratifying those Inclinations is a Prostitution of that holy Ceremony, and must entail a Curse on all who so lightly undertake it. If, therefore, this Haste arises from Impatience, you are to correct, and not give way to it. (307–8)

Adams's insistence that marriage is not 'carnal' seems edged by mockery, but his insistence that marriage is a 'holy Ceremony' and that its service was 'ordained' for purposes of spiritual ennoblement is not ironised. Arguably that is not just because these sentiments affirm Anglican orthodoxy but also because, implicitly, they serve an anti-Erastian/Patriot political programme too.

Indeed, the full meaning and complexity of Adams's relation to wedding protocols becomes apparent when he talks about marriage to a pedlar whom he meets on the road – the man, it turns out, who will reveal that Joseph is a changeling. Before disclosing Joseph's past, the pedlar recounts how he himself was 'married'. While an army drummer, he met a woman on a press gang march with whom he had sex, before going on to live with her 'as Man and Wife':

> 'I suppose', says *Adams* interrupting him, 'you were married with a Licence: For I don't see how you could contrive to have the Banns published while you were marching from Place to Place' – 'No, Sir', said the pedlar, 'we took a Licence to go to Bed together, without any Banns'. ——'Ay, Ay', said the Parson, *'ex Necessitate*, a Licence may be allowable enough; but surely, surely, the other is the more regular and eligible Way'. (325)

The exchange satirises Adams's obsession with wedding banns versus licences, but the joke is not entirely on him. He understands the drummer/pedlar's common/natural law marriage to be based on an act of sexual consummation that is, *ex necessitate*, its own kind of marriage 'Licence'. At this moment Adams reveals himself to be generally less than strict about proper ceremony. It would seem, then, that his insistence on banns in Joseph and Fanny's case is not just a hobby-horse (the obsessive relation between parsons and marriage protocols will be taken further by Goldsmith) or a matter of upholding marriage's full solemnity. Rather, for a poor country curate like Adams, the calling of banns has a social and political charge as an act of clerical autonomy.

Adams's determination that Fanny and Joseph celebrate a public wedding is expressed most forthrightly when he refuses to obey Lady Booby's order for him not to continue with their banns (so as to prevent the wedding from proceeding). In the confrontation that follows, Adams's passive obedience founders:

> 'I desire you will publish [the banns] no more without my Orders.' 'Madam', cries *Adams*, 'if any one puts in sufficient Caution, and assigns a proper Reason against them, I am willing to surcease'. – 'I tell you a Reason', says she, 'he is a Vagabond, and he shall not settle here, and bring a Nest of Beggars into the Parish . . .' 'Madam', answered *Adams*, 'with the utmost Submission to your Ladyship, I have been informed by Lawyer

Scout, that any Person who serves a Year, gains a Settlement in the Parish where he serves'. – 'Lawyer *Scout*', replied the Lady, 'is an impudent Coxcomb; I will have no Lawyer *Scout* interfere with me. I repeat to you again, ... I desire you will proceed no farther'. (282–3)

The exchange initially turns around details of canon law as these were widely available in texts like Joseph Shaw's *The Parish Law* (1733), which helped local lawyers like Scout to resist oligarchical influence, at least to some extent. But Adams opens the discussion up to broader moral and political considerations of the kind that will be recapitulated in the Marriage Act debates:

> 'Madam', returned *Adams*, 'I would obey your Ladyship in every thing that is lawful; but surely the Parties being poor is no Reason against their marrying. G—d forbid there should be any such Law. The Poor have little Share enough of this World already; it would be barbarous indeed to deny them the common Privileges, and innocent Enjoyments which Nature indulges to the animal Creation'. 'Since you understand yourself no better', cries the Lady, 'nor the Respect due from such as you to a Woman of my Distinction, than to affront my Ears by such loose Discourse, I shall mention but one short Word; It is my Orders to you, that you publish these Banns no more; and if you dare, I will recommend it to your Master, the Doctor, to discard you from his Service. (283)

Adams's retort – 'Surely the Parties being poor is no Reason against their marrying' – might seem to be a succinct articulation of Patriot populism but it was also in fact accepted ecclesiastical opinion. For instance, the period's most widely used advice book for country clergy, *The Clergyman's Vade-Mecum*, probably written by the nonjuror John Johnson, but published anonymously, stated the argument like this in its fifth edition of 1723: 'Poverty is no more an Impediment of Marriage, than Riches, and the Kingdom can no more subsist without the Poor, than without the Rich.'[41]

At this point, Lady Booby flatly orders Adams to stop publishing the banns and Adams just as flatly refuses. Here the tensions implicit in the parson-squire relation become explicit and Adams's answer to Lady Booby's threat to report his insubordination to his 'Master, the Doctor', dissolves their complementary relation into 'Civil War':

> I know not what your Ladyship means by the terms *Master* and *Service*. I am in the Service of a Master who will never discard me for doing my Duty: And if the Doctor (for indeed I have never been able to pay for a Licence) thinks proper to turn me from my Cure, G— will provide me, I hope, another. (283)

In disobeying Lady Booby, Adams makes clear that his final responsibility is to his ultimate 'Master', God, and to the divinity that He grants the church, against whom, of course, Lady Booby lacks all authority. It is as if he channels Thomas Ken – or, at any rate, Ken as Dryden presented him: '[The] Prince, tho' great in Arms, the Priest withstood' (323).

Adams's assertion of ecclesiastical autonomy is all the braver because, as he concedes, he does not in fact possess a license to preach, and thus technically has no right to inhabit his office. Actually, against himself, Adams would appear to be over punctilious here. The question of clerical licences had long been a point of contention in the Established Church: licences distinguished Anglican priests from Presbyterian ministers (who needed no licence to practice), yet the requirement had subsided into neglect. *The Clergyman's Vade-Mecum* makes clear that 'so gentle is the present Government in the Church, that even Deacons are, by connivance, generally allow'd to preach without license.'[42] The soft irony, then, that attends Adams's admission that he has no licence draws attention to the politics of this question: as a stickler for Church protocols in the High Church mode he pretends that licences carry more weight than they in fact do, yet as a Patriot populist he is nonetheless willing to perform his duties without a formal licence, operating simply on the basis of support from 'the Cure of whose souls' are 'committed to him', as *The Clergyman's Vade-Mecum* puts it in terms that echo Dryden (54).

Because of Lady Booby's antagonism, Joseph and Fanny are unable to marry in their own (and Adams's) parish. Instead they are married in Mr Booby and Pamela's neighbouring parish church after the curate there agrees 'very kindly [to] exchange . . . Duty' with Adams (342). However, the marriage takes place only after a further delay. After revealing himself to be Joseph's father, Mr Wilson insists that Joseph receive not only his own approval but also that of his wife, Joseph's mother, which Adams whole-heartedly endorses, seeing 'by these means . . . an Opportunity of fulfilling the Church Forms, and marrying his Parishioners without a Licence . . . for such Ceremonies were Matters of no small moment with him' (340). So much so that at Adams's insistence the neighbouring curate rides 'twenty Miles to the Lady *Booby*'s Parish' with the 'particular . . . charge not to omit publishing the banns, being the Third and last Time' (342).

These formalities completed, the wedding at last goes ahead at the 'Squire's Parish Church' (342). The ceremony itself is less elaborately described than Pamela's, and that is because Pamela's subjectivity – her first-person response to the liturgy – lies at the heart of Richardson's novel whereas Joseph and Fanny's thoughts and feelings – religious or otherwise – are of relatively little account. Fielding's emphasis, rather, is on the public nature of the ceremony, its proper and smooth performance (and it runs so smoothly it can be described in a single subordinate clause) along with the modesty of the couple's dress and comportment. Most of all, however, the marriage service provides an opportunity to establish once again Adams's independence from secular authority by virtue of his office:

> At length the happy Day arrived, which was to put *Joseph* in the possession of all his Wishes. He arose and drest himself in a neat, but plain Suit of Mr. *Booby's*, which exactly fitted him; for he refused all Finery; as did *Fanny* likewise, who could be prevailed on by *Pamela* to attire herself in nothing richer than a white Dimity Night-Gown. Her Shift indeed, which *Pamela* presented her, was of the finest Kind, and had an Edging of Lace round the Bosom; she likewise equipped her with a Pair of fine white Thread Stockings, which were all she would accept; for she wore one of her own short round-ear'd Caps, and over it a little Straw Hat, lined with Cherry-coloured Silk, and tied with a Cherry-coloured Ribbon. In this Dress she came forth from her Chamber, blushing, and breathing Sweets; and was by *Joseph*, whose Eyes sparkled Fire, led to Church, the whole Family attending, where Mr. *Adams* performed the Ceremony; at which nothing was so remarkable, as the extraordinary and unaffected Modesty of *Fanny*, unless the true Christian Piety of *Adams*, who publickly rebuked Mr. *Booby* and *Pamela* for laughing in so sacred a Place, and so solemn an Occasion. Our Parson would have done no less to the highest Prince on Earth: For, tho' he paid all Submission and Deference to his Superiors in other Matters, where the least Spice of Religion intervened, he immediately lost all Respect of Persons. It was his Maxim, That he was a Servant of the Highest, and could not, without departing from his Duty, give up the least Article of his Honour, or of his Cause, to the greatest earthly Potentate. Indeed he always asserted, that Mr. *Adams* at church with his Surplice on, and Mr. *Adams* without that Ornament, in any other place, were two very different Persons. (342)

The passage certainly contains elements of parody; it is hard not to read the description of Fanny's dress, as supplied by Pamela, except as wryly mocking Richardson's obsession with his heroine's clothing. The hint of eroticism it borrows from Richardson (Fanny's blushing and 'breathing sweets', Joseph's eyes 'sparkling fire') is also parodic – though not only that, since here Fielding has indeed managed to reconcile the real, the carnal and the spiritual. The passage's primary force, however, is to assert most plainly what lies at the novel's centre: Parson Adams and his 'true Christian Piety'.

Here Adams's sacerdotal and his worldly selves are figured as two bodies: different 'persons' in one material form. That doubleness emphatically does not represent an Erastian theo-politics of church and state of the kind that Warburton theorised, whereby the church supplements the state upon which it depends. Rather it harks back to the older tradition of Anglican Protestant nationhood of the kind envisaged by Richard Hooker, for which church and state are two aspects of a single social constitution. In this regard, the novel's ending in a provincial wedding – its marriage plot – works not merely as a completion of form or plot, but also as an ideological closure just because Adams's authority is uncontestably established in the church, presiding over a wedding service.

Indeed, it is hard not to notice that *Joseph Andrews*'s marriage plot (more than *Pamela*'s) re-enacts Richardson's injunction to 'good clergymen' in *Pamela*'s coda to incur the 'displeasure' of their 'proud patrons'. Adams's insistence on his own spiritual authority is quixotic in an actual Erastian state, or on a smaller scale in a parish owned by the Boobys. But it is not just quixotic: it is also utopian in a Patriot sense. Adams's rejection of the Booby order of things – his defiance of Lady Booby and his silencing of Mr Booby and Pamela's laughter in the context of a rural parish wedding that is not to be theatricalised – points to the idea of a polity in which the English social order is unified by virtue of its acceptance of an authority who transcends interest, protects liberty and combines the religious-moral authority of the church with the power of the state in a fusion that dissolves their differences.

Yet, as noted earlier, the figure of the good squire or the Patriot King barely appears in *Joseph Andrews*. He is glimpsed, perhaps, in the character of Adams's first patron, Sir Oliver Hearty, and again at the novel's close in the figure of the reformed Mr Booby, who shelters Joseph and Fanny from his aunt's best efforts to ruin them by falsely prosecuting them under the Black Acts.[43] The younger Booby hosts Joseph, Fanny and their families at his country 'House' in the custom, we are told, 'of the old *English* Hospitality ... still preserved in some very Few Families in the remote Parts of *England*' (341). After the ceremony and at the novel's end, Booby gifts Fanny £2,000 and offers Adams 'a Living of one hundred and thirty Pounds a Year' (344). Adams refuses at first, not wanting to neglect his old parishioners, but then in what is perhaps a moment of less than soft irony, he decides to 'keep a Curate' while remaining in his original parish (344). That is, to become a pluralist, no less. Nonetheless Booby's largesse foreshadows the pivotal role played by benevolent squires and worthy country gentlemen, alongside good parsons, in marriage plot novels of the 1750s and 1760s.

A final word needs to be said about the formal contours of Fielding's Patriot marriage plot and, in particular, its closure in a parish wedding.

How are we to understand the politics of restoring an old marriage plot convention that Richardson had eschewed? On one hand, the answer would seem simple enough: Joseph and Fanny's wedding magically reconciles the community, overcoming civic discord through religious ritual. To be sure, Fanny and Joseph's wedding engages what might broadly be termed a populist little Englandism. It obeys proper ceremony and is officiated by a Tory parson who is loved by parishioners in a rural parish imagined as quite other to the spaces native to the Whig oligarchy or indeed to metropolitan commercial and clandestine cultures. Yet, like Pamela and Mr B.'s (private) ceremony, Joseph and Fanny's wedding must occur outside their native parish so to avoid the full force and hostility of (in this case, Lady Booby's) oligarchical power. Theirs is a displaced country parish wedding in which the parson, the couple and their respective families stand in for an absent parochial community. This act of substitution is made most obvious when, after the ceremony, the wedding party return to Mr Booby's house:

> *Joseph* led his blooming bride back to Mr. *Booby*'s (for the Distance was so very little that they did not think it proper to use a Coach) the whole Company attended them likewise on foot; and now a most magnificent Entertainment was provided, at which Parson *Adams* demonstrated an Appetite surprizing, as well as surpassing every one present. (343)

The passage is rendered as if Fanny and Joseph are attended by a crowd of well-wishing locals in the manner of their earlier parish homecoming (or of Sir Charles Grandison's public wedding, although that event presents a rather different picture of parish relations). Yet 'the whole Company' that attends them is made up, exactly, of Mr Booby, Pamela, Mr and Mrs Wilson and Adams himself. Their quasi-parish wedding followed by its attendant feasting and 'Merriment' (343) is a fit climax for a text that resists the state-endorsed resacralisation embraced by Richardson in the name of a populist rural Anglicanism, centred on Adams and presented as the essence of Englishness. Yet, because of the text's irony, the parish is presented less a political or governmental instrument than an ideological one: as if Country-Patriot politics were once again (although in another mode than Richardson's) moving out of the world of statecraft into that of fiction and the imagination.

In these terms, Joseph and Fanny's wedding also foregrounds the Patriot utopianism and nostalgia that is threaded through the novel, by neatly sealing its plot. In applying a closure drawn from romance and classical comedy to a socially engaged and mimetic text, the 'comic epic in prose' concedes the fictionality of its theo-politics and legitimates its own dis-placement from practical politics into the ideological. That is why its irony costs so little, and why Richardson's *Pamela* never makes such a concession, since its heroine's virtue, attached to Mr B.'s reformation and Mr Williams's rise in social status, earnestly solicits readerly emulation. We can say, then, that the modern English marriage plot establishes its conditions of possibility, along with its forms and meanings, exactly where Richardson and Fielding intersect: that is, where English theo-politics produces a Christian literature committed to emulative, missionary fic-tions on one side, and on the other a literature committed to the provincial parish-based imaginary of nostalgic English nationalism.

Shebbeare's *The Marriage Act*

In different ways, Richardson's and Fielding's novels of the 1740s played a role in the Marriage Act debate of the 1750s and beyond. Richardson, as we know, lined up behind Hardwicke's legislation, condoning its require-ments for parental consent in the marriages of minors and privately claiming to have influenced its passage. This attitude was shared by one strain of his literary influence too, which is discussed in the next chapter. Fielding, however, remained silent about the Marriage Act, despite his role as a Whig-appointed magistrate and his praise of Hardwicke, to whom he had dedicated his 1751 pamphlet *An Enquiry into the Causes of the Late Increase of Robbers*. However, even if his response to the Marriage Act was muted, Fielding's influence on its literary reception was significant. The period's two most prominent anti-Marriage Act novels – John Shebbeare's *The Marriage Act* (1754) and Oliver Goldsmith's *The Vicar of Wakefield* (1766) – condemned the Marriage Act in fictional forms that depended on him.

Joseph Andrews, in particular, served as a template for literary contribu-tions to the Marriage Act debate because it spoke to that popular-Patriot vein of opposition that objected to the Marriage Act's effects on plebeian welfare. In the context of anti-Marriage Act pamphlet literature too, concerns that the Marriage Act imposed barriers to marriage and thereby created new divisions between the rich and poor and made young women vulnerable to seduction gave rise to a cast of characters that owed a great deal to fiction, and in particular to Fielding.[44] Four social types figured prominently there: one, the libertine squire without checks to his power; two, the seduced and abandoned young woman; three, 'the subaltern cleric' and/or good vicar; and four, the good squire who enters into a more or less equal partnership with the vicar. All these types, in turn, found their way into Shebbeare and Goldsmith's novels, for which the vicar is, nonetheless, once more the primary point of focus.

For Patriot writing of the period the figure of the good squire was near ubiquitous. In Fielding's case, he was fully realised in the character of Squire Allworthy in *Tom Jones* (1749) and then drawn in different terms by Richardson in *Sir Charles Grandison*. One associated strain of moral fiction especially depended upon him: the bluestocking marriage plot, as I call it, spearheaded by Henry Fielding's sister, Sarah Fielding, and further developed by bluestocking writers like Sarah Scott in the 1760s. The heroes of *The Adventures of David Simple* (1744) and *The History of Sir George Ellison* (1766) are men of feeling and, in the case of George Ellison, a Christian gentleman (modelled after Grandison) who engages in benevolent and charitable works in the context of the landed estate and the parish. These novels blend Richardson's Anglican moralism with Fielding's emphasis on sociable charity within a commitment to piety and social reform. Crucially, they do not ironise their protagonists. Vicars are assigned minor character status and, while marriage provides closure, proper ceremony as such is not a matter of concern. Like the female-authored literary marriage plots discussed in the next chapter, bluestocking marriage plots serve as an instructive contrast to the (male-authored) Patriot plots of the anti-Marriage Act movement. For them, the difference is quite simple: good squires rather than vicars rightly preside over the marriage plot.

Fielding's vicar-centred marriage plot, however, found new political traction in the 1750s. Its irony, its rural estate and parish-based English setting, its fictionalisation of the good parson, its appeal to popular Protestant traditions of liberty and its comic-epic closure all fuelled the case against the Marriage Act and ongoing attempts to have it repealed. As we know, the Marriage Act was part of a Court Whig reform programme which aimed to turn the body politic into an administered population, and which controversially did not appeal to the various ideologies that attached to English ethnicity or to English traditions of faith or place. In this context, Fielding's conspicuously English rural settings and self-reflexive gentlemanly wit − not to say his irony − could be weaponised. So when Shebbeare, a Tory and a fervent admirer of Bolingbroke, chose to write a fictional polemic against the Marriage Act, he did so in homage to Fielding, referring to him as 'an Author whom we adore'.[45] Similarly, when Goldsmith turned to the novel form for the first time almost a decade later, he wrote a vicar-centred narrative which William Hazlitt thought an 'almost entire plagiarism' of *Joseph Andrews*.[46]

It hardly need be said that Goldsmith and Shebbeare occupy different places in the novel's history. Goldsmith is an acknowledged innovator who is widely understood to have crafted a beguiling fictional style lying somewhere between Fielding's irony and Richardson's Christian moralism.[47] Shebbeare, by contrast, is usually regarded as a Tory ideologue who used the novel form as a propaganda tool in two nearly forgotten works, *The Marriage Act* and *Lydia, or Filial Piety* (1755).[48] We owe this picture in part to Richardson, who in correspondence with Lady Bradshaigh affirmed her description of Shebbeare as a 'low Imitator of all Novel Writers'.[49] That may be true enough, but it obscures an important insight, namely that authors like Goldsmith and Shebbeare wrote their marriage plot novels as contributions to a political debate. Both men were Tories with Patriot leanings; both had written polemical journalism before turning to fiction; both produced satirical letter collections on British customs in the personae of learned foreign observers (a Mandarin Chinese philosopher in Goldsmith's case, and an Italian Jesuit priest in Shebbeare's) and both deployed Fielding's satire and soft irony in parson-focussed marriage plots that explicitly objected to the Marriage Act.

Shebbeare in particular is an instructive figure in the marriage plot's lineage just because his novel was so entangled in the public policy and literary debates of the day. *The Marriage Act* went into three editions in the decade or so following Hardwicke's Marriage Act (the first reissue of 1755 was retitled *Matrimony, a Novel* to avoid libel charges and the final edition, which appeared in 1766 shortly after the first attempt to repeal the Marriage Act in 1765, was published in the same year as *The Vicar of Wakefield*).[50] The novel played an important role in the Marriage Act's literary uptake and afterlife – so much so that Garrick saw fit to advertise it as a source for his Drury Lane comedy hit *The Clandestine Marriage*, also produced in 1766. Shebbeare also traded off the novel's notoriety, using 'By the Author of *The Marriage Act*' as his literary signature as late as 1763. His own reputation remained forever associated with the text.

The Marriage Act, however, was not only a topical novelty. At the very least, its literary significance is twofold: first it anticipates the repeal debates of the coming decades and in doing so attaches a new politics of liberty to the marriage plot; and second its inventive use of the vicar-squire trope provides an otherwise missing link in the Patriot marriage plot's formal development. The novel closes not with a wedding but by revealing the (fictional) conditions of its own production. Harkening back to Fielding and Gay's self-reflexive meta-theatre, it accounts for an important transformation of the good parson trope as it morphed from Parson Adams to

Dr Primrose, that is, from Fielding's third-person parish-focussed irony to *The Vicar of Wakefield*'s more elusive first-person mode.

The Marriage Act was first and foremost an act of literary-political provocation. Its full title read as a running sheet of complaint against the Marriage Act as recently aired in parliamentary debate: *The Marriage Act. A Novel. In which the Ruin of Female Honour, the Contempt of the Clergy, the Destruction of the Private and Public Liberty, with Other Fatal Consequences, Are Considered in a Series of Interesting Adventures.* Because unlicensed publications on the proceedings of Parliament were illegal, Shebbeare was immediately arrested. (He was soon afterwards released only to remain a prominent enemy of the Whig ministry, which would pillory him for libel in 1758.) The novel's dedication to the Duke of Bedford was another inflammatory gesture, even as it signalled the complexity of Tory-Patriot alliances in the period's fluid factional politics. Bedford, a Whig grandee recently thrown out of the Pelham ministry, had taken up with disaffiliated Whigs Henry Fox and Robert Nugent (an Irish peer, soon to become Goldsmith's patron), and with them assumed parliamentary leadership of the anti-Marriage Act cause. At any rate, that dedication meant there could be no ambiguity about Shebbeare's intention.

As J. C. D. Clark has pointed out, the parliamentary debate of the Marriage Act was an important moment in English political history because it generated a new kind of oppositional alliance.[51] Bedford, Fox and Nugent seized upon the marriage question as a means of arousing popular opinion against the ministry in the broader public sphere. Bedford's role, in particular, was prescient. He recognised that freedom of marriage, especially for minors, was an issue that could energise broad-based opposition to the Court Whigs by joining patrician values to plebeian welfare. In the agitation against the 1753 bill, he was instrumental in yoking it to the already highly unpopular Jewish Naturalisation Act so as to shore up the Tory vote for the opposition. With his backing, the anti-ministerial journal *The Protestor* edited by James Ralph (*The Champion*'s former editor alongside Fielding) launched a virulent public campaign to discredit both bills as measures that undermined the national interest by pandering to foreigners and religious minorities at the expense of English popular liberties.[52] (Of course the Marriage Act made exceptions for Jews and Quakers, both of whom, not coincidentally, are portrayed negatively in Shebbeare's novel.) By joining accusations of Whig venality to entrenched High Church Tory prejudice, especially against Jews, Bedford and the Patriot bloc fanned public hostility against both bills and paved the way for oppositional movements to come.

After the Marriage Act was passed, the proto-nationalist opposition it generated was kept alive by efforts to repeal the Marriage Act across the next three decades (the first repeal initiative, sponsored by Wilkesite radicals in 1765, was followed by Charles James Fox's further campaigns on behalf of a softer, Whig-radical alliance in 1772 and 1781 against the new Tory ministry). In each instance, the Marriage Act's curtailment of the simple right to marry served to rally anti-government coalitions. The freedom to marry was figured as a natural right and as a fundamental English entitlement – for the poor, for women and for minors.[53] The ongoing anti-Marriage Act movement, therefore, was not just opposi-tional. It helped to create new political connections and to politicise sectors of the unfranchised population.

Shebbeare's novel, then, belongs to the early Patriot roots of a growing movement of English radicalism and political opposition. When he aligned himself with the anti-Marriage Act cause in 1754, it was a new and rather fluid discursive field, especially for fiction. It is reasonable to suppose that he wrote *The Marriage Act* to agitate against the Marriage Act's injustices while also leveraging a 'polite' reading audience for the Patriot cause. Such purposes help to explain the novel's paratactic plot, which Lady Bradshaigh described as 'the poorest, low, piece of nonsensical medley that ever was penn'd'.[54] The main plot has a number of inset narratives and satirical sketches which modulate from satire to sentiment (sometimes justifying Lady Bradshaigh's harsh criticism) and, despite its homage to Fielding, it does not end in marriage at all.

The first volume's main plot is straightforward enough. The nouveau riche Mr Barter intends to improve his family's social standing by marrying off his two daughters, Mary and Eliza. His ambition is aided by the new Marriage Act's parental consent clauses, which allow him to control his daughters' choices until they are twenty-one. Mary, who has been raised in fashionable city circles, consents to her parents' proposed match with the impoverished Lord Sapplin so as to acquire a title. Eliza, raised in the family of a virtuous country clergyman, Mr Thoroughgood, and who has since formed an innocent attachment to her father's shop boy, William Worthy, resists her father's demands (Garrick modelled the romance between Fanny and Lovewell in *The Clandestine Marriage* on this part of Shebbeare's plot). When Eliza flees to the country and her childhood friends, she is soon reunited with Worthy, now titled and enriched by his uncle's fortune. Mr Barter's consent to their match is thence easily gained and they are united in a wedding ceremony performed by Thoroughgood. Meanwhile, Mary's marriage ends in divorce after her husband neglects her. She escapes to France with her hairdresser before joining a convent – all of this told with a satirical relish that counter-balances the high tone of Eliza's narrative.

For all its imitation of Fielding, *The Marriage Act*'s first volume does not insist on proper ceremony, neither does it repeat Adams's assertion of clerical autonomy. Above all else, the novel supports heartfelt attachments, unimpeded by law, as the basis for marriage – or, as Roger Lund puts it, 'the laws of the heart must ever take precedence over the laws of the land.'[55] To pose Shebbeare's polemic in topical terms: love matches like Eliza's (as opposed to marriages of interest like Mary's) accord with Tory-Patriot liberty as sanctioned by God's natural law and as staunchly defended at the time by Tory divines like Henry Stebbing. (This understanding of natural law, of course, is rather different from the careful balancing of God's law and the state that characterises Sir Charles Grandison's embodiment of the principle.)

Because marriages are an expression of natural law which aligns British liberty and happiness with love and romance, weddings do not function merely as devices of closure for Shebbeare but proliferate in the course of the narrative. At the halfway mark, no fewer than four have occurred: those of the two Barter daughters as just described, and two more love matches between Mr Thoroughgood's children and those of a local squire, Sir Oliver Hearty (a character borrowed from *Joseph Andrews*). These latter alliances ground the novel's second volume as it focusses on relations between vicars and squires. The novel presents three vicars: the elderly Mr Thoroughgood, Eliza's mentor, who as his name suggests is cast in Parson Adams's mould; his son, George Thoroughgood junior, who has followed his father into the church; and an unrelated character, Parson Farley, who features in an inset narrative about clandestine marriage that illustrates both the hardships of clerical life and the Marriage Act's stric-tures against offending clergymen.

Farley is a poor country curate, struggling to support his wife and family on £30 a year. He and his wife – who 'love one another as well as a Lord and Lady' (1:209) – are £20 in debt with a fourth child on the way. His request for assistance from the rector, a wealthy London-based pluralist who is 'greatly esteemed by the Ministry' (1:201) and who 'wrote in Defence of the *Jews*-Act before it was repealed, and against it since' (1:201), has been flatly refused. So Farley performs a clandestine wedding for Captain Stem and Miss Biddy Lloyd in exchange for fifty guineas, unaware that Stem has seduced Biddy into the marriage on false pretences. When the marriage's illegality is discovered, it is Farley, not Stem, who is charged under the

Marriage Act (1:228). Pleading guilty, he delivers a rousing diatribe against the Marriage Act:

> [This law] has caused the Clergy of *Great-Britain* to be considered of an inferior Race to other Men of this Island, a set of Slaves and not free Men, held by a different kind of Laws, and excluded from an equal Privilege and Right of Liberty with other *Britons*. (1:264)

Here the subaltern cleric speaks. And he does so to lay claim to the rights of ordinary Britons while offering an indictment of the law and the society that treats him as a 'Slave'. We have come a long way from Parson Adams's passive acceptance of mistreatment here, or even from his use of church forms to resist secular authority. Indeed, Farley's rhetoric anticipates the later radical and Foxite critiques of the Marriage Act that figured it precisely as a form of slavery for minors. Farley, like John Wilkinson of Savoy Chapel fame, is transported for his crime. Unlike Wilkinson, however, he is saved by the intervention of a sympathetic Shrewsbury judge who later privately provides funds to establish him in America. There he lived 'loving and beloved, in Happiness and Ease, only sometimes sighing for their native Land which [he] still loves, and laments, as near the Hour of expiring Liberty' (1:277).

While Farley's eventual good fortune in the colonies offers a horizon of hope for England's poor and disenfranchised, the two Thoroughgood vicars model social balance and harmony, and in particular smooth relations between the gentry and the vicarate in the context of another kind of Patriot idyll: the liberty-loving English country parish and estate. Thoroughgood senior is a version of the good parson, a genteel churchman somewhat like Parson Adams but more affluent.[56] His 'happy situation' (1:278) is described as follows:

> In this State passed away the happy Days in the Family of Mr *Thoroughgood*, blessed not only in the Gifts of Fortune but in being beloved by all the People of his Parish. He was become already their common Parent and Physician, he smoothed the rugged Path of Sickness by the soothing Eloquence of Hope for better Hours and happier States hereafter. (1:284)

This rhetoric is familiar. Thoroughgood is more than a good man – he is a shining light of charity and love for his parishioners, a quasi-parent, physician and spiritual advisor. We can detect echoes of Dryden's good parson in this 'true Divine' whose spiritual aura underpins social harmony. 'Of so much Advantage is one good Man to those over whom he is placed; as the Sun gives Colours to all the Objects of the Earth, so does a true

Divine impart Happiness and Character to all those on whom he shines superior' (1:284). At the same time, the measure of Thoroughgood's 'Utility' (1:278) is Addisonian: he is valued not just for his benevolence but also for his ability to ally with Sir Oliver Hearty, the neighbouring squire. As a consequence, 'Peace dwelt amongst the Inhabitants of his Cure' (1:284).

Sir Oliver, however, is a rough and ready 'Baronet of an ancient Family' (1:285), unwilling to countenance a love match between his son Oliver junior and Thoroughgood's daughter Fanny, because they are not social equals. After much adversity – including a moment of weakness between the lovers that leads to Fanny's pregnancy and apparent disgrace – the young couple's love remains constant and Sir Oliver at last relents: 'Ods-heart, ods-heart, I could not have thought they loved one another so well; if I had, they should not have been parted so long: Desperate Love, desperate Love! God bless 'em, God bless 'em' (2:40). Even the old Tory squire gives way to natural law's force. And so a vicar-squire family compact is sealed by the marriage between Fanny and Sir Oliver junior – the vicar's daughter and the young squire – and is cause for collective celebration:

> [U]niversal Joy appeared on every Face, nothing was ever so happy before; they sat down to an elegant and cheerful Meal, and spent such an Evening, that I verily believe . . . in the most splendid Apartment of the Duke of —— House, they could not produce a Thousandth Part of the Soul-felt Felicity which this Company knew this Evening in a Country Parson's little Habitation. (2:40–1)

As he did in Sir William and Lady Eliza's marriage, Thoroughgood himself performs the wedding ceremony once parental consent is given, Sir Oliver declaring himself the world's 'happiest Parent' (2:43). The wedding dinner's conviviality turns out to be an opportunity for Fanny's brother, the younger Thoroughgood clergyman, to make (yet another) lengthy speech on the Marriage Act's injustices and the hardship it has caused the lovers and their families. His speech to Sir Oliver joins Patriot sentiment to ecclesiastical interest: 'Sir Oliver . . . I consider the bill as the most pernicious that has ever passed in any Country; not to say the most disgraceful that ever was enacted against those who are destined to the Office of Religion, held sacred till now, thro' the World' (2:46–7). This acknowledged, the wedding party goes on to toast the Duke of Bedford and the Bishop of W—— as heroic defenders of true love, British youth and matrimonial freedom.

Bedford's noble resistance to the Marriage Act is celebrated in the high Tory-Patriot rhetoric that was Shebbeare's trademark. He is '[t]he Protector of *British* Youth and Beauty' (2:52):

> [O]ne noble duke, who ... protested he would rather see his Daughter married to a Man of the meanest Birth and Fortune, than this Law be passed, to the Enslaving the Youth of *England*. This Name ought to be dear to every *British* virgin, the generous Defender of their free Choice, the Protector of their Virtues, the Vindicator of their Rights. (2:52)

This panegyric is one of several moments in the story that flirt with nuptial resolution before spilling into yet another anti-Marriage Act polemic. Nonetheless, it is hard not to notice that here *The Marriage Act* pre-empts the final scenes of Goldsmith's *The Vicar of Wakefield*, which will also involve a happy reversal triggering multiple weddings all performed by Primrose (Goldsmith's central vicar character) and sealing an alliance between vicar and squire, via ritual toasts and celebrations at a wedding dinner. If the two novels resemble one another – their good vicars strug-gling with adversity, their daughters endangered/seduced by the libertin-ism of the local squires, their eulogising of provincial English domestic virtue – that is because they both draw on the marriage debate's ideology and characterology.

About a third of the way through *The Marriage Act*'s second volume, the narrative moves forward a decade or so as if to imagine an unfolding horizon of anti-Marriage Act politics. Significantly, this future projection takes the form of a country house metanarrative. The three couples at the heart of the Worthy-Thoroughgood-Hearty alliance gather at Worthy Hall, Sir William Worthy's ancestral home, which he has greatly improved in the manner of Lord Cobham's Stowe, that symbolic oppositional country estate. Sir William's garden is graced by a Temple dedicated to *Honour*, housing 'Busts of Sir *Thomas More*, Epaminondas, and *Socrates*' (2:174) – all significant oppositional figures. And next to this temple stands another

> dedicated to conjugal Felicity, in which Sir *William* had caused to be painted in one Piece, the Pourtraits of himself and Wife, sacrificing at the Altar of Venus, *Hymen* being the Priest, the Loves in the Persons of their Children, holding the Offerings and smiling round, and *Venus* herself in the Skies, pointing to the Date of their nuptial Day, with great Expression of Pleasure. This Motto was beneath the Altar:
>
> > Felices ter, et amplius
> > Quos irrupta tenet copula: nec malis

Divulsus querimoniis
Suprema citius solvet Amor Die. (2:174–5)

As an inscription on a family portrait dedicated to happy marriage, this Horatian motto is rather puzzling. On one hand, it is in keeping with the general presentation of the Worthy family and estate as drenched in a Patriot affect. Over and again, the text binds married love to classical refinement and literary sentiment. Thus, in a celebration of his own conjugal bliss, Sir William – a man of feeling – composes an uxorious poem inspired by Eliza, now his wife of twelve years, entitled 'To the BEST of WOMEN' (2:178–9). Yet Sir William's judgement also seems be under question here since, in what appears to be an insider joke, the source of the quotation from Horace, to which Venus points from the portrait, is an Ode (1:13) that celebrates the blessings of married felicity only in light of the tortures of the sexual jealousy, infidelity and frustration it also harbours.

This literary twist, which suggests hubris or at the very least a limited understanding on Sir William's part, only gives rise to further uncertainty since (for non-contemporary readers at least) the Worthy family's elaborate allegorical portrait is strikingly similar to that of the Primrose family in *The Vicar of Wakefield*, which is treated ironically there. So here again, *The Marriage Act* anticipates Goldsmith's narrative, as it does somewhat indirectly when Thoroughgood junior reveals that, like Sir Worthy, he has turned his pen to the defence of marriage, preparing a pamphlet recording 'little histories' (2:299) of the 'grievous effects' (2:182) of the Marriage Act as it gives 'designing People the Power of ruining the open-hearted and honest' (2:180). His literary motivation is further explained in these terms:

> There is an Affair which has been lately discover'd, which shews how fatal this Act has proved to an innocent and virtuous Family; which single Instance is Reason enough for its Repeal. It is so very singular and poetic, that I have inquired into the Circumstances of the whole, and have put them together on purpose to present the Public with the Story; to which I have added two others, on purpose to shew how pernicious this Act of Parliament may prove to this declining Kingdom. (2:182)

Thoroughgood has turned his hand to fiction, not as a gentleman poet, but like Shebbeare himself (and Goldsmith), as an advocate for 'Repeal' presenting 'the Public with [a] story' that exposes the perniciousness of the Marriage Act. He goes on to read his account to the assembled company, first in the 'Temple sacred to conjugal Felicity' (2:183), which stands 'on a rock which overlook'd a River high, steep and craggy' (2:174), and then at vantage points in Sir Worthy's park and gardens, with the couples taking refreshments between the stories being told (2:232).

Three stories are recounted, each more than thirty pages long. The first tells of a legitimate marriage that is annulled so that legitimate heirs are defrauded (2:188–230). The second is a *Clarissa*-inspired elopement narrative, in which Hardwicke's legislation drives a modest young lady into the hands of a seducer who reduces her to whoredom and eventual death (2:233–76). The third, a story of a father's bigamous marriage to a maidservant that is senselessly upheld by the Marriage Act, is told in Sir William's grotto with its view of the Temples of Honour and Hymen (2:279–96). As each case unfolds, it is appropriated for the anti-Marriage Act cause. In this process a new kind of Patriot marriage narrative emerges, one that places marriage and literature (i.e. the liberty-loving Marriage Act repeal movement) at the centre of a Cobhamite vision of the country estate.

When Thoroughgood at last stops telling his stories, a moment of *literary* collaboration between vicar and squire enables closure. Sir Worthy suggests that Thoroughgood add to his narratives a history '[of] the preceding Parts of our Lives [which] might furnish out a Novel not undiverting and certainly useful; as by that means a great many Evils, naturally attending the Marriage-law, might be brought to View, which now lie unobserved by most People' (2:297). The result is precisely the novel we have just been reading. In a Fielding-esque self-reflexive moment, *The Marriage Act* lays bare its purposes and accounts for its own creation. Thoroughgood has narrated the text all along. It is now clear that he is the omniscient narrator of the frame narrative as well as the active reader of his own appended inset narratives. This means that a 'mere Country Parson' and a 'silly . . . Fellow' (2:188), as he calls himself, is Shebbeare's narratorial vehicle, not Sir William, the country gentleman poet (and squire), who is indeed ironised.

In a telling moment for the marriage plot's genealogy, Shebbeare's novel reveals the vicar character as its narrator so as to licence the paratactic plot structure required for the bad consequences of the Marriage Act to be documented in detail. With this gesture, *The Marriage Act* explicitly identifies Patriot literature with the rural parson and reveals marriage's full political significance for mid-century fiction. This double recognition will form the basis of Goldsmith's *The Vicar of Wakefield*.

The Vicar of Wakefield

Marriage in *The Vicar of Wakefield* is not simply a plot device or theme: it is an organising topic. The novel is narrated in the first person by a country vicar, Dr Charles Primrose, who, like Parson Adams and Sterne's Mr Shandy before him, is gripped by a particular obsession. Primrose's hobby-horse is clerical monogamy, a theological term of art associated with William Whiston. Of no particular importance in ecclesiastical or public debate, it denotes an Anglican clergyman's supposed duty to marry only once, even if his spouse has died. Since clerical monogamy is a hopeless cause, its narrative function is simply to mark Primrose (like Adams) as naïve and quixotic; it also teasingly connects Primrose to primitive Christianity since Whiston was a proponent of returning Anglicanism to Christianity's earliest practices.[57] Most of all, however, it self-reflexively frames marriage as a topos for the novel. In this spirit, and like Parson Adams and Sir Charles Grandison, Primrose is also an advocate of what D. A. Miller has called 'compulsory conjugality', in which marriage is a religious and social obligation.[58]

Less obscure or ironical than the 'Whistonean controversy' (61) are the novel's references to the contemporary Marriage Act debate.[59] They are primarily topical but they also serve a literary-formal function. *The Vicar of Wakefield*'s marriage plot draws on two of the Marriage Act opposition's fundamental propositions: first, that the Marriage Act violated marriage's status as a contract sanctified by natural/divine law; and, second, that it put impediments in the way of class mobility. The latter was an argument that Goldsmith had already made in his contributions to the debate in *The Citizen of the World* (1760–1), where he conveyed a bleak picture of English society under the control of corrupt, deistical Whig oligarchs in cahoots with monied urbanites determined to maintain their privilege at whatever cost: 'The laws of this country are finely calculated to promote all commerce ... Marriages are the only commerce that meet with none.'[60] It turns out too that significant continuities underpin the Whistonean and anti-Hardwicke positions: they each share a belief in marriage as an autonomous religious and social contract rather than as a tool of the state. So *The Vicar of Wakefield*'s topical interest in marriage brought together arcane and contemporary polemic.

The novel was written around 1761 – seven years after the Marriage Act became law – but not published until 1766, shortly after the first repeal bill had been defeated and during the period of Goldsmith's own close connection with Robert Nugent, who led parliamentary coalitions against the Marriage Act.[61] *The Vicar of Wakefield* was the last important novel to engage with the marriage debate directly, notwithstanding ongoing efforts to repeal the Marriage Act. In the theatre, by contrast, topical comedies fuelled by anti-Marriage Act polemic remained popular until the century's end.[62] Goldsmith's own intervention in the theatre proved instrumental to yet another recalibration of marriage themes in the wake of Richardson's influence. In challenging sentimentalism's dominance on the popular stage (i.e. the 'fashion' for 'weeping comedy', as he termed it), his essay on 'laughing comedy' proposed a revival of the Aristotelian comic protocols proper to 'low life and middle life'.[63] *She Stoops to Conquer* (1773) – which was initially rejected by Garrick at Drury Lane as too controversial a rejection of sentimentalism – exemplified 'laughter' precisely by reintroducing 'low' themes – including misdirection, deception and disguise – to the comic marriage plot. But it did not revive mock marriage itself, which, however, serves as the key to *The Vicar of Wakefield*'s marriage plot.

Before approaching that plot, it is important to remind ourselves that *The Vicar of Wakefield*'s reception history is part of its literary interest and, indeed, aura. The novel's connection to Fielding was recognised early on, most notably by Hazlitt. During the nineteenth century, however, it was admired across Europe for other reasons, namely, its stylistic virtuosity. Henry James, for instance, called it 'a miracle of style' and situated it at the 'infancy of art' (by which he meant the art of the novel), adding that it was a text which criticism could barely touch because its characters lacked ethical substance.[64] Goethe (who came to Goldsmith via Johann Gottfried Herder) commended its 'high, benevolent irony' and remarked that it was, unlike Sterne's fictions, 'all form'.[65] These views have some echoes in recent academic criticism. Following James, Marshall Brown, for instance, argues that the novel marks the moment of the genre's aestheticisation.[66] More often, modern critics have regarded it as a bridge between the eighteenth-century and nineteenth-century English novel: Ronald Paulson calls Dr Primrose a 'halfway point' between Fielding's Parson Adams and Austen's Mr Bennet.[67] These lines of thought will be taken up in what follows.

For all that, *The Vicar of Wakefield* has lost status over the past century or so because the contemporary academy has found it hard to reach consensus on its meaning and tone. Is the novel religious or not?[68] Is it a retelling of the biblical Job story (or perhaps even an *imitatio Christi*)?[69] Does it ironise Dr Primrose?[70] Does it too critique sentimentalism? How much faith does it evince in literary authorship in the face of the market and the state?[71]

Might its attack on an unjust social order be considered 'an Irishman's response to English life'?[72] While these questions and more must shape any approach to the novel, my task is less to adjudicate them or to resolve *The Vicar of Wakefield*'s many riddles than to make a contribution to understanding its place in literary history. Goldsmith's novel was the last and most influential of the era's oppositional-Patriot marriage plots. It was central to the novel's development in the second half of the eighteenth century and, in the light of its reception, played a key role in aestheticising both the novel form and the conventions of proper ceremony.

A story about a vicar and a squire (in this case, two squires) as mediated by two marriageable young women (in this case, the vicar's own daughters), *The Vicar of Wakefield* displays all the features of the Patriot marriage plot. When the Primrose family lose their fortune because of what looks like an investment failure, Dr Primrose moves to the parish of Wakefield, where he takes a living as a clerical subaltern à la Parson Adams. Olivia, his elder daughter, is pursued by the young squire, Mr Thornhill, and the family as a whole is befriended by Mr Burchell, a poor man towards whom Dr Primrose acts charitably and who forms an attachment to the vicar's younger daughter, Sophia. Mr Thornhill turns out to be a freethinker and a libertine, a more callous version of Richardson's Mr B. before his reformation, who controls an array of libertine techniques, including mock marriage. He seduces Olivia, whom he then treats with cruel contempt, as he does her family.

The formal characteristics of Patriot fiction are present here too. Like Shebbeare's *The Marriage Act*, Goldsmith's story is not just about a vicar but narrated by one. Its first-person narrative is written from an extra-diegetical position (i.e. at some undefined time and place after the story has come to an end) by Dr Primrose, who is also in a technical sense its hero. And like Parson Adams in *Joseph Andrews*, Primrose is treated with soft irony, even if it is a first-person rather than a third-person narrative that is being ironised, which makes its irony more subtle and stylised than Fielding's. Like *Joseph Andrews* too, the irony means that, despite its depiction of Primrose's courage, resignation and charity, the novel does not invite emulation. It has no Richardsonian missionary drive, even as it affirms at least some of its hero's beliefs and actions.

Goldsmith's allegiance to Tory-Patriot politics is perhaps most consistently expressed in the novel's representation of Primrose's relation to his family. Indeed, Primrose tells a story about his family rather than about himself, a family consisting of his wife, Deborah; his two adult sons, George and Moses; his two daughters, Olivia and

Sophia; and two infant boys, Dick and Bill. The story, as we've begun to see, is one of a series of devastating mishaps and blows. At the novel's beginning he is a rich churchman with his own capital; at his lowest ebb, just before its end (when his fortune is suddenly and all but magically restored), he is in prison, his son has been sentenced to death and Olivia (whom he believes dead) has been seduced and abandoned. His rapid fall is in part his own responsibility. His family has been swept into the consumerism and snobbishness of Hanoverian England as seen from the Country perspective, and which now reaches much further socially and geographically than it did in Richardson, Fielding or Shebbeare, where it was still restricted to London.[73] In particular, the Primroses, and especially the women of the family, have aspirations to polite taste that reach above their station in a social order determined as much by money as by rank or filial status. This insistence on a proper correspondence between station and taste is a sign of the novel's nostalgic Toryism, since it relies upon a rigid social hierarchy to determine fit participation in the cultural sphere.

The Primrose family has also been absorbed into a new 'sentimental' affective economy. Dr Primrose cries on occasions when no character in Richardson or Fielding would. But he does not go so far as his friend Mr Burchell once did. In his younger days, Burchell embraced the whole sentimental ethos, so that '[t]he slightest distress, whether real or fictitious, touched him to the quick, and his soul laboured under a sickly sensibility of the miseries of others' (19). This susceptibility led him to give away his fortune, and then when he was broke, to promise charity rather than actually to perform it, just like the 'good-natur'd Man' in *Joseph Andrews* (175). Burchell is a victim of the destruction that sentimentalism wreaks on true Christian charity as Goldsmith (and Dr Primrose) sees it. This too is, loosely, a Tory point of view taken up directly in Goldsmith's later attack on sentimental theatre.

Dr Primrose rules his family as a 'little republic' (22), albeit one regulated by the 'mechanical forms of good breeding' or 'proper cere-mony' (22), as he describes the Primrose household's body politic. This ambiguous state of affairs exposes him to uxuriousness as it too is assessed by Tory paternalism, which in turn leads to some of his lapses.[74] For instance, he gives way to his wife and daughters when they wish to ride in a coach rather than walk to church despite making themselves ridiculous (23–4), or when they commission a pompous and incoherent family portrait, reminiscent of the one displayed in the Worthy estate's Temple of Hymen (70).

But Primrose's fall is also providential in the sense that it cannot simply be accounted for by his incompetence. This mix of sheer providentialism and moral consequentialism in the Primrose family's fate establishes the novel's rather ambiguous religious status. On one side, God (or Fate) is testing Primrose; on the other, his incompetence has consequences that are rationally narrated. This ambiguity also holds for its sudden and surprising happy ending, which is realised in a double wedding ceremony and the confirmation of another marriage, and is positioned between the contingently miraculous and the logic of just desert. It is partly a result of an earlier act of Christian – not sentimental – charity by Dr Primrose and partly an undeserved piece of good luck.

Finally, and once again like Parsons Adams and Thoroughgood before him, the vicar is a spokesperson for Bolingbrokean values. A famous speech that he makes in chapter 19 (and which alludes to the Marriage Act as 'ordain[ing] that the rich shall only marry with the rich' [87]) is about as succinct an expression of that programme as one can find anywhere, although it is no doubt also influenced by John Brown's resuscitation of civic republicanism in *An Estimate of the Times* (1757).[75] (It does not particularly matter, I think, that this speech too is ironised in being addressed not to a social equal but to a servant passing himself off as a master.) At the same time, like *Joseph Andrews*, the novel moves past contemporary Patriot King ideology towards those older principles which form Bolingbroke's political roots. When Dr Primrose is arrested for debt on the say-so of the evil squire Mr Thornhill, his parishioners begin to riot against that action's injustice. But he asks them to disperse, and does so by appealing to old Tory doctrines of non-resistance and passive obedience:

> 'What! my friends', cried I, 'and is this the way you love me! Is this the manner you obey the instructions I have given you from the pulpit! Thus to fly in the face of justice, and bring down ruin on yourselves and me! Which is your ring-leader? Shew me the man that has seduced you. As sure as he lives he shall feel my resentment. Alas! My dear deluded flock, return back to the duty you owe to God, to your country, and to me.' (123–4)

Here religious duty enjoins political passivity. Here too Dr Primrose adopts a paternalist position like Parson Adams, but one that veers towards sheer authoritarianism. It is difficult, after all, to imagine Parson Adams threatening his flock with his 'resentment'. In the end, Primrose's appeal to a cosmic structure in which divine, social and national authority are fused persuades the crowd to cease their rebellious agitation; in a strange sentimental mood they then 'melt ... into tears' (124).

The Vicar of Wakefield presents readers with an extraordinary, if rather puzzling, dénouement. The narrative culminates in an irony-touched, nostalgia-soaked, vicar-officiated double wedding ceremony that Hazlitt felt borrowed too much from *Joseph Andrews*. Certainly Goldsmith reinstates Fielding's mode of comic-epic closure. But much more daringly than Fielding, and in a spirit quite opposed to Richardson, he constructs a new form of nuptial closure that recuperates clandestine marriage – in the form of mock marriage, no less – alongside proper parish ceremony. As he does so, however, his novel's meaning and politics dissolve into ambiguity.

How does this disjunction work? In the novel's closing chapters, set in Primrose's prison cell and then at a local inn, Dr Primrose's poor friend Mr Burchell reveals himself to be Mr Thornhill's uncle Sir William Thornhill, the owner of the local estate upon whom Mr Thornhill himself is dependent. Sir William has been keeping tabs on his estate by circulating in disguise – like François Fénelon's good prince, Télémaque, in that then widely read romance. Mr Thornhill's nefarious guiles and plots are now revealed and his brutality towards the Primrose family is rectified by Sir William, who reverses – and then some – the family's fall. In this act, Sir William takes the same position of benevolent mastery as had Sir Charles Grandison. This time, however, given Dr Primrose's politics, he is not just a saintly, all-powerful squire but an image of the Patriot King himself: 'a man of large fortune and great interest . . . who was a friend of his country, but loyal to his king' (152–3). Crucially, Thornhill's sham marriage to Olivia – involving a 'false licence and a false priest' (164) – is revealed to have been a reverse mock marriage along the lines of the young Booby squire's wedding in Gay's *The What D'ye Call It*. Thornhill was gulled by his own underling, Jenkinson, who had procured a real licence and real priest for the secret wedding, and who now announces to the assembled company: ''Squire, as sure as you stand there this young lady is your lawful wedded wife . . . here is the licence by which you were married together' (164).

In the rush of weddings and reunions that follow from these revelations Primrose's daughter Sophia is united with Sir William; his son George is reunited with Arabella Wilmot, the beautiful daughter of a rich neighbouring clergyman to whom he was once betrothed; and, of course, Olivia and Mr Thornhill are acknowledged as man and wife. The composite picture formed by these unions would seem to restore the Primrose family to prosperity and happiness in an enactment of traditional comic closure. Yet, like the inset narratives that appear at the end of Shebbeare's novel, each of these unions speaks with distinct force and meaning to the contemporary marriage debate.

George and Arabella have long loved each other, but when the Primroses lose their money and Arabella's father, Mr Wilmot, a rich Anglican divine wholly delivered up to gentility, falls out with Dr Primrose over clerical monogamy, their marriage is forestalled. Mr Thornhill then courts Arabella for her fortune while also pursuing and abandoning Olivia. After the family's fall, George Primrose has a haphazard career (based partly on Goldsmith's own life), ending up in imperial military service;[76] Arabella falsely believes that he has married another. Only when the Primrose family fortune is restored and Mr Thornhill is unmasked can the couple's love – much tried, much delayed – be sealed in a marriage. This, then, is a case of a marriage of social equals grounded in natural law: true love, not interest, governs it. As was the case for Joseph and Fanny and for Sir William and Lady Worthy, what counts is the lovers' original promise to marry. It is the basis of a relationship that is wholly binding in the face of prevailing Whiggish social arrangements, the preferences of parents, guardians or social superiors, or the loss of worldly status or fortune.

Sophia and Sir William's relationship works differently. In this case, the Primrose family have discountenanced any relationship between the two since Mr Burchell is too poor for them. But Mr Burchell has not declared his love anyway, and even after he is revealed to be Sir William Thornhill, just to test her, he suggests that Sophia marry another man. Theirs is not a case of thwarted true love, all the more so because neither character is granted even the minimal interiority that Arabella and George have by virtue of their love for one another. Instead, a bond of mutual regard and affection is gradually established through objective demonstrations of virtue (i.e. Thornhill's kindness and bravery, Sophia's good sense and constancy). Theirs is a deliberative union that confirms the Richardsonian identification of spousal choice with moral worth. It is also an alliance between two gentry families, albeit of different means and status. On one hand, it exemplifies anti-Marriage Act arguments for the importance of unregulated marriage to the circulation of wealth throughout the larger body politic. On the other, and no less importantly, it is the culmination of the novel's vicar-squire narrative in a union between the squire himself and the vicar's daughter, which brings landed interest and clerical order together under the sign of mutual respect.[77] As such, it expresses not so much natural law (it is not primarily a love match) as a personification of the good Tory-Patriot social order.

Finally, in the case of Mr Thornhill and Olivia's clandestine union, Goldsmith charts new territory for the novel's marriage plot. Here an unreformed rake and an impetuous young woman who has been blinded by the glamour of money and authority find themselves married to one another just because they have gone through the proper ceremonial form under the guise of a sham wedding. What counts here is neither love, nor morality, nor happiness, nor family life, nor social reproduction but marriage as a legal institution that restores the penitent Olivia to her honour, to her family and to respectable social life – making an 'honest . . . woman' of her, as Jenkinson puts it (164). Yet this recuperation is only partial since she and Thornhill do not – yet – live together as husband and wife (indeed it is a sign of his diminished and anomalous status as an unreformed rake that he 'resides in [the] quality of [a] companion at a relation's house' and learns 'to blow the French-horn' [169]). Here the novel channels the anti-Marriage Act cause's defence of the indeterminacies of the old consensual marriage code as they sheltered women from the worst consequences of predatory male desire and illicit passion. Indeed, in the story of Olivia's fall a new form of seduction narrative emerges for which clandestine marriage is both a sign of sexual transgression and a means of its social containment.

So, the closing scenes of the novel present an array of unions – natural, deliberative and remedial – that restore social justice in the novel's fictional world. As is the case in *Joseph Andrews*, a description of the wedding ceremony brings the narrative to its end and illuminates the whole. But in this instance, the description is touched by the subtlest of ironies to suggest a polemic against the Marriage Act and its regime. The double wedding ceremony is performed on the authority of marriage licences that have been summarily organised not by Dr Primrose, or by the couples themselves, but by Sir William Thornhill, as if to concede that power has indeed shifted from the Church to the secular sphere (in a manner that Adams fiercely resisted).[78]

When the licences arrive, Dr Primrose goes down to meet the company whom, it would seem, have had no advance warning that the weddings are to take place. The ensuing description, for which the weddings themselves are almost incidental, is worth analysing at length:

> I found the whole company as merry as affluence and innocence could make them. However, as they were now preparing for a very solemn ceremony, their laughter entirely displeased me. I told them of the grave, becoming and sublime deportment they should assume upon this mystical occasion, and read them two homilies and a thesis of my own

composing, in order to prepare them. Yet they still seemed perfectly refractory and ungovernable. Even as we were going along to church, to which I led the way, all gravity had quite forsaken them, and I was often tempted to turn back in indignation. In church a new dilemma arose, which promised no easy solution. This was, which couple should be married first; my son's bride warmly insisted, that Lady Thornhill (that was to be) should take the lead; but this the other refused with equal ardour, protesting she would not be guilty of such rudeness for the world. The argument was supported for some time between both with equal obstinacy and good breeding. But as I stood all this time with my book ready, I was at last quite tired of the contest, and shutting it, 'I perceive', cried I, 'that none of you have a mind to be married, and I think we had as good go back again; for I suppose there will be no business done here to-day'. – This at once reduced them to reason. The Baronet and his Lady were first married, and then my son and his lovely partner. (168)

In the first instance, what is striking about this description is that, beyond its pointed reference to the licences, it shows no interest in proper ceremony. Primrose makes no mention of ceremonial dress (indeed there is no preparation for the ceremony) and offers no description of the liturgy's performance. Nor is the reader offered entry into the consciousness of the participants, as in *Pamela*. The church business is covered in a single, banal sentence: 'The Baronet and his Lady were first married, and then my son and his lovely partner.' The forms of marriage and its relation to God and Christian soul-making are absent.

The vicar's erasure of the wedding ceremony's religious aspects is, I argue, heavily ironic. For what replaces any significant description of the wedding ritual, which might concretely represent the fusion of the divine and the worldly, is a squabble about social status and precedence. Which couple should marry first: the entitled daughter or the commoner son? Both enact their politeness by elaborately deferring to the other. This indicates little likelihood of thoroughgoing moral reformation in the Primrose family. All the more so because, in a concrete reminiscence of *Joseph Andrews*, Dr Primrose has to rebuke the company for their levity – a levity which takes on wider political overtones than in Fielding's novel. For here Primrose is barely able to impose solemnity upon them. That proper ceremony is *not* mock, *not* theatre, *not* a mere act of mimesis – or indeed, a 'laughing comedy' – requires more than the vicar's mere insistence on correct deportment.

Indeed, the company are 'ungovernable' in large part because they are not chastened by Dr Primrose's efforts to instruct them. As he puts it: 'I told them of the grave, becoming and sublime deportment they should assume upon this mystical occasion, and read them two homilies and a thesis of my own composing, in order to prepare them.' The two clauses of this sentence pull away from each other: reading homilies will not encourage solemnity (especially if that solemnity is predicated on sublimity as it is here). Indeed, the tension between the marriage ceremony's ritual weight and the social conditions of the lives of its participants – that is, between Dr Primrose's intellectual unworldliness, his bookish and eccentric religiosity, on one hand, and the Primroses' polite worldliness and dependency on Sir William's secular power, on the other – breaks the account in two, leaving only irony.

Dr Primrose continues to experience the wedding mainly as a struggle to assert his authority. As was the case in *Sir Charles Grandison*, the local community – the wider parish – is not present at the ceremony but wishes to participate in the celebrations:

> We were no sooner returned to the inn, but numbers of my parishioners, hearing of my success, came to congratulate me, but among the rest were those who rose to rescue me, and whom I formerly rebuked with such sharpness. I told the story to Sir William, my son-in-law, who went out and reproved them with great severity; but finding them quite disheartened by his harsh reproof, he gave them half a guinea a piece to drink his health and raise their dejected spirits.
>
> Soon after this we were called to a very genteel entertainment, which was drest by Mr Thornhill's cook. (168–9)

The parishioners have to be reproved all over again for their earlier rebellion, and at this moment the wedding ceremony becomes secondary to this political act. However, importantly for the novel's broader vicar-squire thematic, it is not Dr Primrose who does the reproving this time, because he lacks sufficient authority. At this point in the narrative it has become clear that Primrose is barely a good parson in the loose Addisonian sense, much less in Dryden's terms. The text offers no evidence that he has substantive relationships with any of his parishioners, based on sharing or alleviating their everyday struggles as Parson Adams does (although he does have such a relation to his fellow prisoners, many of whom he succeeds in bringing to repentance). His role depends, rather, on formal charity and the authority of office alone. And so it is left to the squire, Sir William Thornhill, to rebuke the ordinary folk, in an act that places him firmly in control of matters yet able to offer them no part in the wedding celebrations (solemn or otherwise), or any reward for their 'dejected' compliance beyond a round of drinks.

The act of correction over, the wedding party immediately attend a 'genteel entertainment', as if to insist that Primrose's evacuation of spiritual office, Sir Williams's monopoly on power and their shared culture of affluent – implicitly commercial – gentility are joined together. The entertainment is as important as the wedding ceremony itself in providing closure, if only as a ritual performance of polite sociability and as a prelude to the novel's closure in an equally ritualised sentimental tableaux of the newly extended Primrose family assembled by the 'chearful fireside ... according to [the vicar's] old custom' (169). But it is difficult to judge the meaning of this sequence of events. Are readers to take them (in the spirit of satire) as a piece of anti-Whiggism, gesturing at the extent of contemporary social confusion and degradation? Or is the novel's ending more complicit than that? Has Goldsmith, like the Primroses, accepted the values and lifestyles of a hierarchised secular gentility, propped up by merely formal Anglican institutions and practices, and reproduced through filiations organised around Hardwicke's marriage regime?

These questions cannot be answered satisfactorily. At this point of the novel, Goldsmith's soft irony dissolves into that ambiguity which modern criticism has recognised. It is an ambiguity that relies on the sheer style, tone and form of the marriage plot itself, which can thus be understood as inaugurating the aestheticisation of the novel form as James, Marshall Brown and others have suggested. It invites the implied reader's disengaged but complex response to the text's rehearsal of the conventions of closure (which might include amusement, pleasure, condescension, puzzlement and so on) and in a manner that harks back to Fielding's and Gay's early meta-theatrical marriage plots.

It is no coincidence that Goldsmith's turn to ambiguity appears just as the Marriage Act's requirements became hegemonic, and in the context of a subgenre of the novel – the Patriot marriage plot – which had stood against the Whig's new social order as anchored in that legislation. *The Vicar of Wakefield* is an 'aestheticised' novel – all form – because it is the last of the Patriot marriage plots. The aftermath of the novel's publication coincided with the transformation of the political field that had sheltered the Patriot movement. When the (new) Tories returned to power under Lord North's ministry in 1770, Britain's politics became ordered by an increasingly clear division between conservatism and radicalism in which the marriage plot would find a different role.

So, while *The Vicar of Wakefield*'s ambiguity – its aestheticisation of form – turns upon its marriage plot, that plot's social and religious underpinnings and consequences are so weakened, various and confused that the novel itself can neither resist nor endorse them. For literature, this conjunction establishes the marriage plot as the realist novel's template more firmly than before. Its sheer fictionality – which was already apparent in *Joseph Andrews*'s ending – is here intensified, just because, as the novel makes clear, there is so little ethical and religious substance apparent in the world, so little goodness. Goldsmith's marriage plot is imposed on a corrupted society with minimal moral and Christian justification, as if for its own sake, or rather for the sake of the novel as a literary form. This move provides the backdrop of Burney and Austen's extension of the device, as the final chapter argues.

CHAPTER 5

Literary Marriage Plots
Burney, Austen and Gretna Green

Frances Burney and Jane Austen both wrote their era's definitive marriage plot novels, yet it is obvious that their heroine-centred courtship fiction stands at a distance from Fielding, Goldsmith and Shebbeare's clerical and gentlemanly fictions – and even from Richardson's *Pamela*. Most strikingly, proper ceremony holds no interest for Austen and Burney. In their novels conjugal attachment does not express Anglican piety or natural law; rather it promotes a literary subjectivity firmly aligned with moral virtue (and very often at odds with the commercial public sphere). Austen's courtship narratives are widely regarded as a high point of the 'serious' modern realist novel, understood precisely as a secular literary mode.[1] To acknowledge Burney and Austen's departures from their Anglican and Patriot predecessors is not to forget the legacy that shapes their work; it is, instead, to notice that in their hands the English marriage plot undergoes a profound and enduring transformation.

This chapter accounts for how Burney and Austen, drawing on earlier women's fiction, shaped a new kind of marriage plot in the last decades of the eighteenth century. Three related factors underpin their innovations. The first is political. As the previous chapter showed, by 1766, when Goldsmith published *The Vicar of Wakefield*, the old Court Whig hegemony was losing force and a new political structure which divided modern progressivism from conservatism was emerging. In this context, the marriage plot became a formal convention (rather than a topical subgenre) for the novel, and its original theo-politics became less central. Second, English marriage was changing too: after the failure of the parliamentary repeal initiative in 1781, the Hardwicke regime effectively triumphed. Its regulations solidly in place, the clandestine marriage trade, which had contributed so much to the early marriage plot's development, was also significantly transformed and (mostly) relocated to the Scottish border, especially to Gretna Green. Finally, and perhaps most importantly, from the 1760s and especially after 1774, when perpetual copyright ended and

circulating libraries became more common, literary culture itself was
reorganised.[2] As the novel form became commercialised, it developed
specialist genres and niche markets, many of which were mainly written
by and aimed at women.[3] At the same time, in a countermove, a new
awareness of literary tradition and formal innovation entered the genre.

Burney and Austen's fiction reflects these changes, not least by subsuming the old church-state politics of the first-wave English marriage plot into
new realist techniques tethered primarily to civil-secular values. With
them, the marriage plot becomes feminised and, at the same time, an
enduring marker of the realist novel's ethical and literary seriousness. It
does so against the new commercialisms – both of fiction and of the
irregular marriage market (i.e. Gretna Green). Burney draws on earlier
heroine-focussed courtship fiction as well as her male predecessors to
reconfigure the genre for new literary readerships, while she also secularises,
extends and urbanises its characterology and settings. Austen builds on
Burney's legacy at the same time as she reinvents the older Patriot genre,
expanding its formal range. In that move, she sets the marriage plot firmly
into the mainstream of English literary history. Both authors extend the
marriage plot's mimetic and critical capacities through formal innovations,
reaching towards what Kathryn Sutherland has called 'perfected
verisimilitude'.[4] In the process, they fuse the English marriage plot with
new forms of literary subjectivity that help to elevate the realist novel by
marking it off from more thoroughly commodified forms.

This chapter identifies four novels – Burney's *Cecilia* (1782) and *Camilla*
(1796) and Austen's *Pride and Prejudice* (written 1796–7, published 1813)
and *Mansfield Park* (1814) – as recasting the first-wave English marriage
plot by refiguring vicar-squire relations and/or clandestine marriage intrigue in new contexts. Collectively, their most striking feature is that they
consign proper ceremony, once definitive of the form, to quiet redun-
dancy. Courtship's dramas and deliberations (rather than matters of ceremony per se) define an emergent literary marriage plot which becomes the
realist novel's default mode.

Haywood's Inadvertency

In providing a context for Burney and Austen, we need to take two
histories forward into the post-Court Whig era: first, the history of clandestine marriage after the Marriage Act (as it spawned the Gretna Green
romance); and second, the ongoing efforts to repeal the Marriage Act (as
they helped to energise a new political spectrum and in particular a new

radicalism). In each case and importantly, women were the focus of the new politics of marriage. For this reason, it is helpful to backtrack briefly to address the heroine-focussed courtship fiction that provided a foundation for Burney's fiction in particular, and for women writers' engagement with the marriage plot generally. Haywood's *The History of Miss Betsy Thoughtless* (1751) is the key text here. Arguably it was pivotal for the history of the English novel, not least because by fusing Richardson's realist marriage plot with elements of amatory fiction, it produced a narrative of female reform that would shape the novel's later development.[5]

Haywood was the most prominent female writer of the mid-century era and one of its most successful fiction writers. She wrote across a number of genres, including drama, dramatic criticism, journalism and political pamphleteering (her politics were broadly Tory and, as some argue, shaded into Jacobite).[6] Like Fielding (with whom she worked at the Haymarket and who later called her 'Mrs Novel'), she also produced a satirical parody of *Pamela* soon after it appeared.[7] She was, however, best known for amatory novels such as her bestseller, *Love in Excess* (1720), for fictions which included 'scandalous memoirs' such as *The Adventures of Eovaai* (1736), which combined political satire with orientalist fantasy, and for 'translations' of the Continental erotic novella such as those collected in *Love in Its Variety* (1727).

Quite late in a career characterised by considerable entrepreneurial flair, Haywood published something different again – *Betsy Thoughtless*, a story of an independently minded but careless (or 'inadvertent') young woman who, without sufficient guidance and support, must negotiate her own survival in London's polite society and marriage market. The novel ends happily when – after several close shaves with libertine desire and some bad decision-making, including a disastrous, loveless marriage – she marries a good man, Mr Trueworth, whom, somewhat haphazardly, she comes to realise she loves.

In genealogical terms, *Betsy Thoughtless* is significant for this study. Written in the wake of *Pamela* and *Joseph Andrews*, it draws much from amatory fiction, including several seduction scenes and Betsy's own (inadvertent) friendship with a prostitute. But these improprieties are now contained within a plot of female reform.[8] More relevant still, Haywood's marriage plot contributes neither to a religious mission (à la Richardson) nor to an anti-Erastian political argument (à la the patriot novelists). Like the older romances it channels, *Betsy Thoughtless* floats free of political and ecclesiastical topicality, at least with regard to the marriage debate.[9] At the same time, it reassembles a number of Anglican and Patriot fiction's formal and thematic elements. Like Richardson and Fielding's marriage plots, it is realist in the sense that it is set in a recognisable, quite thickly described England, time now. Yet it is mostly metropolitan, set neither in a landed estate nor in a rural parish (in the early stages of the narrative Betsy leaves boarding school for London's balls, masquerades, shops and urban sociability from which she retreats only in the narrative's final stages). That setting seals the novel's secularity: its primary interest is neither Richardson's Anglican virtue, nor Fielding's image of a good parson, nor the country parish as organic community, nor indeed the populace at large. Rather it is centred on the adventures of a single young woman on the elite marriage market.

As scholars have long noticed, *Betsy Thoughtless* is an early narrative of female development, a genre for which happy marriage functions as the endpoint of education or reform.[10] An unworldly, coquettish young woman, Betsy improves her self-knowledge and understanding in the process of choosing among a field of suitors. This means that she develops morally and socially in ways that Fielding or Goldsmith's marriage plot heroines, for instance, do not. For all that she is no heroine of virtue in Pamela's mould, since she entirely lacks piety or moral authority. Her character is tellingly defined by 'inadvertency' (27, 356, 387, 442–3, 557), an equivocal trait that turns out to be something like natural intelligence crossed with thoughtlessness.

Arguably, Betsy's inadvertency is an insightful nod on Haywood's part to the self-opacity that made Pamela a sufficiently deep and complex character to ground Richardson's marriage plot. As we noted earlier, that opacity or self-division is most fully revealed in the first-person reflection that marked Pamela's moment of realisation of her love for Mr B. – as triggered by her memorable encounter with sham marriage. Betsy too struggles to understand her own heart. She too has a significant close encounter with sham marriage, as finagled by a fake baronet, Sir Frederick Fineer, who engages not just the requisite phoney priest but also a mock surgeon to stage an elaborate deathbed scene designed to force Betsy to succumb to an impromptu wedding (422–6). And as in *Pamela*, the sham encounter is a narrative turning point – one which prompts not the heroine's self-realisation of love but a dawning recognition of the perils of inadvertency, and which thus sets into play the self-understanding that will eventually lead to marriage with Trueworth.

Structurally, then, Betsy's is a narrative of reform, but it is not sub-jectivised or spiritualised like Pamela's: the narration of her 'development' bypasses the first-person, soulful self-reckoning that had worked for

Richardson's Anglican missionary purposes. In order to characterise Betsy herself, as well as to reveal a larger conflict between chastity and desire, self-restraint and agency that defines courtship for women per se, Haywood's omniscient third-person narration relies not on the epistolary mode's interiority or depth effects, but rather on the comic trope of inadvertency. It follows that the novel shows no interest in proper ceremony; the rituals of Betsy's two weddings are not described. Haywood offers no fusing of subjective depth with Anglican liturgy as in *Pamela*; no conferring of public significance on the couple as in *Sir Charles Grandison*; and no ironic reference to the diminishment of ecclesiastical authority as in Fielding, Shebbeare or Goldsmith.

Instead, Betsy's misadventures are narrated in a third-person mode that, like Fielding's comic-epic fiction, embraces learning, wit and literary taste. The measure of her development – the antidote, as it were, to her inadvertency in the context of the world of self-display and consumption she has entered – is, finally, literary. The alignment of Betsy's moral development with literature is not just diegetic (i.e. in her reunion and marriage with Trueworth as closure) but also extra-diegetic. As David Oakleaf argues, Haywood is at her most self-consciously writerly in *Betsy Thoughtless*, presenting elaborate (Fielding-esque) self-reflexive chapter headings and using literary allusion as a form of satiric commentary throughout the novel – most notably in an allegorisation of the failure of Betsy's first courtship as a conflict between her taste for the fashionable entertainments of the town – 'Plays, – operas, – and masquerades' (214) – and Trueworth's gentlemanly preference for pastoral forms (225–6).[11] At critical moments of the narrative too the narrator cites verse – John Dryden and Abraham Cowley's in particular – as if to underscore a shared polite literary/rhetorical education and cultivated taste that binds her to her readers.

Haywood's penchant for literary allusion is not unusual; it enacts a fairly conventional neoclassical alignment of civility and moral value with literary sensibility. Coupled with a narrative of female development, however, I argue that it represents something new for the marriage plot. By aligning female education with literary values, Haywood moved away from Richardson's Anglican moralism, on one hand, and from Fielding's parish- and vicar-focussed irony, on the other. Instead, she charted a path forward for the English marriage plot that was both more fully secular and specifically gendered, one that could be transmitted to realist novelists concerned with female courtship in the post-Court Whig era. Haywood heralds a new subgenre that will take form as female *Bildung*, largely though not exclusively written by women (including Charlotte Lennox, Frances Sheridan, Amelia Opie and Elizabeth Inchbald) and primarily concerned with courtship (rather than ceremony per se) as a vexed arena of female subjectivity and agency.

In the context of our account of the English marriage plot, we might also say that because Haywood's heroine-focussed reform plot retained a relation to older romance and scandal fiction genres which eschewed the topical theo-politics of Richardson and Fielding's novels, its literary influence increased as those politics retreated. Certainly, *Betsy Thoughtless* laid the ground for Burney and Austen's later deliberative courtship narratives even as they went on to configure the relationship between marriage and literary values quite differently. They use their literary marriage plots to push back against the forms of commercial romance that had been Haywood's domain while nonetheless carrying forward her secular, heroine-focussed marriage plot.

The Gretna Green Romance

By the last three decades of the eighteenth century, no trope signified modern consumer culture's pleasures and dangers for women more powerfully than clandestine marriage. That was because clandestine marriage itself had been transformed. No longer associated with the old urban marriage market, it was now figured in distinctly post-Hardwicke forms: in the northern elopement, the so-called Scotch marriage, and most famously the Gretna Green wedding. Gretna Green was the first village on the new western turnpike road as it crossed from England into neighbouring Scotland, where the old code of consent tolerating clandestine marriage remained in place even after Hardwicke's legislation.[12] There, English couples could continue to be married instantaneously without banns, and under-aged English couples could be married without parental consent.

Initially, Scotch marriages catered to the local peasantry who crossed the border to avoid the expense and publicity of parish weddings, as well as to a small number of religious Dissenters and underage couples who ventured to Edinburgh's Canongate district for instant marriage services.[13] After 1770, when the turnpike network reached Scotland, regular traffic included marriage-bound couples from England who could reach Gretna Green by coach within three days from London. The elopement trade thrived at Gretna until 1856, when Parliament imposed a three-week residency requirement on all marriages north of the border, which put an end to the instant marriage business in Scotland.

Scotch marriages belonged to the modern British economy and to the new domestic tourism industry reliant on late Georgian Britain's improved transport infrastructure: macadamised roads, turnpikes, faster coaches, more efficient relay stations or 'posts'. Like Fleet weddings, Scotch marriages – and Gretna weddings in particular – became topical. Representations of them formed a staple of the popular media – in newspapers and magazines, prints, ballads, stage entertainments, conduct books, scandal sheets, travel writing and, not least, novels. It is important to note that these representations of the Gretna marriage trade were disjunct from its actual material conditions, just as those of Fleet weddings had been. The media were most interested in elite, under-aged couples who travelled to Scotland to marry without permission from parents or guardians. As young 'fugitives' from English law, their so-called runaway marriages or northern elopements became the focus of an elaborate romance culture which retains its place in popular memory. Today there is still a thriving tourist and marriage trade at Gretna Green dedicated to their memory.

Representations of Gretna weddings quickly developed a romance iconography, which channelled old clandestine tropes of itinerancy, fortune-hunting and improper femininity to new ends. Young lovers fled north along the turnpike to be married secretly after a breakneck carriage ride to the Scottish border. The groom was usually a dashing adventurer, often a military officer, and his bride-to-be an heiress, love-struck and underage. Angry parents or guardians followed in hot pursuit. In later incarnations, the Gretna chase typically ended in a hasty, rustic wedding at the village blacksmith's forge. Here the subaltern cleric resurfaced as a 'blacksmith-priest', moonlighting in a spirit of 'Scotch' roguery.

High-profile cases sealed Gretna's reputation for scandal, much as they had done for Keith's earlier London-based genteel wedding trade at the Mayfair chapel. These included Richard Brinsley Sheridan, grandson of the playwright, married at Gretna Hall to the heiress Marcia Maria Grant in 1835; the elderly Lord Erskine, former Lord Chancellor, who married his housemaid, also at Gretna Hall in 1819; and Percy Bysshe Shelley's marriage to Harriet Westbrook in Edinburgh in 1811. None, however, rivalled the 1782 elopement of the heir of the Earl of Westmorland, Lord Burghersh, with Sarah Child, the seventeen-year-old heiress to the Child banking fortune. The couple were married on 20 May at Gretna Green, possibly by Joseph Paisley, the village's most famous 'priest', after Sarah escaped from her father's house in Berkeley Square. Enraged, Mr Child had chased the couple at a furious pace and shot dead one of Westmorland's carriage horses. But he failed to prevent the marriage.[14] The sheer daring of the elopement – its speed, violence and recklessness – was memorialised in Thomas Rowlandson's satiric print 'Fillial Affection, or a Trip to Gretna Green' (1785), which depicted it as a triumph of youth over patriarchy. It was still remembered as such thirty years later.[15]

It is easy to dismiss the Gretna wedding as a species of romance, forgetting that it was a vehicle for powerful, often transgressive, social energies. It bypassed marriage markets, flouted courtship norms and reimagined the social meanings of marriage itself. Typically involving risk, flight, seduction and sex before marriage, its social consequences were uncertain.[16] At its heart lay desire – the young couple's desire for freedom, autonomy and sexual satisfaction. More than anything else, this sealed Gretna's place as romance's destination in the social imaginary of the period. Popular imagery of the old Fleet weddings had emphasised their rough plebeian vitality as shadowed by fraud, drunkenness and violence. The Gretna elopement, by contrast, was elite, glamorous and modern. And as a new iteration of the old theme of romantic love straining against patriarchal authority, Gretna was multifaceted: it transgressed national and sexual boundaries; it fermented family conflict; it threatened fortunes; it engaged internal colonial relations; it overlapped with popular domestic tourist routes and practices; and not least it heralded a new cultural nexus of romance, commerce and novelty, centred on youth. In these last terms, in particular, Gretna quickly became associated both with unlicensed female desire and with the sentimental novel in its more commodified forms, and thus came to play a key role in the English marriage plot's history.

Media fascination with Gretna Green coincided not just with the print market's growth after 1770 but also with the development of innovative new print ventures aimed at women readers and writers. The staples of commercial fiction at this time were new genres such as the Gothic, oriental tales, sentimental romances, novels of sensibility and Shandyean travel fiction – many focalised from a woman's point of view and more often than not presented as marriage plots. At the same time, new mis-cellaneous serial publications like George Robinson's monthly *Lady's Magazine* (1770–1830) or the short-lived *Matrimonial Magazine* (1775) stood at the vanguard not just of such fiction (and similar journalism) but also of popular print's niche and fashion-driven expansion.[17] They did so by creating rakish, youth-oriented modes of address, by eliciting reader contributions and by circulating vernacular news, politics, opinion, gossip

Illustration 5 Thomas Rowlandson, 'Fillial Affection, or a Trip to Gretna Green', 1785.

and scandal (very often about, once again, seduction, adultery, elopement and marriage) as well as by focussing on consumption and fashion.

'Charlotte Bateman, a Tale' (1782), a lavishly illustrated elopement narrative serialised in three parts in *Lady's Magazine*, stands as an example of the new fashion-oriented fiction. It reads as a highly condensed, sentimentalised revision of Richardson's *Clarissa*, in which the heroine, Charlotte, chooses secretly to elope with her beau, Captain Melvil, in defiance of her father. (He later comes to reconcile himself to their illicit union, offering the couple his retrospective consent and blessings.) The romantic appeal of Charlotte's breathless, first-person narrative and its fantasy of sexual desire, freedom and fulfilment was standard fare at *Lady's Magazine*, heightened by an accompanying lavish copperplate engraving. It showed not Charlotte's (presumably Scotch) wedding (the precise details of which we do not learn) but her flight from her father's house straight into her uniformed lover's arms. Descending a rope ladder in full travel dress, she appears all at once as a daring, emancipated heroine and a fetching up-to-the-moment fashion plate.[18] Here, an iconography of elopement – as a thrilling, genteel mode of female adventure – blends seamlessly with the pleasures of consumption.

Because its popular appeal was exploited by new print genres like *Lady's Magazine*, elopement – Scotch or otherwise – featured in the literary backlash that those genres provoked. Scotch marriages first emerge on the popular stage in satirical attacks on commodity fiction. The key instance is William Whitehead's 1770 farce afterpiece, *A Trip to Scotland*, whose anti-heroine, Miss Flack, is an inveterate, romance-struck novel reader who runs away with a strolling player. Poet laureate Whitehead had earlier joined Chesterfield, Horace Walpole and Joseph Warton in denouncing the growing taste for fiction concerned with 'low subjects' and written 'in a low manner', or what he termed tellingly 'modern romance'.[19] Readers should be forbidden, he opined, 'to open any novel or romance ... unless it should happen to be stamped RICHARDSON or FIELDING'.[20] Scotch elopement relayed a soft comic version of that critique onto the popular stage. The joke embedded in the play's title, *A Trip to Scotland*, linked elopement to new modes of middle-class leisure, to domestic travel and not least to sentimental fiction, as exemplified by Sterne's *Sentimental Journey* (1768). The play became a Drury Lane staple, which Garrick regularly staged as an afterpiece to *The Clandestine Marriage*, as if to double down on efforts to overwrite the old Fleet marriage tradition with new romance tropes, whether sentimental or comic.

Whitehead was one of the earliest writers to associate the Scotch marriage satirically with modern consumer culture – with turnpike roads, shopping, fashion, commodity fiction (especially novels) and circulating libraries. The play's main plot featured the landlady of a Yorkshire inn made rich by marriage traffic to Scotland, while the subplot spelt out the fiction craze's dire consequences. According to the comic stereotypes that Whitehead joined together (only partly ironically), elopement was the disastrous outcome of reading popular fiction. Miss Flack's appetite for unlicensed romance has been cultivated within countless novels supplied by her local circulating library, supplemented by a regular diet of 'sentimental comedies' at the playhouse which, in the play's exaggerated estimation, have motivated anywhere between five and 500 couples to set off from London to the border alongside the hapless pair.[21] Within this 'modern romance' scenario – which recalls Restoration stage jokes about the scale of 'lawless' weddings – the institutions of the novel and the institutions of elopement intersect and overlap so as to be indistinguishable from each other. It is as if the 'circulation' of the circulating library becomes both a trope for and a cause of elopement's own perilous mobility. Fittingly, however, Miss Flack's Gretna romance grinds to a halt when she finds herself abandoned on the road to Scotland.

Miss Flack is a female Quixote, a character type satirists routinely used to push back against sentimentalism and romance on the popular stage and beyond. Arguably, such satire was itself double-edged, channelling the very commodity pleasures it critiqued. Lydia Languish, the heroine of Richard Sheridan's Goldsmith-inspired 'laughing comedy' *The Rivals* (1775), is a case in point. Her love of reading causes her to wish for a 'sentimental elopement', complete with 'so becoming a disguise! – so amiable a ladder of ropes! – Conscious moon – four horses – Scotch parson … and such paragraphs in the News-papers!' (act 5, scene 1). She knowingly desires not just a Scotch elopement but also the whole commercial assemblage that surrounds it, including media publicity. She is a genteel, late-century reprisal of the prostitute-bride of earlier Fleet satire, an improper woman who has given herself over to public spectacle and display. Sheridan's critique is directed less at sexual transgression than consumer desire per se, yet even as Lydia's dream of elopement marks her as a dupe of modern romance – a frivolous woman seduced by a hollow, consumerist contemporaneity – it also attests to a new kind of female agency enabled by commodity culture.

Whitehead and Sheridan's plays participate in a wider literary critique of sentimentalism and romance culture which features Goldsmith too (and to which his earlier characterisation of Primrose's daughters in *The Vicar of Wakefield* of course belongs). This context helps to make sense of why Goldsmith published a (now-forgotten) 'Register of Scotch marriages' as a follow-up to his laughing comedy essay in the *Westminster Review* in 1773. For him, Scotch marriage and theatrical sentimentalism belong to the same debased commercial culture. The 'Register' catalogues no fewer than twenty-five cases of Scotch elopement – all fictional – in which couples depart for Scotland in a happy and hopeful frame of mind – 'whirling off to the land of promise' – before returning to England 'gloomy and out of temper . . . the gentlemen . . . sullen, and the ladies discontented'.[22] Here once again the crux of Scotch marriage, its central conceit, is unlicensed female desire, now tabulated in such a way as to allow Goldsmith's punitive moral to unfold in a series of blackly comic reversals: Miss Rachel leaves triumphantly with her grenadier and returns with his knapsack on her back; Miss Racket is for 'holding the whip' before becoming a victim to it; an unnamed bride appears as 'one of the prettiest, modestest ladies' before turning out to be a 'common woman of the town' (348); and so on.

Goldsmith's Scotch marriage essay makes explicit what was at stake in the literary attack upon Scotch marriage and what would become a commonplace of Gretna discourse. He figures the return trip from Scotland to England in an opposition between romance and realism which gives spatial form to an emerging anti-sentimental literary polemic. If Scotland is romance's destination, England is aligned with a sobering, corrective return to realism, especially for women. Here romance and realism are projected onto a British geography which locates their threshold at the internal colonial border, forging a literary conceit that informs the work of many Romantic-era travel writers and aestheticians, including William Gilpin, Walter Scott and Dorothy Wordsworth. It enters the discourse of the novel too, emerging as an important and suggestive element of the English marriage plot, but not before the Gretna trope is politicised in the wake of continuing attempts to have Hardwicke's Marriage Act repealed.

Radicalism and the Repeal Debates

By the 1770s, Scotch marriage functioned not just as a satirical trope for contemporary romance and commerce but also as a vehicle for a radical politics of liberty increasingly addressed to women. This confluence happened within a new political landscape which reshaped both the public politics of marriage and the politics of the novel form.

After the Seven Years' War (1756–63) between France and Britain (and its Continental allies), and more especially after George III's succession in 1760, the old Court Whigs lost influence. New power bases and political divisions emerged, with Pitt leading the way to a new Tory movement – one less dependent on the rural clergy – from out of the old Whig Party's Patriot wing. This movement stabilised after 1770, when Lord North became prime minister. Simultaneously, a new mode of popular radicalism appeared, most vociferously among London Tory politicians like the elder William Beckford or disaffected Whigs like John Wilkes. This populism was partly triggered when the new monarch, himself at first appealing to Bolingbrokean ideology, took an interventionist role in government. Dissatisfaction with the ministry was intensified by the American rebellion and the eventual loss of the colonies, as well as by the post-revolutionary radicalisation of republican ideals there.[23] This dissatisfaction was articulated through the old discourses of 'true patriotism' and English constitutional freedom, but it took advantage of a growing sense of Old Corruption's baleful influence. Thus, it had practical political aims that were new, or at any rate had been lost sight of after the Whigs came to power in 1714: most notably, to reform the Parliament, secure legal rights, reduce national debt and relieve widespread immiseration.[24]

In this situation, the marriage debate provided a means by which oppositional forces could radicalise themselves. Hardwicke's Marriage Act, introduced by the Court Whigs, now came to be associated with a Tory administration, fuelling three repeal bills in as many decades (in 1765, 1772 and 1781). Opposition to the measure, once based in informal connections between high churchmen, hard-line Tories, disaffiliated Whigs, Country Patriots and the merely disaffected, transmuted into a broad-based coalition between refigured Tory patriots, Wilkesites, Rockingham Whigs and other nationally based radical groupings with an anti-corruption, parliamentary reform agenda. As had been the case for the earlier Patriot opposition, repeal advocates viewed the Marriage Act as an encroachment on the people's rights and freedom to marry as a fundamental English entitlement, but now (more radically again) they posed the desire to marry against parental will as an expression of liberty.

The key moment of transition between the original Marriage Act debate (turning on relations of church and state) and a new, more politically radical rights and liberties rhetoric was in 1765 when the Commons debated the first repeal bill. Sir John Glynne, Wilkes's lawyer, introduced the bill.[25] It stated that the Marriage Act had proved 'inconvenient, and ineffectual', particularly insofar as 'divers of his Majesty's Subjects ...

have ... repaired to Scotland, and there have been married', producing
confusion as to 'whether such Marriage is lawful or not'.[26] Glynne proposed a set of looser regulative measures to replace the Marriage Act,
retaining its rules for wedding procedures and registration while seeking
to abolish its residency and nullity provisions, as well as to confirm the
validity of Scottish marriages in England since their legal status remained
uncertain.

Glynne's argument engaged an entangled set of national and parochial
loyalties. As one pro-repeal pamphlet, *Reflections on the Marriage Act*
(1764), noted, the discrepancy between Scotch and English marriage law
'seems not to be agreeable to the *comitas* which should take place between
the sister-realms'[27] – not least, of course, because Scotland's nuptial freedom offered a rebuke to restrictions on English liberty. The discrepancy
provided an occasion for radical rhetorical intensity in which Stebbing's
old theological discourse of individual natural rights was marshalled in the
service not of Patriot anti-statism but of a burgeoning democratic reform
movement addressed to 'every subject, in every part of the kingdom' (37).
Love, youth, liberty and natural rights are joined together not just against
oligarchy and state corruption but also against private, parental 'caprice or
avarice' (37). In these terms, the repeal cause became attached both to lived
familial relations and to broader political demands taken up by the
Wilkesite movement: the right to report parliamentary debates, the
empowerment of juries, the reduction of press censorship, the reform of
the franchise and so on. The radical programme would come to absorb and
use all the romantic affect that images of 'distressed and loving' couples and
'connubial joy' could invoke for these political ends (37).

The links between romance and radicalism were further popularised in
Charles James Fox's campaign to repeal the Marriage Act on behalf of
a softer, Whig-radical alliance in the 1770s and 1780s. Following his father,
Henry Fox, who had led the crusade against Hardwicke's Marriage Act in
the 1750s, the younger Fox used the controversial Royal Marriage Act of
1772 as an opportunity to resign from North's ministry and to stand as an
independent Whig, in a move that foreshadowed his role as parliamentary
radicalism's champion after the French Revolution.[28] Fox's early career was
shaped by the politics of marriage; he introduced private bills proposing
the repeal of the Marriage Act in 1772 and again in 1781 (both were
unsuccessful, although the 1781 attempt was only narrowly defeated).
These commitments allowed Fox to style himself as a man of the people
who lived his political cause, since his own heterodox amorous adventures
(including a clandestine marriage) were widely known. Fox's oratory

during the repeal debate of 1781, in particular, exploited the pro-marriage cause's popular appeal, associating the Marriage Act with royal and ministerial abuses of power and arguing that it was 'totally inconsonant with the genius of the people, and ... opposite to every principle of the constitution'.[29] Proposing to lower the age of consent from twenty-one to sixteen for women and eighteen for men, he figured the marriage market as a home-grown slave trade violating the rights of England's youth, and once again used tropes of young love and free choice in marriage to figure English political liberty.

More than anything else, Foxite repeal rhetoric feminised the anti-Marriage Act cause by connecting it to the language of sentiment and emphasising the plight of daughters subject to parental tyranny. It thereby significantly extended the marriage debate's discursive range and literary influence. We can cite two significant examples. *Lady's Magazine*, which had been quick to take up the Foxite cause in a flood of elopement fictions, editorials and letters championing the marriage rights of minors, published a letter (signed 'Aurelia') in the aftermath of the failure of Fox's first repeal attempt:

> The legislature was mighty prudent, truly, to make a law to keep all their money in their own hands ... Sir, I assume the boldness, though a woman, to aver, no law was ever made in these realms, since the revolution, that has occasioned so many broken hearts, unhappy lives, and accumulated distresses as this has. When children have worthy parents who have their real good at heart, there is little occasion to call in the aid of parliament to enable them to govern their families; and if they are arbitrary and cruel, they ought not to have it in their power to make their children miserable for life.[30]

Aurelia's language of 'broken hearts' and 'unhappy lives' soon modulates into a rhetoric of liberty and political reform that ventures into startling new territory:

> [P]ray, Sir, are not English women *Britons*, as well as the men? If so, why after all this rout about *liberty* for so many years, are *we* to be deprived of it, and have no shadow of a right to it till after we are obliged to give it away. (132)

Here the repeal effort rallies a female readership figured not as a community of breathless wedding-goers as Richardson had imagined an emergent female public sphere in *Sir Charles Grandison*, but as a concerned community of public-minded Britons driven to broach the nascent question of women's 'right[s]'. Yet for *Lady's Magazine*, such a reckoning with the politics of 'liberty' was typically forestalled by the magazine's avalanche of consumer-driven content. As was the case for Charlotte Bateman's elopement adventure, which coincided with the failure of Fox's second repeal bill, the politics of filial disobedience was readily subsumed into fiction and fashion's pleasures.

When the Foxite campaign spilled into musical theatre in the 1780s, however, the Gretna elopement itself was figured unequivocally as a mode of marriage choice and agency for young women. Charles Stuart's Haymarket afterpiece, *Ripe Fruit, or, The Marriage Act*, was a novelty piece staged by George Colman in August 1781 in support of Fox's proposal to lower the age of consent.[31] It featured a pair of sisters, Sally, aged sixteen, and Nancy, fifteen, who are 'ripe' to wed by the laws of nature but cruelly prevented by the Marriage Act's parental consent clauses. Nancy and her beau intend to flee to Scotland while Sally awaits the outcome of the parliamentary debate of Fox's bill, which would allow her to marry immediately. Upon receiving news of the bill's defeat in the Lords, the two sisters depart for Scotland with their lovers, singing in rhyming couplets:

> This country for freedom by heav'n design'd,
> Throws the fetters of law o'er the hearts of mankind!
> . . .
> For us we'll relinquish this tyrannous scene;
> To enjoy Hymen's Freedom on Gretna Green.[32]

Reversing the satiric meanings that had attached to Scotch marriage on the stage up to this time, *Ripe Fruit* recoded the Gretna romance for Foxite purposes – for radicalism – as a refuge for England's forsaken youth, and especially for liberty-loving young women.

Stuart's comic operetta, *Gretna Green* (1783), a Haymarket hit of the 1780s and 1790s, presented the youthful Gretna elopement in new terms again: as part of a rousing musical celebration of Britain's naval victory against the Spanish at Gibraltar. The play provided audiences with the first stage representation of Gretna Green and its weddings, popularising the myth of Gretna's blacksmith priest performing weddings at the village forge. Its comic satire of the Scottish wedding trade – rendered ironically as a hub of empire – was supplemented by a sentimental marriage plot that transformed the old historical connections between clandestine marriage, itinerancy and war into the stuff of imperial romance. Captain Gorget, a gallant Irish naval officer and hero at Gibraltar, returns from active service to Gretna Green so as to marry his under-aged English sweetheart Maria Pedigree, who has awaited his safe return in defiance of her guardians.

Framed by British patriotism, her elopement is linked neither to novel reading nor to sexual impetuosity, commercial excess or, indeed, filial disobedience; rather it is the reward of her own good sense and constancy and, above all, an expression of female public spirit.[33] Similarly, Gorget's love for Maria only enhances his martial spirit: 'Secure in my Maria's heart, No longer shall we live asunder? Tho' I yield to Cupid's dart, I always brav'd great Mars's thunder!'[34] Energised by a love of freedom and country, their Gretna union furthers Britain's glorious cause while also pressing the popular case against the English Marriage Act's tyrannies.

If Fox feminised and popularised the repeal cause, binding it to refigured tropes of youthful liberty and British patriotism, it was Edmund Burke who revivified the Marriage Act's defence in the post-Hardwicke era. As a young MP and an influential Rockingham Whig, like Fox he had opposed the Royal Marriage Act. Channelling High Church-Tory anti-statism, he argued that the Marriage Act failed to recognise marriage as a divinely ordained institution subject only to the laws of nature.[35] At this time too his *Thoughts on the Cause of the Present Discontents* (1770), something of a manifesto for the Rockingham Whigs, served as a model for the Foxite repeal pamphlet, *Considerations on the Causes of the Present Stagnation of Matrimony* (1772).[36] In 1781, however, Burke switched sides in the marriage debate, breaking with political allies to oppose Fox's second repeal effort. Importantly, he defended the Hardwicke Marriage Act in what later became familiar Burkean terms: that is, by arguing for the necessity to respect established authority, both aristocratic and parental, as a matter of social utility. Like the repealists, he marshalled intensely sentimental rhetoric but this time on the side of provident fathers. Overturning the familial relations invoked in Charles Townsend's parliamentary speech against the original Hardwicke Marriage Act, Burke put this question to his fellow MPs:

> Would you suffer the sworn enemy of [a father's] family, his life, and his honour, possibly the shame and scandal and blot of human society, to debauch from his care and protection the dearest pledge that he has on the earth, the sole comfort of his declining years, almost in infantine imbecility, – and with it to carry into the hands of his enemy, and the disgrace of Nature, the dear-earned substance of a careful and laborious life? Think of the daughter of an honest, virtuous parent allied to vice and infamy. Think of the hopeful son tied for life by the meretricious arts of the refuse of mercenary and promiscuous lewdness. Have mercy on the youth of both sexes; protect them from their ignorance and inexperience . . . by the wisdom of laws and the care of Nature.[37]

Burke's defence of the Marriage Act relies on familiar novelistic tropes, now available to both sides of the marriage debate (Goldsmith, for instance, had used the seduced maid to argue against the Marriage Act in *The Vicar of Wakefield*). Discourses of liberty, choice and national freedom were used to radicalise the anti-Marriage Act cause by the 1770s, and injunctions regarding the reproduction of labour, society and culture that had long informed the marriage debate now mobilised populist critique in new commercialised forms that addressed women. But as Hardwicke's legislation increasingly came to require conservative defence, that too could harness up-to-date figures of sentiment and melodrama – now in order to sweeten paternal (and by implication state) authority.

Burke's intervention demonstrates that by the last decades of the eighteenth century the politics of marriage, once primarily the domain of church and state, had been refigured around emergent causes – progressive, conservative and contingent. Arguably the repeal debates played an important role in that transformation by helping to spell out possibilities for new discursive intersections and positions in which social relations – and especially the position of dependent daughters – could be politicised. They articulated possibilities, that is, for a politics which was becoming the domain not just of church and state, or even of the struggle for liberty and autonomy, but which increasingly extended to familial and domestic-erotic ties as well as to internal colonial and imperial relations.

By the 1790s the Gretna Green elopement had become a leitmotif of the marriage plot, especially in British women's fiction, where it served as a point of departure for new commercial, political and literary engagements with the genre; for instance, William Lane's Minerva Press, the period's leading women's fiction publisher, made the Gretna plot its own. Lane specialised in romance and in particular the Rousseauvian novel of 'sensibility' adapted for English readers by pairing highly moralised marriage plots with pathos-drenched subplots of female ruin.[38] The Gretna-inflected sensibility narrative usually told of a young woman's seduction ending in betrayal, unhappiness or death, as was the case for Maria Dorville, the Gretna-bound bride-cum-fallen woman of *The Fair Cambrians* (1790), an anonymous Minerva publication; or for Lady Mary Lumly, abandoned by her feckless lover on the road to Gretna in Susannah Rowson's *Charlotte's Daughter* (1828), the posthumous sequel to *Charlotte Temple* (1791), a bestselling trans-Atlantic seduction tale.[39] Minerva Press established Gretna's romance currency as it was later certified in popular fiction by writers such as Hannah Maria Jones, Sarah Green and Susannah Reynolds, and adapted to the first genuine mass print market.[40]

Conversely, novelists who distanced themselves from commodity culture also turned to the Gretna plot. In the 1790s political upheaval, when sensibility became associated with revolutionary thought and behaviour, moderate writers like Amelia Opie used the Gretna elopement sympathetically to explore the consequences of female desire (*Father and Daughter*, 1801), while conservative writers like Elizabeth Hamilton folded the Gretna plot into a caricature of women's rights (*Memoirs of Modern Philosophers*, 1800). These polemical re-appropriations of the Gretna romance charted two different courses for the English marriage plot: first, as a full-blown, emancipatory narrative allied to progressive politics; and second, as a Burkean retreat into conservative moral-literary values. The novels of Charlotte Smith stand as key examples of the first, Burney and Austen of the second.

Charlotte Smith, who was connected to radical circles, put Scotch marriages at the centre of her political fiction. Her novels present elopement as a signifier of wider social liberation, and hence as an individual choice linked to freedom in the Foxite spirit. She made this move within a genre, the sentimental Gothic, that was her own, reassigning the Gothic novel's themes of tyranny and sexual violence from the feudal past to the British present. In Smith's novels, characters without power and (in some cases) money are validated because of the fineness and fluency of their emotional responses to one another (sentiment being a more legitimate index of personhood than status or riches). These emotional responses regularly flow over into desire and desire into elopement and clandestine marriage, according to the logic with which we are by now familiar.

Thus in *Emmeline: The Orphan of the Castle* (1788), Delamere, a wealthy heir who wishes to marry Emmeline Mowbray (his poor, orphaned cousin) against his father's (Lord Montraville's) will, intends to 'solicit [her] to consent to a Scottish expedition'.[41] Similarly in *The Old Manor House* (1793), the impoverished young couple, Orlando and Monimia, are reunited and privately married at Guernsey, the journey to Scotland being too expensive.[42] These marriages are not expressions of desire out of bounds, or of a failure to accept proper social regulation; rather they are strategies by which young couples of goodwill and in love can avoid their families' illegitimate control. *The Young Philosopher* (1798), centred on George Delmont, a man of reason and radical sensibility, involves two digressions that detail the experiences of Laura and Medora Glenmorris, Delmont's friends, as 'victims of British society'.[43] Both women elope to Scotland, Laura willingly for a marriage of love, Medora unwillingly, abducted by a Gothic villain, although she is rescued by Delmont before the knot has been tied. At the novel's end, the fugitive couples prepare for a new life in America, leaving cruelty, poverty and grief behind.

The so-called Burney school of literary innovators treats Scotch marriage very differently: as a foil for the realist marriage plot. In Burney's *Camilla* (1796), for instance, Eugenia Tyrold, the heroine's virtuous sister and sole heiress of the family fortune, is carried away by the villainous Mr Bellamy to be married against her will at Gretna Green. Here the Gretna elopement is reduced – miniaturised even – to the status of a secondary plot line for the primary narrative and the 'good' marriages with which it ends. But Burney school authors used Gretna subplots not just for moral but also for literary ends, namely to separate fine feeling and moral sense from mere romance, and to thereby differentiate their own fictions from the popular sensibility plot. In Austen's *Mansfield Park* (1814), for instance, Julia Bertram's flight to Scotland with Mr Yates functions as a milder version of her sister Maria's disgrace, and as a point of contrast for the forbearance and suffering that mark Fanny Price's heartfelt attachment to Edmund. Here Whitehead and Goldsmith's satiric attacks on elopement undergo an important adjustment: Scotch marriage is no longer identified with the novel form as a whole or with sentimentalism per se, but with the modes of sensibility and superficial feeling associated most often with Minerva Press genres. And what was merely satiric for earlier dramatists now becomes realistic: in Burney and Austen's female-focussed fictional worlds, described through the developing codes of literary realism, marriage is a serious and careful business distinct from the reckless folly of the Gretna romance.

Burney's Literary Marriage Plot

When William Hazlitt famously dismissed Burney's fiction as involving 'too much "Female Difficulties"', he set the tone for the ambivalent reception of her marriage plots.[44] As critics tirelessly observe, her novels deny readerly satisfaction even as they provide conventional closure. Take *Cecilia*'s (1782) self-declared 'imperfect' ending, for example, where the heroine cheerfully 'resign[s]' herself to a mix of 'general felicity' and 'partial evil' that is her married fate.[45] The problem dogs Burney's happier endings too, since the 'female difficulties' that characterise courtship in *Evelina* (1778) or *Camilla*, for instance, would seem to foreclose closure itself, rendering their heroines' marriages merely phatic and seemingly incomplete.[46] This situation has given rise to a perennial set of questions about Burney's fiction: are her ambivalent endings emblematic of the fundamentally 'divided' nature of her writing, its uneasy, equivocal presentation of female compliance and critique, as a generation of feminist critics have contended?[47] Or are they rather, as revisionists argue, another instance of her conservatism or even her ironic 'over-compliance' with received values?[48]

I want to take a different line of approach by suggesting that *Cecilia's* imperfect ending be taken at face value: as an instance of the realist – or as Burney herself put it, 'real life' – thrust that drove that novel, and her marriage plots more generally. In the context of the commercial fiction market, Burney's realism carried polemical force, precisely as a literary commitment to 'Nature', 'Reason' and 'sober Probability', as against 'Romance', as she put it in *Evelina's* preface.[49] For Burney, this commitment took shape as a steady project of formal experimentation with the marriage plot, now understood as a central convention of the literary novel, albeit one that also anchors rival commodity forms. As I began this chapter by arguing, Burney is one of the first novelists to treat the marriage plot as a mark of the novel's ethical and literary seriousness (as opposed to a merely formal convention, a mode of Anglican outreach or a Patriot critique), and she departs from both earlier female practitioners of heroine-focussed romance and courtship fiction and her male literary predecessors to do so. Against Hazlitt, we might argue that 'female difficulties' – or the troubles of courtship – are for Burney the very stuff of realism, the 'filler' of an emergent literary mode of 'serious' fiction, as Franco Moretti (borrowing from Roland Barthes) would have it, out of which narrative turning points and resolutions only occasionally emerge.[50]

Genealogically, Burney follows Haywood in freeing the marriage plot from topical theo-political concerns, emphasising not matters of faith, nation or society-in-general but rather a young woman's experience in the social economy of courtship and marriage. (Thus she had a special animus against Shebbeare, the most intensely politically engaged of all the novelists we have discussed.)[51] This young woman's story, however, is not a return to Richardsonian soul-making; like Betsy Thoughtless, hers is a secular, worldly story, or more precisely, as Burney famously put it in *Evelina's* subtitle, one that centres on a young woman's 'Entrance into the world'. Evelina's story begins when she leaves a cloistered life in rural Berry Hill, the residence of her guardian, Reverend Mr Villars, for London's world of elite sociability, fashion and leisure. In this context, the 'world' is, de facto, a marriage market, in which choice is an exercise in female desire and autonomy. Here, however, we are not offered the liberatory forms that marriage choice takes in modern romance à la Charlotte Bateman or the Gretna elopement, or in the modes of desire, forwardness or coquetry that

shape Haywood's amatory world (both of which for Burney are improper);
it operates in the interests of a stable filiative establishment whose reproduction Burney somewhat hesitantly endorses.

Like Betsy Thoughtless, Burney's heroines are upper-class young
women who come 'out' into the world without adequate support or
preparation. An absence of proper authority and guidance forms the
crux of their 'female difficulties' – the fraught, extended courtships –
that structure Burney's fictions in a manner reminiscent of Haywood's
inadvertency. Her novels are marriage plots insofar as they end when
this young woman finally marries the right man for her. Yet Burney's
heroines achieve their realist/real-life marriages, as we might call them,
under certain constraints. First, they fall in love with the right man
early on in the story. This means that Burney's marriage plots, like
those of *Sir Charles Grandison* and *Joseph Andrews*, are narratives
structured primarily around deferral, the delay between meeting (or
falling in love with) the right man and marrying him. They are less
centrally narratives of development (i.e. of misrecognition and moral
transformation) than are *Betsy Thoughtless* or *Pamela*, whose characters'
perceptions and judgements have to change before they can marry
well. Mitzi Myers long ago termed Burney's narratives ones of 'female
non-development' for this reason.[52] Non-development, like
Haywood's inadvertency, names a conflict between desire and self-
restraint that haunts the heroine-centred marriage plot. Yet Burney's
fiction reduces the impact of this conflict since, as Deidre Lynch has
argued, the culture of money and commodification that explicitly
frames her heroines' passage to marriage knows no real distinction
between the processes of female self-definition and self-objectification:
indeed, literary inwardness and psychological complexity take shape
precisely in the interstices of commercial culture.[53]

Despite knowing whom they love for much of the plot, and despite their
financial independence, Burney's heroines have limited agency because
they cannot express their desire publicly. The codes of female modesty that
underpin the elite marriage market dictate that they must not choose but
be chosen. This marks out their distance once again from *Betsy Thoughtless*,
as well as the radicalism expressed, for instance, in Charlotte Smith's
Scotch marriage fictions or more pointedly again in Mary Hays's
Memoirs of Emma Courtney (1796), which allowed its heroine both to
express her desire for the man she loves and to propose marriage to him.
For all her realist affirmation of her heroines' subjectivity, independence
and desire, Burney's ban on active choosing distinguishes her marriage

plots from the incipient modes of female emancipation associated with the Gretna wedding.

Burney learns much from Goldsmith and she is on record as particularly admiring *The Vicar of Wakefield*.[54] Behind Goldsmith, of course, lay Richardson and Fielding, whose legacies she dutifully (although anonymously) acknowledged in her preface to *Evelina*, and whose interest in 'the pathetic' on one side and in comic 'wit' on the other she continues and indeed intensifies (10). As Betty Schellenberg notes, Burney most readily names her male literary forebears as a means both of authorising her work and of charting a course for herself within emerging models of literary professionalism. On one hand, she wishes to avoid the taint of genre fiction and print commerce and, on the other, of (bluestocking) coterie writing.[55] In this context, it would not be wrong to say that Burney wrote conservative rather than Patriot or radical marriage plots, despite her fiction's retreat from topicality compared to Goldsmith or Fielding. Many critics have pointed out that her novels uphold received social values while condemning the culture of sensibility.[56] Yet it would be more accurate still to say that the politics of her marriage plots were truly ambivalent, absorbing elements of the anti-Marriage Act movement (even as it shaded into radicalism) into their conservatism.

Parsing Burney's politics like this, however, risks marginalising her most significant contribution to the history of the marriage plot, since her fiction initiated precisely a literary repurposing of that plot. Burney attaches marriage to new discourses of literary inwardness, to associated practices of 'reading character' (to borrow Lynch's term), and creates new character types based on a love of literature in and against mundane society.[57] As Catherine Gallagher observes, unlike her predecessors Burney writes with a sense of the novel as a tradition behind her (which paradoxically is an effect of the commodity market's expansion via the recirculation of earlier texts).[58] This awareness allows her to treat the marriage plot as a well-defined novelistic device against which new realist experiments with form can be created. These include new modes of narration, new subjectivity effects, new character types, new levels of narrative complexity, and finally, a new scrutiny of – and scepticism towards – closure itself.

Narration is the most significant of the formal innovations that underpin Burney's realist marriage plot. After *Evelina*, she replaced both Richardson's epistolary form and the essayistic omniscient narrator of Fielding/Haywood with a new kind of third-person narration which, to use Catherine Gallagher's catch-all term for Burney's mode of address, seemed to be uttered by 'Nobody'.[59] That is to say, it was a third-person

narration whose persona lay somewhere between what D. A. Miller identifies as the 'noisy personality' of Fielding's (or Haywood's) narration, and
the dematerialised voice of no one in particular that was to become Jane
Austen's signature style.[60] In this sense, Burney's persona is a nascent form
of the 'absolute impersonality' (96, n. 2) that Miller associates with 'the
great world-historical achievement' of Austen's realism as it transcends
gender, conjugality and personhood itself (75).

More modestly, we can note that Burney's impersonal mode of
narration lent itself particularly to experiments with free-indirect
style, which created a 'third voice' between narrator and character.
Moreover, it was a mode that rarely uttered explicit moral judgements
or expressed a social or political vision. It allowed moral intent to be
articulated mainly indirectly, just through plot and character. To the
degree that the novels did directly express moral judgements these were
articulated by characters: in *Cecilia*, for example, the 'monitor' (130) Mr
Albany is a character designed to do that and nothing much more;
against verisimilitude, he intermittently appears in public places like
an Old Testament prophet to denounce the luxury, decadence and
backsliding which characterise London society from his (and the text's
own) perspective. Burney's impersonal style of narration may ultimately
have been driven by her well-known reluctance to put herself forward
into the public sphere, but I'd suggest that it was also enabled by the
power of the marriage plot itself. After Richardson, Fielding, Haywood
and Goldsmith, her novels' most effective ethical work could be carried
out simply by the story itself – by telling who married whom, when, how
and why.

Additionally, Burney's third-person form, used in this way, belonged to
and assumed that literary space which was already invoked in *Pamela*. Now
the narration was not itself diegetically motivated (there was no internal
account of why its manuscript exists), neither did it express the views of an
essayistic narratorial persona (in Haywood's distinctive style, or
Fielding's). It just was: it existed by virtue of a familiar literary convention
(the marriage plot) through which the procedures of fictionality could
smoothly proceed. But for Burney it was not simply fictionality that could
be assumed in this way: moralising and sermonising themselves became
literary as much as ethical modes of address; they too were absorbed into
the narration and thus into a willing suspension of disbelief. In being
fictionalised like this, the original sermonic and missionary power of the
Richardsonian marriage plot was muted insofar as it was confined to
literature.

If Burney's narration lacked a convincingly endorsed ethical persona and voice, the social world that she described itself lacked sanctioned authorities and standards. The strong patriarchal structures that ordered the world of her predecessors' fictions (*Sir Charles Grandison*, for example, which Burney especially admired) were manifestly absent or flawed. This absence is the condition of possibility of her heroines' 'Female Difficulties' – their vulnerability and lack of support as they entered society – and hence of their moral loneliness and tendency to head towards what we can call, without exaggeration, the abyss – towards madness and suicide. In this regard, her heroines are significantly different from those of earlier marriage plots: they are more exposed to existential crisis, to psychological ambivalences, pathologies and confusions. Burney takes Pamela's self-opacity and Betsy Thoughtless's inadvertency to new levels, while also, at least intermittently, flirting with new genres – melodrama and the Gothic – of the increasingly commercialised literary market.[61] Crucially, however, these situations of psychological/moral stress are described in relation to a passage to marriage, the generic inevitability of which frames (and distances) the heroine's temporary collapse.

Burney also brought a new social world into realist representation. Because her plots were organised around a device which performed significant literary/ethical work (i.e. the marriage plot), and because their settings were not confined to the landed estate and the parish, she had command of a narrative structure capable of connecting and regulating a larger fictional world. Like Tobias Smollett, to whom she felt indebted, she extended the novel form's characterology.[62] In the first instance, she renovates, transforms and supplements the old theatrical stereotypes: the fops, spendthrifts and libertines that crowd the post-Restoration stage. She also invents – or at any rate brings into literary representation for the first time – new social types: *Cecilia's* Mr Meadows, for example, who constantly pretends to what will become that crucial nineteenth-century affect, ennui; or in the same novel, Miss Larolle's scatty cynicism, which can properly be called radical because it is so dismissive of all conventional values and wisdom; or *Camilla's* more subtly depicted Sir Sedley Clarendel, a rich, bored and good-natured landed gentleman whose privilege detaches him, in a relaxed manner, from actual experience, feeling and concerns. It is notable how many of these character types operate from a diluted version of what would later come to be called 'alienation'. While Burney is primarily, if especially in *Cecilia*, a novelist of Society in the old sense of the term – i.e. the elite public sphere of balls, theatre, court presentations and so on, organised around the metropolitan 'season' and the marriage market – yet Society is very far from exclusive and very far from winning respect from all those attached to it.

Moreover, Burney's characters were not confined to the polite sphere, as her fiction echoes the modes of social inclusion that marked the radicalism of the Marriage Act repeal movement. Most famously, she brings the urban lower-middle classes into focus: *Evelina*'s Branghton family, for instance, are Cockney tradespeople who are the heroine's blood relations and who aspire to gentility; they seem to have come as a revelation to her contemporaries.[63] With this shift, a variety of new intimacies and connections across classes, centred on money, also became possible. Take *Camilla*'s Mr Dubster, a wig-maker, who has sufficient capital for a £500 p.a. income and who can thus tentatively seek Camilla's hand; or in the same novel, Mrs Mittin, who, socialising with polite society, acts as an agent between the gentry and the Tunbridge Wells retail trade, and through whom Camilla falls into the debt that nearly destroys her. More significantly still, and again with an implicit reference to political radicalism, Burney also invented a number of damaged, unjustly treated people: *Cecilia*'s Hill family stands as an example, starving because the father was unpaid for his carpentry by the callous gambler Mr Harrel.[64]

Burney's proliferation of character types constitutes 'the world' into which her heroines enter: the epic exteriority (or as Samuel Johnson put it, the 'huge canvas') against and through which her heroines' inner lives come into view.[65] If the dramas and difficulties of courtship constitute her marriage plots' crux, then choosing friends among the crowd of minor characters is also key to her heroines' (non-)development, along with readers' judgements of it. To this end, Burney's array of characters also includes, importantly, a new kind of urban aesthete whom the heroine typically befriends. *Evelina*'s depressive Scottish poet, Mr Macartney, is the first such figure, but the type is further developed in *Cecilia*'s Mr Belfield, a gifted son of a tradesman and sometime author. His literary 'propensities' set him at odds with the world of patronage and preferment he has entered and, in this regard, he mirrors Cecilia's anomalous social status on the marriage market (since she is an heiress who must keep her own family name at marriage or lose her fortune) and underscores, once again, Burney's own less than full endorsement of the status quo.[66]

Literary personhood and subjectivity are explored more fully in *Camilla*, where Mr Melmond, a young Oxonian and ardent poetry fan (Akenside, Collins, Thompson), is granted sufficient ethical substance to marry Camilla's sister, Eugenia. In general terms, however, Burney's literary characters are important not just as signs of the uncertainty that attended literary endeavour in the burgeoning world of professional authorship, as Schellenberg argues, but also of the increased cultural status of a particular kind of romantic (or proto-romantic) literary subjectivity with which Burney's readers are invited to identify and against which the consumers of cheap fiction are to be measured negatively.[67] It is they who work to ally the marriage plot, now absorbing radicalism into conservatism, with a taste for serious poetry, against which the actual social world and its modes of authority stand wanting.

Burney's marriage plots display a wider range of narrative possibilities and choices than was the case for her predecessors. In formal terms, they depend on complex situational *donnés* that turn on clandestine marriage. Her stories begin by positioning her heroines in unusual, obscure or artificial familial situations, which complicate their social standing and open the narrative to many different resolutions, at least in theory. *Evelina*'s narrative is shaped by her disinheritance and the hidden story of her mother's secret marriage to Sir John Belmont;[68] Cecilia, on the other hand, is left with no choice but to enter into a (disastrous) secret union with the man she loves. Burney's heroines must negotiate an array of suitors and acquaintances and a proliferation of misunderstandings and delays that prevent the disclosure of their true feelings; from the beginning, however, they must also contend with the consequences of a troubled family history (and associated matters of money, property, debt, legitimacy and inheritance)[69] that severely constrains their choices.

Cecilia demonstrates the point. The heroine's backstory is indeed a tangle of anomalies. She is both an heiress and a double orphan: her parents died when she was young and her uncle (an Anglican dean, known just as 'the Dean'), whose ward she is, has died too. In his will, he has insisted that anyone Cecilia marries (and who will acquire his own fortune since Cecilia is his heir) must take his and her family name, Beverley. He has also appointed three unsuitable guardians for his ward. One, Mr Delvile, is an appalling snob; one, Mr Briggs, is a miser; the third, Mr Harrel, is an immoral gambler. Importantly none of these men knows each other: they do not form a social network, in Caroline Levine's sense.[70] Without familial support, Cecilia is set adrift in London under her guardians' different modes of care before being rescued by the younger Mr Delvile, with whom she falls in love. They are unable to marry, however, because his parents, distorted by class pride, cannot allow their son to forfeit the family name. So, when Cecilia, pressed by rival suitors, reaches her majority, he proposes a clandestine wedding to which she reluctantly agrees.

This narrative set-up allows *Cecilia* to upend marriage plot conventions. After a botched earlier wedding in which an anonymous interloper falsely declares the existence of an impediment, Cecilia marries the younger Mr Delvile in a private ceremony well before the novel's end. Each occasion recalls *Pamela*'s own sham and private marriages, and each is narrated in free-indirect style, creating striking depth effects (the sham marriage, in particular, being imbued with a grotesque, phantasmic power that channels the extravagantly dark history of Fleet marriages, as it did for Richardson).[71] Crucially, however, relations between sham marriage and proper ceremony are reversed so that Cecilia's proper ceremony precipitates not deep soul-making or subjectivity but mental breakdown and psychosis. The marriage – which cannot be publicly recognised because it is not condoned by the elder Mr Delvile and is in violation of the conditions of her inheritance – propels Cecilia into the abyss. Dispossessed of her fortune and temporarily cut adrift from her new husband, she loses her mind, runs amok on the streets of London and spends days locked in a pawnbroker's shop after having been mistaken for a patient escaped from Bedlam.

All is eventually reset within the novel's insistently realist ending, where closure depends not on a wedding ceremony but on the eventual public recognition and parental endorsement of Cecilia's marriage. The ambivalence of the novel's conclusion, however, turns not just on the irony of its famous invocation of marriage as a 'partial evil' serving 'general felicity' but also on the belatedness of the parental sanction of Cecilia's wedding. This resequencing of proper ceremony positions the novel ambivalently between supporters of the Marriage Act and its repeal because, while it accedes to parental authority, it does not respect the reasons that Delvile's parents give for forbidding the marriage. In this regard, *Cecilia*'s conclusion is another example of that doubleness in relation to the politics of marriage which characterises Burney's contribution to the marriage plot.

Indeed, *Cecilia*'s experiment with closure heralds a significant shift for the English marriage plot. As we know, Fielding and Goldsmith described the wedding ceremonies that ended their novels in some detail; that was necessary within the Erastian theo-politics in which they wrote and took positions. But Burney, following Haywood, does nothing of the kind. Hers are proper marriage plots that do *not* represent their heroines' weddings. The whole problematic of Tory Anglicanism which made matters of ceremony relevant for her predecessors does not matter to Burney, just as it no longer centrally animates late Georgian politics. This absence is, of course, a sign of how much political and social agency the Church has lost.

Because proper ceremony no longer represents a coming together of religion, community and tradition, because marriage is primarily an institution over which parents and children struggle, because over the border its ceremony is not religious at all, and because too fashionable weddings are matters of media interest, Burney can write definitive marriage plot novels in which weddings per se do not figure.

Arguably, Burney's demurral with regard to proper ceremony moves beyond Goldsmith's Patriot aestheticisation of the marriage plot to reach towards a new protocol for closure: one rooted less in matters of ceremony than in the loose, elliptical and almost casual reference to a wedding. In this regard, Burney's convoluted courtship plots and fraught marriage endings set the stage (albeit negatively) for what becomes a characteristic of the female-authored literary marriage plot: the self-conscious citation of what we, as readers, are assumed already to know about closure. So, in Austen, weddings will happen in a minimalist nod consistent with her stylistic economy: *Pride and Prejudice* makes no mention at all of the weddings with which it ends, while *Emma*'s final paragraph remarks in passing that Emma and Knightley's wedding 'was very much like other weddings, where the parties have no taste for finery or parade'.[72] (Indeed, over-attention to ceremony and show in the case of Maria Bertram and Mr Rushworth's wedding in *Mansfield Park* is a sign that their marriage is doomed.)[73] *Jane Eyre* (1847) offers another telling example. Charlotte Bronte's narrative famously turns on proper ceremony (and borrows Mr Mason's interruption of Jane and Rochester's union from *Cecilia*'s own botched wedding scene). Nonetheless, its much-delayed nuptial closure occurs as a mere first-person aside – 'Reader, I married him' – that confirms proper *marriage* in the absence of a representation of proper *ceremony* itself. The realist novel's shift away from ceremony is important: it attests to both the novel form's literary consolidation of the English marriage plot (in terms that eschew a merely superficial interest in weddings) and a subsumption of that plot's original theo-political conditions of possibility. Burney, channelling Haywood's old romance secularism, is arguably the first to put Richardsonian proper ceremony truly to rest in these terms.

If *Cecilia* reset the marriage plot's relation to proper ceremony, *Camilla* recast its Patriot themes and settings around emergent literary values. As Burney's third novel, written after the French Revolution (and her own marriage to an *émigré* French aristocrat), it marks a shift in Burney's writing, as is widely noted.[74] Unlike *Cecilia* and *Evelina*, it is not set in London but on a landed estate and parish, with important scenes set in the commercialised spa town of Tunbridge Wells. More than that, the novel is interested in relations between vicars and squires, although on new secular terms. In line with this partial return to the received settings of the marriage plot, an anti-romantic, moralising narrative voice is more apparent than in the earlier novels. Indeed, *Camilla* has been read as a concession to the literary marketplace and, in the wake of *Cecilia*'s experimentation with the form, as a retreat into established marriage plot conventions as they sanction a patriarchal social order.[75] I want to suggest otherwise: the novel's turn to literary values secures a new trajectory for the marriage plot by refiguring the old clandestine marriage and clerical subplots fundamental to the form. Importantly, this change happens within an implied critique of Anglican authority that more emphatically foregrounds the irony and secularism of Burney's literary marriage plot than her earlier novels had done.

Certainly *Camilla* reprises old themes. Its narrative *donné* shares much with those of *Evelina* and *Cecilia*, while its scenario of a respectable family brought down by the vagaries of the commercial-credit economy is borrowed from *The Vicar of Wakefield*.[76] The heroine, Camilla, and her three siblings (two sisters, Lavinia and Eugenia, and an elder brother, Lionel) are born into a situation where parental authority is inadequate and dispersed. Their father, Mr Tyrold, is a younger son and country parson with a good living, and therefore a gentleman in ways that neither Richardson's Mr Williams or Fielding's Parson Adams were. In keeping with the increasing social status of the beneficed Anglican parson in the period, however, he is not seen to interact with his parishioners.

Camilla's uncle is the local squire, Sir Hugh Tyrold, who significantly has not inherited his estate: he has bought it quite recently in order to be close to his brother's parish. Sir Hugh, however, lacks both self-confidence and ordinary astuteness, being obsessed by the silly idea that his lack of erudition means that he receives insufficient social respect. So he, the squire, is no adequate mentor or authority – indeed his unworldliness is reminiscent of Parson Adams and Dr Primrose. He is unmarried, but his niece and Camilla's cousin, Indiana Lynmere, lives with him, as does his favourite, Camilla herself, whom, at the novel's beginning, he designates his heir. But Eugenia is soon disabled by accidents caused by Lionel and Sir Hugh's carelessness, and out of guilt Sir Hugh writes Camilla out of his will and names Eugenia, her younger sister, his heir instead.

This complex set-up reveals that neither father nor uncle – vicar nor squire – possesses effective authority. From it, four marriage plots unfold: Camilla's, Eugenia's, Lavinia's and Indiana's;[77] those of Camilla and

Eugenia count most. Camilla's is of course the featured marriage but, for the first time among the texts we discuss, it shares the foreground with another marriage plot, that of her sister Eugenia; indeed, Eugenia's marriages (she marries twice in an important echo of Haywood's *Betsy Thoughtless*) are arguably as significant as Camilla's. Two of the marriages – Eugenia's first marriage and Indiana's – involve Gretna elopements, although neither is a love match. The novel is structured around the difference between the Gretna and the regular English wedding, just as earlier marriage plots had been structured around the contrast between sham marriage and proper ceremony.

Camilla also recapitulates the *Vicar of Wakefield*'s neat multi-plot ending, presenting a series of marriages that map the characters' fates according to a moral hierarchy (which now floats free from its original allusion to the Marriage Act debate): Eugenia's second union is sanctioned by nature (and literature, as we see in what follows); Camilla's by virtue and constancy, although sorely tested; and finally Indiana's in the remedial terms usually assigned to the Gretna plot. Only Lavinia marries a good man without delay or tension, but nothing rests on this outcome except the marriage plot's neatness and reach. Indiana, however, elopes to Gretna with Mr Macdersey, a penniless Irish ensign, curiously described as 'wild and eccentric' but 'by no means wanting in parts'.[78] As this equivocation suggests, he turns out to be a more than adequate husband for her – exactly what she deserves. In this instance, and just as for the radicals, Gretna enables practical morality to be served.

Before the novel's story is well under way Camilla falls in love with Edgar Mandlebert, a neighbouring squire and her father's ward, and he with her. So her plot turns not on who she will marry but on the reasons to delay the disclosure of that choice and its resolution – which are often improbable and irritating, as Hazlitt long ago pointed out. The first important such reason is that Edgar, although an attractive, good and capable man in the style of a young Sir Charles Grandison, is unwilling to decide on a wife for himself. He is still under tutelage and appeals for help to his mentor, the Anglican churchman Dr Marchmont. A sceptic and misogynist, Marchmont suggests that Edgar test Camilla before proposing to her by observing how she comports herself as she enters the world. This, then, is a courtship staged as surveillance, allowing Edgar himself to take on the role of 'monitor' or of 'heroine-watch[er]', as Lynch puts it, under the auspices of a distanced Anglican authority.[79]

The test backfires. Camilla is, after all, deprived of proper moral and practical support from her family while prey to her brother's demands for money to offset his gambling debts. She is left to rely on newfound friends – Mrs Arlbery and Mrs Berlinton – who unintentionally lead her towards disaster. These glamorous older women are the novel's most complex and ambiguous characters because, although chaste and good-natured, they live on the far side of social and enlightened virtue. Mrs Arlbery is morally careless; Mrs Berlinton (sister to Melmond, the poetry fan) has not found established social structures that fulfil her. The dilemma has political resonance too since theirs is a mildly radicalised femininity which (as Burney makes clear) cannot adequately model virtue for Camilla. Caught, then, between her own youthful 'imprudence', on one hand, and the relentless and watchful 'distrust' of Edgar and Dr Marchmont on the other, Camilla steadily falls into debt and, like Cecilia before her, heads towards madness (913). Eventually all is put right, when Edgar, having posed as a clergyman summoned to administer the last rites to Camilla in her delirium, learns of her innocence and constancy.

Once again, young love is almost derailed. This time, however, it is not parental tyranny but a remote clerical arrogance which is to blame, since Marchmont's negative judgement of 'the whole female sex' (903) had effectively sanctioned Camilla's decline. It is with some irony, then, that in the novel's final scenes Marchmont presides in part over Edgar and Camilla's double wedding, held at the Cleves estate of Sir Hugh, who after a period of exile has only recently returned, Parson Adams-like, 'to the clamorous rejoicings of the assembled poor of the neighborhood' (908). Marchmont unites Camilla's sister Lavinia and Harry Westwyn, but not Camilla and Edgar; that role is reserved for Camilla's father, Mr Tyrold. This arrangement is partly a reference to earlier marriage plots, of course, and the symmetry by which they assigned double roles to clerical characters like Williams, Adams and Primrose himself (as rivals, friends, fathers and priests, respectively). Marchmont's partial inclusion is also in keeping with that symmetry: he has been nothing less than a spoiler in this marriage plot, so the novel's closing sentences duly note that he regrets the 'injustice', 'arrogance' and 'narrowness' with which he condemned Camilla during her time of trial (913). Coming after Camilla's harrowing experiences, however, his apology seems gestural – another of Burney's unsatisfying closures. Considered too, in light of the novel's homage to *The Vicar of Wakefield*, it carries more than a whiff of Anglican critique. Certainly, such a conclusion is embedded neither in Christian faith nor in any securely affirmed and institutionalised authority. It offers, rather, a secular and literary citation of proper ceremony in Burney's signature style.

Against this background, Eugenia's marriage plot functions as a supplement to and commentary on Camilla's. Here Burney subjects not the Church but literary sensibility itself to careful scrutiny in two intertwined courtship-cum-elopement narratives. Eugenia, we recall, is an heiress and a classical scholar who has been maimed by smallpox in her youth. Because of her learning and her disability, she is deemed an unworthy object of male desire and an anomaly in the marriage market. For all that, she has 'the mind of an angel' (804), commands the respect and admiration of all, and is sought by Melmond in what initially unfolds as a literary courtship. He, however, as a literary type, is equally susceptible to nature's 'exquisite workmanship' (800) and soon falls for Indiana, the 'beautiful automaton' (191). Just as his appreciation of Eugenia's sensibility overcame any physical repugnance towards her, he is able simply to imagine away Indiana's stupidity and narcissism.

At this juncture, Eugenia is abducted by a charming and deceptive fortune-seeker, Alphonso Bellamy (born plain Nicholas Gwigg), who carries her off to Gretna Green. The elopement repeats elements of popular romance: Melmond hotly pursues the couple, arriving too late to stop the wedding (which is not described); Bellamy plays the role of passionate lover, wholly insincerely threatening suicide if Eugenia does not consent to their marriage; she is shaken by the event, 'a living picture of grief' (802); and her father, Mr Tyrold, is a broken man. More telling still are the reasons for Eugenia's capitulation to Bellamy. Although she is no debased novel reader, she is undone by her own 'credulous goodness' (808) and easily deceived. Seemingly out of literary idealism (her 'love of literature' [800], as Melmond terms it) rather than religious faith, she regards her forced vows to Bellamy as 'sacred' and refuses any attempt at legal redress, even when he turns out to be a brutal husband of the worst kind.

It is only when Bellamy dies unexpectedly in the novel's final stages that Eugenia can return to the marriage plot that was always hers and marry Melmond. He has adjusted to reality after Indiana's own elopement with Macdersey, just as Eugenia's brief marriage to Bellamy tempers her innocence and ardour with melancholy. The point of their marriage, then, is that at last a narrative and social space has been cleared in which they can unite for and by themselves, reflectively, on the basis of mutual 'sympathy', 'taste' and 'turn of mind' (912). Melmond is not a good match for Eugenia by conventional criteria since he has no money and she is an heiress. Similarly, her disfigured body and bluestocking mind make her a poor catch by romantic – Gretna – criteria. Rather their wedding (once again not described) sanctions a moral and social space outside the established order for persons whose subjectivities are structured by the cultural field to which the novel itself belongs. In this way, the marriage plot, which does so much to forward moral judgement in Burney's fictions, is here also placing itself in a cultural zone outside theo-politics, outside the Patriot imaginary, outside radicalism and outside commercial romance – that of the literary imagination itself.

Against Eugenia's literary marriage plot, Camilla's more conventional, deliberative marriage plot rings somewhat hollow. In *Camilla*, however, the literary marriage plot is emergent: it stands in the place of the older Anglican and Patriot plots, while also remaining secondary, convoluted, tentative and, indeed, in close proximity to the Gretna romance. Nonetheless, the kind of subjectivity it represents and aims to activate in its readers will come more fully into play in the context of later fiction, especially Austen's.

Austen's Vicars and Squires

Jane Austen's unique literary prestige and, indeed, her Englishness, turn on her marriage plots. That she is central to the development of the novel form and its realist marriage plot is, of course, a literary-historical commonplace.[80] Of all the authors treated in this study, her novels come closest to defining the modern English marriage plot as we began by theorising it, that is, as marking a coalescence of social status, states of feeling, Christian virtue and moral worth in marriage. If Burney's realism consolidates and extends this English marriage plot around 'Female Difficulties', Austen's represent its culmination within a stylistic economy animated by the 'non-contested subjectivity' of heroines such as Elizabeth Bennet, Emma Woodhouse or Fanny Price.[81]

Austen's canonicity too owes everything to the perceived moral-literary gravitas of her marriage plots: F. R. Leavis sanctioned them as a master discourse of the novel form and a touchstone of literary value (she inaugurates the Great Tradition); Ian Watt judged them as representing the moment at which the novel had, indeed, achieved its 'rise'.[82] More recently and rather differently, Franco Moretti considers Austen a novelist of 'serious' bourgeois-conservative realism alongside Balzac, Flaubert and other European greats on the grounds that, like no other fiction, her marriage plots bring together the two key indices of the mode – *Bildung* and free indirect style.[83] Moretti cites Elizabeth's realisation that Mr Darcy is 'exactly the man, who . . . would most suit her' in chapter 50 of *Pride and Prejudice* (1818) as an example of Austen's extended deployment of free indirect style in the context of *Bildung*.[84] In this moment of subjective reflection, Elizabeth comes to see herself with 'the eyes of the narrator' (396), an adjustment which sets into play her eventual union with Darcy and which, by aligning her self-perception with 'the achieved social contract' (396), models, for Moretti, the realist novel's commitment to rigid normativity.

Yet Austen's marriage plots are less flawless distillations of literary realism than experiments with form itself, just like Burney's. While it is true enough, for instance, that Elizabeth, like Pamela or Betsy Thoughtless, undergoes a reversal of feeling that enables her marriage plot, that reversal first occurs not in the realist context of everyday household affairs at Longbourn (as identified by Moretti in chapter 50) but earlier in the narrative, when she is travelling in Derbyshire with the Gardiners and receives the wholly unexpected news that her sister Lydia has 'gone to Gretna' with Mr Wickham. That news, channelling the spectre of clandestine marriage though at some remove, almost immediately triggers Elizabeth's own (romance) reversal/recognition that she 'could have loved' Mr Darcy (306).

Lydia's elopement subplot mixes modes too, unfolding as something of a realist variation of the Gretna romance. She and Wickham, after all, are the stereotypical Gretna couple: a giddy under-aged bride and a caddish officer groom. Yet the crisis their flight causes is compounded by word that 'they are certainly not gone to Scotland' – that they 'left Brighton together on Sunday night, and were traced almost to London, but not beyond' (306). Knowing what we know about the topography of modern romance, it is clear that Lydia comes perilously close to falling off the edge of the map here – it is bad enough that she has gone to Gretna, still worse that she has not. The inevitable conclusion is that 'W[ickham] never intended . . . to marry [her] at all' (303). As Elizabeth absorbs the news, Darcy breaks in upon her, prompting the following exchange:

> 'I have just had a letter from Jane, with such dreadful news. It cannot be concealed from any one. My youngest sister has left all her friends – has eloped; – has thrown herself into the power of – of Mr Wickham . . . She has no money, no connections, nothing that can tempt him to – she is lost forever.' . . . Darcy made no answer. He seemed scarcely to hear her, and was walking up and down the room in earnest meditation; his brow contracted,

his air gloomy. Elizabeth soon observed, and instantly understood it. Her
power was sinking; every thing *must* sink under such a proof of family
weakness, such an assurance of the deepest disgrace. She could neither
wonder nor condemn, but the belief of his self-conquest brought nothing
consolatory to her bosom, afforded no palliation of her distress. It was, on
the contrary, exactly calculated to make her understand her own wishes; and
never had she so honestly felt that she could have loved him, as now, when
all love must be in vain. (305–6)

The drama of interiority that unfolds here takes the form of anti-Gretna
discourse. Darcy meditates and conquers himself. Elizabeth observes him,
(mis)calculates his thoughts and belatedly comes to understand a deeper
self hidden within her. Stylistically, the representation of her realisation
depends upon the narrative technique of free indirect style. That technique
places an extra-characterological presence (i.e. the narrator) between fictional characters and the reader, which in this case functions as
a discriminating subjectivity between readers and the romance story.[85]
Here, the technique offers an indemnity against the volatile speech/action
nexus represented by elopement. Darcy, of course, will disprove Elizabeth's
surmise that she is sinking under disgrace, and he will do so by taking bold
action behind the scenes: compelling Wickham to make an honest woman
of Lydia. But that bold action is itself the result of deliberation; it is based
on the history of his own relation to Elizabeth, which has involved
a prudential calculation of the gains and risks he will court in marrying
her. In removing herself from the Gretna nexus, Austen is careful to fuse
deep subjectivity not with passiveness or sheer contemplation, but with
resolution and action in Darcy's case and with hard-won self-knowledge in
Elizabeth's.

There was nothing new in the alignment of deep subjectivity with the
deliberative marriage plot, or in the realist novel using the Gretna romance
to mark that differentiation. While Austen's plots echo and reverberate
with the marriage plot's history as outlined here, at the same time she was
a literary innovator. For her, like Burney, the marriage plot is inherited,
and as such it functions as a given formal frame in which she is free to
experiment rather than as an ideological weapon or an expression of
a religious mission.[86] At the same time, for her too the marriage plot is
primarily directed against the culture of romance, spontaneity and sensibility, as the near disaster of Lydia's Gretna romance underscores. Unlike
Burney, however, she rearranges and extends the marriage plot's key
elements – its moral and female-focus on one side, and the Patriot novel's
interest in parishes, vicars and squires on the other – so as to establish forms

and techniques that enable the genre to be claimed as a moral basis of national life.[87]

Among Austen's generic borrowings, perhaps the most notable is her revivification of the Patriot imaginary. Several of her novels (*Pride and Prejudice, Mansfield Park, Emma*) are set in idealised rural parishes run by vicars and squires, even if the organic community such parishes represented for Fielding and Goldsmith no longer holds in them: no whole and connected community is represented. Both *Sense and Sensibility* (1811) and *Mansfield Park* (1814), for instance, present morally perceptive and mature young women who are rewarded by marrying parsons in social situations where the merely rich and powerful have, by and large, evacuated their ethical responsibilities. In *Sense and Sensibility*, which once again turns to *The Vicar of Wakefield*'s double marriage plot, Marianne Dashwood (an ardent sentimentalist who learns the error of her ways) marries a good squire (Colonel Brandon) while her elder sister, Elinor (realist and deliberative by nature), marries her brother-in-law Edward Ferrars, a vicar to whom Brandon has granted his parish living. Here a condensed form of the vicar-squire narrative is organised not around Court Whig theo-politics but around literary and affective styles – and in particular around the temptations of sensibility.

Importantly, however, for Austen's heroines, marriage is no longer determined just by love, money, status, literary taste and moral exemplarity but also, sometimes, by profession. In this context, it matters that the eligible heroes of *Northanger Abbey, Sense and Sensibility* and *Mansfield Park* are, precisely, clergymen (and that, for instance, Frederick Wentworth in *Persuasion* is a naval officer). Historically, the marriage plot's professionalisation in Austen reflects England's militarisation during the Napoleonic wars and much of the discussion of placement and profession in her novels concerns military officers (just as Burney showed a persistent interest in anomalous literary characters, which Austen does not revisit).[88] But in relation to *Mansfield Park*, and its renovation of the Patriot marriage plot, what matters more is that becoming a clergyman is no longer a calling in the traditional sense, or a mere patronage opportunity. Rather the priesthood is a choice of profession.

Because Austen returns to the Patriot marriage plot setting of the rural parish, her fictional worlds are narrower than Burney's and her heroines' marriage choices more socially restricted. Typically, Austen's fictional worlds, 'little bit[s] ... of Ivory (two Inches wide)', as she famously termed them, consist of a handful of local gentry or near-gentry families along with itinerant military men and perhaps richer professionals who live in a neighbouring town.[89] Her heroines do not enter metropolitan marriage markets (indeed they are not 'out' at all in terms of London's Season), neither do they usually move in new social circles in order to meet a husband. Some of Austen's heroines barely move beyond their childhood home and family to marry: *Mansfield Park*'s Fanny Price marries a cousin who has been a brother to her; Emma marries her father's best friend, Mr Knightley, who has known her since she was a child and who is her brother-in-law. As the criticism has often remarked, here endogamous marriage becomes something like incestuous.[90]

In these texts, the representatives of virtue have not just retreated behind the 'park gates', as Patrick Parrinder contends.[91] Rather the parish itself has shrunk into a rarefied 'gentry world' enabled by the steady tightening of vicar-squire relations. This world is very nearly without plebeians or parishioners, and without that community whose stratified heterogeneity Fielding and Goldsmith both celebrated as *English*. Yet just because the parish ideal and the country clergy no longer possess substantive political agency, they have ossified into a literary setting that signifies another – genteel – ideal of Englishness. Their function for Austen seems to be, in part, just to refer back to Fielding and Goldsmith under the assumption that the old Patriot marriage plot and its image of rural community and nation can provide a (somewhat equivocal, as we see later) standard against which both the culture of commercial sensibility and political radicalism can be measured.[92] Understood in these terms, Austen's reinvention of the vicar-squire plot is anything but radical. At best, it bears the hope that if gentlemanly parsons carry out their Christian pastoral duties sensitively and responsibly, then oligarchical corruption can be kept at bay.

Good Reading in *Mansfield Park*

Like *Camilla*, *Mansfield Park* explicitly returns to the Patriot marriage plot's themes and settings, inflecting them with new literary value. As a novel 'about ordination', as Austen herself put it, it turns upon relations between parsons and squires, and the life of the landed estate and the parish.[93] Its narrative base, like that of *Pride and Prejudice*, is Richardsonian: a poor, intelligent and virtuous young woman (Fanny Price) converts a backsliding young man (Edmund Bertram, insofar as he is in love with Mary Crawford) and marries him. It energises this narrative with ambiguous characters (in Burney's style): first, by having Edmund fall in love with Mary, a character perhaps modelled on Burney's Mrs

Berlinton (Mary's cynicism and lack of principles also struggle with her intelligence and good nature), and then by having Mary's brother Henry, who shares Mary's moral ambiguity, fall in love with Fanny. Fanny herself, however, remains immune to Henry's charms – she has, after all, loved Edmund since she was ten, and it is simply love's advertency and steadfastness, grounded in feeling more than principle, that allows her to decline Henry's marriage proposal.

Fanny's loyalty to Edmund provides the novel's moral basis. But her steadiness, moral acuity and courage in resisting the various temptations that beset her are not, like Pamela's, based on a conventional piety or on political or philosophical principle. Rather, they develop slowly in subtly plotted everyday-life interactions with the Bertrams and the Crawfords. She learns to be reserved because she has been humiliated as a child. Obedient for all that, she emulates authority-figures – Sir Thomas and Edmund – while also coming to appreciate their limits. Often left to her own devices, she finds sustenance in literature, especially in William Cowper's poetry – a love which she shares with Edmund.[94] Living in a grand country house, she also comes to appreciate that elegance, privacy and freedom from want are required to live the good life. In sum, her immersion in the ordinary, combined with her affective complexion and literary sensibility, secures her loyalty to Edmund and grounds her marriage plot itself.

Mansfield Park is another self-referential – and literary – twist on the genre. In formal terms, Fanny is a character whose moral worth is staked on narrative delay instead of principle or faith. But like Burney's heroines she lives in a community that is less than self-contained and morally ordered. Admittedly, Mansfield Park is a landed estate and parish more like those that Fielding and Goldsmith imagined than Burney's. But famously, its squire, Sir Thomas Bertram, draws income from estates in Antigua, presumably from a sugar plantation worked by slaves. This matters not just because it puts moral pressure on Mansfield Park (the slave trade is under discussion there, as it is more critically in *Emma*) but also because the estate is not at the centre of a traditional landed parish as the old Country interest imagined it. As an estate without land, newly bought like Sir Hugh's estate in *Camilla*, Mansfield Park is maintained by capital at least partly earned in a morally compromised business. Slavery was by 1814 widely recognised as such in England; abolitionism by this time had become a key element of radicalism, while slavery itself, as we have had several occasions to note in this study, was a widely used signifier of oppression in general.[95]

Nonetheless ownership of the estate includes ownership of a clerical living, which Sir Thomas intends for his second son, Edmund, but which until the novel's end is in the hands of the gentlemanly bon vivant Dr Grant. Grant brings the ambiguous Crawfords into the parish – with momentous consequences. (Mrs Grant, Henry and Mary's aunt, is the daughter of Admiral Crawford, a Whig grandee and libertine, whose distant presence in the narrative harkens back to the corruptions of the old Whig ascendency and accounts for the family's continuing impiety.) So, at Mansfield Park, the relationship between the vicar and the squire has reverted to a polite friendship between gentlemen and their extended families. The old sense of spiritual vocation and the old moments of clerical unworldliness and charisma which animated Patriot fictions such as *Joseph Andrews* and *The Vicar of Wakefield* no longer exist.[96] This situation sets certain questions of authority into play. How are we to view Edmund's clerical vocation? Is it just an oligarchical gift, is it genuinely a vocation or is it a choice of profession? Where does real authority in the parish lie, if anywhere? With Sir Thomas as oligarch, slave-owner and squire? With the gentlemanly vicar? In literature itself? Or elsewhere?

On the face of it, Sir Thomas is a just and effective patriarch in the spirit of Sir Charles Grandison, rather than, say, Goldsmith's bad squire, Mr Thornhill, or indeed Admiral Crawford. His insistence upon moral standards is demonstrated most of all by the manner in which he brings the private theatricals to an end on his surprise return from Antigua. His authority matters not least because the other adults in the household – Lady Bertram and Fanny's Aunt Norris – are manifestly incapable. Aunt Norris, in particular, has spoiled Fanny's cousins and Edmund's sisters, Maria and Julia, which is a primary cause of Maria's running off with Henry Crawford at the novel's end, and Julia's eloping to Gretna Green, albeit with an acceptable man. In *Mansfield Park*, as in *Camilla*, a strand of anti-Marriage Act argument has been absorbed: in the absence of proper authority, Gretna marriages can work to secure a certain justice.

Sir Thomas, however, is an absent patriarch removed from the everyday life in which the marriage plot unfolds. His parliamentary duties take him regularly to London, and falling returns in Antigua further remove him from much of the action. While the household stands in awe of him, he is not sufficiently engaged in the exchanges, conversations, outings, problems and plans which constitute the daily affairs of his family to be able to exercise effective power and judgement over them.[97] The life of the household is precisely Fanny's arena and the source of her growing moral authority. Moreover, Sir Thomas is also removed from the life of the parish, which, arguably and to repeat, is not an organic community in Fielding and Goldsmith's sense, and in which visiting rights among gentlemanly properties stand in the place of full communal life.

In this ambiguous situation, the question of how moral and religious authority is to be instituted becomes pressing. It is probed most directly in one of the novel's key scenes: a discussion about 'good reading' among Fanny, Henry Crawford and Edmund during the period when Henry pursues Fanny as a sanctioned suitor and Edmund is in love with Mary. The amateur theatricals provided an occasion for the squire to reassert his political/familial power, thereby allowing Austen to take a back-handed swipe at the theatre by aligning it (once more) with sensibility, immorality and the Bertram sisters' improper marriage plots, which the episode foreshadows; in contrast, the 'good reading' scene stands as its future-directed analogue. It brings matters of clerical vocation and literary subjectivity to the fore, while suggesting the terms upon which the pulpit and the novel form might come to accommodate each other.

The scene begins with a literary discussion about Shakespeare. In his up-to-date manner, Henry, thinking nationally and politically, notes that Shakespeare is 'part of an Englishman's constitution', and that his 'thoughts and beauties are so spread abroad that one touches them everywhere' (390–1). He reads aloud a passage from *Henry VIII*. As we know from the private theatricals episode, Henry is a consummate actor while Fanny is suspicious of his talent, which is after all an expression of his capacity to roleplay and occupy different value systems. Even she, however, is drawn into this performance:

> All her attention was for her work. She seemed determined to be interested by nothing else. But taste was too strong in her. She could not abstract her mind five minutes; she was forced to listen; his reading was capital, and her pleasure in good reading extreme. To *good* reading, however, she had been long used; her uncle read well – her cousins all – Edmund very well; but in Mr Crawford's reading there was a variety of excellence beyond what she had ever met with. The King, the Queen, Buckingham, Wolsey, Cromwell, all were given in turn; for with the happiest knack, the happiest power of jumping and guessing, he could always light, at will, on the best scene, or the best speeches of each; and whether it were dignity or pride, or tenderness or remorse, of whatever were to be expressed, he could do it with equal beauty. It was truly dramatic. (389–90)

The passage, in free indirect style, privileges Fanny's point of view and enacts a literary subjectivity which she, Henry and Edmund all share. That subjectivity is a matter of performance of course, but also of critical

judgement and intuition: Henry skilfully chooses the 'best' passages as he
skips from scene to scene, character to character, mood to mood.[98]

In his performance's aftermath, the two men begin discussing the
rhetorical principles behind reading aloud, agreeing that the education
system ('the ordinary school-system for boys') is a failure in this regard
(392). They are discussing a controversial topic. As Lucy Newlyn has
shown, competing styles of 'reading aloud' (chanting versus speaking)
were at stake in the bitter struggle between the Bell and Lancaster systems,
that is, between established Anglican practices and emerging non-
denominational models of educational reform, respectively.[99] Indeed, the
dispute over reading foreshadowed a decisive moment in the dismantling
of the old Erastian compact. In preparing for a national education system,
the Lancaster system brought into question the Anglican Church's default
role as the state's pedagogical and administrative instrument. Under its
reforms, the state alone would take control of primary education, in
a victory key to the secular turn of nineteenth-century governmentality
in England.

The Church's incipient failure in this regard becomes apparent when
Edmund is moved to speak about his own professional training as
a clergyman:

> 'Even in my profession', – said Edmund with a smile – 'how little the art of
> reading has been studied! How little a clear manner, and good delivery have
> been attended to! I speak rather of the past, however, than the present.
> There is now a spirit of improvement abroad; but among those who were
> ordained twenty, thirty, forty years ago, the larger number, to judge by their
> performance, must have thought reading was reading, and preaching was
> preaching. It is different now. The subject is more justly considered. It is felt
> that distinctness and energy may have weight in recommending the most
> solid truth; and, besides, there is more general observation and taste, a more
> critical knowledge diffused, than formerly; in every congregation, there is
> a larger proportion who know a little of the matter, and who can judge and
> criticize'. (392–3)

Edmund's understanding of clerical life is a long way from the 'good
parson' tradition discussed in Chapter 4. That tradition had in fact been
invoked by Sir Thomas himself earlier in the novel when he insisted that
Edmund live in his parish on the grounds that 'human nature needs more
lessons than a weekly sermon can convey' and that without 'constant
attention' to his parishioners a parson 'does very little either for their
good or his own' (288). Curiously enough, although Sir Thomas is inclined
to the Whig interest, he does not see the Church's role in pragmatic

Erastian or Addisonian terms. Both Henry and Edmund, on the other hand, view the clergyman in new terms: as a professionally trained oral communicator who draws on learned skills of the kind that Henry has demonstrated in his Shakespeare reading. This good parson needs not just a fine voice, not just taste, not just observation, but also critical judgement, the standards of which are 'distinctness and energy'. Such a mastery of rhetorical forms, which bleeds into literary subjectivity, is required to communicate effectively in a parish community that is increasingly 'heterogeneous' (as Henry later puts it).

The implicit tension between Sir Thomas's traditional understanding of the rural parson's role and Edmund's modern professional one turns out to be significant. From sermonising, Edmund and Henry's conversation turns to liturgy itself. Surprisingly, Henry Crawford has as strong a sense of liturgy as he does of dramatic literature. He has thought carefully about how to make the Anglican service, with 'its redundancies and repetitions' (393), as he calls them, work better for the congregation. Warming to his theme, he repeats and extends Edmund's own argument, returning almost despite himself to the question of how to deliver a sermon, enacting once again his capacity to become other to himself:

> 'A sermon, well delivered, is more uncommon even than prayers well read . . . It is more difficult to speak well than to compose well: that is, the rules and trick of composition are oftener an object of study. A thoroughly good sermon, thoroughly well delivered, is a capital gratification. I can never hear such a one without the greatest admiration and respect, and more than half a mind to take orders and preach myself. There is something in the eloquence of the pulpit, when it is really eloquence, which is entitled to the highest praise and honour. The preacher who can touch and affect such an heterogeneous mass of hearers, on subjects limited, and long worn threadbare in all common hands . . . is a man whom one could not . . . honour enough. I should like to be such a man . . . But then, I must have a London audience. I could not preach, but to the educated; to those who were capable of estimating my composition. And I do not know that I should be fond of preaching often; now and then, perhaps . . . but not for a constancy; it would not do for a constancy'. (394–5)

This exchange is curious and revealing. It assumes not just that most Anglican congregations are 'heterogeneous', and that speaking well is harder than composing, but also that the Church's teachings have 'long worn thread-bare'. In effect, Henry calls into question Anglicanism's doctrinal basis by replacing theology with rhetorical performance. At this point, Henry begins to imagine himself not so much preaching as acting the part of a preacher to an elite Anglican metropolitan audience. Crucially, Edmund does not openly demur, although he laughs a little cynically when Henry claims that he too would like to be a clergyman.

It is Fanny who jibes when Henry declares his dislike of 'constancy', by which he means the commitment to the regular weekly preaching required of a beneficed parson (in this respect, his preference might be for the less regular life of a subaltern cleric). She understands the word in a different sense than Henry intended: that is to say, as denoting a virtue. At this point in the conversation, Edmund withdraws, burying himself in newspaper advertisements for 'a most desirable Estate in South Wales', and school advertisements addressed 'To Parents and Guardians' – advertisements that signify a social order very different from that of the Anglican parish ideal. Alone with Fanny, Henry pounces: 'What did that shake of the head mean?' he asks, insisting that Fanny explain herself. So now, at last, she openly declares her opinion of Henry, and with no Edmund in support throws off her submissiveness. Here is their exchange, beginning with Henry's inquiry of her:

> 'You shook your head at my acknowledging that I should not like to engage in the duties of a clergyman always for a constancy. Yes, that was the word. Constancy: I am not afraid of the word. I would spell it, read it, write it with any body. I see nothing alarming in the word. Did you think I ought?' (396)

To which Fanny replies:

> 'Perhaps, Sir . . . I thought it was a pity you did not always know yourself as well as you seemed to do at that moment.' (397)

Fanny's reproof is multilayered and, indeed, a turning point. At one level, her support for the grind of being a parson (and by implication for the Church's continued moral and social significance) is an oblique rejection of Mary Crawford's dislike of Edmund's profession (which is not yet fully known to Edmund, who is still in love with her). That support is also directed against Henry's changeability, his lack of ethical substance. More importantly, however, the virtue upon which Fanny's own marriage plot rests – her constancy, her unalterable commitment to Edmund during the long delay between falling in love with him and marrying him – is affirmed in a situation where her intelligence and observational powers are fully displayed (after all she, as a young woman, is joining in a discussion about professional matters).

Fanny's marriage plot thus begins its final phase in her negative judgement of Henry, bringing to fruition all that it implies. Having finally revealed why she dislikes him, the process of her and Edmund's disentanglement from other potential partners can begin. Importantly, the two pillars of formal social authority – Sir Thomas, the squire, with his traditional standards, and Edmund, the soon-to-be vicar, with his new professional values – are equally marginalised in this process. Foregrounded, rather, is Fanny's insight into Henry's flawed character, and the irony that attends his reduction of religious doctrine to rhetorical performance (a reduction which, it would appear, both Edmund and his father might accept). Fanny's disclosure of her judgement of Henry, then, is structurally the equivalent of Parson Adams's defiance of Lady Booby in *Joseph Andrews* or Dr Primrose's rebuke to his parishioners before being carted off to jail. It lies at the novel's religio-moral centre. That a young woman of relatively little means or status delivers that judgement matters a great deal, of course, not the least because in that *Mansfield Park* echoes *Pamela*.

Fanny's good judgement and constancy thus emerge as primary virtues for the novel. And they do so against the implied backdrop of a social order beset by moral ambivalence and change in which, for instance, wars are fought, estates bought and sold, slaves traded, fortunes won and lost, spoilt young women recklessly endanger their reputations, a national education system is a prize to be fought over by religious denominations, social status is disjoined from capability, improvements are destructive, clergymen are trained into a profession rather than a vocation, and so on. Constancy, by contrast and as exemplified by Fanny, belongs to love and to nature as the Tory tradition understood it, to female modesty and self-denial, as well as to a steady passion for poetry. Female constancy also belongs to the English novel's marriage plot as it is reimagined by Burney and Austen, for whom it is both an affect and a virtue.

In this way too the marriage plot itself comes to belong to the literary field in which, as Austen makes clear, Shakespeare is another constant ornament. But Fanny's constancy actually stands as something of a rebuke to Shakespeare, who is, after all, championed by that virtuoso of ambiguity and changeability, Henry Crawford. Yet it is Shakespeare who has inserted literature itself into the nation's 'constitution', as Henry has it, and as the powerful effect of his own (too?) good reading skills on Fanny and Edmund would seem to prove. Indeed, the good reading scene in *Mansfield Park* is not just a neat allegory of or turning point for Fanny's marriage plot. It suggests that the literary marriage plot itself can form a basis for the representation of English life and values. On these grounds, the novel genre can claim both a moral authority lacking in its old rival, the theatre, and more capacity than any sermon – than the Church – to reach and affect a 'heterogeneous' British audience.

Afterword

This study has made the case that the secularism of the English marriage plot has been too readily assumed. That assumption dissolves as soon as the genre's early political contexts are more fully taken into account: Court Whig hegemony, the passage of and intense resistance to Hardwicke's Marriage Act and the marriage debates that follow. Yet the origins of the English marriage plot are nothing if not layered. The novels of Richardson, Fielding, Shebbeare and Goldsmith shaped the genre and retain connections to improper marriage cultures. Old urban clandestine wedding markets and theatrical mock marriages continue to haunt them even as, promoting various Anglican and political interests, they invent a genre for which proper church ceremony is central.

Only later in the century does the English marriage plot take the shape most familiar to modern readers, in heroine-focussed secular narratives which understand themselves to be a mode of 'literature' possessing substantive moral and cultural force. In Burney and Austen's courtship novels (which draw much from Haywood especially) nuptial topoi that once carried a theo-political charge – clandestine marriage, vicars, squires, the country estate and the parish – are reconfigured for new purposes, perhaps most notably the containment of radicalism, commercialism and female desire. In them, proper ceremony recedes. At the same time, the marriage plot becomes literary realism's default mode. For later novelists like Walter Scott and George Eliot, this literary marriage plot, now a subspecies of the *Bildungsroman*, provides a platform for the novel genre's 'serious' engagement with national life.[1]

However, even as proper ceremony lost authority and status in the novel form across the eighteenth century, its aura – inherited from the stage – persisted. Few texts attest to this more powerfully than Maria Edgeworth's *Belinda* (1801). Edgeworth's novel tells the story of a 'rational heroine' whose courtship choices engage a colonialism and inter-racialism that remained merely implicit in Austen. As critics have noted, *Belinda*'s attention to slavery and creole culture was unusual, and under pressure Edgeworth would later all but erase it.[2] The novel's dénouement, however, remained largely unrevised and was delivered with an outré comic flourish.

Belinda ends happily enough, with its heroine about to be married to the young aristocrat Clarence Hervey, whom she has always loved but until now believed engaged to another. Its closing passages, however, take the form not of a description of Belinda's wedding ceremony, nor even of a minimalist, materialist account of the terms of her marriage settlement, but rather of a mock literary commentary which suggests, facetiously, that what matters most about her wedding is not how it will proceed but how it might best be narrated. The marriage plot's literariness here is expressed in an overt self-consciousness reminiscent of Gay, Fielding and Shebbeare's self-reflexive marriage narratives.

On the face of it, Edgeworth's closing joke situates proper ceremony in a worldly, secular domain. In a spirit of drollery, Belinda's erstwhile mentor Lady Delacour (a society hostess after Burney's ambivalent older female characters) delivers to her guests a roll call of literary genres and their wedding protocols, naming the novel, the letter and the dramatic tableaux, respectively. As her mock commentary unfolds, it offers a timely and extended reflection on the English marriage plot as written and read by women.

Lady Delacour begins with a surprise, a self-referential proposal – 'shall I finish the novel for you?' (477) – to which Belinda offers her qualified consent:

> [T]here is nothing in which novelists are so apt to err, as in hurrying things toward the conclusion. In not allowing *time* enough for that change of feeling, which change of situation cannot instantly produce. (477)

Belinda, true to character and in the manner of a 'serious' reader or writer, insists on a realist marriage plot – one that inculcates a moral, offers a developmental narrative and holds little or no regard for proper ceremony.

Lady Delacour's nondescript sister-in-law Mrs Margaret Delacour responds differently, and in a way which evokes the marriage plot's history. She hankers after the narrative pleasure of a 'mere wedding' in the old Richardsonian style:

> I am of the old school, and though I could dispense with the description of miss Harriet Byron's worked chairs and fine china ... I like to hear something of the preparation for marriage, as well as of the mere wedding. I like to hear *how* people become happy in a rational manner, better than to be

told in the huddled style of an old fairy tale – *and so they were all married, and they lived very happily all the rest of their days.* (477)

In light of Belinda and Mrs Delacour's preferences – which also reflect the literary-commercial divisions of the women's fiction market – Lady Delacour proposes a compromise:

> Something must be left to the imagination. Positively I will not describe the wedding dresses, or a procession to church. I have no objection to saying, that the happy couples were united by the worthy Mr Moreton; that Mr Percival gave Belinda away; and that immediately after the ceremony, he took the whole party down with him to Oakly-park. Will this do? (477–8)

It will, indeed, do. Belinda and Clarence will be wedded by Mr Moreton (the vicar) under the sanction of Mr Percival of Oakly-park (a benefactor and in days gone by Lady Delacour's suitor). In communicating these details, Lady Delacour telegraphs the English marriage plot's essential lexicon in which weddings involve not just a couple but also a vicar, a squire and a country estate too. She goes on to complete her mock narration with a final, reflexive twist, offering her own reformation as the 'moral' (478) of Belinda's marriage plot.

Belinda treats proper ceremony elliptically and comically while also acknowledging its elemental status for the English marriage plot's development. Edgeworth's irony is salutary because it reminds us that, as the genre became feminised and secularised, it often continued to reference rural parishes where relations between vicars and squires remained central. George Eliot's *Adam Bede* (1859) stands as a key later example of this nostalgia (or inertia): the old eighteenth-century topoi are there used for distinctly nineteenth-century purposes. In this light, we can conclude that the realist marriage plot's secularism is limited. For all its later irony and secular moral seriousness, the genre could not quite shake off its origins in an early eighteenth-century religious mission as well as in church-state politics. In its bones, the English marriage plot is not so much secular as post-secular.

Notes

Introduction: Historicising the English Marriage Plot

1. A newspaper clipping, dated 10 June 1814, 'A scrapbook ... compiled by William Beckford between 1805 and 1814', Beckford 409, Beinecke Library, Yale University.

2. '[T]hrough the same Jesus Christ our Lord, who liveth and reigneth with thee and the Holy Spirit ever, one God, world without end'. *The Book of Common Prayer* (New York: Church Pension Fund, 1945), 303 (orig. 425).

3. Biester argued that tying marriage to religion was contrary to Enlightenment ideals: 'Vorschlag, die Geistlichen nicht mehr bei Vollziehung der Ehen zu bemühen', *Berlinische Monatsschrift* (1783): 265–75. Zöllner's reply: 'Ist es rathsam, das Ehebündniß nicht ferner durch die Religion zu sanciren?' *Berlinische Monatsschrift* (1783): 508–17.

4. Literary scholars routinely understand the Marriage Act of 1753 to have instituted a 'contractual, secular definition of marriage' corresponding to the rise of companionate marriage in the period. The quotation is from Joseph Allen Boone, *Tradition Counter Tradition: Love and the Form of Fiction* (Chicago: Chicago University Press, 1987), 59. See also Robert D. Hume, *The Rakish Stage: Studies in English Drama, 1660–1800* (Carbondale: Southern Illinois University Press, 1983), 181; Christopher Flint, *Family Fictions: Narrative and Domestic Relations in Britain, 1688–1798* (Stanford: Stanford University Press, 1998), 54; Ruth Perry, *Novel Relations: The Transformation of Kinship in English Literature and Culture, 1748–1818* (Cambridge: Cambridge University Press, 2004), 278; and Bonnie Latimer, *Making Gender, Culture, and the Self in the Fiction of Samuel Richardson* (London: Ashgate, 2013), 166.

5. Watt's chapter on *Pamela* remains the standard account of the marriage plot's centrality to the novel's development. See Ian Watt, *The Rise of the Novel: Studies in Defoe, Richardson and Fielding* (Berkeley: University of California Press, 1957), 140–79.

6. Scholarship includes: Katherine Sobba Green, *The Courtship Novel 1740–1820: A Feminized Genre* (Lexington: University of Kentucky Press, 1991); Ruth Bernard Yeazell, *Fictions of Modesty: Women and Courtship in the English Novel* (Chicago: University of Chicago Press, 1991); John P. Zomchick, *Family and the Law in Eighteenth-Century Fiction: The Public Conscience in the Private Sphere* (Cambridge: Cambridge University Press, 1993); Eve Tavor Bannet, *The Domestic Revolution: Enlightenment Feminisms and the Novel* (Baltimore: Johns Hopkins University Press, 2000); Wendy S. Jones, *Consensual Fictions: Women, Liberalism, and the English Novel* (Toronto: University of Toronto Press, 2005); Helen Thompson, *Ingenuous Subjection: Compliance and Power in the Eighteenth-Century Domestic Novel* (Philadelphia: University of Pennsylvania Press, 2005); Chris Roulston, *Narrating Marriage in Eighteenth-Century England and France* (Farnham: Ashgate, 2010); Laura E. Thomason, *The Matrimonial Trap: Eighteenth-Century Women Writers Redefine Marriage* (Lewisburg: Bucknell University Press, 2014); Talia Schaffer, *Romance's Rival: Familiar Marriage in Victorian Fiction* (Oxford: Oxford University Press, 2016); Perry, *Novel Relations*; and Flint, *Family Fictions*. While these accounts construct different lineages for the marriage plot, and offer a rich variety of interpretive approaches, their modes of contextualisation are, for the most part, social, literary and legal rather than political.

7. On the early novel's transnationalism, see Mary Helen McMurran, *The Spread of Novels: Translation and Prose Fiction in the Eighteenth Century* (Princeton: Princeton University Press, 2008) and Srinivas Aravamudan, *Enlightenment Orientalism: Resisting the Rise of the Novel* (Chicago: Chicago University Press, 2012).

8. See Margaret Anne Doody, *The True Story of the Novel* (New Brunswick, NJ: Rutgers University Press, 1996), 67–72, for a discussion of ancient marriage and literature. On traditional comic form and its resolution in festive ritual, usually a wedding or multiple weddings, see Northrop Frye, *Anatomy of Criticism: Four Essays* (Princeton: Princeton University Press, 1957), 163–5.

9. Charlotte Elizabeth Morgan, *The Rise of the Novel of Manners: A Study of English Prose Fiction between 1600 and 1740* (New York: Columbia University Press, 1911), 3ff.

10. Richardson describes *Pamela* as 'a new species of writing' in a letter to Aaron Hill dated 1 February 1741. *Correspondence with Aaron Hill and the Hill Family*, ed. Christine Gerrard (Cambridge: Cambridge University Press, 2013), 90. Subsequent in-text citations are to this edition. The phrase is also applied to Fielding in *An Essay on the New Species of Writing Founded by Mr. Fielding* (1751), usually attributed to Frances Coventry.

11. Walter Scott, *Lives of the Eminent Novelists and Dramatists* (London: Frederick Warne, 1886), 398.

12. For example, Manley's critique of romance in her preface to *The Secret History of Queen Zarah* (1705). On pre-Richardsonian claims to 'historicity', see Ros Ballaster, *Seductive Forms: Women's Amatory Fiction from 1684–1740* (Oxford: Clarendon, 1992), 49–53.

13. Toni Bowers, 'Sex, Lies, and Invisibility: Amatory Fiction from the Restoration to Mid-Century', in *The Columbia History of the British Novel*, ed. John J. Richetti (New York: Columbia University Press, 1994), 58.

14. Thomas Keymer and Peter Sabor, eds, *The Pamela Controversy: Criticisms and Adaptations of Samuel Richardson's 'Pamela', 1740–1750*, 6 vols (London: Pickering and Chatto, 2001) and Thomas Keymer and Peter Sabor, *'Pamela' in the Marketplace: Literary Controversy and Print Culture in Eighteenth-Century Britain and Ireland* (Cambridge: Cambridge University Press, 2005).

15. John J. Richetti, *The English Novel in History 1700–1800* (London: Routledge, 1999), 84.

16. Watt, *Rise of the Novel*, 173ff.

17. Rebecca Probert, *Marriage Law and Practice in the Long Eighteenth Century: A Reassessment* (Cambridge: Cambridge University Press, 2009), 1–18.

18. On marriage and Reformation theology, see John Witte Jr, *From Sacrament to Contract: Marriage, Religion, and Law in the Western Tradition* (Louisville: Westminster John Knox Press, 1997), 42ff.

19. Michel Foucault, *The History of Sexuality*, vol. 1: *The Will to Knowledge* (London: Penguin, 1988), 140ff.

20. Charles Taylor, *A Secular Age* (Cambridge, MA: Belknap, Harvard University Press, 2007) and Hans Blumenberg, *The Legitimacy of the Modern Age*, trans. Robert M. Wallace (Cambridge, MA: MIT Press, 1983).

21. Brent S. Sirota, *The Christian Monitor: The Church of England and the Age of Benevolence, 1680–1730* (New Haven: Yale University Press, 2014), 2–7 and 257–9.

22. Patrick Parrinder, *Nation and Novel: The English Novel from Its Origins to the Present Day* (Oxford: Oxford University Press, 2006).

1 Church, State and the Public Politics of Marriage

1. James Boswell's journal entry for Tuesday 25 July 1769. James Boswell, *Boswell in Search of a Wife, 1766–1769*, ed. Frank Brady and Frederick A. Pottle (New York: McGraw-Hill, 1956), 239–40.

2. Quoted in Boswell, *Search of a Wife*, 240.

3. Boswell, *Search of a Wife*, 279.

4. Boswell's mock marriage contract is reproduced in Boswell, *Search of a Wife*, 348.

5. Samuel Richardson, *The History of Sir Charles Grandison*, ed. Jocelyn Harris (Oxford: Oxford University Press, 1986), 1: 25. Unless otherwise stated, subsequent references in the text, by part and page number, refer to this edition.

6. Harriet's remarks, in particular, are informed by Reformation theology – specifically the Anglican absorption of the Lutheran 'social' and Calvinist 'convenantal' models of marriage.

7. Montgomerie, a regular reader of the Book of Common Prayer, confessed herself 'something of an Episcopal at heart' (Boswell, *Search of a Wife*, 341).

8. Witte coins the term 'commonwealth model' for the Anglican conception of marriage's foundational place within the network of domestic and political institutions understood to comprise the commonwealth. 'Church, State and Marriage: Four Early Modern Protestant Models', *Oxford Journal of Law and Religion* 1, no. 1 (2012): 8–9.

9. The term is originally William Cobbett's. See W. D. Rubinstein, 'The End of "Old Corruption" in Britain 1780–1860', *Past and Present* 101, no. 1 (1983): 55–86.

10. Sirota, *Christian Monitor*, 1–7; Tony Claydon, *William III and the Godly Revolution* (Cambridge: Cambridge University Press, 2004); Steve Pincus, *1688: The First Modern Revolution* (New Haven: Yale University Press, 2009).

11. Claydon, *William III*, 83.

12. E. P. Thompson, *The Poverty of Theory* (London: Merlin, 1978), 252.

13. Mark Goldie, 'The English System of Liberty', in *The Cambridge History of Eighteenth-Century Political Thought*, ed. Mark Goldie and Robert Wokler (Cambridge: Cambridge University Press, 2006), 50.

14. J. C. D. Clark, *English Society, 1660–1832: Religion, Ideology, and Politics during the Ancien Regime* (Cambridge: Cambridge University Press, 2000), 30–2. Against Clark's 'confessional state' model, others insist on the slow, partial and ongoing nature of Anglican confessionalisation. See Jeremy Gregory, *Restoration, Reformation and Reform: Archbishops of Canterbury and Their Diocese* (Oxford: Clarendon, 2000), 3–4 and Eamon Duffy, 'The Long Reformation: Catholicism, Protestantism and the Multitude', in *England's London Reformation 1500–1800*, ed. Nicholas Tyacke (London: Routledge, 1998), 33–70.

15. Goldie, 'System of Liberty', 50–2.

16. See G. F. A. Best, *Temporal Pillars: Queen Anne's Bounty, the Ecclesiastical Commissioners, and the Church of England* (Cambridge: Cambridge University Press, 1964), 95ff.

17. As J. H. Plumb argued, large estate holders increasingly dominated the less wealthy country gentry economically and politically. See *England in the Eighteenth Century* (New York: Penguin, 1963), 18–19.

18. Following Robert Harris, I call the opposition to the Court Whigs the 'Country interest' in order to pass over difficulties in classifying the various groups, interests and ideologies arrayed against them. Certainly by 1750, old-style Jacobite Tories were a spent force, and the old 'Country Whig' interest that had resisted Walpole's policies (it was against 'war, high taxes and government by patronage and finance', to use J. G. A. Pocock's words) had been defanged. See Robert Harris, *Politics and the Nation: Britain in the Mid-Eighteenth Century* (Oxford: Oxford University Press, 2002), 67–101 and Pocock, *Virtue, Commerce, and History: Essays on Political Thought and History, Chiefly in the Eighteenth Century* (Cambridge: Cambridge University Press, 1985), 77.

19. Reed Browning, *Political and Constitutional Ideas of the Court Whigs* (Baton Rouge: Louisiana State University Press, 1982), 1–5, 169–70. Patriot rhetoric and values were also sourced in civic humanism. See Quentin Skinner, 'The Principles and Practices of Opposition: The Case of Bolingbroke versus Walpole', in *Historical Perspectives: Essays in Honour of J. H. Plumb*, ed. N. McKendrick (London: Europa, 1974), 93–218.

20. Christine Gerrard, *The Patriot Opposition to Walpole: Politics, Poetry, and Myth, 1725–1742* (Oxford: Clarendon, 1994), 10–12.

21. See H. T. Dickinson on Court Whig philosophy in *Liberty and Property: Political Ideology in Eighteenth-Century Britain* (New York: Holmes and Meier Publishers, 1977), 158.

22. Eliga H. Gould, *The Persistence of Empire: British Political Culture in the Age of the American Revolution* (Chapel Hill: University of North Carolina Press, 2000), 88.

23. Linda Colley, *Britons: Forging the Nation, 1707–1837* (New Haven: Yale University Press, 1992), 11.

24. Browning, *Political and Constitutional Ideas*, 11–14.

25. See B. W. Young, 'William Warburton, a Polemic Divine', in *Religion and Enlightenment in Eighteenth-Century England: Theological Debate from Locke to Burke* (Oxford: Clarendon, 1998), 167–212.

26. William Warburton, *The Alliance between Church and State: Or, The Necessity and Equity of an Established Religion and a Test Law Demonstrated*, 4th edn (London: A. Millar and J. and R. Tonson, 1766), 170. On its influence, see Edward R. Norman, *Church and Society in England 1770–1970: A Historical Study* (Oxford: Clarendon, 1976), 16.

27. William Warburton, 'Preface to Volume III of *Clarissa Harlowe*, 1748', in *Novel and Romance 1700–1800: A Documentary Record*, ed. Ioan Williams (London: Routledge Revivals, 2010), 92.

28. That revival effort dated back to the post-revolutionary period. It championed England's moral and religious renewal through public

association and charitable endeavour in the civil sphere. Retrospectively, the period was known as 'the age of benevolence'. See Sirota, *Christian Monitor*, 1–7, and, differently, Claydon, *William III*, 236.

29. See Warburton, 'Preface', 92.
30. Peter Brown, *The Chathamites* (London: Macmillan, 1967), 235.
31. David Philip Miller, 'Birch, Thomas (1705–1766)', in *Oxford Dictionary of National Biography*, www.oxforddnb.com/view/article/2436.
32. E. P. Thompson, *Whigs and Hunters: The Origin of the Black Act* (London: Allen Lane, 1975), 208.
33. Peter D. G. Thomas, 'Yorke, Philip, First Earl of Hardwicke (1690–1764)', in *Oxford Dictionary of National Biography*, www.oxforddnb.com/view/article/30245.
34. See Browning's chapter on Hardwicke in *Political and Constitutional Ideas*, 151–74. The decision sealed his reputation as 'the man who did so much to make equity a scientific system'. See Ian Simpson Ross, *The Life of Adam Smith* (Oxford: Oxford University Press, 1996), 292.
35. Peter Linebaugh, *The London Hanged: Crime and Civil Society in the Eighteenth Century* (Cambridge: Cambridge University Press, 1992), 70–3.
36. P. C. Yorke, *The Life and Correspondence of Philip Yorke, Earl of Hardwicke, Lord High Chancellor of Great Britain* (Cambridge: Cambridge University Press, 1913), 2:472–4.
37. The term 'fiscal-military state' originates from John Brewer's influential argument that the English state and its fiscal system were shaped by the demands of war. See *The Sinews of Power: War, Money and the English State 1688–1793* (London: Century Hutchinson, 1989).
38. The quotation is from Paul Langford, *A Polite and Commercial People: England 1727–1783* (Oxford: Oxford University Press, 1989), 41.
39. Quoted in Best, *Temporal Pillars*, 72. On Hardwicke's discouragement of pluralism, see W. M. Jacob, *Lay People and Religion in the Early Eighteenth Century* (Cambridge: Cambridge University Press, 1996), 25.
40. On Fielding's involvement in the campaign to ban 'heritable Jurisdictions', see Martin C. Battestin, *Henry Fielding: A Life* (London: Routledge, 1989), 418. Also see J. A. Downie, *A Political Biography of Henry Fielding* (London: Pickering and Chatto, 2009), 193–4.
41. Thomas R. Cleary, *Henry Fielding: Political Writer* (Waterloo, ON: Wilfrid Laurier University Press, 1984), 209. Much of Fielding's anti-Jacobite propaganda extolled the virtues of English Protestantism and liberty against Papist absolutism.
42. J. G. A. Pocock (borrowing from J. C. Beckett) uses the term 'the Age of the Three Kingdoms' to speak inclusively of English, Scottish and Irish history in the century before the Union of 1707. See *The Discovery of Islands: Essays in*

British History (Cambridge: Cambridge University Press, 2005), 28, 97 and 74–6.

43. Browning, *Political and Constitutional Ideas*, 170.
44. Five years later, in 1758, a second registration bill was defeated in Parliament.
45. See Thomas W. Perry, *Public Opinion, Propaganda, and Politics in Eighteenth-Century England: A Study of the Jew Bill of 1753* (Cambridge, MA: Harvard University Press, 1962). Dana Y. Rabin, 'The Jew Bill of 1753: Masculinity, Virility, and the Nation', *Eighteenth-Century Studies* 39, no. 2 (2006): 157–71.
46. D. V. Glass, *Numbering the People: The Eighteenth-Century Population Controversy and the Development of Censes and Vital Statistics in Britain* (Farnborough: Saxon House, 1973), 11. For William Brackenridge, Robert Wallace and William Bell, England's population was in decline. Their opponents included David Hume and William Temple.
47. See Maxine Berg and Elizabeth Eger, eds, *Luxury in the Eighteenth Century: Debates, Desires, and Delectable Goods* (New York: Palgrave Macmillan, 2003). Charles Churchill's Wilkesite satirical poem 'The Times' (1764) explicitly tied the Marriage Act to a culture of sodomy and unnatural law: 'Vile Pathicks read the Marriage Act with pride/And fancy that the Law is on their side.' (lines 551–6), *The Poetical Works of Charles Churchill*, ed. and intro. by Douglas Grant (Oxford: Clarendon, 1956), 405.
48. Glass, *Numbering the People*, 19–20.
49. The Act belonged with previous attempts, in 1747, 1748 and 1751, to attract foreign immigrants to offset a perceived labour shortage. Langford, *Polite and Commercial*, 224.
50. *The Gentleman's Magazine*, London, October 1753, 452.
51. This claim is made by Hannah Arendt in *The Origins of Totalitarianism* (New York: Harcourt Brace, 1973), 11–15.
52. Harris, *Politics and the Nation*, 82.
53. Rabin, 'The Jew Bill of 1753', 166ff and Perry, *Public Opinion*, 8.
54. Quoted in Linda Colley, *Defiance of Oligarchy: The Tory Party 1714–1760* (Cambridge: Cambridge University Press, 1982), 131.
55. Harris, *Politics and the Nation*, 82–3. The quotation is from *The London Evening Post*, 23 June 1753, 27. Hardwicke's letter to Secker is reprinted in Yorke, *Life and Correspondence*, 2:128.
56. Perry, *Public Opinion*, 132.
57. An Act for the Better Preventing of Clandestine Marriages, 1753, 26 Geo II cap. 33. The Act is reproduced in R. B. Outhwaite, *Clandestine Marriage in England, 1550–1850* (London: The Hambleton Press, 1995), 173–80. Subsequent citations of the Act refer to section numbers and are given in the text.

58. The case of *Cochran* v *Campbell* reached the House of Lords in 1753. Captain John Campbell of Carrick had bigamously married Jean Campbell in 1725 and lived with her for twenty years while keeping his first wife, Magdalen Cochran, whom he had married in 1724, as his mistress. Upon the captain's death in 1746, Cochran claimed a pension as his widow, prompting Campbell to take her to court. The Lords found in favour of Campbell as the publicly acknowledged wife. Both marriages had been irregular unions. See Leah Leneman, 'The Scottish Case That Led to Hardwicke's Marriage Act', *Law and History Review* 17, no. 1 (1999): 161–9.

59. Outhwaite, *Clandestine Marriage*, 86.

60. Hardwicke's private notes on the Marriage Act debate indicate that he was deeply concerned about the inadequacy of registration practices: '[t]he security of some Publick Register seems necessary: and of one that shall be better kept than the Parochial Registers are.' Quoted in Outhwaite, *Clandestine Marriage*, 80–2.

61. Commentary on the nullity clauses includes O. R. McGregor, *Divorce in England* (London: Heinemann, 1957), 14 and Roger Lee Brown, 'The Rise and Fall of Fleet Marriages', in *Marriage and Society: Studies in the Social History of Marriage*, ed. R. B. Outhwaite (London: Europa, 1981), 136. Probert cautions that the Marriage Act's nullity clauses and punitive measures were interpreted liberally in the courts and applied selectively. 'The Judicial Interpretation of Lord Hardwicke's Act of 1753', *Legal History* 23, no. 2 (2002): 129–51 and 'The Impact of the Marriage Act of 1753: Was It Really "A Most Cruel Law for the Fair Sex"?' *Eighteenth-Century Studies* 38, no. 2 (2005): 257.

62. McGregor (*Divorce in England*, 14) and Flint (*Family Fictions*, 54) view the Marriage Act as progressive legislation. Those who view it as regressive include Lawrence Stone, *Road to Divorce. England 1530–1987* (Oxford: Oxford University Press, 1990), 135–7; John R. Gillis, *For Better, for Worse: British Marriages, 1600 to the Present* (New York: Oxford University Press, 1985), 140–2; Erica Harth, 'The Virtue of Love: Lord Hardwicke's Marriage Act', *Cultural Critique* 9 (1988): 123–54; Belinda Meteyard, 'Illegitimacy and Marriage in Eighteenth-Century England', *Journal of Interdisciplinary History* 10 (1980): 486–7; Eve Tavor Bannet, 'The Marriage Act of 1753: "A Most Cruel Law for the Fair Sex"', *Eighteenth-Century Studies* 30, no. 3 (1997): 250; and Perry, *Novel Relations*, 277–8.

63. Probert, 'Impact of the Marriage Act', 257–8 and *Marriage Law and Practice*, 6–20.

64. Outhwaite, *Clandestine Marriage*, 84.

65. From the 1520s, German Protestant states introduced civil marriage ordinances based on three fundamental reforms: 1) legal requirements for

public weddings involving the participation of parents, witnesses and the church; 2) the curtailment of the number of impediments to betrothal and marriage; and 3) the introduction of divorce on proof of cause and provisions for remarriage. See Witte, *From Sacrament to Contract*, 51–4.

66. The Anglican Church's position on marriage was an anomalous blend of Anglo-Catholic and reformist thought. Witte, 'Church, State and Marriage', 3–5, 8–9.

67. Quoted in Outhwaite, *Clandestine Marriage*, 87. For Secker's role in the passage of the Marriage Act, see 79–80.

68. Some of these objections are repeated by modern commentators, e.g. Eve Tavor Bannet, 'The Marriage Act of 1753', 250 and Perry, *Novel Relations*, 277–8.

69. My emphasis on the 'polite' nature of the Marriage Act debate is not intended to underplay the significance of popular protests during its passage. See David Lemmings, 'Marriage and the Law in the Eighteenth Century: Hardwicke's Marriage Act of 1753', *The Historical Journal* 39, no. 2 (1996): 340.

70. Reverend Alexander Keith and John Shebbeare were among those who linked the two bills.

71. Outhwaite, *Clandestine Marriage*, 92–3.

72. See his letter to Elizabeth Carter, 17 August 1753, published posthumously in *Monthly Magazine* 33 (1812): 541.

73. Three of Mulso's letters survive; the third is most relevant. See Hester Mulso Chapone, *The Works of Mrs. Chapone: Now First Collected. In Four Volumes* (London: John Murray, 1807), 2:29–143. For this quote 2:113–14.

74. Chapone, *Works*, 2:114. For commentary on Mulso and Richardson's exchange, see Thomas Keymer, *Richardson's 'Clarissa' and the Eighteenth-Century Reader* (Cambridge: Cambridge University Press, 1992), 98–104 and Thomason, *Matrimonial Trap*, 67–84.

75. 'Duty is reciprocal: there is a duty owing by parents to their children, as well as by children to their parents' (61). For Townshend's speech, see William Cobbett, *Parliamentary History of England, from the Earliest Period to the Year 1803* (London: T. C. Hansard, 1813), 15:49–62.

76. Horace Walpole believed Townshend's speech to be autobiographical. His remarks appear in a letter (24 May 1753) to Henry Seymour Conway. (Cobbett, *Parliamentary History*, 15:32–3.)

77. Quoted in Yorke, *Life and Correspondence*, 2:65.

78. On Court Whig understandings of natural law, as adumbrated by Thomas Herring, Samuel Squire and Lord Hardwicke, see Browning, *Political and Constitutional Ideas*, 241–51. On the origins of the natural law tradition, see

J. B. Schneewind, *The Invention of Autonomy: A History of Modern Moral Philosophy* (Cambridge: Cambridge University Press, 1998), 17–21.

79. Browning, *Political and Constitutional Ideas*, 249–52.

80. Quoted in T. C. Duncan Eaves and Ben D. Kimpel, *Samuel Richardson: A Biography* (Oxford: Clarendon, 1971), 549.

81. I am indebted to recent scholarly conceptions of early modern natural law not as a doctrine but as a language that set in play rival juridical and political programmes. See Knud Haakonssen, 'Protestant Natural-Law Theory: A General Interpretation', in *New Essays on the History of Autonomy: A Collection Honoring J. B. Schneewind*, ed. Natalie Brender and Larry Krasnoff (Cambridge: Cambridge University Press, 2004), 92–109 and Ian Hunter, 'Natural Law As Political Philosophy', in *The Oxford Handbook of Philosophy in Early Modern Europe*, ed. Desmond Clarke and Catherine Wilson (Oxford: Oxford University Press, 2011), 476.

82. Henry Gally, *Some Considerations upon Clandestine Marriages*, 2nd edn (London: J. Hughs, 1750). Citing George Elliot Howard's *A History of Matrimonial Institutions* (Chicago: Chicago University Press, 1904), Bannet dates the first edition 1729 ('The Marriage Act of 1753', 252, n. 22). However, neither the *Oxford Dictionary of National Biography* nor *Eighteenth-Century Collections Online* cites a first edition.

83. Gally, *Some Considerations*, preface. On the corruption of the clergy, see Humphrey Prideaux, *The Case of Clandestine Marriages Stated Wherein Are Shewn the Causes from Whence This Corruption Ariseth* (London: 1691).

84. Gally, *Some Considerations*, 12–13.

85. Gally, *Some Considerations*, 15.

86. Yorke, *Life and Correspondence*, 2:60.

87. Pufendorf's work, widely translated throughout Europe, was taken up in Britain most directly by Scottish Enlightenment thinkers (Hutcheson, Millar and Smith). English translations of *De jure naturae et gentium* had appeared in seven editions by 1750. See Ian Hunter and David Saunders, 'Bringing the State to England: Andrew Tooke's Translation of Samuel Pufendorf's *De Officio Hominis et Civis*', *History of Political Thought* 24, no. 2 (2003): 218–19. Pufendorf was also regularly cited as an authority in English debates about the limits of kindred marriage (or incest). See Ellen Pollak, *Incest and the English Novel 1684–1814* (Baltimore: Johns Hopkins University Press, 2003), 36–9.

88. Locke defines marriage as 'a voluntary compact between man and woman' on which the social contract is based. John Locke, *Two Treatises of Government*, ed. Peter Laslett (Cambridge: Cambridge University Press, 1998), 2.§78, 319. For commentary on Locke's understanding of marriage, see Witte, 'Church, State and Marriage', 10–18. The quoted text is from Samuel Pufendorf, *The*

Law of Nature and Nations: or, A General System of the Most Important Principles of Morality, Jurisprudence, and Politics, 8 books, 5th edn (London: J. and J. Bonwicke, 1749), 563.

89. Ian Hunter and David Saunders, introduction to *Natural Law and Civil Sovereignty: Moral Right and State Authority in Early Modern Political Thought* (New York: Palgrave, 2002), 2.

90. Pufendorf, *Law of Nature*, 558, 561.

91. Pufendorf, *Law of Nature*, 559, 564.

92. Pufendorf, *Law of Nature*, 565.

93. Gally, *Some Considerations*, 6.

94. Gally, *Some Considerations*, 6–7.

95. Cobbett, *Parliamentary History of England*, 15: 22 (Nugent); 69–70, 74 (Fox); 78 (Murray rebuttal). Fox makes his High Church comments on 69–70.

96. For a more straightforward High Church rebuttal of the Marriage Act, see Marshall Montague Merrick's *Marriage a Divine Institution* (London: E. Withers, 1754).

97. Warburton all but accused Stebbing of crypto-Jacobitism in *An Apologetical Dedication to the Reverend Dr Henry Stebbing* (London: J. and P. Knapton, 1746), a rebuttal of Stebbing's earlier attack on Warburton's *The Divine Legation of Moses* (1738–41). See B. W. Young, 'Warburton, William (1698–1779)', in *Oxford Dictionary of National Biography*, www.oxforddnb.com/view/article/28680.

98. Henry Stebbing, *An Enquiry into the Force and Operation of the Annulling Clauses in a Late Act for the Better Preventing of Clandestine Marriages, with Respect to Conscience in which the Rights of Marriage both in and out of Society Are Briefly Discussed* (London: M. Cooper, 1754), 13.

99. Stebbing also referred to earlier writings on matrimony by Latitudinarian bishops Edward Stillingfleet and William Fleetwood. *Enquiry*, 5 and 16.

100. Stebbing, *Enquiry*, 19.

101. My dating of Warburton's sermon is based upon his remarks in a letter to Richard Hurd, dated 30 September 1754. Quoted in John Nicols, *Literary Anecdotes of the Eighteenth Century: Comprising Biographical Memoirs of William Bowyer*, 6 vols (London: Nichols, Son, and Bentley, 1812), 2:269.

102. William Warburton, 'On the Nature of the Marriage Union. Matt. Xix. 6: Sermon XVII', in *The Works of the Right Reverend William Warburton, D.D., Lord Bishop of Gloucester*, 12 vols, ed. Richard Hurd (London: T. Cadell and W. Davies, 1811), 9:348.

103. Warburton, 'Marriage Union', 349.

104. Warburton, 'Marriage Union', 350. Warburton here draws on doctrine advanced by Benjamin Hoadly in his *The Nature of the Kingdom, or Church, of Christ* (1717), which argued against the autonomy of the

Church on the grounds that 'Christ left behind him no visible human authority' so that any claim to it was a dangerous denial of civil authority. See Stephen Taylor, 'Hoadly, Benjamin (1676–1761)', in *Oxford Dictionary of National Biography*, www.oxforddnb.com/view/arti cle/13375.

105. Warburton, 'Marriage Union', 352.
106. Warburton, 'Marriage Union', 352–3.

2 Clandestine Marriage, Commerce and the Theatre

1. Outhwaite, *Clandestine Marriage*, 31–5 and Donald A. Spaeth, *The Church in an Age of Danger: Parsons and Parishioners, 1660–1740* (Cambridge: Cambridge University Press, 2000), 211–12.

2. Because consent was fundamental to the sacramental doctrine of marriage, scholastic theologians held that while clandestine marriage was wrong, it was nonetheless valid. Philip L. Reynolds, *How Marriage Became One of the Sacraments: The Sacramental Theology of Marriage from Its Medieval Origins to the Council of Trent* (Cambridge: Cambridge University Press, 2016), 981–2.

3. *The Craftsman* (London, 18 December 1736). On the corruption of the licence system, see David Cressy, *Birth, Marriage, and Death: Ritual, Religion, and the Life-Cycle in Tudor and Stuart England* (Oxford: Oxford University Press, 1997), 310. Horace Walpole notes that banns were unfashionable among the elite: 'Publication of banns was . . . totally in disuse except amongst the inferior people, who did not blush to obey the law. Persons of quality . . . were constantly married by special licence.' Walpole is quoted in Walter Besant, *The Survey of London: London in the Eighteenth-Century* (London: Adam and Charles Black, 1902), 268.

4. Lawrence Stone, *Uncertain Unions: Marriage in England 1660–1753* (Oxford: Oxford University Press, 1992), 29. Jeremy Boulton tracks significant incremental changes in the proportion of London's population marrying at the Fleet in 'Clandestine Marriages in London: An Examination of a Neglected Urban Variable', *Urban History* 20, no. 2 (1993): 202–3.

5. Probert, *Marriage Law and Practice*, 189–90. Spaeth also notes that clandestine marriage rates may have declined in the early eighteenth century (*Age of Danger*, 203).

6. Gill Newton, 'Clandestine Marriage in Early Modern London: When, Where and Why?' *Continuity and Change* 29, no. 2 (2014): 152–3, 157–62. To capture marriages outside the home parish, Newton supplements parish records with the records of inhabitants' weddings that took place elsewhere. The expression 'commonest means' is Boulton's ('Clandestine Marriages in London', 202–3).

7. Spaeth, *Age of Danger*, 203.

8. The priest's role in marriage was a matter of debate: Protestant reformers argued that although matrimony was a holy state, it was not made so by clerical solemnisation. The Anglican Church, however, maintained that marriage required a minister. See Cressy, *Birth, Marriage, and Death*, 320–1.

9. Lawrence Stone, *The Family, Sex and Marriage in England, 1500–1800* (New York: Harper & Row, 1977), 30.

10. Henry Swinburne, *A Treatise of Spousals or Matrimonial Contracts* (London: S. Roycroft for Robert Clavell, 1686), 15.

11. Probert, *Marriage Law and Practice*, 46.

12. Warburton, 'Marriage Union', 352.

13. Roger Lee Brown, 'The Rise and Fall', 118–19; Probert, 'Impact of the Marriage Act', 248.

14. Probert, *Marriage Law and Practice*, 184. By the 1730s some common law judges, including Hardwicke, had begun to reject as evidence irregular marriage certificates and register entries because of their unreliability (Stone, *Road to Divorce*, 115–16).

15. Spaeth, *Age of Danger*, 203. For Lawrence Stone and John R. Gillis, clandestine marriage belongs to a pattern of irregular marriage associated with plebeian sociability and noncompliance. See Stone, *Uncertain Unions*, 30 and Gillis, *For Better, for Worse*, 6–8.

16. Outhwaite estimates that 6 per cent of clandestine weddings were amongst Dissenters and 1 per cent amongst Catholics (*Clandestine Marriage*, 36–7). Probert gives the figure as no more than 2 per cent (*Marriage Law and Practice*, 165).

17. The political changes wrought by the Restoration added to the number of ministers willing to perform clandestine weddings. In 1662 more than 1,000 left their livings because they would not subscribe to the new Prayer Book. Probert, *Marriage Law and Practice*, 171.

18. For Humphrey Prideaux, clandestine marriage was an abuse of the system committed by 'indigent Curates or unpreferr'd Chaplains … who have nothing to lose [and] are out of the Reach of … penalty'. *Case of Clandestine Marriages*, 2.

19. On the Church of England's modification of the Catholic wedding ceremony and emphasis on public witnessing, see Cressy, *Birth, Marriage, and Death*, 321, 338–42. The civil marriage statutes of various German Protestant states mandated parental consent, witnesses, public church solemnisation and registration with church officials (Witte, *From Sacrament to Contract*, 59–61).

20. Probert, *Marriage Law and Practice*, 182–3, 175–6.

21. Quoted in Norman Sykes, *Church and State in England in the XVIII Century* (Hamden, CT: Archon Books, 1962), 221.

22. Gillis, *For Better, for Worse*, 218; Linebaugh, *London Hanged*, 141–2.

23. In 1712 *The Spectator* noted the volume of weddings at St Pancras: 'We are inform'd from Pankridge, that a dozen Weddings were lately celebrated in the Mother Church of that Place.' *The Spectator*, ed. Donald F. Bond, 5 vols (Oxford: Clarendon, 1965), 4:93.

24. John Southerden Burn, *The Fleet Registers. Comprising the History of Fleet Marriages and Some Account of the Parsons and Marriage-House Keepers, with Extracts from the Registers* (London: Rivingtons, Butterworth and Suter, 1833), 4.

25. *The Works of William Congreve*, ed. D. F. McKenzie, 3 vols (Oxford: Oxford University Press, 2011), 1.1.103–9.

26. *The Tatler*, ed. Donald F. Bond, 3 vols (Oxford: Clarendon, 1987), 1:66–7.

27. Boulton claims that the occupations of those marrying clandestinely reflected 'a cross-section of London society' ('Clandestine Marriages in London', 208). Brown's sample figures confirm this ('Rise and Fall', 126). See also Probert, *Marriage Law and Practice*, 208.

28. Probert, *Marriage Law and Practice*, 189.

29. Probert, *Marriage Law and Practice*, 172–3, 186–8. A statement of her methodology appears on 15–16.

30. Probert, *Marriage Law and Practice*, 208; Newton, 'When, Where and Why', 175.

31. On the literature of London, see Penelope J. Corfield, 'Walking the City Streets: The Urban Odyssey in Eighteenth-Century England', *Journal of Urban History* 16, no. 2 (1990): 132–74.

32. The first recorded Fleet marriage was as early as 1613. See Ben Weinreb and Christopher Hibbert, *The London Encyclopaedia* (London: Macmillan, 1983), 283.

33. Brown, 'Rise and Fall', 128.

34. Legislation of 1695 (6 and 7 Will. 3 c. 6) and 1696 (7 and 8 Will. 3 c. 6, s. 52) imposed fines and suspensions on clergymen who performed church weddings without banns or licence (Probert, *Marriage Law and Practice*, 175).

35. The Act is 10 Anne c. 18.

36. On parsons travelling to the Fleet, see Probert, *Marriage Law and Practice*, 192. Miles Ogborn estimates that the area contained about twenty marriage shops. See 'This Most Lawless Space: The Geography of the Fleet and the Making of Lord Hardwicke's Marriage Act of 1753', *New Formations* 37 (1999): 16. Quoting figures from Jeremy Boulton and Roger Lee Brown, Ogborn notes that from 1694 to 1754 between 200,000 and 300,000 marriages were performed in and around the Fleet prison. As early as 1700, there were more than 2,500 marriages at the Fleet per annum, and by 1740 some 6,600, accounting for somewhere between half and three-quarters of the marriages in London (16).

37. On the legal status of debtors, London's debtors' sanctuaries and the 'Rules', see Ogborn, 'Lawless Space', 20–1.
38. Ogborn, 'Lawless Space', 13.
39. Alex Smith, *A Compleat History of the Lives and Robberies of the most Notorious Highway-Men, Foot-Pads, Shop-Lifts, and Cheats, of both Sexes*, 3 vols (London: Sam Briscoe, 1719), 2:218.
40. Linebaugh, *London Hanged*, 141–2.
41. Linebaugh, *London Hanged*, 138–41.
42. John Gay, *Dramatic Works*, ed. John Fuller, 2 vols (Oxford: Clarendon, 1983), 2: introduction, line 15.
43. Burn, *Fleet Registers*, 53–4.
44. Brown, 'Rise and Fall', 129–30.
45. Thomas Pennant, *Some Account of London*, 3rd edn (London: Robert Faulder, 1793), 232–3.
46. William H. Draper, *The Morning Walk, or, City Encompassed* (London: 1751), 42. Burn details the careers of several clandestine parsons, including Elliott, Keith and Gaynam, active from 1709 to 1740 (*Fleet Registers*, 92–100).
47. Cited in Burn, *Fleet Registers*, 6–7.
48. As cited in Charles Knight, *London*, vol. 4: 'London: Virtue' (London: Charles Knight & Company, 1875–77), 58. Also see Burn, *Fleet Registers*, 6–7.
49. See Jessica Warner, *Craze: Gin and Debauchery in the Age of Reason* (London: Random House, 2002).
50. Knight, *London*, 52.
51. Ogborn, 'Lawless Space', 29–30.
52. Draper, *Morning Walk*, 42–3.
53. The prints were published in 1745; the original paintings (1743–5) are held in the National Gallery, London, catalogue nos. 113–18.
54. For Ogburn, the first plate deploys an iconography of deception and the second turns on themes of wanton femininity and cuckoldry ('Lawless Space', 18–19). For Newton, June's second print underscores the exuberance of Fleet weddings ('When, Where and Why', 156–7).
55. On clandestine marriage to avoid debt, see Stone, *Road to Divorce*, 122. On pregnancy, the Fleet registers record brides 'big with child' (Burn, *Fleet Registers*, 54). Also Outhwaite, *Clandestine Marriage*, 60–1 and, differently, Newton, 'When, Where and Why', 172–5.
56. Russel was a High Church divine with Jacobite sympathies. See Battestin, *Henry Fielding*, 132–3.
57. *The Grub-Street Journal*, London, 27 February 1735.
58. Burn, *Fleet Registers*, 76. Burn notes that some Fleet parsons kept records 'not to be registered in ye yearly book' (47). In one such secret register, dated

1748–53, 'nearly all the contracting parties were of a superior station in life' (48).

59. Anne Pimlott Baker, 'Keith, Alexander (*d.* 1758)', in *Oxford Dictionary of National Biography*, www.oxforddnb.com/view/article/15260.

60. These figures are provided by Outhwaite, *Clandestine Marriage*, 52. See also George J. Armytage, ed., *Register of Baptisms and Marriages at St. George's Chapel, May Fair* (London: Mitchell and Hughes, 1889).

61. *The Daily Advertiser*, London, 16 April 1743. Keith threatened to excommunicate Gibson and Trebeck in turn.

62. Baker, 'Keith, Alexander (*d.* 1758)'. Burn estimates that Keith's patrons averaged some 6,000 couples a year. Just fifty regular contracts were solemnised in the neighbouring St Anne's Church (*Fleet Registers*, 98). Outhwaite disputes these figures (*Clandestine Marriage*, 106).

63. *Old England*, London, 3 March 1750. Similar advertisements appeared in *The Country Journal or The Craftsman*, London, 2 June 1744; *The London Post or The Morning Advertiser*, 25–27 November 1748; and *The London Gazetteer*, 5 March 1751.

64. *The Remembrancer*, London, 7 October 1749. Outhwaite provides a facsimile of a lengthy advertisement concerning the preservation of Keith's wife's corpse from *The Daily Advertiser*, 23 January 1750 (*Clandestine Marriage*, 53).

65. Quotation from Walpole's letter to Montagu of October 1754. Cited in Burn, *Fleet Registers*, 100.

66. Quotation from Walpole's memoirs, cited in Knight, *London*, 59.

67. Quotation from Walpole's letter to George Montagu of 17 July 1753. *The Yale Edition of Horace Walpole's Correspondence*, ed. W. S. Lewis, 48 vols (New Haven: Yale University Press, 1937–83), 9:154.

68. Baker, 'Keith, Alexander (*d.* 1758)'.

69. Horace Walpole: 'The event that has made most noise since my last, is the extempore wedding of the youngest of the two Gunnings … they were married with a ring of the bed-curtain at half an hour after twelve at night, at Mayfair Chapel' (*Correspondence*, 20:302–3).

70. Alexander Keith, *Observations on the Act for Preventing Clandestine Marriages* (London: M. Cooper, 1753), 4. Subsequent citations in the text refer to this edition.

71. Quoted in Ogburn, 'Lawless Space', 29.

72. On mock wedding practices in London's molly houses, see Rictor Norton, *Mother Clap's Molly House: The Gay Subculture in England, 1700–1830* (London: Gay Men's Press, 1982).

73. As described in the *dramatis personae*. Ben Jonson, *Epicoene, or The Silent Woman*, ed. L. A. Beaurline (London: Edward Arnold, 1967), 6.

74. Jonson, *Epicoene*, 5.4.183–93.
75. Female playwrights show particular interest in irregular marriages, as Misty Anderson notes (citing figures from Alleman). *Female Playwrights and Eighteenth-Century Comedy: Negotiating Marriage on the London* Stage (New York: Palgrave, 2002), 33 and 214, n. 55.
76. Gellert Spencer Alleman, *Matrimonial Law and the Materials of Restoration Comedy* (Wallingford, PA: privately published, 1942), 74.
77. Alleman, *Matrimonial Law*, 78. Cressy cites two relevant Elizabethan cases (*Birth, Marriage and Death*, 320).
78. Alleman, *Matrimonial Law*, 39.
79. John Dryden, *The Wild Gallant*, in *The Works of John Dryden* [1662–1663], ed. John Harrington Smith and Dougald MacMillan, vol. 8 (Berkeley: University of California Press, 1967), 5.3.1.
80. Alleman, *Matrimonial Law*, 41.
81. Collier devoted the third chapter of his treatise to 'The Clergy Abused by the Stage'. *A Short View of the Immorality, and Profaneness of the English Stage* [1698] (New York: Routledge, 1989), 133–4.
82. *An Account of Marriage, or, the Interests of Marriage Considered and Defended against the Unjust Attacques of this Age* (London: B. G. for Allen Bancks, 1672), 54.
83. Alleman, *Matrimonial Law*, 41.
84. Susan Staves, *Players' Scepters: Fictions of Authority in the Restoration* (Lincoln: University of Nebraska Press, 1979), 191.
85. Aphra Behn, *The False Count* [1682], in *The Plays, Histories, and Novels of the Ingenious Mrs. Aphra Behn with Life and Memoirs*, vol. 3 (London: John Pearson, 1871), 5.1.154.
86. This quotation is from the 1751 edition of *Clarissa*. Samuel Richardson, *Clarissa*, 3rd edn, ed. Florian Stuber, *The Clarissa Project*, 8 vols (New York: AMS Press, 1990), Letter 58, 3:412, 6:230.
87. John L. Austin, *How to Do Things with Words* (Oxford: Clarendon, 1962), 16.
88. Vincent J. Liesenfeld, *The Licensing Act of 1737* (Madison: University of Wisconsin Press, 1987), 226, n. 4.
89. Odell's theatre postdated the new theatre in the Haymarket which opened in 1720. See Liesenfeld, *Licensing Act*, 16–17, 58.
90. Robert D. Hume notes that the Marriage Act caused 'an immediate and precipitate decline in the production of new plays' (*Rakish Stage*, 307).
91. The disturbances that marked the 1736 season enabled Walpole to argue that the drama endangered his government and national security (Liesenfeld, *Licensing Act*, 60–3).
92. *The Daily Gazetteer*, London, 8 June 1737.
93. On Richardson's contribution to the early eighteenth-century theatre controversy, see Keymer, *Richardson's 'Clarissa'*, 142–3; Darryl P. Domingo,

'Richardson's Unfamiliar Quotations: *Clarissa* and Early Eighteenth-Century Comedy', *RES* 66, no. 277 (2015): 939–42. On the flood of pamphlets on the topic, see Sister Rose Anthony, *The Jeremy Collier Stage Controversy, 1698–1726* (New York: Benjamin Blom, 1966).

94. Richardson, *A Seasonable Examination of the Pleas and Pretensions of the Proprietors of, and Subscribers to, Play-Houses, Erected in Defiance of the Royal Licence* [1735], in *Early Works*, ed. Alexander Pettit (Cambridge: Cambridge University Press, 2012), 61–85, at 69 and 65, respectively. Subsequent citations in the text refer to this edition.

95. Commentary on Richardson's anti-theatricalism includes Keymer (*Richardson's 'Clarissa'*, 143–50) and Domingo ('Richardson's Unfamiliar Quotations', 939–42).

96. Richardson, *The Apprentice's Vade Mecum or Young Man's Pocket Companion*, in *Early Works,* ed. Alexander Pettit (Cambridge: Cambridge University Press, 2012), 1–60, at 19. Subsequent citations in the text refer to this edition.

97. Pamela's remarks on the theatre's 'proper Regulation' appear in Richardson, *Pamela in Her Exalted Condition*, ed. Albert J. Rivero (Cambridge: Cambridge University Press, 2012), 314.

98. For the details of Barnard's bill, see Liesenfeld, *Licensing Act*, 33–4 and Alexander Pettit's General introduction to Samuel Richardson, *Early Works*, l.

99. See John A. Dussinger, '"Ciceronian Eloquence": The Politics of Virtue in Richardson's *Pamela*', *Eighteenth-Century Fiction* 12, no. 1 (1999): 47–8, esp. n. 21. See also Keymer, *Richardson's 'Clarissa'*, 145–9.

100. On Richardson's use of the phrase, see John A. Dussinger, '"The Working Class of People": An Early Eighteenth-Century Source', *Notes and Queries* 43, no. 3 (1996): 299–302. On eighteenth-century debates about commercialised leisure, see Darryl P. Domingo, 'Unbending the Mind: Or, Commercialized Leisure and the Rhetoric of Eighteenth-Century Diversion', *Eighteenth-Century Studies* 45, no. 2 (2012): 207–36.

101. 'Irregular drama' is Albert J. Rivero's term. See *The Plays of Henry Fielding: A Critical Study of His Dramatic Career* (Charlottesville: University Press of Virginia, 1989), 31ff.

102. Aparna Gollapudi, *Moral Reform in Comedy and Culture 1696–1747* (Burlington, VT: Ashgate, 2011), 5–15.

103. Lisa A. Freeman, *Character's Theatre: Genre and Identity on the Eighteenth-Century Stage* (Philadelphia: University of Pennsylvania Press, 2002), 76.

104. *The What D'ye Call It* predates Gay's formal collaborations with the Scriblerians, although Pope may have been a co-author. See John Fuller, introduction to John Gay, *Dramatic Works*, vol. 1 (Oxford: Clarendon, 1983), 16.

105. Despite its success, *Pasquin* was not performed after 1736 and never achieved repertory status. See Thomas Lockwood's introduction to *Pasquin*, in Henry Fielding, *Plays Volume III, 1734–1742* (Oxford: Clarendon, 2011), 229.

106. On the doubleness of Fielding's satire, see Freeman, *Character's Theatre*, 61 and Thomas Keymer, 'Fielding's Theatrical Career', in *The Cambridge Companion to Henry Fielding*, ed. Claude Rawson (Cambridge: Cambridge University Press, 2007), 19.

107. Freeman, *Character's Theatre*, 41.

108. John Gay, preface to *The What D'ye Call It*, in *Dramatic Works*, ed. John Fuller, vol. 1 (Oxford: Clarendon, 1983), preface, 136. Subsequent citations in the text refer to this edition.

109. See Fuller, introduction, 18–19.

110. Chesterfield and others understood *Pasquin* to have provoked the Licensing Act by exceeding the boundaries of acceptable political satire. See 'Lord Chesterfield's Speech against the Licensing Bill', in Henry Fielding, *Contributions to 'The Champion' and Related Writings*, ed. W. B. Coley (Oxford: Clarendon, 2003), 628 and Thomas Lockwood, 'Fielding and the Licensing Act', *Huntington Library Quarterly* 50, no. 4 (1987): 379. On the Haymarket, see Jane Moody, *Illegitimate Theatre in London, 1770–1840* (Cambridge: Cambridge University Press, 2000), 15.

111. Fielding's political allegiances changed significantly over the course of his life. For the most part, I accept Keymer's argument that they were 'pragmatic and mobile' ('Fielding's Theatrical Career', 18–19). Chapter 4 contains more on this in relation to *Joseph Andrews*.

112. On *Pasquin*'s marketing campaign, see Lockwood, introduction, 219.

113. Lockwood, introduction, 221.

114. Lockwood, introduction, 223.

115. Lockwood, introduction, 223–4.

116. The stage direction reads: 'Each Mob on each Side of the Stage, crying out promiscuously, Down with the Rump! no Courtiers! no Jacobites! down with the Pope! no Excise! a Place and a Promise! a Fox-Chace [*sic*] and a Tankard! At last they fall together by the Ears and cudgel one another off the Stage.' See Henry Fielding, *Pasquin*, in *Plays Volume III, 1734–1742*, ed. Thomas Lockwood (Oxford: Clarendon, 2011), 249–315, at 271. Page numbers are cited for Lockwood's edition, which does not contain line numbers. Subsequent citations in the text refer to this edition.

117. See Keymer, 'Fielding's Theatrical Career', 18–19.

118. Martin Battestin argues that Fielding's satire on bribery and corruption echoes the 'patriot' thinking of George Lyttelton and the Cobham circle of dissident Whigs, itself drawn from Bolingbroke's *Dissertation on Parties* (1733–4). Battestin, *Henry Fielding*, 197–8. J. A. Downie challenges this view,

arguing that *Pasquin*'s satire cannot be distinguished meaningfully from everyday opposition propaganda (*Political Biography*, 72–4, 246).

119. On *Pasquin* as 'a dramatic Dunciad', see John Loftis, *Comedy and Society from Congreve to Fielding* (Stanford: Stanford University Press, 1959), 41–2. For a re-evaluation of Fielding's Scriblerian ties, see Ashley Marshall, 'Henry Fielding and the "Scriblerians"', *Modern Language Quarterly* 72, no. 1 (2011): 19–48.

120. Pope's *Essay on Man* was later deemed to be Spinozist and we know that Fielding owned copies of Spinoza's works. Lockwood, introduction, 228.

121. W. B. Coley, General introduction to Henry Fielding, *Contributions to 'The Champion' and Related Writings* (Oxford: Clarendon, 2003), xxvi–xxvii. Lockwood also notes that this part of the play, which was generally believed to be an attack on clerical power and institutions, gave particular offence (introduction, 228).

122. Freeman, *Character's Theatre*, 195. Thomas Keymer, 'Domestic Servitude and the Licensed Stage', in *'Pamela' in the Marketplace: Literary Controversy and Print Culture in Eighteenth-Century Britain and Ireland*, ed. Thomas Keymer and Peter Sabor (Cambridge: Cambridge University Press, 2005), 114.

123. Moody, *Illegitimate Theatre*, 1–9.

124. Battestin, *Henry Fielding*, 464.

125. See Simon Trefman, *Sam. Foote, Comedian 1720–1777* (New York: New York University Press, 1971), 45.

126. William Beatty Warner, *Licensing Entertainment: The Elevation of Novel Reading in Britain, 1684–1750* (Berkeley: University of California Press, 1998), 176–230.

127. Giffard's *Pamela* debuted on 9 November 1741, starring David Garrick in a newly created role as Jack Smatter, the foppish-rake nephew of Lady Davers. Keymer, 'Domestic Servitude', 116.

128. Once again, Keymer's research is instructive: Garrick staged his friend Edward Moore's comedy, a *Pamela*-like main piece titled *The Foundling*, in an all-star production at Drury Lane in his first season as manager at the theatre in 1748 ('Domestic Servitude', 126–7, 30). *Rosina* was staged again at Drury Lane in 1749 and 1750 (127).

129. *The London Stage 1600–1800*, Part 3: 1729–1747, ed. Arthur H. Scouten, 2 vols (Carbondale: Southern Illinois University Press, 1961), 2: 1115.

130. *The London Stage 1600–1800*, Part 4: 1747–1776, ed. George Winchester Stone Jr, 3 vols (Carbondale: Southern Illinois University Press, 1962), 3:lxv.

131. Moody, *Illegitimate Theatre*, 1–9.

132. Moody, *Illegitimate Theatre*, 4–6. As Moody notes, 'the illegitimate seems to resist both institutional and even generic boundaries' (6).

133. Tate Wilkinson, *Memoirs of His Own Life*, vol. 1 (York: Wilson, Spence, and Mawman, 1790), 74–5. Subsequent citations in the text refer to this edition.

134. Quoted in Weinreb and Hibbert, *London Encyclopaedia*, 773.
135. Outhwaite, *Clandestine Marriage*, 126.
136. George Winchester Stone Jr and George M. Kahrl, eds, *David Garrick: A Critical Biography* (Carbondale: Southern Illinois University Press, 1979), 742.
137. Stone and Kahrl, *Critical Biography*, 742.
138. George M. Kahrl, introduction to *The Letters of David Garrick*, ed. David M. Little and George M. Kahrl, vol. 1 (Cambridge, MA: Belknap, Harvard University Press, 1963), xxvii.
139. Quoted in Carola Oman, *David Garrick* (Suffolk: Hodder and Stoughton, 1958), 141.
140. Stone and Kahrl, *Critical Biography*, 742.
141. Quoted in Outhwaite, *Clandestine Marriage*, 127.
142. Stone and Kahrl, *Critical Biography*, 742.
143. The four oil paintings alluded to the Oxfordshire election of 1754. *A New Description of Sir John Soane's Museum*, 9th edn (London: published by the Trustees, 1991), 27.
144. Quoted from Stone and Kahrl, *Critical Biography*, 46.
145. Stone and Kahrl, *Critical Biography*, 205–6.
146. Although Colman has generally been believed to be the play's predominant author, F. L. Bergmann's scholarship on the Folger Library's manuscript of the play has established that Garrick wrote the last half of it and devised the character of Lord Ogleby and much of the plot (Stone and Kahrl, *Critical Biography*, 242–3). Fanny Burney makes frequent mention of the play in her early diary, singling out Lord Ogleby as one of her favourite characters. *The Early Journals and Letters of Fanny Burney*, ed. Lars E. Troide, 2 vols (Oxford: Clarendon 1990–1991), 1:94, 2:137.
147. David Garrick and George Colman, *The Clandestine Marriage*, ed. Noel Chevalier (Peterborough: Broadview, 1995), 4.2.156–7.
148. Freeman, *Character's Theatre*, 195.
149. Garrick and Colman, *Clandestine Marriage*, 1.1.183–4.
150. Garrick and Colman, *Clandestine Marriage*, 1.2.18–19.
151. *The Elopement* was first produced on 26 December 1767 as an afterpiece to *The London Merchant*. Its authorship is unknown, although sometimes attributed to James Messink.
152. *The London Stage 1600–1800*, Part 5: 1776–1800, 3 vols, edited by C. B. Hogan (Carbondale: Southern Illinois University Press, 1968), 2:702.
153. *The Clandestine Marriage* was an instant success, and was performed eighteen times in the remaining part of the 1765/6 season before entering repertory. *A Trip to Scotland* was regularly staged at Drury Lane from 1770 to 1784/5, while *The Elopement* continued there from 1767 to 1783/4, missing

only the 1769/70 season. The latter was also performed at the Hammersmith and Haymarket theatres during the 1785/6 season.

154. Stuart wrote *Gretna Green*'s libretto. Samuel Arnold composed the score. John O'Keeffe added alterations and songs. It debuted at the Haymarket on 28 August 1783 and was performed regularly up to and including the 1795/6 season. Relevant entries appear in Hogan, *The London Stage*, vols 1, 2 and 3.

3 The New Fiction: Samuel Richardson and the Anglican Wedding

1. Letter to Elizabeth Carter, 17 August 1753 (published posthumously in *Monthly Magazine* 33 [1812]: 541).
2. Critics who view Richardson as a supporter of Court Whig marriage reform include Watt, Stone, Lemmings, Keymer (*Richardson's 'Clarissa'*, 103) and David Macey, '"Business for the Lovers of Business": *Sir Charles Grandison*, Hardwicke's Marriage Act and the Specter of Bigamy', *Philological Quarterly* 84, no. 3 (2005): 337 and Thomason, *Matrimonial Trap*, 80.
3. Scholarly consensus ends here, however. Accounts of Richardson's politics range from Rosemary Bechler's emphasis on his High Church Toryism to Dussinger's insistence on his non-aligned, business-minded pragmatism. See Bechler, '"Triall by What Is Contrary": Samuel Richardson and Christian Dialectic', in *Samuel Richardson: Passion and Prudence*, ed. Valerie Grosvenor Myer (London: Vision Press, 1986), 94ff and Dussinger, 'Politics of Virtue', 41–3. Toni Bowers surveys the relevant scholarship, offering her own (largely allegorical) reading of Richardson's fiction in light of his residual Toryism in *Force or Fraud: British Seduction Stories and the Problem of Resistance, 1660–1760* (Oxford: Oxford University Press, 2011), 251–2. For Rachel Carnell, Richardson's fiction belongs to 'moderation politics' and realism per se is the aesthetic of Whig dominance. See *Partisan Politics, Narrative Realism, and the Rise of the British Novel* (London: Palgrave, 2006), 8–9, 103–28.
4. Eaves and Kimpel, *Samuel Richardson*, 21.
5. Richardson was the sole official printer of bills and committee reports for the House of Commons from 1733 and the exclusive printer of the *Journals of the House of Commons* from 1742. See William M. Sale, *Samuel Richardson: Master Printer* (Ithaca: Cornell University Press, 1950), 76–85 and Thomas Keymer, 'Parliamentary Printing, Paper Credit, and Corporate Fraud: A New Episode in Richardson's Early Career', *Eighteenth-Century Fiction* 17, no. 2 (2005): 183–206.
6. Margaret Anne Doody, 'Richardson's Politics', *Eighteenth Century Fiction* 2, no. 2 (1990): 113–28 sees Richardson's Tory affiliations reaching into the 1750s.

In his introduction to *Pamela*, Keymer outlines Richardson's early Jacobite allegiances (x–xi). He dates Richardson's accommodation of Whig establishment from the 1730s (*Richardson's 'Clarissa'*, 168–70).

7. Rosemary Bechler traces connections between Richardson, Law and John Bryom, the Manchester High Church Tory, poet and Jacobite plotter. 'Samuel Richardson and Christian Dialectic', 94ff. Dussinger disputes her conclusions: '"Stealing the Great Doctrines of Christianity": Samuel Richardson As Journalist', *Eighteenth-Century Fiction* 15 (2003): 453–9.

8. Eaves and Kimpel, *Samuel Richardson*, 81 and 549.

9. For example, Cynthia Griffin Wolff, *Samuel Richardson and the Eighteenth-Century Puritan Character* (Connecticut: The Shoe String Press, 1972).

10. Thomas Keymer and Peter Sabor connect *The Apprentice's Vade Mecum* to the outflow of anti-deistical pamphlets in response to Anthony Collins's *Discourse of the Grounds and Reasons of the Christian Religion* (1724). See *'Pamela' in the Marketplace*, 1–17. A *Seasonable Examination* reused the *Vade Mecum*'s discussion of the theatre's unsuitability for young tradesmen. See Pettit's introduction to Samuel Richardson, *Early Works*, l–lii. Dussinger further notes that *The Infidel Convicted* (1730), printed by Richardson, was a source for the *Vade Mecum*'s third section ('Richardson As Journalist', 459–61).

11. See G. V. Bennett, *The Tory Crisis in Church and State 1688–1730: The Career of Francis Atterbury Bishop of Rochester* (Oxford: Clarendon, 1975).

12. Richardson, *Vade Mecum*, 19.

13. Richardson, *Vade Mecum*. The third part runs 44–60. Quote appears on 57.

14. Louise Curran, *Samuel Richardson and the Art of Letter Writing* (Cambridge: Cambridge University Press, 2016), 21–2.

15. For Keymer, Richardson's blending of religion and morality with national productivity is 'cynical at root' (*Richardson's 'Clarissa'*, 146). Latimer aligns Richardson with Latitudinarianism's emphasis on piety's worldly purposes (*Making Gender*, 112–45).

16. Jeremy Gregory, 'The Eighteenth-Century Reformation: The Pastoral Task of Anglican Clergy after 1689', in *The Church of England c. 1689 – c. 1833: From Toleration to Tractarianism*, ed. John Walsh, Colin Haydon and Stephen Taylor (Cambridge: Cambridge University Press, 1993), 69.

17. See W. R. Dudley, *The Moral Revolution of 1688* (New Haven: Yale University Press, 1982). The quotation is from John Spurr, 'The Church, the Societies and the Moral Revolution of 1688', in *The Church of England c. 1689–c. 1833*, ed. John Walsh, Colin Haydon and Stephen Taylor (Cambridge: Cambridge University Press, 1993), 127.

18. For early Oxford Methodism, see Richard Heitzenrater, introduction to *Diary of an Oxford Methodist: Benjamin Ingham, 1733–34* (Durham, NC:

Duke University Press, 1985), 1–48. I point to this connection despite Richardson's own ambivalent attitude towards Methodism. See Eaves and Kimpel, *Samuel Richardson*, 553–4 and Richardson, *Sir Charles Grandison*, 3:116.

19. Boone and Armstrong are among those who, following Watt, view Richardson as part of a Puritan tradition that includes Daniel Defoe. See Boone, *Tradition Counter Tradition*, 58–9; Watt, *Rise of the Novel*, 160–2 and Nancy Armstrong, *Desire and Domestic Fiction: A Political History of the Novel* (Oxford: Oxford University Press, 1987), 7.

20. Curran, *Art of Letter Writing*, 50.

21. Richardson's marriage plots typically feature clergymen as significant minor characters: *Pamela* presents a romance triangle of the altar-bound couple and Mr Williams, the clergyman who will marry them, and *Sir Charles Grandison*'s eponymous hero selects as his mentor a wise clergyman, Dr Bartlett. *Clarissa*'s clergyman, Mr Brand, by contrast, is a strangely shadowy figure, who possesses spiritual and moral authority but does not act on it.

22. Eliza Haywood, *The History of Miss Betsy Thoughtless* [1751], ed. Christine Blouch (Peterborough: Broadview, 1998), 252.

23. This and all subsequent quotations are from *The Weekly Miscellany*, London, 11 October 1740. Reproduced in Keymer and Sabor, *Pamela Controversy*, 1: xliii.

24. Hill went on fulsomely to praise the novel's 'Good-breeding, Discretion, Good-nature, Wit, Fancy, Fine Thought, and Morality'. Letter to Richardson, 17 December 1740. *Correspondence with Aaron Hill and the Hill Family*, 63. The letter was included in the prefatory material of *Pamela*'s second edition (14 February 1741).

25. Eaves and Kimpel, *Samuel Richardson*, 89.

26. Letters XCV–CI. See Richardson, *Letters Written to and for Particular Friends on the Most Important Occasions* [1741] in *Early Works*, ed. Alexander Pettit (Cambridge: Cambridge University Press, 2012), 321–526, at 430–6.

27. Seven letters address remarriage; all advise against it. See Letters CXL, CXLI, CXLII and CXLIII in Richardson *Letters*, 464–74.

28. Letter LIV, in Richardson, *Letters*, 381–2.

29. See Letters CLXI, CLXII, CLXIII, CLXIV and CLXV in Richardson, *Letters*, 506–13.

30. Letters CXXXVIII and CXXXIX, Richardson, *Letters*, 463–4.

31. Fictions consisting of love letters were routine from about 1670. See Ruth Perry, *Women, Letters and the Novel* (New York: AMS Press, 1980), x–xi and Ballaster, *Seductive Forms*, 61. My discussion of Richardson's use of the epistolary device draws on Keymer, *Richardson's 'Clarissa'*, 1–56; Curran, *Art of*

Letter Writing, 19–50 and Joe Bray, *The Epistolary Novel: Representations of Consciousness* (London: Routledge, 2003), 58ff.

32. Curran, *Art of Letter Writing,* 25–7; Richardson, *Letters,* 316 and Eaves and Kimpel, *Samuel Richardson,* 597.
33. Review of the first edition of Richardson's letters. Quoted in Curran, *Art of Letter Writing,* 2.
34. Thomas G. Pavel, *The Lives of the Novel: A History* (Princeton: Princeton University Press, 2013), 124; Watt, *Rise of the Novel,* 140–5.
35. For Watt, Richardson's realism is a departure from the romance tradition's rhetorical and narrative idealism. The subsequent pattern of the English novel is to emphasise love *within* marriage, while the French novel retains romance's privileging of romantic love and adultery. *Rise of the Novel,* 140–5.
36. For example, Ballaster, *Seductive Forms.*
37. For McKeon, this is one of the novel's 'progressivist' narrative scripts. See *The Origins of the English Novel, 1600–1740* (Baltimore: Johns Hopkins University Press, 1987), 256–9.
38. This line of argument is posed most influentially by Armstrong in *Desire and Domestic Fiction,* 108–34.
39. See Samuel Richardson, *Pamela; or, Virtue Rewarded* [1740], ed. Thomas Keymer and Alice Wakely (Oxford: Oxford University Press, 2001), 211. Unless otherwise indicated, subsequent citations in the text refer to this edition.
40. Samuel Richardson, *Pamela; or, Virtue Rewarded* [1801, incorporating corrections from the 1810 edition], ed. Peter Sabor, introduction Margaret A. Doody (London: Penguin, 1980), 83.
41. Armstrong, *Desire and Domestic Fiction,* 121.
42. Richardson, *Pamela* (ed. Sabor), 219.
43. This line of argument is pursued by Toni Bowers, who argues, rightly I think, that Pamela's story is an allegory of the trajectory through which the virtuous (Tory) subject becomes reconciled to the worldly mercantilist state administered by the Court Whigs (*Force or Fraud,* 4–6, 252–62).
44. McKeon, *Origins,* 361.
45. One influential line of commentary continues to express scepticism about Pamela's change of heart. Eaves and Kimpel conclude that 'marriage kills [Pamela] as a character' (*Samuel Richardson,* 184). For Ann Louise Kibbie, by the novel's end, 'Pamela's will has been both rewarded and dissolved.' See 'Sentimental Properties: *Pamela* and *Memoirs of a Woman of Pleasure*', *ELH* 58, no. 3 (1991): 566. By contrast, a rich vein of contemporary commentary reads into Richardson's text the contingencies of passion and (political) power that unsettle any simple opposition between resistance and complicity on Pamela's part. Toni Bowers analyses the modes of 'collusive resistance' that

operate in *Pamela* and other (Tory-inflected) seduction stories of the period (*Force or Fraud*, 4–6). For Helen Thompson, on the other hand, Pamela's transformation from servant to wife is 'compelled by [Humean] passion' (*Ingenuous Subjection*, 96–106). In not taking account of the mock marriage trope, however, these lines of argument are also unable to account for Pamela's change of heart at the level of plot and personhood.

46. Armstrong, *Desire and Domestic Fiction*, 130–1. This kind of analysis draws upon Lawrence Stone's influential historiography of family which poses a distinction between love and alliance in marriage that corresponds to competing historical models of the family (nuclear affectionate and the feudal patriarchal) and that understands the former to reflect a modern bourgeois critique of the latter (i.e. of status-based forms of social authority).

47. Richardson, *Pamela* (ed. Sabor), 277.

48. This nomenclature is used in the 1801 revised edition. Richardson, *Pamela* (ed. Sabor), 307.

49. The historical person to whom Mr B. refers may be William, first Earl Cowper, Whig politician and twice Lord Chancellor of Britain (1665–1723). His sham marriage seduction of Elizabeth Culling was fictionalised in Delarivier Manley's *New Atlantis* (1709). See Alan D. McKillop, 'The Mock Marriage Device in *Pamela*', *Philological Quarterly* 26 (1947): 285. Edward Hyde (later Earl of Clarendon) is another possible referent. He was complicit in the secret marriage of his daughter Anne (Duchess of York, 1637–71) to the Duke of York (afterwards James II) in 1660. See Keymer and Wakely eds., *Pamela*, 533, n. 269.

50. Richardson, *Pamela* (ed. Sabor), 307.

51. Peter Sabor remarks in his note on the passage that it was inserted to show that 'Pamela loves B. for himself, not for his fortune.' See Sabor's notes to Richardson's *Pamela; or, Virtue Rewarded* (London: Penguin, 1980), 531.

52. For Charlotte Sussman, the silenced body of 'poor Miss Sally Godfrey' is the basis for a call to feminist cultural historians to revivify the identities, bodies and lives that have fallen outside of marriage. Charlotte Sussman, '"I Wonder Whether Poor Miss Sally Godfrey Be Living or Dead": The Married Woman and the Rise of the Novel', *diacritics* 20, no. 1 (1990): 101.

53. See Paul Langford, *Public Life and the Propertied Englishman 1689–1798* (Oxford: Oxford University Press, 1991), 568–9 and Viviane Barrie-Curien, 'The Clergy in the Diocese of London in the Eighteenth Century', in *The Church of England, c. 1689–c. 1833: From Toleration to Tractarianism*, ed. John Walsh, Colin Haydon and Stephen Taylor (Cambridge: Cambridge University Press, 1993), 88.

54. Best, *Temporal Pillars*, 61. Best's thesis is further developed by Alan D. Gilbert, *Religion and Society in Industrial England: Church, Chapel, and*

Social Change, 1740–1914 (London: Longman, 1976), 13 and Paul Virgin, *The Church in an Age of Negligence* (Cambridge: Cambridge University Press, 1991).

55. Joseph Addison, Essay No. 21, 24 March 1711, in *The Spectator*, ed. Donald F. Bond, 5 vols (Oxford: Clarendon, 1965), 1:88.

56. As John Richetti aptly remarks of Mr Williams, he is 'the ineffectual Parson' (*English Novel*, 94).

57. Keymer, introduction to *Pamela*, xx.

58. See Watt, *Rise of the Novel*, 157, for a discussion of this scene.

59. Latimer, *Making Gender*, 142–3. On the rehabilitation of church buildings in the early eighteenth century, see Jacob, *Lay People*, 209–19.

60. Cressy, *Birth, Marriage, and Death*, 342–7.

61. Most influentially, for Armstrong and McKeon *Pamela* is a prototype of modern domestic subjectivity. See *Desire and Domestic Fiction*, 108–34 and *Origins of the English Novel*, 357–81, respectively.

62. During the planning of Sir Charles and Harriet's public wedding, Uncle Selby declares 'chamber marriages' 'neither *decent*, nor *godly*'; Sir Charles claims that he would take 'glory' in receiving Harriet's hand 'before ten thousand witnesses' (3:193). David Macey details the novel's 'contrasting depictions of abuses typical under the old marriage laws [with] scenes that demonstrate the rational pleasures associated with well-regulated marriage' ('Spectre of Bigamy', 333).

63. Bowers, *Force or Fraud*, 296ff. For Bowers, *Grandison*'s shift away from Tory themes of seduction towards 'manners' fiction reflects Richardson's accommodation of Hanoverianism.

64. John Allen Stevenson observes that Richardson 'never allows a wedding to be his last image' and so his courtship narratives are best understood as 'anti-courtship narratives', which evoke but deny the possibility of conventional structure. '"A Geometry of His Own": Richardson and the Marriage Ending', *SEL* 26, no. 3 (1986): 469–83. Jacob Sider Jost reiterates the point in structural-theological terms: 'Life does not end with marriage in Richardson because life does not end, period. And telling the story of a life with no imagined end – a life lived in view of Christian immortality – requires a fundamental shift in the concepts of plot and narrative closure.' *Prose Immortality 1711–1819* (Charlottesville: University of Virginia Press, 2015), 98.

65. Macey offers a rich discussion of the novel's 'bigamous' (336) ending ('Spectre of Bigamy', 335–44).

66. On 'affective community', see Tita Chico, 'Details and Frankness: Affective Relations in *Sir Charles Grandison*', *Studies in Eighteenth-Century Culture* 38 (2009): 45–68.

67. For Erin Mackie, Sir Charles's 'resolutely private' exercise of virtue is an aspect of the text's revision of aristocratic honour codes 'in line with the domestic and sentimental orientation of the modern gentleman'. *Rakes, Highwaymen and Pirates: The Making of the Modern Gentleman in the Eighteenth Century* (Baltimore: Johns Hopkins University Press, 2009), 170.

68. I draw here on two discussions of *Grandison*'s natural law themes. For Macey, the novel balances the rationalising demands of the law with the complications of the heart (see 'Spectre of Bigamy', 352). For Alison Conway, it does not: 'Richardson could not entertain a political solution to the inequalities of religious and sexual difference without undermining his commitment to the cultural authority of paternalist governance.' See '*Sir Charles Grandison* and the Sexual Politics of Toleration', *Lumen* 30 (2011): 16.

69. On the Christian background of Sir Charles's character, see Margaret Anne Doody, *A Natural Passion: A Study of the Novels of Samuel Richardson* (Oxford: Clarendon, 1974), 249–50; Mackie, *Rakes, Highwaymen and Pirates*, 169–74; and Mary V. Yates, 'The Christian Rake in *Sir Charles Grandison*', *SEL* 24, no. 3 (1984): 545–61.

70. On Sir Charles's lack of interiority as an effect of perfect virtue, see Eaves and Kimpel, *Samuel Richardson*, 397; Conway, 'Sexual Politics', 11 and Chico, 'Details and Frankness', 54–5. For negative readings of his character, see Latimer, *Making Gender*, 151, 121–37 and Tassie Gwilliam, *Samuel Richardson's Fictions of Gender* (Stanford: Stanford University Press, 1993), 150. On Harriet Byron as the novel's emotional centre, see Chico, 'Details and Frankness', 50–8 and on her religious life and 'affective' zealotry as components of her subjectivity, see Conway, 'Sexual Politics', 3–9.

71. See Pufendorf, *Law of Nature and Nations*, book 2, chapter 5, 'Of Self-Defence', ix, xii.

72. Jacob, *Lay People*, 209–19.

73. On Sir Charles's advocacy of marriage and 'the married state' (1:290, 3:408), see Macey, 'Spectre of Bigamy'; Sider Jost, *Prose Immortality*, 100–6; and Bonnie Latimer, 'Popular Fiction after Richardson', *Eighteenth-Century Fiction* 29, no. 2 (2016): 256–7.

74. Leah Price argues that Sir Charles's role as legal executor diminishes the importance of marriage in the novel. Arguably, the inverse is true: his competence in business matters finally bolsters his eligibility for marriage, allowing his practical capabilities, Christian and secular, domestic and financial, to be amplified and inserted into a plot whose ultimate significance is fixed around a wedding. Price, '*Sir Charles Grandison* and the Executor's Hand', *Eighteenth-Century Fiction* 8, no. 3 (1996): 331–42.

75. On the second attachment motif, see Betty A. Schellenberg, 'Using "Femalities" to "Make Fine Men": Richardson's *Sir Charles Grandison* and the Feminization of Narrative', *SEL* 34, no. 3 (1994): 599–616.

76. Patrick Mello, '"Piety and Popishness": Tolerance and the Epistolary Reaction to Richardson's *Sir Charles Grandison*', *Eighteenth-Century Fiction* 25, no. 3 (2013): 519–21. On Catholicism in the novel, see Sylvia Kasey Marks, *'Sir Charles Grandison': The Compleat Conduct Book* (Lewisburg: Bucknell University Press, 1986), 59; Teri Doerksen, '*Sir Charles Grandison*: The Anglican Family and the Admirable Roman Catholic', 15, no. 3 (2003): 539–58; and Doody, *Natural Passion*.

77. My argument partially concurs with Mello's claim that the novel's Catholic subplot is 'an expression of an emergent cosmopolitanism' grounded in 'human emotion and sympathy'. See 'Tolerance and the Epistolary', 527, 531.

78. Doerksen rightly argues that a comparative logic structures the text's representation of 'admirable Catholics' who ultimately serve to underscore the virtues of its central Protestant couple ('Anglican Family', 556). I am less convinced by her further supposition that Sir Charles's Protestant tolerance ultimately functions as a pretext for an imperialist assimilation of the Italian Catholics into his English 'moral community' (557). Such a reading passes over the text's reliance on a discourse of natural law that enables it to posit universal bonds of human sympathy between the Italian and English characters even as it foregrounds their confessional and cultural differences.

79. Mary Wortley Montagu, *The Letters and Works of Lady Mary Wortley Montagu*, ed. Lord Wharncliffe (London: Richard Bentley, 1837), letter of 20 October 1752 (3:38). Montagu had earlier remarked that *Pamela* was 'the joy of the chambermaids of all nations' (25 October 1749, 2:389).

80. Volume 6, Letter 52, Lady G., Miss Selby, To Lady L.; Thursday Morning, 16 November (3:218–29).

81. As Chico notes, frankness is the attribute most used to characterise Harriet in the novel. It is contrasted with Sir Charles's 'reserve' ('Details and Frankness', 56–7, 54–5).

82. The ecclesiastical calendar prohibited marriage during holy seasons reserved for prayer, fasting and spiritual contemplation. Almost 40 per cent of the year – including Lent, Ascension and Advent – was designated unsuitable for weddings. Marriages performed at these times required dispensation by special licence. Cressy, *Birth, Marriage, and Death*, 298–301.

83. Conway, 'Sexual Politics', 11.

84. Sider Jost, *Prose Immortality*, 103. For him, 'the marriage is … both metonymy and metaphor for divine justice as a whole' (105).

85. On wedding dress see, see Cressy, *Birth, Marriage, and Death*, 356, 361–2. Elizabeth Freeman dates the white wedding dress from around 1650. *The Wedding Complex: Forms of Belonging in Modern American Culture* (Durham, NC: Duke University Press, 2002), 19.
86. Cressy, *Birth, Marriage, and Death*, 352–3.
87. Hunter and Saunders, *Natural Law*, 2.

4 The Patriot Marriage Plot: Fielding, Shebbeare and Goldsmith

1. Gerrard, *Patriot Opposition*, 10–12.
2. Thomas Lockwood, 'Did Fielding Write for *The Craftsman?*', *RES* 59, no. 1 (2008): 86–117. Martin C. Battestin attributed forty-one essays published in *The Craftsman* to Henry Fielding. See Battestin, with Michael G. Farrindon, *New Essays by Henry Fielding* (Charlottesville: University of Virginia Press, 1989), 188. W. B. Coley disputed the attribution in his introduction to Henry Fielding's *Contributions*, xxx–xxxi.
3. Bertrand A. Goldgar, 'Fielding's Periodical Journalism', in *The Cambridge Companion to Henry Fielding*, ed. Claude Rawson (Cambridge: Cambridge University Press, 2007), 110 and Jenny Uglow, 'Fielding, Grub Street, and Canary Wharf', in *Grub Street and the Ivory Tower: Literary Journalism and Literary Scholarship from Fielding to the Internet*, ed. Jeremy Treglown and Bridget Bennett (Oxford: Clarendon, 1998), 9.
4. See Frederick G. Ribble, 'Fielding and William Young', *Studies in Philology* 98, no. 4 (2001): 457–501.
5. *Shamela* also includes a notable, extended satirical inversion of Richardson's injunction to 'good clergymen' in *Pamela*. Fielding, *Joseph Andrews and Shamela*, ed. Judith Hawley (London: Penguin, 1999), 42.
6. Downie, *Political Biography*, 125; also Roger D. Lund, 'The Problem with Parsons: *Joseph Andrews* and the "Contempt of the Clergy" Revisited', in *Henry Fielding in Our Time: Papers Presented at the Tercentenary Conference*, ed. J. A. Downie (Newcastle: Cambridge Scholars, 2008), 257–8.
7. In 1751, Fielding wrote an explicit critique of Bolingbroke's thought. See Battestin, *Henry Fielding*, 582–3 and Fielding, 'A Fragment of a Comment of Lord Bolingbroke's Essays', in *A Journal of a Voyage to Lisbon* (Dublin: James Hoey, 1756), 221–45.
8. Fielding speaks of a 'Species of writing ... hitherto unattempted in our Language' in the preface to *Joseph Andrews*, echoing Richardson's earlier reference to *Pamela* as 'a new species of writing'. See Henry Power, *Epic into Novel: Henry Fielding, Scriblerian Satire, and the Consumption of Classical Literature* (Oxford: Oxford University Press, 2015), 43.

9. As Power argues, *Joseph Andrews* recreated the epic for a consumerist age. *Epic into Novel*, 2. A full discussion appears on pages 1–4 and 41–3.

10. McKeon, *Origins*, 407–8.

11. Paula McDowell, 'Why Fanny Can't Read: *Joseph Andrews* and the (Ir) relevance of Literacy', in *A Companion to the Eighteenth-Century English Novel and Culture*, ed. Paula R. Backscheider and Catherine Ingrassia (Oxford: Blackwell, 2005), 172–3, 186.

12. I borrow this use of the term from Paul Morrison's 'Enclosed in Openness: *Northanger Abbey* and the Domestic Carceral', *Texas Studies in Literature and Language* 33, no. 1 (1991): 1–23.

13. Fielding, *Joseph Andrews*, ed. Martin C. Battestin (Middletown, CT: Wesleyan University Press, 1984), 48. All subsequent references to *Joseph Andrews* are to Battestin's edition and are given in the text.

14. Nancy Armstrong and Leonard Tennenhouse, 'The Network Novel and How It Unsettled Domestic Fiction', in *A Companion to the English Novel*, eds. Stephen Arata, Madigan Haley, J. Paul Hunter and Jennifer Wicke (Hoboken: Wiley-Blackwell, 2015), 314.

15. Jacob, *Lay People*, 11. The following account of the parish is drawn also from W. M. Jacob and N. J. G. Pounds, *A History of the English Parish: The Culture of Religion from Augustine to Victoria* (Cambridge: Cambridge University Press, 2000) and K. D. M. Snell, *Parish and Belonging: Community, Identity and Welfare in England and Wales, 1700–1950* (Cambridge: Cambridge University Press, 2006).

16. Long-standing Poor Laws that gave ratepayers responsibility for the local poor. Jacob, *Lay People*, 9–12, 191–6.

17. Colley, *Defiance of Oligarchy*, 18.

18. On the parson, see Geoffrey S. Holmes, *Augustan England: Professions, State and Society, 1680–1730* (London: G. Allen & Unwin, 1982), 83–114 and Gregory, 'Eighteenth-Century Reformation', 67–85.

19. The service, on a Tuesday morning, is noted as the occasion of the second calling of the banns for Joseph and Fanny's wedding.

20. In *Britons*, Colley argues that the idea of Britain as an elect nation, distinct from Catholic Continental Europe, was key to the self-definition of eighteenth-century Britons. For a different view, see Jeremy Black, 'Confessional State or Elect Nation? Religion and Identity in Eighteenth-Century England', in *Protestantism and National Identity: Britain and Ireland, c. 1650–c. 1850*, ed. Tony Claydon and Ian McBride (Cambridge: Cambridge University Press, 1998), 53–74.

21. Langford, *Public Life*, 568–9.

22. Lund, 'The Problem with Parsons', 264–6.

23. Geoffrey S. Holmes, *Politics, Religion and Society in England, 1679–1742* (London: Hambledon Press, 1986), 103 and Sykes, *Church and State*, 201ff.

24. Although rural vicars' incomes increased in the second half of the century owing to the boom in agricultural productivity (partly as a result of enclosure), the division between an impoverished majority and a richer elite remained. See Sykes, *Church and State*, 206–9.

25. On the novel's ironical treatment of Adams's clerical dress, see Lund, 'The Problem with Parsons', 262–3.

26. Sykes, *Church and State*, 206.

27. Richardson shared these concerns. See *Letters*, ed. Pettit, Letter 76, 409.

28. John Dryden, 'The Character of a Good Parson', in *Fables Ancient and Modern Translated into Verse from Homer, Ovid, Boccace, & Chaucer* (London: Jacob Tonson, 1700). Subsequent citations in the text refer to this edition.

29. James Kinsley, 'Dryden's "Character of a Good Parson" and Bishop Ken', *RES* 3, no. 10 (1952): 155–8.

30. The following quotations come from Addison's 'Essay no. 106', published 2 July 1711; 'Essay no. 111', published 7 July 1711 and 'Essay no. 112', published 9 July 1711, reproduced in Bond's edition of *The Spectator*. Subsequent citations of *The Spectator* in this chapter refer to this edition.

31. Sykes, *Church and State*, 234–3. Jacob, *Lay People*, 209–19.

32. 'An Apology for the Clergy', *The Champion*, London, 29 March and 5, 12 and 19 April 1740. See Fielding, *Contributions*, 256–60, 266–71, 271–8 and 283–6, respectively. Subsequent citations of this series of essays are to this edition, edited by W. B. Coley, and are given in the text.

33. On Fielding's deist tendencies, see Ronald Paulson, 'Henry Fielding and the Problem of Deism', in *The Margins of Orthodoxy: Heterodox Writing and Cultural Response, 1660–1750*, ed. Roger D. Lund (Cambridge: Cambridge University Press, 1995), 247–70.

34. For commentary on the *Champion* essays' influence on the characterisation of Adams, see Martin C. Battestin, *The Moral Basis of Fielding's Art: A Study of Joseph Andrews* (Middletown, CT: Wesleyan University Press, 1967), 136–43; George A. Drake, 'Ritual in *Joseph Andrews*', in *Henry Fielding in Our Time: Papers Presented at the Tercentenary Conference*, ed. J. A. Downie (Newcastle: Cambridge Scholars, 2008), 134 and Lund, 'The Problem with Parsons', 258–62, 285.

35. See Judith Hawley's introduction to Henry Fielding's *Joseph Andrews and Shamela* (London: Penguin, 1999), xxi. On Adams's quixotism, see Ronald Paulson, *Don Quixote in England: The Aesthetics of Laughter* (Baltimore: Johns Hopkins University Press, 1998), 71; Lund, 'The Problem with Parsons', 259 and Drake, 'Ritual in *Joseph Andrews*', 133–46. On Adams's 'inconsistencies', see Drake, 'Ritual in *Joseph Andrews*', 134–5.

36. On Adams's flirtation with deist and anticlerical thought, see Lund, 'The Problem with Parsons', 276–83. On his church politics as a blend of High Church reaction and Low Church radicalism, see Lund, 'The Problem with Parsons,' 259 and 275–86.

37. On the attribution of the *Prometheia*, see Kristine Louise Haugen, *Richard Bentley: Poetry and Enlightenment* (Cambridge, MA: Harvard University Press, 2011), 23, 53.

38. Scott Mackenzie offers a different account of the scene's relation to parish governance. '"Stock the Parish with Beauties": Henry Fielding's Parochial Vision', *PMLA* 125, no. 3 (2010): 612.

39. On the idea of the Patriot King, see David Armitage, 'A Patriot for Whom? The Afterlives of Bolingbroke's Patriot King', *Journal of British Studies* 36, no. 4 (1997): 403–6. On the complexities of the oppositional Whig-Tory nexus underpinning Adams's characterisation, see Treadwell Ruml II, 'Henry Fielding and Parson Adams: Whig Writer and Tory Priest', *Journal of English and Germanic Philology* 97, no. 2 (1998): 205–25 and Lund, 'The Problem with Parsons', 274–86.

40. Discussions of Adams's insistence upon the publication of banns and his subsequent confrontation with Lady Booby include Murial Brittain Williams, *Marriage: Fielding's Mirror of Morality* (Tuscaloosa: University of Alabama Press, 1973), 59; Lund, 'The Problem with Parsons', 261 and Drake, 'Ritual in *Joseph Andrews*', 139.

41. Anon. [John Johnson], *The Clergyman's Vade-Mecum: Or, An Account of the Ancient and Present Church of England; The Duties and Rights of the Clergy; and of Their Privileges and Hardships*, 5th edn (London: Robert Knaplock and Sam. Ballard, 1723), 203.

42. *The Clergyman's Vade-Mecum*, 54.

43. For Ruml, Booby is the 'image of the benevolent squirearch of Tory propaganda' ('Henry Fielding', 209).

44. For example, *Reflections on the Marriage Act* (London, 1764); *Reflections on the Repeal of the Marriage Act* (London, 1765); *A Scheme to Pay Off, in a Few Years, the National Debt, by a Repeal of the Marriage Act* (London, 1767). *Reflections on the Marriage Act* is further discussed in Chapter 5.

45. John Shebbeare, *The Marriage Act: A Novel*, 2 vols (London: J. Hodges, 1754), 1:288. Subsequent citations in the text refer to this edition.

46. Quoted in G. S. Rousseau, ed., *Oliver Goldsmith: The Critical Heritage* (London: Routledge and Kegan Paul, 1974), 258.

47. See George E. Haggerty, 'Satire and Sentiment in *The Vicar of Wakefield*', *The Eighteenth Century* 32, no. 1 (1991): 25–38.

48. Roger D. Lund, 'John Shebbeare (1709–1788)', in *Dictionary of Literary Biography*, vol. 39: *British Novelists, 1660–1800*, ed. Martin C. Battestin, Part 2: M–Z (Detroit: Gale Research Company, 1985), 420.

49. Lady Bradshaigh, Letter to Richardson, 23 May 1756 and Richardson, Letter to Lady Bradshaigh, 29 May 1756. *Correspondence with Lady Bradshaigh and Lady Echlin*, ed. Peter Sabor (Cambridge: Cambridge University Press, 2016), 2:621, 624.

50. The third edition was also published under the revised title for T. Lowndes in 1766. See James R. Foster, 'Smollett's Pamphleteering Foe Shebbeare', *PMLA* 57, no. 4 (1942): 1071, n. 70.

51. See J. C. D. Clark, *The Dynamics of Change: The Crisis of the 1750s and English Party Systems* (Cambridge: Cambridge University Press, 1982), 39–40.

52. The relevant commentary appears in *The Protestor*, June–November, 1753.

53. On the limits of the Patriot defence of women's rights, see Ann Campbell, 'The Limits of "Laudable Action": Women's Marital Choice in John Shebbeare's *The Marriage Act*', *Topic* 55 (2007): 13–24.

54. Lady Bradshaigh, Letter to Richardson, 23 May 1756, *Correspondence with Lady Bradshaigh*, 621.

55. Lund, 'John Shebbeare', 422.

56. For Lund, Thoroughgood is a Patriot squire figure, after *Tom Jones*'s Allworthy ('John Shebbeare', 422). But this is to forget that he is, after all, a clergyman.

57. See Eric Rothstein and Howard D. Weinbrot, '*The Vicar of Wakefield*, Mr. Wilmot, and the "Whistonean Controversy"', *Philological Quarterly* 55 (1976): 225–40.

58. See Oliver Goldsmith, *The Vicar of Wakefield*, ed. Arthur Friedman (Oxford: Oxford University Press, 2006), 12. Subsequent citations in the text refer to this edition. And see D. A. Miller, *Jane Austen, or, The Secret of Style* (Princeton: Princeton University Press, 2003), xxx.

59. As Robert H. Hopkins observed long ago in 'Matrimony in *The Vicar of Wakefield* and the Marriage Act of 1753', *Studies in Philology* 74, no. 3 (1977): 322–39.

60. Oliver Goldsmith, 'Letter LXXII: The Marriage Act Censured' (1760) and 'Letter CXIV: Against the Marriage Act. A Fable' (1761), in *Collected Works of Oliver Goldsmith*, ed. Arthur Friedman, vol. 2: *The Citizen of the World; or Letters from a Chinese Philosopher, Residing in London to His Friends in the East* (Oxford: Clarendon, 1966), 298–303; 440–5. This quote is from Letter CXIV, 302–3.

61. On Goldsmith's ten-year connection with Nugent, see Norma Clarke, *Brothers of the Quill: Oliver Goldsmith in Grub Street* (Cambridge, MA: Harvard University Press, 2016), 13, 25.

62. For example, Charles Stuart, *Ripe Fruit, or, The Marriage Act* [1781], ms. Larpent 566, Henry E. Huntingdon Library and Art Gallery, 9 and 11. See also his *Gretna Green* (staged at the Haymarket Theatre, 1783–96).

63. Oliver Goldsmith, 'An Essay on the Theatre; Or, A Comparison between Laughing and Sentimental Comedy', *The Westminster Magazine*, January 1773 (1): 4–6.

64. Quoted in Rousseau, ed., *Oliver Goldsmith*, 66–7.

65. Quoted in Rousseau, ed., *Oliver Goldsmith*, 278.

66. Marshall Brown, *Preromanticism* (Stanford: Stanford University Press, 1991), 151.

67. Ronald Paulson, *Satire and the Novel in Eighteenth-Century England* (New Haven: Yale University Press, 1967), 269. Also Stephen Derry, 'Jane Austen's Use of *The Vicar of Wakefield* in *Pride and Prejudice*', *English Language Notes* 28, no. 3 (1991): 25–7.

68. Patrick Müller disputes religious readings of the text in *Latitudinarianism and Didacticism in Eighteenth-Century Literature: Moral Theology in Fielding, Sterne, and Goldsmith* (Frankfurt: Peter Lang, 2009), 328–51.

69. For the novel as a typology of Christ, see Paul J. Korshin, *Typologies in England, 1650–1820* (Princeton: Princeton University Press, 1982), 259–60. Also see Jonathan Lamb, *The Rhetoric of Suffering: Reading the Book of Job in the Eighteenth Century* (Oxford: Clarendon, 1995) and James Lehmann, '*The Vicar of Wakefield*: Goldsmith's Sublime, Oriental Job', *ELH* 46, no. 1 (1979): 97–121.

70. Nicholas Seager offers an account of the shifting reception of the text's sincerity and irony. See 'Providence, Futurity and Typology in Oliver Goldsmith's *The Vicar of Wakefield*', in *Theology and Literature in the Age of Johnson: Resisting Secularism*, ed. Melvyn New and S. J. Reedy (Newark: University of Delaware Press, 2012), 163–4.

71. Maureen Harkin, 'Goldsmith on Authorship in *The Vicar of Wakefield*', *Eighteenth-Century Fiction* 14, nos. 3–4 (2002): 325–44.

72. Clarke, *Brothers of the Quill*, 22–4. The quotation, which paraphrases James Joyce's response to the novel, is on 23.

73. On the novel's commercial themes, see Christopher K. Brooks, 'Goldsmith's Commercial Vicar: Spectacles and Speculation', *CLA Journal* 41, no. 3 (1998): 319–34 and Harkin, 'Goldsmith on Authorship'.

74. For an alternative reading, see James P. Carson, '"The Little Republic" of the Family: Goldsmith's Politics of Nostalgia', *Eighteenth-Century Fiction* 16, no. 2 (2004): 177. Carson contests the notion that the family's republicanism stands against Primrose's monarchism.

75. Carson, 'Politics of Nostalgia', 186.

76. George Primrose's narrative draws from Goldsmith's biography. See Clarke, *Brothers of the Quill*, 18.

77. Seager makes a similar observation about this match in 'Providence, Futurity, and Typology', 178.

78. Hopkins also views this as an aspect of Sir William's privilege. See 'Matrimony', 338.

5 Literary Marriage Plots: Burney, Austen and Gretna Green

1. Franco Moretti, 'Serious Century', in *The Novel, Volume 1: History, Geography, and Culture*, ed. Franco Moretti (Princeton: Princeton University Press, 2006), 396. Moretti draws his use of the term from Erich Auerbach's influential conception of realism as the 'serious imitation of the everyday' in *Mimesis: The Representation of Reality in Western Literature* (Princeton: Princeton University Press, 2003). See also Kathryn Sutherland, 'Jane Austen and the Invention of the Serious Modern Novel', *The Cambridge Companion to English Literature, 1740–1830*, ed. Thomas Keymer and Jon Mee (Cambridge: Cambridge University Press, 2004), 244–62.

2. On the expansion of the commercial book trade dating from the 1760s, see James Raven, *Judging New Wealth: Popular Publishing and Responses to Commerce in England, 1750–1800* (Oxford: Clarendon, 1992), 31–4 and *The Business of Books: Booksellers and the English Book Trade, 1450–1850* (New Haven: Yale University Press, 2007), 222–5.

3. On marketing aimed at women, see Raven, *The Business of Books*, 255. On female authorship, see Raven, 'Historical Introduction: The Novel Comes of Age', in *The English Novel, 1770–1829: A Bibliographical Survey of Prose Fiction Published in the British Isles*, vol. 1: *1770–1799*, ed. Peter Garside, James Raven and Rainer Schöwerling (Oxford: Oxford University Press, 2000), 42–9. It is worth noting that the scholarship on gender and the literary marketplace in the period has not reached consensus.

4. Kathryn Sutherland, *Jane Austen's Textual Lives: From Aeschylus to Bollywood* (Oxford: Oxford University Press, 2007), 11.

5. Paula R. Backscheider, 'The Story of Eliza Haywood's Novels: Caveats and Questions', in *The Passionate Fictions of Eliza Haywood: Essays on Her Life and Work*, ed. Kirsten T. Saxton and Rebecca P. Bocchicchio (Lexington: University of Kentucky Press, 2000), 19–47; Kathryn R. King, 'The Afterlife and Strange Surprising Adventures of Haywood's Amatories (with Thoughts on Betsy Thoughtless)', in *Masters of the Marketplace: British Women Novelists of the 1750s*, ed. Susan Carlile (Bethlehem, PA: Lehigh University Press, 2011), 203–18; and Aleksondra Hultquist, 'Haywood's Re-Appropriation of the Amatory Heroine in *Betsy Thoughtless*', *Philological Quarterly* 85 (2006): 141–65.

6. On Haywood's alliances and patronage networks, see Kathryn R. King, *A Political Biography of Eliza Haywood* (London: Pickering and

Chatto, 2012). On her putative Jacobitism, see Carnell, *Partisan Politics*, 129–61.

7. Eliza Haywood, *Anti-Pamela; or, Feign'd Innocence Detected* (London: J. Huggonson, 1741).

8. The status of Haywood's reform plot is much debated. See Helen Thompson, 'Betsy Thoughtless and the Persistence of Coquettish Volition', *Journal for Early Modern Cultural Studies* 4, no. 1 (2004): 102–26; Stuart Shea, 'Subversive Didacticism in Eliza Haywood's *Betsy Thoughtless*', *SEL* 42, no. 3 (2002): 559–75 and Aleksondra Hultquist, 'Marriage in Haywood; or, Desire Rewarded', in *Masters of the Marketplace: British Women Novelists of the 1750s*, ed. Susan Carlile (Lanham, MD: Lehigh University Press, 2011), 31–46.

9. This is not to suggest that the amatory tradition was apolitical but rather that the politics of the roman à clef, or secret history, worked by means of allegory rather than by topicality per se. Toni Bowers, for instance, places Manley, Haywood and Richardson in a tradition of Tory-oriented prose fiction about seduction and frames Haywood as a political writer (*Force or Fraud*, 223–7).

10. Jane Spencer credits *Betsy Thoughtless* as the first major English novel of female education, or the 'reformed heroine plot'. See *The Rise of the Woman Novelist: From Aphra Behn to Jane Austen* (Oxford: Basil Blackwell, 1986), 141. Mary Davys's *The Reformed Coquet* (1724) predates it, however, as Deborah J. Nestor notes in 'Virtue Rarely Rewarded: Ideological Subversion and Narrative Form in Haywood's Later Fiction', *SEL* 34, no. 3 (1994): 595, n. 7. See also Josephine Donovan, *Women and the Rise of the Novel* (London: Palgrave, 1999), 106–11.

11. On Haywood's literary allusions, see David Oakleaf, '"Shady bowers! And purling streams! – Heavens, how insipid!": Eliza Haywood's Artful Pastoral', in *The Passionate Fictions of Eliza Haywood: Essays on Her Life and Work*, ed. Kirsten T. Saxon and Rebecca P. Bocchicchio (Lexington: University of Kentucky Press, 2000), 285. Also see Nestor, 'Virtue Rarely Rewarded', 581.

12. Lord Hardwicke exempted Scotland from his legislation on the understanding that the Lords in Session in Scotland would introduce their own bill to prevent clandestine marriages. Such a bill was debated in 1755, but opponents successfully argued that its regulations would interfere with Scottish religious freedom as protected by the 1707 Union settlement. See T. C. Smout, 'Scottish Marriage, Regular and Irregular 1550–1940', in *Marriage and Society: Studies in the Social History of Marriage*, ed. R. B. Outhwaite (London: Europa, 1981), 208.

13. See J. C. Jeaffreson, *Brides and Bridals*, vol. 2 (London: Hurst and Blackett, 1872), 205–6.

14. Robert Elliot, *The Gretna Green Memoirs* (London: published by the Gretna Green Parson, 1842), 17–18.

15. It was 'metrically illustrated' by William Combe in a satiric poem entitled 'Gretna Green', published in his collaboration with Thomas Rowlandson: *The English Dance of Death*, 2 vols (London: J. Diggens, 1815–16), vol. 2.

16. A Gretna wedding could mean social reincorporation or ruin – all the more so because a union enabled by violence or abduction could be legally contested and nullified.

17. On the *Lady's Magazine*, see Raven, 'Historical Introduction: The Novel Comes of Age', 76–7; Robert D. Mayo, *The English Novel in the Magazines 1740–1815* (Evanston: Northwestern University Press, 1962), 213 and Edward Copeland, 'Money Talks: Jane Austen and the *Lady's Magazine*', in *Jane Austen's Beginnings: The Juvenilia and Lady Susan*, ed. J. David Grey (Ann Arbor: University of Michigan Research Press, 1989), 153–72.

18. 'Charlotte Bateman, A Tale', *Lady's Magazine*, Nov., Dec. & supp. 1782, 579–83, 625–7, 692–4. My discussion draws on Edward Copeland, *Women Writing about Money: Women's Fiction in England, 1790–1820* (Cambridge: Cambridge University Press, 1995), 127–9. Elopement narratives were standard fare for the *Lady's*. See for example 'Julia; or the Clandestine Marriage', *Lady's Magazine*, 26 May 1795, 231–6.

19. The articles appeared in Dodsley's *World* magazine in the mid-1750s. Quoted in Mayo, *English Novel*, 120.

20. Quoted in Mayo, *English Novel*, 121.

21. William Whitehead, *A Trip to Scotland* (London: J. Dodsley, 1770), 38, 16.

22. See 'A Register of Scotch Marriages', in *The Miscellaneous Works of Oliver Goldsmith* (London: Macmillan, 1923), 347–8. Subsequent citations in the text refer to this edition.

23. See Colin Bonwick, *English Radicals and the American Revolution* (Chapel Hill: University of North Carolina Press, 1977), 199–215.

24. On Wilkes's protest movement, see Frank O'Gorman, *The Long Eighteenth Century: British Political and Social History 1688–1832* (London: Arnold, 1997), 227. One Wilkesite pamphlet framed the repeal debate in terms of the crisis in the American colonies, precipitated by the Sugar and Stamp Acts of 1764 and 1765. See *A Scheme to Pay Off, in a Few Years, the National Debt.*

25. Glynne's bill passed by a small majority in the Commons but was defeated in the House of Lords.

26. Quoted in Outhwaite, *Clandestine Marriage*, 112–13, 134.

27. *Reflections on the Marriage Act with Some Hints for a New Law: Humbly Offered to the Consideration of Parliament* (London: printed for G. Woodfall, 1764), 37. The author noted that, unlike Scottish Presbyterians, English Dissenters were unable to be 'married in their own

meeting-houses, nor by their own clergy' (37). Subsequent citations in the text refer to this edition.

28. The Royal Marriage Act prevented royal family members under the age of twenty-five from marrying without the monarch's consent. See Langford, *Polite and Commercial*, 579–80.

29. Cobbett, *Parliamentary History of England*, 22:413–21. Also see Outhwaite, *Clandestine Marriage*, 115.

30. 'Defence of Marrying the Younger Part of the Sex', *Lady's Magazine* 4 (1773): 131. Subsequent citations in the text refer to this edition.

31. Hogan, ed., *The London Stage*, 1:446–7. The play ran for just two nights on 22 and 24 August 1781.

32. Stuart, *Ripe Fruit*.

33. On the discourse of female patriotism, see Colley, *Britons*, 262–73, and Harriet Guest, *Small Change: Women, Learning and Patriotism, 1750–1810* (Chicago: Chicago University Press, 2000), 155–291.

34. Charles Stuart, *Gretna Green, a Comic Opera*, in *Scottish Ballad Operas III: Farce and Satire*, compiled by Walter H. Rubsamen (New York: Garland, 1974), 21.

35. See Langford, *Polite and Commercial*, 580.

36. Sometimes attributed to the miscellaneous writer and pamphleteer Francis Douglas. *Considerations on the Causes of the Present Stagnation of Matrimony* (London: T. Silsbury, for J. Ridley, 1772).

37. Quoted in Isaac Kramnick, ed., *The Portable Edmund Burke* (New York: Penguin, 1999), 97–8.

38. Garside, Raven and Schöwerling, *English Novel*, includes reference to the full catalogue of Minerva Press novels.

39. Andrew Davies suggests that *The Fair Cambrians* was authored by a woman, on the basis of the handwritten inscription on the fly-leaf of the first volume, presumed a personal copy. '"The Gothic Novel in Wales" Revisited: A Preliminary Survey of the Wales-Related Romantic Fiction at Cardiff University', *Cardiff Corvey: Reading the Romantic Text* 2, no. 1 (1998): www .romtext.org.uk/articles/cc02_n01/#foot1

40. Hannah Maria Jones, *Gretna Green; or, The Elopement of Miss D– with a Gallant Son of Mars* (1821); Sarah Green, *Gretna Green Marriages, or, The Nieces* (1823); Susannah Frances Reynolds, *Gretna Green, or, All for Love* (1848) and Ellen Wood, *East Lynne* (1861).

41. Charlotte Smith, *Emmeline: The Orphan of the Castle*, ed. Loraine Fletcher (Ontario: Broadview, 2003), 77.

42. Charlotte Smith, *The Old Manor House*, ed. Anne Henry Ehrenpreis (Oxford: Oxford University Press, 1989).

43. Elizabeth Kraft, introduction to Charlotte Smith, *The Young Philosopher*, (Lexington: University of Kentucky Press, 1999), xxvi.

44. '[T]hey are difficulties created out of nothing' (124), Hazlitt went on to say. 'On the English Novelists', in *The Complete Works of William Hazlitt*, vol. 6, ed. P. P. Howe (London: Dent, 1931), 106–32.

45. Frances Burney, *Cecilia, Or Memoirs of an Heiress*, ed. Peter Sabor and Margaret Anne Doody (London: Oxford University Press, 1988), 941. Subsequent citations in the text refer to this edition.

46. Critics dissatisfied by Burney's courtship resolutions include Mitzi Myers, 'The Dilemmas of Gender as Double-Voiced Narrative; Or Maria Edgeworth Mothers the Bildungsroman', in *The Idea of the Novel in the Eighteenth Century*, ed. Robert W. Uphaus (East Lansing: Colleagues, 1988), 67–96 and Margaret Doody, 'Burney and Politics', in *The Cambridge Companion to Frances Burney*, ed. Peter Sabor (Cambridge: Cambridge University Press, 2007), 97. Gallagher notes the disappointment of Burney's contemporary readers with *Cecilia*'s ending. *Nobody's Story: The Vanishing Acts of Women Writers in the Marketplace 1670–1820* (Berkeley: University of California Press, 1994), 248–9.

47. Kristina Straub is paradigmatic in this regard. See *Divided Fictions: Fanny Burney and the Feminine Strategy* (Lexington: University of Kentucky Press, 1987), 53–77. Or more recently, Ann Campbell, 'Clandestine Marriage and Frances Burney's Critique of Matrimony in *Cecilia*', *Eighteenth-Century Life* 37, no. 2 (2013): 96–9.

48. These are the revisionist positions of Miranda J. Burgess and Claudia L. Johnson, respectively. Claudia L. Johnson, *Equivocal Beings: Politics, Gender, and Sentimentality in the 1790s: Wollstonecraft, Radcliffe, Burney, Austen* (Chicago: University of Chicago Press, 1995), 141–90, 145 and Miranda J. Burgess, *British Fiction and the Production of Social Order, 1740–1830* (Cambridge: Cambridge University Press, 2000), 104–5, 259, n. 82.

49. *Evelina or The History of a Young Lady's Entrance into the World*, ed. Edward A. Bloom (Oxford: Oxford University Press, 2002), 10. Subsequent citations in the text refer to this edition.

50. Moretti, 'Serious Century', 396.

51. Burney recounts Shebbeare's odious manners in her journal, remarking that the man and his novel were 'antidote' enough for anyone's desire for marriage. *The Early Diary of Frances Burney 1768–1778*, 2 vols, ed. Anne R. Ellis (London: Bell and Sons, 1907), 1:285–9.

52. Myers, 'Dilemmas of Gender', 67–98, especially 69.

53. As Deidre Shauna Lynch remarks, 'consumer culture is not the cancelation of psychological complexity but simply the state of its operations'. *The Economy of Character: Novels, Market Culture, and the Business of Inner Meaning* (Chicago: University of Chicago Press, 1998), 168.

54. Burney, *Early Diary*, 1:13–14. Also reproduced in Rousseau, *Oliver Goldsmith*, 52–3.

55. Behind them lie a significant number of unnamed women writers whom she read and admired, including Elizabeth Griffith, Frances Brooke and Charlotte Lennox. Betty A. Schellenberg, *The Professionalization of Women Writers in Eighteenth-Century Britain* (Cambridge: Cambridge University Press, 2010), 172.

56. Burney scholars are not in agreement about her politics: for Burgess, she is 'conservative' (see *British Fiction*, 87–9); Doody sees glimpses of radical politics in the novels (see 'Burney and Politics', 93–110).

57. Lynch, *Economy of Character*, 126–32.

58. Gallagher, *Nobody's Story*, 221.

59. Gallagher, *Nobody's Story*, 213–14.

60. Miller, *Jane Austen*, 33.

61. Doody makes the latter observation in *Frances Burney: The Life in the Works* (New Brunswick, NJ: Rutgers University Press, 1988), 147–8.

62. On Burney's use and proliferation of character types, see Lynch, *Economy of Character*, 164–207 and Leanne Maunu, *Women Writing the Nation: National Identity, Female Community, and the British-French Connection, 1770–1820* (Lewisburg: Bucknell University Press, 2007), 43–8.

63. See Hazlitt, 'On Londoners and Country People', in *The Complete Works of William Hazlitt*, vol. 12, ed. P. P. Howe (London: J. M. Dent, 1931), 66–77.

64. See Margaret Doody's discussion of the Hill family in 'Burney and Politics', 93–110. And for her assertion that *Cecilia* is a Jacobin novel before the fact, see *Frances Burney*, 147.

65. The quote is from Johnson, *Equivocal Beings*, 19. The point is elaborated by Lynch, *Economy of Character* and by Julie Park, *The Self and It: Novel Objects in Eighteenth-Century England* (Stanford: Stanford University Press, 2010).

66. Schellenberg makes a similar point about Belfield (*Professionalization of Women*, 156–8).

67. On romantic literary subjectivity, see Lynch, *Economy of Character*, 131–2.

68. Burney originally wrote, and destroyed, the narrative of Miss Evelyn (whose 'improper' ceremony contrasts with Evelina's proper marriage plot). Letter two of *Evelina* fully discusses the improper marriages of her mother with Sir John Belmont and her grandfather to Madame Duval ('then a waiting-girl at a tavern').

69. As Lynch, Burgess and others note, Burney's romance plots are simultaneously economic plots. See Lynch, *Economy of Character*, 167–8 and Burgess, *British Fiction*, 75, 92–5.

70. See Caroline Levine, *Forms: Whole, Rhythm, Hierarchy, Network* (Princeton: Princeton University Press, 2015).

71. On *Cecilia*'s clandestine marriage, see Campbell, 'Clandestine Marriage', 85–103 and Melissa J. Ganz, 'Clandestine Schemes: Burney's *Cecilia* and the Marriage Act', *The Eighteenth Century: Theory and Interpretation* 54, no. 1 (2013): 25–51.

72. Jane Austen, *Emma*, ed. Richard Cronin and Dorothy McMillan (Cambridge: Cambridge University Press, 2005), 475.

73. Laura Mooneyham White makes this observation in *Jane Austen's Anglicanism* (Farnham: Ashgate, 2011), 57–9.

74. See, for instance, Johnson's discussion of Camilla's 'densely textured irony' in *Equivocal Beings*, 146. The full discussion runs on pages 141–64.

75. Gallagher, *Nobody's Story*, 255. For a contrary reading: Elizabeth Rose Gruner, 'Loving the Difference: Sisters and Brothers from Frances Burney to Emily Bronte', in *The Significance of Sibling Relationships in Literature*, ed. JoAnna Stephens Mink and Janet Doubler Ward (Bowling Green: Bowling Green State University Popular Press, 1993), 34.

76. Michael Cohen discusses the echoes of *The Vicar of Wakefield* in *Camilla* in 'First Sisters in the British Novel: Charlotte Lennox to Susan Ferrier', in *The Significance of Sibling Relationships in Literature*, ed. JoAnna Stephens Mink and Janet Doubler Ward, 99, 103. He notes that Lennox was the first to use sisters comparatively in her *History of Harriet and Sophia* (1760–1) (which predates Goldsmith's novel).

77. Actually five, since another young friend of the family, the very foolish Miss Dennel, runs away to marry aged fifteen. Her role is to remind readers what a completely thoughtless but socially acceptable marriage might be. For Lynch's discussion of *Camilla*'s multi-plot, see *Economy of Character*, 172–3.

78. Frances Burney, *Camilla, or A Picture of Youth* [1796], ed. Edward A. Bloom and Lillian D. Bloom (Oxford: Oxford University Press, 1983), 821. Subsequent citations in the text refer to this edition.

79. Lynch, *Economy of Character*, 176.

80. This is a modified version of an observation made by William Galperin in *The Historical Austen* (Philadelphia: University of Pennsylvania Press, 2003), 139. Scholarship on Austen's marriage plots includes: William H. Magee, 'Instrument of Growth: The Courtship and Marriage Plot in Jane Austen's Novels', *The Journal of Narrative Technique* 17, no. 2 (1987): 198–208; Julie Shaffer, 'Not Subordinate: Empowering Women in the Marriage-Plot: The Novels of Frances Burney, Maria Edgeworth, and Jane Austen', *Criticism: A Quarterly for Literature and the Arts* 34, no. 1 (1992): 51–73; Laura Mooneyham White, 'Jane Austen and the Marriage Plot: Questions of Persistence', in *Jane Austen and the Discourses of Feminism*, ed. Devoney Looser (New York: St. Martin's Press, 1995), 71–86; Charles H. Hinnant, 'Jane Austen's "Wild Imagination": Romance and the

Courtship Plot in the Six Canonical Novels', *Narrative* 14, no. 3 (2006): 294–310 and Eric C. Walker, *Marriage, Writing, and Romanticism: Wordsworth and Austen after War* (Stanford: Stanford University Press, 2009).

81. The term is Claudia Johnson's (*Equivocal Beings*, 18–19).
82. Watt, *Rise of the Novel*, 296–9.
83. Moretti, 'Serious Century', 395.
84. Jane Austen, *Pride and Prejudice*, ed. Pat Rogers (Cambridge: Cambridge University Press, 2006), 344. All subsequent citations in the text refer to this edition.
85. On Austen's use of free indirect style, see Linda Bree, 'The Literary Context', in *The Cambridge Companion to 'Pride and Prejudice'*, ed. Janet Todd (Cambridge: Cambridge University Press, 2013), 56–66; and Frances Ferguson, 'Jane Austen, *Emma*, and the Impact of Form', *MLQ*, 61, no. 1 (2000): 157–80.
86. The classic account of Austen's relation to her precursors is Kenneth Moler's *Jane Austen's Art of Allusion* (Lincoln: University of Nebraska Press, 1968). On the particular influence of Richardson's *Grandison* on Austen, see Jocelyn Harris's *Jane Austen's Art of Memory* (Cambridge: Cambridge University Press, 1989), 35, 40–1.
87. Discussions of Austen's 'national marriage plot' include Patrick Parrinder, *Nation and Novel*, 180–212 and Vlasta Vranjes, 'Jane Austen, Lord Hardwicke's Marriage Act, and the National Courtship Plot', *CLIO* 43, no. 2 (2014): 197–223.
88. On Austen's representation of the professions and their role in the changing social order of Regency Britain, see Alice Drum, 'Pride and Prestige: Jane Austen and the Professions', *College Literature* 36, no. 3 (2009): 92–115.
89. *Jane Austen's Letters to Her Sister Cassandra and Others*, ed. R. W. Chapman, 2nd edn (London: Oxford University Press, 1959), 469.
90. See, for instance, Mary Jean Corbett, *Family Likeness: Sex, Marriage, and Incest from Austen to Virginia Woolf* (Ithaca: Cornell University Press, 2008): 30–57; Parrinder, *Nation and Novel*, 195–202 and Pollak, *Incest and the English Novel*, 162–199.
91. Parrinder, *Nation and Novel*, 195.
92. Austen's politics remain a matter of critical debate. Contemporary political readings of Austen's oeuvre more or less begin with Marilyn Butler's *Jane Austen and the War of Ideas* (Oxford: Oxford University Press, 1975). Very recently, her novels have been taken up by the alt-right, as well as by conservatives such as Theresa May. See Spencer Jackson's unpublished talk, 'Austen in the Age of Trump', University of Queensland Art Museum, 27 July 2017.

93. See *Jane Austen's Letters*, ed. Deirdre Le Faye, 3rd edn (Oxford: Oxford University Press 1995), 202. Parrinder suggests that Austen's statement has been misread (*Novel and Nation*, 195). See also Michael Karounos, 'Ordination and Revolution in *Mansfield Park*', *SEL* 44, no. 4 (2004): 715–36 and Pamela Regis, 'Vows in *Mansfield Park*: The Promises of Courtship', *Persuasions* 28 (2006): 166–75.

94. Fanny twice quotes the poetry of Cowper. Jane Austen, *Mansfield Park*, ed. John Wiltshire (Cambridge: Cambridge University Press, 2005), 66, 499. Subsequent citations in the text refer to this edition. See William Deresiewicz, *Jane Austen and the Romantic Poets* (New York: Columbia University Press, 2004), 8, 56ff. On Austen's relation to Wordsworth and Gilpin, see Frank W. Bradbrook, *Jane Austen and Her Predecessors* (Cambridge: Cambridge University Press, 1966), 78–9.

95. Relevant scholarship includes Edward Said, 'Jane Austen and Empire', in *Culture and Imperialism* (London: Chatto and Windus, 1993), 95–115; Moira Ferguson, '*Mansfield Park*: Slavery, Colonialism and Gender', *Oxford Literary Review* 13 (1991): 118–39; Joseph Lew, '"That Abominable Traffic": *Mansfield Park* and the Dynamics of Slavery', in *History, Gender and Eighteenth-Century Literature*, ed. Beth Fowkes Tobin (Athens: University of Georgia Press, 1994), 271–300; Gabrielle D. V. White, *Jane Austen in the Context of Abolition: 'A Fling at the Slave Trade'* (New York: Palgrave Macmillan, 2006) and Catherine Ingrassia, '*Emma*, Slavery, and Cultures of Captivity', *Persuasions* 38 (2016): 95–106.

96. On Austen's own Anglicanism and her representation of the clergy, see Irene Collins, *Jane Austen and the Clergy* (London: Hambledon, 1994); Michael Giffin, *Jane Austen and Religion: Salvation and Society in Georgian England* (Hampshire: Palgrave Macmillan, 2002) and White, *Austen's Anglicanism*.

97. On Sir Thomas's role as a patriarch, see Paula M. Cohen, 'Stabilizing the Family System at Mansfield Park', *ELH* 54 (1987): 669–93.

98. As Kate Rumbold observes, Henry Crawford's choices echo William Dodd's immensely popular *Beauties of Shakespear* (1752), which collected 'the finest passages of the finest poet'. *Shakespeare and the Eighteenth-Century Novel: Cultures of Quotation from Samuel Richardson to Jane Austen* (Cambridge: Cambridge University Press, 2016), 167.

99. Lucy Newlyn, *Reading, Writing and Romanticism: The Anxiety of Reception* (Oxford: Oxford University Press, 2000), 356–8.

Afterword

1. Ian Duncan, 'The Bildungsroman, the Romantic Nation, and the Marriage Plot', in *Replotting Marriage in Nineteenth-Century British Literature*, ed. J. Galvan and E. Michie (Columbus: Ohio State University Press, 2018), 16–17.
2. Maria Edgeworth, *Belinda*, ed. Kathryn J. Kirkpatrick (Oxford: Oxford University Press, 1994). Subsequent citations in the text refer to this edition. *Belinda*'s revised 1810 edition effectively censored two marriage plots involving West Indian characters: Belinda's courtship with Mr Vincent, a creole landowner, and a union between Lucy, an English farm girl, and Juba, Mr Vincent's African slave. See Kirkpatrick's introduction, xxii, xxvi–xxxii.

Bibliography

Primary Sources

Account of Marriage, or, the Interests of Marriage Considered and Defended against the Unjust Attacques of this Age, An. London: B. G. for Allen Bancks, 1672.

Act for the Better Preventing of Clandestine Marriage, An. 1753. 26 Geo. II. c. 33. Reproduced in R. B. Outhwaite, *Clandestine Marriage in England, 1550–1850*, 173–80. London: Hambleton Press, 1995.

Armytage, George J., ed. *Register of Baptisms and Marriages at St. George's Chapel, May Fair.* London: Mitchell and Hughes, 1889.

Austen, Jane. *Emma* [1816]. Edited by Richard Cronin and Dorothy McMillan. Cambridge: Cambridge University Press, 2005.

 Jane Austen's Letters. Edited by Deirdre Le Faye. 3rd edn. Oxford: Oxford University Press, 1995.

 Jane Austen's Letters to Her Sister Cassandra and Others. Edited by R. W. Chapman. 2nd edn. London: Oxford University Press, 1959.

 Mansfield Park [1814, 1816]. Edited by John Wiltshire. Cambridge: Cambridge University Press, 2005.

 Pride and Prejudice [1813]. Edited by Pat Rogers. Cambridge: Cambridge University Press, 2006.

Behn, Aphra. *The False Count* [1682]. In *The Plays, Histories, and Novels of the Ingenious Mrs. Aphra Behn with Life and Memoirs.* Vol. 3. London: John Pearson, 1871.

Beister, Johann Erich. 'Vorschlag, die Geistlichen nicht mehr bei Vollziehung der Ehen zubemühen'. *Berlinische Monatsschrift* (1783): 265–75.

Book of Common Prayer, The. New York: Church Pension Fund, 1945.

Boswell, James. *Boswell in Search of a Wife, 1766–1769.* Edited by Frank Brady and Frederick A.Pottle. New York: McGraw-Hill, 1956.

Burn, John Southerden. *The Fleet Registers. Comprising the History of Fleet Marriages, and Some Account of the Parsons and Marriage-House Keepers, with Extracts from the Registers.* London: Rivingtons, Butterworth and Suter, 1833.

Burney, Frances. *Camilla, or A Picture of Youth* [1796]. Edited by Edward A. Bloom and Lillian D. Bloom. Oxford: Oxford University Press, 1983.

 Cecilia, or Memoirs of an Heiress [1782]. Edited by Peter Sabor and Margaret Anne Doody. London: Oxford University Press, 1988.

The Early Diary of Frances Burney, 1768–1778. Edited by Anne R. Ellis. 2 vols. London: Bell and Sons, 1907.

Early Journals and Letters of Fanny Burney. Edited by Lars E. Troide. 2 vols. Oxford: Clarendon, 1990.

Evelina, or The History of a Young Lady's Entrance into the World [1778]. Edited by Edward A. Bloom. Oxford: Oxford University Press, 2002.

Chapone, Hester Mulso. *The Works of Mrs. Chapone: Now First Collected. In Four Volumes*. London: John Murray, 1807.

'Charlotte Bateman, a Tale'. *Lady's Magazine* 13 (Nov., Dec. & supp. 1782): 579–83, 625–7, 692–4.

Churchill, Charles. *The Times* [1764]. In *The Poetical Works of Charles Churchill*. Edited by Douglas Grant, 389–409. Oxford: Oxford University Press, 1956.

Cobbett, William, ed. *The Parliamentary History of England, from the Earliest Period to the Year 1803*. 36 vols. London: R. Bagshaw, 1806–20.

Collier, Jeremy. *A Short View of the Immorality, and Profaneness of the English Stage* [1698]. New York: Routledge, 1989.

Congreve, William. *The Works of William Congreve*. Edited by D. F. McKenzie. 3 vols. Oxford: Oxford University Press, 2001.

'Defence of Marrying the Younger Part of the Sex'. *Lady's Magazine* 4 (1773): 131.

[Douglas, Francis?]. *Considerations on the Causes of the Present Stagnation of Matrimony*. London: T. Silsbury, for J. Ridley, 1772.

Draper, William H. *The Morning Walk, or, City Encompassed*. London: M. Cooper, 1751.

Dryden, John. 'The Character of a Good Parson'. In *Fables Ancient and Modern Translated into Verse from Homer, Ovid, Boccace, & Chaucer*, 320–4. London: Jacob Tonson, 1700.

The Wild Gallant. In *The Works of John Dryden* [1662–3]. Edited by John Harrington Smith and Dougald MacMillan. Vol. 8. Berkeley: University of California Press, 1967.

Edgeworth, Maria. *Belinda* [1801]. Edited by Kathryn J. Kirkpatrick. Oxford: Oxford University Press, 1994.

Elliot, Robert. *The Gretna Green Memoirs*. London: Gretna Green Parson, 1842.

Fielding, Henry. 'A Fragment of a Comment of Lord Bolingbroke's Essays'. In *A Journal of a Voyage to Lisbon*, 221–45. Dublin: James Hoey, 1756.

Contributions to 'The Champion' and Related Writings. Edited by W. B. Coley. Oxford: Clarendon, 2003.

Joseph Andrews [1742]. Edited by Martin C. Battestin. Middletown, CT: Wesleyan University Press, 1984.

Joseph Andrews and Shamela [1742, 1741]. Edited by Judith Hawley. London: Penguin, 1999.

New Essays by Henry Fielding. Edited by Martin C. Battestin and Michael G. Farrindon. Charlottesville: University of Virginia Press, 1989.

Plays Volume III, 1734–1742. Edited by Thomas Lockwood. Oxford: Clarendon, 2011.

Gally, Henry. *Some Considerations upon Clandestine Marriages.* 2nd edn. London: J. Hughs, 1750.

Garrick, David and George Colman. *The Clandestine Marriage* [1766]. Edited by Noel Chevalier. Peterborough: Broadview, 1995.

Gay, John. *Dramatic Works.* Edited by John Fuller. 2 vols. Oxford: Clarendon, 1983.

Goldsmith, Oliver. *Collected Works of Oliver Goldsmith.* Edited by Arthur Friedman. Vol. 2: *The Citizen of the World; or Letters from a Chinese Philosopher, Residing in London to His Friends in the East.* Oxford: Clarendon, 1966.

'An Essay on the Theatre; Or, A Comparison between Laughing and Sentimental Comedy'. *The Westminster Magazine* 4 (January 1773): 4–6.

'A Register of Scotch Marriages' [1773]. In *The Miscellaneous Works of Oliver Goldsmith*, 347–8. London: Macmillan, 1923.

The Vicar of Wakefield [1766]. Edited by Arthur Friedman. Oxford: Oxford University Press, 2006.

Haywood, Eliza. *Anti-Pamela; or, Feign'd Innocence Detected.* London: J. Huggonson, 1741.

The History of Miss Betsy Thoughtless [1751]. Edited by Christine Blouch. Peterborough: Broadview, 1998.

Hazlitt, William. 'On the English Novelists'. In *The Complete Works of William Hazlitt.* Edited by P. P. Howe. Vol. 6, 106–32. London: Dent, 1931.

'On Londoners and Country People'. In *The Complete Works of William Hazlitt.* Edited by P. P. Howe. Vol. 12, 66–77. London: Dent, 1931.

Jeaffreson, J. C. *Brides and Bridals.* Vol. 2. London: Hurst and Blackett, 1872.

Johnson, John. *The Clergyman's Vade-Mecum.* 5th edn. London: Robert Knaplock and Sam. Ballard, 1723.

Jonson, Ben. *Epicoene, or The Silent Woman* [1609]. Edited by L. A. Beaurline. London: Edward Arnold, 1967.

Keith, Alexander. *Observations on the Act for Preventing Clandestine Marriages.* London: M. Cooper, 1753.

Knight, Charles. *London.* Vol. 4: *London: Virtue.* London: Charles Knight & Company, 1875–7.

Locke, John. *Two Treatises of Government* [1689]. Edited by Peter Laslett. Cambridge: Cambridge University Press, 1998.

Merrick, Montague. *Marriage a Divine Institution.* London: E. Withers, 1754.

Montagu, Mary Wortley. *The Letters and Works of Lady Mary Wortley Montagu.* 3 vols. Edited by Lord Wharncliffe. London: Richard Bentley, 1837.

Nicols, John. *Literary Anecdotes of the Eighteenth Century: Comprising Biographical Memoirs of William Bowyer.* 6 vols. London: Nichols, Son, and Bentley, 1812.

Pennant, Thomas. *Some Account of London.* 3rd edn. London: Robert Faulder, 1793.

Prideaux, Humphrey. *The Case of Clandestine Marriages Stated Wherein Are Shewn the Causes from Whence This Corruption Ariseth.* London: 1691.

Pufendorf, Samuel. *The Law of Nature and Nations: or, A General System of the Most Important Principles of Morality, Jurisprudence, and Politics*. 8 books. 5th edn. London: J. and J. Bonwicke, 1749.

Reflections on the Marriage Act with Some Hints for a New Law: Humbly Offered to the Consideration of Parliament. London: printed for G. Woodfall, 1764.

Richardson, Samuel. *Clarissa*. 3rd edn. Edited by Florian Stuber. *The Clarissa Project*. 8 vols. New York: AMS Press, 1990.

    Clarissa, or The History of a Young Lady 1747–48. 1st edn. Edited by Angus Ross, Penguin, 1985.

    Correspondence with Aaron Hill and the Hill Family. Edited by Christine Gerrard. Cambridge: Cambridge University Press, 2013.

    Correspondence with Lady Bradshaigh and Lady Echlin. Edited by Peter Sabor. Cambridge: Cambridge University Press, 2016.

    Early Works. Edited by Alexander Pettit. Cambridge: Cambridge University Press, 2012.

    The History of Sir Charles Grandison. 7 vols. London: C. Hitch and L. Hawes, 1754.

    The History of Sir Charles Grandison [1753–4]. Edited by Jocelyn Harris. 7 vols. Oxford: Oxford University Press, 1986.

    Pamela in Her Exalted Condition. Edited by Albert J. Rivero. Cambridge: Cambridge University Press, 2012.

    Pamela; or, Virtue Rewarded [1801, incorporating corrections from the 1810 edition]. Edited by Peter Sabor. Introduction by Margaret A. Doody. London: Penguin, 1980.

    Pamela; or, Virtue Rewarded [1740]. Edited by Thomas Keymer and Alice Wakely. Oxford: Oxford University Press, 2001.

Rowlandson, Thomas and William Combe. *The English Dance of Death*. 2 vols. London: J. Diggens, 1815–16.

Scheme to Pay Off, in a Few Years, the National Debt, by a Repeal of the Marriage Act, A. London: T. Becket & P. A. De Hondt, 1767.

Scott, Walter. *Lives of the Eminent Novelists and Dramatists*. London: Frederick Warne, 1886.

Shebbeare, John. *The Marriage Act: A Novel*. 2 vols. London: J. Hodges, 1754.

Smith, Alex. *A Compleat History of the Lives and Robberies of the Most Notorious Highway-Men, Foot-Pads, Shop-Lifts, and Cheats, of Both Sexes*. 3 vols. London: Sam Briscoe, 1714–20.

Smith, Charlotte. *Emmeline: The Orphan of the Castle* [1788]. Edited by Loraine Fletcher. Ontario: Broadview, 2003.

    The Old Manor House [1793]. Edited by Anne Henry Ehrenpreis. Oxford: Oxford University Press, 1989.

Spectator, The. Edited by Donald F. Bond. 5 vols. Oxford: Clarendon, 1965.

Stebbing, Henry. *An Enquiry into the Force and Operation of the Annulling Clauses in a Late Act for the Better Preventing of Clandestine Marriages, with Respect to Conscience in which the Rights of Marriage both in and out of Society Are Briefly Discussed*. London: M. Cooper, 1754.

Stuart, Charles. *Gretna Green, a Comic Opera* [1783]. In *Scottish Ballad Operas III: Farce and Satire*, compiled by Walter H. Rubsamen. New York: Garland, 1974.

  Ripe Fruit, or, The Marriage Act [1781]. Ms. Larpent 566. Henry E. Huntingdon Library and Art Gallery.

Swinburne, Henry. *A Treatise of Spousals or Matrimonial Contracts*. London: S. Roycroft for Robert Clavell, 1686.

Tatler, The. Edited by Donald F. Bond. 3 vols. Oxford: Clarendon, 1987.

Walpole, Horace. *The Yale Edition of Horace Walpole Correspondence*. Edited by W. S. Lewis. 48 vols. New Haven: Yale University Press, 1937–83.

Warburton, William. *The Alliance between Church and State: Or, The Necessity and Equity of an Established Religion and a Test Law Demonstrated*. 4th edn. London: A. Millar and J. and R. Tonson, 1766.

  'On the Nature of the Marriage Union, Matt. Xix. 6: Sermon XVII'. In *The Works of the Right Reverend William Warburton, D. D., Lord Bishop of Gloucester*, 12 vols. Edited by Richard Hurd, 9:345–64. London: T. Cadell and W. Davies, 1811.

  'Preface to Volume III of *Clarissa Harlowe*, 1748'. In *Novel and Romance 1700–1800: A Documentary Record*, edited by Ioan Williams, 91–2. London: Routledge Revivals, 2010.

Whitehead, William. *A Trip to Scotland*. London: J. Dodsley, 1770.

Wilkinson, Tate. *Memoirs of His Own Life*. Vol. 1. York: Wilson, Spence, and Mawman, 1790.

Yorke, P. C. *The Life and Correspondence of Philip Yorke, Earl of Hardwicke, Lord High Chancellor of Great Britain*. 3 vols. Cambridge: Cambridge University Press, 1913.

Zöllner, Johann Friedrich. 'Ist es rathsam, das Ehebündniß nicht ferner durch die Religion zu sanciren?' *Berlinische Monatsschrift* (1783): 508–17.

Secondary Sources

Alleman, Gellert Spencer. *Matrimonial Law and the Materials of Restoration Comedy*. Wallingford, PA: privately published, 1942.

Anderson, Misty G. *Female Playwrights and Eighteenth-Century Comedy: Negotiating Marriage on the London Stage*. New York: Palgrave, 2002.

Anthony, Sister Rose. *The Jeremy Collier Stage Controversy, 1698–1726*. New York: Benjamin Blom, 1966.

Aravamudan, Srinivas. *Enlightenment Orientalism: Resisting the Rise of the Novel*. Chicago: Chicago University Press, 2011.

Arendt, Hannah. *The Origins of Totalitarianism*. New York: Harcourt Brace, 1973.

Armitage, David. 'A Patriot for Whom? The Afterlives of Bolingbroke's Patriot King'. *Journal of British Studies* 36, no. 4 (1997): 397–418.

Armstrong, Nancy. *Desire and Domestic Fiction: A Political History of the Novel*. Oxford: Oxford University Press, 1987.

Armstrong, Nancy and Leonard Tennenhouse. 'The Network Novel and How It Unsettled Domestic Fiction'. In *A Companion to the English Novel*. Edited by Stephen Arata, Madigan Haley, J. Paul Hunter and Jennifer Wicke, 306–20. Hoboken: Wiley-Blackwell, 2015.

Auerbach, Erich. *Mimesis: The Representation of Reality in Western Literature*. Princeton: Princeton University Press, 2003.

Austin, John L. *How to Do Things with Words*. Oxford: Clarendon, 1962.

Backscheider, Paula R. 'The Story of Eliza Haywood's Novels: Caveats and Questions'. In *The Passionate Fictions of Eliza Haywood: Essays on Her Life and Work*. Edited by Kirsten T. Saxton and Rebecca P. Bocchicchio, 19–47. Lexington: University of Kentucky Press, 2000.

Ballaster, Ros. *Seductive Forms: Women's Amatory Fiction from 1684–1740*. Oxford: Clarendon, 1992.

Bannet, Eve Tavor. *The Domestic Revolution: Enlightenment Feminisms and the Novel*. Baltimore: Johns Hopkins University Press, 2000.

'The Marriage Act of 1753: "A Most Cruel Law for the Fair Sex"'. *Eighteenth-Century Studies* 30, no. 3 (1997): 233–54.

Barrie-Curien, Viviane. 'The Clergy in the Diocese of London in the Eighteenth Century'. In *The Church of England, c. 1689–c. 1833: From Toleration to Tractarianism*. Edited by John Walsh, Colin Haydon and Stephen Taylor, 86–109. Cambridge: Cambridge University Press, 1993.

Battestin, Martin C. *Henry Fielding: A Life*. London: Routledge, 1989.

The Moral Basis of Fielding's Art: A Study of Joseph Andrews. Middletown, CT: Wesleyan University Press, 1967.

Bechler, Rosemary. '"Triall by What Is Contrary": Samuel Richardson and Christian Dialectic'. In *Samuel Richardson: Passion and Prudence*. Edited by Valerie Grosvenor Myer, 93–113. London: Vision Press, 1986.

Bennett, G. V. *The Tory Crisis in Church and State 1688–1730: The Career of Francis Atterbury Bishop of Rochester*. Oxford: Clarendon, 1975.

Berg, Maxine and Elizabeth Eger, eds. *Luxury in the Eighteenth Century: Debates, Desires, and Delectable Goods*. New York: Palgrave Macmillan, 2003.

Besant, Walter. *The Survey of London: London in the Eighteenth-Century*. London: Adam and Charles Black, 1902.

Best, G. F. A. *Temporal Pillars: Queen Anne's Bounty, the Ecclesiastical Commissioners, and the Church of England*. Cambridge: Cambridge University Press, 1964.

Black, Jeremy. 'Confessional State or Elect Nation? Religion and Identity in Eighteenth-Century England'. In *Protestantism and National Identity*. Edited by Tony Claydon and Ian McBride, 53–74. Cambridge: Cambridge University Press, 1998.

Blumenberg, Hans. *The Legitimacy of the Modern Age*. Translated by Robert M. Wallace. Cambridge, MA: MIT Press, 1983.

Bonwick, Colin. *English Radicals and the American Revolution*. Chapel Hill: University of North Carolina Press, 1977.

Boone, Joseph Allen. *Tradition Counter Tradition: Love and the Form of Fiction*. Chicago: Chicago University Press, 1987.

Boulton, Jeremy. 'Clandestine Marriages in London: An Examination of a Neglected Urban Variable'. *Urban History* 20, no. 2 (1993): 191–210.

Bowers, Toni. *Force or Fraud: British Seduction Stories and the Problem of Resistance, 1660–1760*. Oxford: Oxford University Press, 2011.

'Sex, Lies, and Invisibility: Amatory Fiction from the Restoration to Mid-Century'. In *The Columbia History of the British Novel*. Edited by John J. Richetti, 50–72. New York: Columbia University Press, 1994.

Bradbrook, Frank W. *Jane Austen and Her Predecessors*. Cambridge: Cambridge University Press, 1966.

Bradley, James E. *Religion, Revolution, and English Radicalism: Nonconformity in Eighteenth-Century Politics and Society*. Cambridge: Cambridge University Press, 1990.

Bray, Joe. *The Epistolary Novel: Representations of Consciousness*. London: Routledge, 2003.

Bree, Linda. 'The Literary Context'. In *The Cambridge Companion to 'Pride and Prejudice'*. Edited by Janet Todd, 56–66. Cambridge: Cambridge University Press, 2013.

Brewer, John. *The Sinews of Power: War, Money and the English State 1688–1793*. London: Century Hutchinson, 1989.

Brooks, Christopher K. 'Goldsmith's Commercial Vicar: Spectacles and Speculation'. *CLA Journal* 41, no. 3 (1998): 319–34.

Brown, Marshall. *Preromanticism*. Stanford: Stanford University Press, 1991.

Brown, Peter. *The Chathamites*. London: Macmillan, 1967.

Brown, Roger Lee. 'The Rise and Fall of Fleet Marriages'. In *Marriage and Society: Studies in the Social History of Marriage*. Edited by R. B. Outhwaite, 117–36. London: Europa, 1981.

Browning, Reed. *Political and Constitutional Ideas of the Court Whigs*. Baton Rouge: Louisiana State University Press, 1982.

Burgess, Miranda J. *British Fiction and the Production of Social Order, 1740–1830*. Cambridge: Cambridge University Press, 2000.

Butler, Marilyn. *Jane Austen and the War of Ideas*. Oxford: Oxford University Press, 1975.

Campbell, Ann. 'Clandestine Marriage and Frances Burney's Critique of Matrimony in *Cecilia*'. *Eighteenth-Century Life* 37, no. 2 (2013): 85–103.

'The Limits of "Laudable Action": Women's Marital Choice in John Shebbeare's *The Marriage Act*'. *Topic* 55 (2007): 13–24.

Carnell, Rachel. *Partisan Politics, Narrative Realism, and the Rise of the British Novel*. New York: Palgrave Macmillan, 2006.

Carson, James P. '"The Little Republic" of the Family: Goldsmith's Politics of Nostalgia'. *Eighteenth-Century Fiction* 16, no. 2 (2004): 173–96.

Chico, Tita. 'Details and Frankness: Affective Relations in *Sir Charles Grandison*', *Studies in Eighteenth-Century Culture* 38 (2009): 45–68.

Clark, J. C. D. *The Dynamics of Change: The Crisis of the 1750s and English Party Systems*. Cambridge: Cambridge University Press, 1982.

English Society, 1660–1832: Religion, Ideology, and Politics during the Ancien Regime. 2nd edn. Cambridge: Cambridge University Press, 2000.

Clarke, Norma. *Brothers of the Quill: Oliver Goldsmith in Grub Street.* Cambridge, MA: Harvard University Press, 2016.

Claydon, Tony. *William III and the Godly Revolution.* Cambridge: Cambridge University Press, 2004.

Cleary, Thomas R. *Henry Fielding: Political Writer.* Waterloo, ON: Wilfrid Laurier University Press, 1984.

Cohen, Michael. 'First Sisters in the British Novel: Charlotte Lennox to Susan Ferrier'. In *The Significance of Sibling Relationships.* Edited by JoAnna Stephens Mink and Janet Doubler Ward, 98–109. Bowling Green: Bowling Green State University Popular Press, 1993.

Cohen, Paula M. 'Stabilizing the Family System at Mansfield Park'. *ELH* 54 (1987): 669–93.

Coley, W. B., General introduction to Henry Fielding, *Contributions to 'The Champion' and Related Writings*, xxiii–cxix. Oxford: Clarendon, 2003.

Colley, Linda. *Britons: Forging the Nation, 1707–1837.* New Haven: Yale University Press, 1992.

In Defiance of Oligarchy: The Tory Party 1714–1760. Cambridge: Cambridge University Press, 1982.

Collins, Irene. 'Displeasing Pictures of Clergymen'. *Persuasions* 18 (1996): 109–19.

Jane Austen and the Clergy. London: Hambledon, 1994.

Conway, Alison. '*Sir Charles Grandison* and the Sexual Politics of Toleration'. *Lumen* 30 (2011): 1–19.

Copeland, Edward. 'Money Talks: Jane Austen and the *Lady's Magazine*'. In *Jane Austen's Beginnings: The Juvenilia and Lady Susan.* Edited by J. David Grey, 153–72. Ann Arbor: University of Michigan Research Press, 1989.

Women Writing about Money: Women's Fiction in England, 1790–1820. Cambridge: Cambridge University Press, 1995.

Corbett, Mary Jean. *Family Likeness: Sex, Marriage and Incest from Austen to Virginia Woolf.* Ithaca: Cornell University Press, 2008.

Corfield, Penelope J. 'Walking the City Streets: The Urban Odyssey in Eighteenth-Century England'. *Urban History* 16, no. 2 (1990): 132–74.

Cressy, David. *Birth, Marriage, and Death: Ritual, Religion, and the Life-Cycle in Tudor and Stuart England.* Oxford: Oxford University Press, 1997.

Curran, Louise. *Samuel Richardson and the Art of Letter Writing.* Cambridge: Cambridge University Press, 2016.

Davies, Andrew. '"The Gothic Novel in Wales" Revisited: A Preliminary Survey of the Wales-Related Romantic Fiction at Cardiff University', *Cardiff Corvey: Reading the Romantic Text* 2, no. 1 (1998): www.romtext.org.uk/articles/cc02_n01/#foot1.

Deresiewicz, William. *Jane Austen and the Romantic Poets.* New York: Columbia University Press, 2004.

Derry, Stephen. 'Jane Austen's Use of *The Vicar of Wakefield* in *Pride and Prejudice*'. *English Language Notes* 28, no. 3 (1991): 25–7.

Dickinson, H. T. *Liberty and Property: Political Ideology in Eighteenth-Century Britain*. New York: Holmes and Meier Publishers, 1977.

Doerksen, Teri. '*Sir Charles Grandison*: The Anglican Family and the Admirable Roman Catholic'. *Eighteenth-Century Fiction* 15, no. 3 (2003): 539–58.

Domingo, Darryl P. 'Richardson's Unfamiliar Quotations: *Clarissa* and Early Eighteenth-Century Comedy'. *RES* 66, no. 277 (2015): 936–53.

'Unbending the Mind: Or, Commercialized Leisure and the Rhetoric of Eighteenth-Century Diversion'. *Eighteenth-Century Studies* 45, no. 2 (2012): 207–36.

Donovan, Josephine. *Women and the Rise of the Novel*. London: Palgrave, 1999.

Doody, Margaret Anne. 'Burney and Politics'. In *The Cambridge Companion to Frances Burney*. Edited by Peter Sabor, 93–110. Cambridge: Cambridge University Press, 2007.

Frances Burney: The Life in the Works. New Brunswick, NJ: Rutgers University Press, 1988.

A Natural Passion: A Study of the Novels of Samuel Richardson. Oxford: Clarendon, 1974.

'Richardson's Politics'. *Eighteenth-Century Fiction* 2, no. 2 (1990): 113–28.

The True Story of the Novel. New Brunswick, NJ: Rutgers University Press, 1996.

Downie, J. A. *A Political Biography of Henry Fielding*. London: Pickering and Chatto, 2009.

Downie, J. A., ed. *Henry Fielding in Our Time: Papers Presented at the Tercentenary Conference*. Newcastle: Cambridge Scholars, 2008.

Drake, George A. 'Ritual in *Joseph Andrews*'. In *Henry Fielding in Our Time: Papers Presented at the Tercentenary Conference*. Edited by J. A. Downie, 133–46. Newcastle: Cambridge Scholars, 2008.

Drum, Alice. 'Pride and Prestige: Jane Austen and the Professions'. *College Literature* 36, no. 3 (2009): 92–115.

Dudley, W. R. *The Moral Revolution of 1688*. New Haven: Yale University Press, 1982.

Duffy, Eamon. 'The Long Reformation: Catholicism, Protestantism and the Multitude'. In *England's London Reformation 1500–1800*. Edited by Nicholas Tyacke, 33–70. London: Routledge, 1998.

Duncan, Ian. 'The Bildungsroman, the Romantic Nation, and the Marriage Plot'. In *Replotting Marriage in Nineteenth-Century British Literature*. Edited by J. Galvan and E. Michie, 15–34. Columbus: Ohio State University Press, 2018.

Dussinger, John A. '"Ciceronian Eloquence": The Politics of Virtue in Richardson's *Pamela*'. *Eighteenth-Century Fiction* 12, no. 1 (1999): 39–60.

'"Stealing the Great Doctrines of Christianity": Samuel Richardson as Journalist'. *Eighteenth-Century Fiction* 15 (2003): 451–506.

'"The Working Class of People": An Early Eighteenth-Century Source'. *Notes and Queries* 43, no. 3 (1996): 299–302.

Eaves, T. C. Duncan and Ben D. Kimpel. *Samuel Richardson: A Biography*. Oxford: Clarendon, 1971.

Ferguson, Frances. 'Jane Austen, *Emma*, and the Impact of Form'. *MLQ* 61, no. 1 (2000): 157–80.

Ferguson, Moira. '*Mansfield Park*: Slavery, Colonialism and Gender'. *Oxford Literary Review* 13 (1991): 118–39.

Flint, Christopher. *Family Fictions: Narrative and Domestic Relations in Britain, 1688–1798*. Stanford: Stanford University Press, 1998.

Foster, James R. 'Smollett's Pamphleteering Foe Shebbeare'. *PMLA* 57, no. 4 (1942): 1053–1100.

Foucault, Michel. *The History of Sexuality*. Vol. 1: *The Will to Knowledge*. London: Penguin, 1988.

Freeman, Elizabeth. *The Wedding Complex: Forms of Belonging in Modern American Culture*. Durham, NC: Duke University Press, 2002.

Freeman, Lisa A. *Character's Theatre: Genre and Identity on the Eighteenth-Century Stage*. Philadelphia: University of Pennsylvania Press, 2002.

Frye, Northrop. *Anatomy of Criticism: Four Essays*. Princeton: Princeton University Press, 1957.

Fuller, John. Introduction to John Gay, *Dramatic Works*. Vol. 1, 1–76. Oxford: Clarendon, 1983.

Gallagher, Catherine. *Nobody's Story: The Vanishing Acts of Women Writers in the Marketplace 1670–1820*. Berkeley: University of California Press, 1994.

Galperin, William. *The Historical Austen*. Philadelphia: University of Pennsylvania, 2003.

Ganz, Melissa J. 'Clandestine Schemes: Burney's *Cecilia* and the Marriage Act'. *The Eighteenth Century: Theory and Interpretation* 54, no. 1 (2013): 25–51.

Garside, Peter, James Raven and Rainer Schöwerling, eds. *The English Novel, 1770–1829: A Bibliographical Survey of Prose Fiction Published in the British Isles*. Vol. 1: *1770–1799*. Oxford: Oxford University Press, 2000.

Gerrard, Christine. *The Patriot Opposition to Walpole: Politics, Poetry, and Myth, 1725–1742*. Oxford: Clarendon, 1994.

Giffin, Michael. *Jane Austen and Religion: Salvation and Society in Georgian England*. Hampshire: Palgrave Macmillan, 2002.

Gilbert, Alan D. *Religion and Society in Industrial England: Church, Chapel, and Social Change, 1740–1914*. London: Longman, 1976.

Gillis, John R. *For Better, for Worse: British Marriages, 1600 to the Present*. New York: Oxford University Press, 1985.

Glass, D. V. *Numbering the People: The Eighteenth-Century Population Controversy and the Development of Censes and Vital Statistics in Britain*. Farnborough: Saxon House, 1973.

Goldgar, Bertrand A. 'Fielding's Periodical Journalism'. In *The Cambridge Companion to Henry Fielding*. Edited by Claude Rawson, 109–21. Cambridge: Cambridge University Press, 2007.

Goldie, Mark. 'The English System of Liberty'. In *The Cambridge History of Eighteenth-Century Political Thought*. Edited by Mark Goldie and Robert Wokler, 40–78. Cambridge: Cambridge University Press, 2006.

Gollapudi, Aparna. *Moral Reform in Comedy and Culture 1696–1747*. Burlington, VT: Ashgate, 2011.

Gould, Eliga H. *The Persistence of Empire: British Political Culture in the Age of the American Revolution*. Chapel Hill: University of North Carolina Press, 2000.

Gregory, Jeremy. 'The Eighteenth-Century Reformation: The Pastoral Task of Anglican Clergy after 1689'. In *The Church of England c. 1689–c. 1833: From Toleration to Tractarianism*. Edited by John Walsh, Colin Haydon and Stephen Taylor, 67–85. Cambridge: Cambridge University Press, 1993.

Restoration, Reformation and Reform: Archbishops of Canterbury and Their Diocese. Oxford: Clarendon, 2000.

Gruner, Elisabeth Rose. 'Loving the Difference: Sisters and Brothers from Frances Burney to Emily Bronte'. In *The Significance of Sibling Relationships in Literature*. Edited by JoAnna Stephens Mink and Janet Doubler Ward, 32–57. Bowling Green: Bowling Green State University Popular Press, 1993.

Guest, Harriet. *Small Change: Women, Learning and Patriotism, 1750–1810*. Chicago: Chicago University Press, 2000.

Gwilliam, Tassie. *Samuel Richardson's Fictions of Gender*. Stanford: Stanford University Press, 1993.

Haakonssen, Knud. 'Protestant Natural-Law Theory: A General Interpretation'. In *New Essays on the History of Autonomy: A Collection Honoring J. B. Schneewind*. Edited by Natalie Brender and Larry Krasnoff, 92–109. Cambridge: Cambridge University Press, 2004.

Haggerty, George E. 'Satire and Sentiment in *The Vicar of Wakefield*'. *The Eighteenth Century* 32, no. 1 (1991): 25–38.

Harkin, Maureen. 'Goldsmith on Authorship in *The Vicar of Wakefield*'. *Eighteenth-Century Fiction* 14, nos. 3–4 (2002): 325–44.

Harris, Jocelyn. *Jane Austen's Art of Memory*. Cambridge: Cambridge University Press, 1989.

Harris, Robert. *Politics and the Nation: Britain in the Mid-Eighteenth Century*. Oxford: Oxford University Press, 2002.

Harth, Erica. 'The Virtue of Love: Lord Hardwicke's Marriage Act'. *Cultural Critique* 9 (1988): 123–54.

Haugen, Kristine Louise. *Richard Bentley: Poetry and Enlightenment*. Cambridge, MA: Harvard University Press, 2011.

Hawley, Judith. Introduction to *Joseph Andrews and Shamela*, by Henry Fielding, vii–xxix. London: Penguin, 1999.

Heitzenrater, Richard. Introduction to *Diary of an Oxford Methodist: Benjamin Ingham, 1733–34*, 1–48. Durham, NC: Duke University Press, 1985.

Hinnant, Charles H. 'Jane Austen's "Wild Imagination": Romance and the Courtship Plot in the Six Canonical Novels'. *Narrative* 14, no. 3 (2006): 294–310.

Hogan, C. B., ed. *The London Stage 1600–1800*, Part 5: 1776–1800. 3 vols. Carbondale: Southern Illinois University Press, 1968.

Holmes, Geoffrey S. *Augustan England: Professions, State and Society, 1680–1730*. London: G. Allen & Unwin, 1982.

Politics, Religion and Society in England, 1679–1742. London: Hambledon Press, 1986.

Hopkins, Robert H. 'Matrimony in *The Vicar of Wakefield* and the Marriage Act of 1753'. *Studies in Philology* 74, no. 3 (1977): 322–39.

Hultquist, Aleksondra. 'Haywood's Re-Appropriation of the Amatory Heroine in *Betsy Thoughtless*'. *Philological Quarterly* 85 (2006): 141–65.

'Marriage in Haywood; or, Desire Rewarded'. In *Masters of the Marketplace: British Women Novelists of the 1750s*. Edited by Susan Carlile, 31–46. Lanham, MD: Lehigh University Press, 2011.

Hume, Robert D. *The Rakish Stage: Studies in English Drama, 1660–1800*. Carbondale: Southern Illinois University Press, 1983.

Hunter, Ian. 'Natural Law as Political Philosophy'. In *The Oxford Handbook of Philosophy in Early Modern Europe*. Edited by Desmond Clarke and Catherine Wilson, 475–99. Oxford: Oxford University Press, 2011.

Hunter, Ian and David Saunders. 'Bringing the State to England: Andrew Tooke's Translation of Samuel Pufendorf's *De Officio Hominis et Civis*'. *History of Political Thought* 24, no. 2 (2003): 218–34.

Hunter, Ian and David Saunders, eds. *Natural Law and Civil Sovereignty: Moral Right and State Authority in Early Modern Political Thought*. New York: Palgrave, 2002.

Hunter, J. Paul. *Before Novels: The Cultural Contexts of Eighteenth-Century Fiction*. New York: Norton, 1990.

Ingrassia, Catherine. '*Emma*, Slavery, and Cultures of Captivity'. *Persuasions* 38 (2016): 95–106.

Jackson, Spencer. 'Austen in the Age of Trump', unpublished talk, University of Queensland Art Museum, 27 July 2017.

Jacob, W. M. *Lay People and Religion in the Early Eighteenth Century*. Cambridge: Cambridge University Press, 1996.

Jacob, W. M. and N. J. G. Pounds. *A History of the English Parish: The Culture of Religion from Augustine to Victoria*. Cambridge: Cambridge University Press, 2000.

Johnson, Claudia L. *Equivocal Beings: Politics, Gender, and Sentimentality in the 1790s: Wollstonecraft, Radcliffe, Burney, Austen*. Chicago: University of Chicago Press, 1995.

Jones, Wendy S. *Consensual Fictions: Women, Liberalism, and the English Novel*. Toronto: University of Toronto Press, 2005.

Kahrl, George M. Introduction to *The Letters of David Garrick*, edited by David M. Little and George M. Kahrl. Vol. 1, xxiii–lxiv. Cambridge, MA: Belknap, Harvard University Press, 1963.

Karounos, Michael. 'Ordination and Revolution in *Mansfield Park*'. *SEL* 44, no. 4 (2004): 715–36.

Keymer, Thomas. 'Domestic Servitude and the Licensed Stage'. In *'Pamela' in the Marketplace: Literary Controversy and Print Culture in Eighteenth-Century Britain and Ireland.* Edited by Thomas Keymer and Peter Sabor, 114–42. Cambridge: Cambridge University Press, 2005.

'Fielding's Theatrical Career'. In *The Cambridge Companion to Henry Fielding.* Edited by Claude Rawson, 17–37. Cambridge: Cambridge University Press, 2007.

Introduction to Samuel Richardson, *Pamela; Or, Virtue Rewarded,* Edited by Thomas Keymer and Alice Wakely, vii–xxxiv. London: Oxford University Press, 2001.

'Parliamentary Printing, Paper Credit, and Corporate Fraud: A New Episode in Richardson's Early Career'. *Eighteenth-Century Fiction* 17, no. 2 (2005): 183–206.

Richardson's 'Clarissa' and the Eighteenth-Century Reader. Cambridge: Cambridge University Press, 1992.

Keymer, Thomas and Peter Sabor, eds. *The Pamela Controversy: Criticisms and Adaptations of Samuel Richardson's 'Pamela', 1740–1750.* 6 vols. London: Pickering and Chatto, 2001.

'Pamela' in the Marketplace: Literary Controversy and Print Culture in Eighteenth-Century Britain and Ireland. Cambridge: Cambridge University Press, 2005.

Kibbie, Ann Louise. 'Sentimental Properties: *Pamela* and *Memoirs of a Woman of Pleasure'. ELH* 58, no. 3 (1991): 561–77.

King, Kathryn R. 'The Afterlife and Strange Surprising Adventures of Haywood's Amatories (with Thoughts on Betsy Thoughtless)'. In *Masters of the Marketplace: British Women Novelists of the 1750s.* Edited by Susan Carlile, 203–18. Bethlehem, PA: Lehigh University Press, 2011.

A Political Biography of Eliza Haywood. London: Pickering and Chatto, 2012.

Kinsley, James. 'Dryden's "Character of a Good Parson" and Bishop Ken'. *RES* 3, no. 10 (1952): 155–8.

Kirkpatrick, Kathryn, J. Introduction and Note on the Text to Maria Edgeworth, *Belinda* [1801], ix–xxv, xxvi–xxxii. Oxford: Oxford University Press, 1994.

Korshin, Paul J. *Typologies in England, 1650–1820.* Princeton: Princeton University Press, 1982.

Kraft, Elizabeth. Introduction to Charlotte Smith, *The Young Philosopher* [1798], ix–xxxii. Lexington: University of Kentucky Press, 1999.

Kramnick, Isaac, ed. *The Portable Edmund Burke.* New York: Penguin, 1999.

Lamb, Jonathan. *The Rhetoric of Suffering: Reading the Book of Job in the Eighteenth Century.* Oxford: Clarendon, 1995.

Langford, Paul. *A Polite and Commercial People: England 1727–1783.* Oxford: Oxford University Press, 1989.

Public Life and Propertied Englishmen 1689–1798. Oxford: Oxford University Press, 1991.

Latimer, Bonnie. *Making Gender, Culture, and the Self in the Fiction of Samuel Richardson.* London: Ashgate, 2013.

'Popular Fiction after Richardson'. *Eighteenth-Century Fiction* 29, no. 2 (2016): 241–60.

Lehmann, James. '*The Vicar of Wakefield*: Goldsmith's Sublime, Oriental Job'. *ELH* 46, no. 1 (1979): 97–121.

Lemmings, David. 'Marriage and the Law in the Eighteenth Century: Hardwicke's Marriage Act of 1753'. *The Historical Journal* 39, no. 2 (1996): 339–60.

Leneman, Leah. 'The Scottish Case That Led to Hardwicke's Marriage Act'. *Law and History Review* 17, no. 1 (1999): 161–9.

Levine, Caroline. *Forms: Whole, Rhythm, Hierarchy, Network*. Princeton: Princeton University Press, 2015.

Lew, Joseph. '"That Abominable Traffic": *Mansfield Park* and the Dynamics of Slavery'. In *History, Gender, and Eighteenth-Century Literature*. Edited by Beth Fowkes Tobin, 271–300. Athens: University of Georgia Press, 1994.

Liesenfeld, Vincent J. *The Licensing Act of 1737*. Madison: University of Wisconsin Press, 1987.

Linebaugh, Peter. *The London Hanged: Crime and Civil Society in the Eighteenth Century*. London: Penguin, 1991.

Lockwood, Thomas. 'Did Fielding Write for *The Craftsman?*' *RES* 59, no. 1 (2008): 86–117.

'Fielding and the Licensing Act'. *Huntington Library Quarterly* 50, no. 4 (1987): 379–93.

Introduction to *Pasquin*. In Henry Fielding, *Plays Volume III, 1734–1742*, 217–48. Oxford: Clarendon, 2011.

Loftis, John. *Comedy and Society from Congreve to Fielding*. Stanford: Stanford University Press, 1959.

Lund, Roger D. 'John Shebbeare (1709–1788)'. In *Dictionary of Literary Biography*. Vol. 39: *British Novelists, 1660–1800*. Edited by Martin C. Battestin, 2 parts, 1:418–28. Detroit: Gale Research Company, 1985.

'The Problem with Parsons: *Joseph Andrews* and the "Contempt of the Clergy" Revisited'. In *Henry Fielding in Our Time: Papers Presented at the Tercentenary Conference*. Edited by J. A. Downie, 257–86. Newcastle: Cambridge Scholars, 2008.

Lynch, Deidre Shauna. *The Economy of Character: Novels, Market Culture, and the Business of Inner Meaning*. Chicago: University of Chicago Press, 1998.

Macey, David. '"Business for the Lovers of Business": *Sir Charles Grandison*, Hardwicke's Marriage Act and the Specter of Bigamy'. *Philological Quarterly* 84, no. 3 (2005): 333–55.

Mackenzie, Scott. '"Stock the Parish with Beauties": Henry Fielding's Parochial Vision'. *PMLA* 125, no. 3 (2010): 606–21.

Mackie, Erin. *Rakes, Highwaymen and Pirates: The Making of the Modern Gentleman in the Eighteenth Century*. Baltimore: Johns Hopkins University Press, 2009.

Magee, William H. 'Instrument of Growth: The Courtship and Marriage Plot in Jane Austen's Novels'. *The Journal of Narrative Technique* 17, no. 2 (1987): 198–208.

Marks, Sylvia Kasey. *'Sir Charles Grandison': The Compleat Conduct Book*. Lewisburg: Bucknell University Press, 1986.

Marshall, Ashley. 'Henry Fielding and the "Scriblerians"'. *Modern Language Quarterly* 72, no. 1 (2011): 19–48.

Maunu, Leanne. *Women Writing the Nation: National Identity, Female Community, and the British-French Connection, 1770–1820*. Lewisburg: Bucknell University Press, 2007.

Mayo, Robert D. *The English Novel in the Magazines 1740–1815*. Evanston: Northwestern University Press, 1962.

McDowell, Paula. 'Why Fanny Can't Read: *Joseph Andrews* and the (Ir)relevance of Literacy'. In *A Companion to the Eighteenth-Century English Novel and Culture*. Edited by Paula R. Backscheider and Catherine Ingrassia, 167–90. Oxford: Blackwell, 2005.

McGregor, O. R. *Divorce in England*. London: Heinemann, 1957.

McKeon, Michael. *The Origins of the English Novel, 1600–1740*. Baltimore: Johns Hopkins University Press, 1987.

McKillop, Alan D. 'The Mock Marriage Device in *Pamela*'. *Philological Quarterly* 26 (1947): 285–8.

    Samuel Richardson: Printer and Novelist. Chapel Hill: University of North Carolina Press, 1936.

McMurran, Mary Helen. *The Spread of Novels: Translation and Prose Fiction in the Eighteenth Century*. Princeton: Princeton University Press, 2008.

Mello, Patrick. '"Piety and Popishness": Tolerance and the Epistolary Reaction to Richardson's *Sir Charles Grandison*'. *Eighteenth-Century Fiction* 25, no. 3 (2013): 511–31.

Meteyard, Belinda. 'Illegitimacy and Marriage in Eighteenth-Century England'. *Journal of Interdisciplinary History* 10 (1980): 479–89.

Miller, D. A. *Jane Austen, or, The Secret of Style*. Princeton: Princeton University Press, 2003.

Moler, Kenneth. *Jane Austen's Art of Allusion*. Lincoln: University of Nebraska Press, 1968.

Moody, Jane. *Illegitimate Theatre in London, 1770–1840*. Cambridge: Cambridge University Press, 2000.

Moretti, Franco. 'Serious Century'. In *The Novel, Volume 1: History, Geography, and Culture*. Edited by Franco Moretti, 364–400. Princeton: Princeton University Press, 2006.

    The Way of the World: The Bildungsroman in European Culture. London: Verso, 1987.

Morgan, Charlotte Elizabeth. *The Rise of the Novel of Manners: A Study of English Prose Fiction between 1600 and 1740*. New York: Columbia University Press, 1911.

Morrison, Paul. 'Enclosed in Openness: *Northanger Abbey* and the Domestic Carceral'. *Texas Studies in Literature and Language* 33, no. 1 (1991): 1–23.

Müller, Patrick. *Latitudinarianism and Didacticism in Eighteenth-Century Literature: Moral Theology in Fielding, Sterne, and Goldsmith.* Frankfurt: Peter Lang, 2009.

Myers, Mitzi. 'The Dilemmas of Gender as Double-Voiced Narrative; or, Maria Edgeworth Mothers the Bildungsroman'. In *The Idea of the Novel in the Eighteenth Century.* Edited by Robert W. Uphaus, 67–96. East Lansing: Colleagues, 1988.

Nestor, Deborah J. 'Virtue Rarely Rewarded: Ideological Subversion and Narrative Form in Haywood's Later Fiction'. *SEL* 34, no. 3 (1994): 579–98.

Newlyn, Lucy. *Reading, Writing and Romanticism: The Anxiety of Reception.* Oxford: Oxford University Press, 2000.

Newton, Gill. 'Clandestine Marriage in Early Modern London: When, Where and Why?' *Continuity and Change* 29, no. 2 (2014): 151–80.

Norman, Edward R. *Church and Society in England 1770–1970: A Historical Study.* Oxford: Clarendon, 1976.

Norton, Rictor. *Mother Clap's Molly House: The Gay Subculture in England, 1700–1830.* London: Gay Men's Press, 1982.

Oakleaf, David. '"Shady bowers! And purling streams! – Heavens, how insipid!": Eliza Haywood's Artful Pastoral'. In *The Passionate Fictions of Eliza Haywood: Essays on Her Life and Work.* Edited by Kirsten T. Saxon and Rebecca P. Bocchicchio, 283–99. Lexington: University of Kentucky Press, 2000.

Ogborn, Miles. 'This Most Lawless Space: The Geography of the Fleet and the Making of Lord Hardwicke's Marriage Act of 1753'. *New Formations* 37 (1999): 11–32.

O'Gorman, Frank. *The Long Eighteenth Century: British Political and Social History 1688–1832.* London: Arnold, 1997.

Oman, Carola. *David Garrick.* Suffolk: Hodder and Stoughton, 1958.

Outhwaite, R. B. *Clandestine Marriage in England, 1550–1850.* London: The Hambleton Press, 1995.

Oxford Dictionary of National Biography. Print edition edited by H. C. G. Matthew and Brian Harrison. Oxford: Oxford University Press, 2004. Online edition edited by Lawrence Goldman. www.oxforddnb.com.

Park, Julie. *The Self and It: Novel Objects in Eighteenth-Century England.* Stanford: Stanford University Press, 2010.

Parrinder, Patrick. *Nation and Novel: The English Novel from Its Origins to the Present Day.* Oxford: Oxford University Press, 2006.

Paulson, Ronald. *Don Quixote in England: The Aesthetics of Laughter.* Baltimore, MD: Johns Hopkins University Press, 1998.

'Henry Fielding and the Problem of Deism'. In *The Margins of Orthodoxy: Heterodox Writing and Cultural Response, 1660–1750.* Edited by Roger D. Lund, 247–70. Cambridge: Cambridge University Press, 1995.

Satire and the Novel in Eighteenth-Century England. New Haven: Yale University Press, 1967.

Pavel, Thomas G. *The Lives of the Novel: A History.* Princeton: Princeton University Press, 2013.

Perry, Ruth. *Novel Relations: The Transformation of Kinship in English Literature and Culture, 1748–1818*. Cambridge: Cambridge University Press, 2004.
  Women, Letters and the Novel. New York: AMS Press, 1980.
Perry, Thomas W. *Public Opinion, Propaganda, and Politics in Eighteenth-Century England: A Study of the Jew Bill of 1753*. Cambridge, MA: Harvard University Press, 1962.
Pettit, Alexander. General introduction to Samuel Richardson, *Early Works*. xxxi–civ. Cambridge: Cambridge University Press, 2012.
Pincus, Steve. *1688: The First Modern Revolution*. New Haven: Yale University Press, 2009.
Plumb, J. H. *England in the Eighteenth Century*. New York: Penguin, 1963.
Pocock, J. G. A. *The Discovery of Islands: Essays in British History*. Cambridge: Cambridge University Press, 2005.
  Virtue, Commerce, and History: Essays on Political Thought and History, Chiefly in the Eighteenth Century. Cambridge: Cambridge University Press, 1985.
Pollak, Ellen. *Incest and the English Novel 1684–1814*. Baltimore, MD: Johns Hopkins University Press, 2003.
Power, Henry. *Epic into Novel: Henry Fielding, Scriblerian Satire, and the Consumption of Classical Literature*. Oxford: Oxford University Press, 2015.
Price, Leah. '*Sir Charles Grandison* and the Executor's Hand'. *Eighteenth-Century Fiction* 8, no. 3 (1996): 329–42.
Probert, Rebecca. 'The Impact of the Marriage Act of 1753: Was It Really "A Most Cruel Law for the Fair Sex"?' *Eighteenth-Century Studies* 38, no. 2 (2005): 247–62.
  'The Judicial Interpretation of Lord Hardwicke's Act of 1753'. *Legal History* 23, no. 2 (2002): 129–51.
  Marriage Law and Practice in the Long Eighteenth Century: A Reassessment. Cambridge: Cambridge University Press, 2009.
Rabin, Dana Y. 'The Jew Bill of 1753: Masculinity, Virility, and the Nation'. *Eighteenth-Century Studies* 39, no. 2 (2006): 157–71.
Raven, John. *The Business of Books: Booksellers and the English Book Trade, 1450–1850*. New Haven: Yale University Press, 2007.
  'Historical Introduction: The Novel Comes of Age'. In *The English Novel, 1770–1829: A Bibliographical Survey of Prose Fiction Published in the British Isles. Vol. 1: 1770–1799*. Edited by Peter Garside, James Raven and Rainer Schöwerling, 15–121. Oxford: Oxford University Press, 2000.
  Judging New Wealth: Popular Publishing and Responses to Commerce in England, 1750–1800. Oxford: Clarendon, 1992.
Regis, Pamela. 'Vows in *Mansfield Park*: The Promises of Courtship'. *Persuasions* 28 (2006): 166–75.
Reynolds, Philip L. *How Marriage Became One of the Sacraments: The Sacramental Theology of Marriage from Its Medieval Origins to the Council of Trent*. Cambridge: Cambridge University Press, 2016.

Ribble, Frederick G. 'Fielding and William Young'. *Studies in Philology* 98, no. 4 (2001): 457–501.

Richetti, John J. *The English Novel in History 1700–1800*. London: Routledge, 1999.

Rivero, Albert J. *The Plays of Henry Fielding: A Critical Study of His Dramatic Career*. Charlottesville: University Press of Virginia, 1989.

Ross, Ian Simpson. *The Life of Adam Smith*. Oxford: Oxford University Press, 1996.

Rothstein, Eric and Howard D. Weinbrot. '*The Vicar of Wakefield*, Mr. Wilmot, and the "Whistonean Controversy"'. *Philological Quarterly* 55 (1976): 225–40.

Roulston, Chris. *Narrating Marriage in Eighteenth-Century England and France*. Farnham: Ashgate, 2010.

Rousseau, G. S., ed. *Oliver Goldsmith: The Critical Heritage*. London: Routledge and Kegan Paul, 1974.

Rubinstein, W. D. 'The End of "Old Corruption" in Britain 1780–1860', *Past and Present* 101, no. 1 (1983): 55–86.

Rumbold, Kate. *Shakespeare and the Eighteenth-Century Novel: Cultures of Quotation from Samuel Richardson to Jane Austen*. Cambridge: Cambridge University Press, 2016.

Ruml, Treadwell, II. 'Henry Fielding and Parson Adams: Whig Writer and Tory Priest'. *Journal of English and Germanic Philology* 97, no. 2 (1998): 205–25.

Said, Edward. 'Jane Austen and Empire'. In *Culture and Imperialism*, 95–115. London: Chatto and Windus, 1993.

Sale, William M. *Samuel Richardson: Master Printer*. Ithaca: Cornell University Press, 1950.

Schaffer, Talia. *Romance's Rival: Familiar Marriage in Victorian Fiction*. Oxford: Oxford University Press, 2016.

Schellenberg, Betty A. *The Professionalization of Women Writers in Eighteenth-Century Britain*. Cambridge: Cambridge University Press, 2010.

'Using "Femalities" to "Make Fine Men": Richardson's *Sir Charles Grandison* and the Feminization of Narrative'. *SEL* 34, no. 3 (1994): 599–616.

Schneewind, J. B. *The Invention of Autonomy: A History of Modern Moral Philosophy*. Cambridge: Cambridge University Press, 1998.

Scouten, Arthur H., ed. *The London Stage 1600–1800*, Part 3: 1729–1747. 2 vols. Carbondale: Southern Illinois University Press, 1961.

Seager, Nicholas. 'Providence, Futurity and Typology in Oliver Goldsmith's *The Vicar of Wakefield*'. In *Theology and Literature in the Age of Johnson: Resisting Secularism*. Edited by Melvyn New and S. J. Reedy, 163–82. Newark: University of Delaware Press, 2012.

Shaffer, Julie. 'Not Subordinate: Empowering Women in the Marriage-Plot: The Novels of Frances Burney, Maria Edgeworth, and Jane Austen'. *Criticism* 34, no. 1 (1992): 51–73.

Shea, Stuart. 'Subversive Didacticism in Eliza Haywood's *Betsy Thoughtless*'. *SEL* 42, no. 3 (2002): 559–75.

Sider Jost, Jacob. *Prose Immortality 1711–1819*. Charlottesville: University of Virginia Press, 2015.

Sirota, Brent S. *The Christian Monitor: The Church of England and the Age of Benevolence, 1680–1730*. New Haven: Yale University Press, 2014.

Skinner, Quentin. 'The Principles and Practices of Opposition: The Case of Bolingbroke versus Walpole'. In *Historical Perspectives: Essays in Honour of J. H. Plumb*. Edited by N. McKendrick, 93–218. London: Europa, 1974.

Smout, T. C. 'Scottish Marriage, Regular and Irregular 1550–1940'. In *Marriage and Society: Studies in the Social History of Marriage*. Edited by R. B. Outhwaite, 204–36. London: Europa, 1981.

Snell, K. D. M. *Parish and Belonging: Community, Identity and Welfare in England and Wales, 1700–1950*. Cambridge: Cambridge University Press, 2006.

Sobba Green, Katherine. *The Courtship Novel 1740–1820: A Feminized Genre*. Lexington: University of Kentucky Press, 1991.

Spaeth, Donald A. *The Church in an Age of Danger: Parsons and Parishioners, 1660–1740*. Cambridge: Cambridge University Press, 2000.

Spencer, Jane. *The Rise of the Woman Novelist: From Aphra Behn to Jane Austen*. Oxford: Basil Blackwell, 1986.

Spurr, John. 'The Church, the Societies and the Moral Revolution of 1688'. In *The Church of England c. 1689–c. 1833*. Edited by John Walsh, Colin Haydon and Stephen Taylor, 127–42. Cambridge: Cambridge University Press, 1993.

Staves, Susan. *Players' Scepters: Fictions of Authority in the Restoration*. Lincoln: University of Nebraska Press, 1979.

Stevenson, John Allen. '"A Geometry of His Own": Richardson and the Marriage Ending'. *SEL* 26, no. 3 (1986): 469–83.

Stone, George Winchester, Jr, ed. *The London Stage 1600–1800*, Part 4: 1747–1776. 3 vols. Carbondale: Southern Illinois University Press, 1962.

Stone, George Winchester, Jr, and George M. Kahrl, eds. *David Garrick: A Critical Biography*. Carbondale: Southern Illinois University Press, 1979.

Stone, Lawrence. *The Family, Sex and Marriage in England, 1500–1800*. New York: Harper & Row, 1977.

   Road to Divorce. England 1530–1987. Oxford: Oxford University Press, 1990.

   Uncertain Unions: Marriage in England 1660–1753. Oxford: Oxford University Press, 1992.

Straub, Kristina. *Divided Fictions: Fanny Burney and the Feminine Strategy*. Lexington: University of Kentucky Press, 1987.

Sussman, Charlotte. '"I Wonder Whether Poor Miss Sally Godfrey Be Living or Dead": The Married Woman and the Rise of the Novel,' *diacritics* 20, no. 1 (1990): 86–102.

Sutherland, Kathryn. 'Jane Austen and the Invention of the Serious Modern Novel'. In *The Cambridge Companion to English Literature, 1740–1830*. Edited by Thomas Keymer and Jon Mee, 244–62. Cambridge: Cambridge University Press, 2004.

   Jane Austen's Textual Lives: From Aeschylus to Bollywood. Oxford: Oxford University Press, 2007.

Sykes, Norman. *Church and State in England in the XVIII Century*. Hamden, CT: Archon Books, 1962.

Taylor, Charles. *A Secular Age*. Cambridge, MA: Belknap, Harvard University Press, 2007.

Thomason, Laura E. *The Matrimonial Trap: Eighteenth-Century Women Writers Redefine Marriage*. Lewisburg: Bucknell University Press, 2014.

Thompson, E. P. *The Poverty of Theory*. London: Merlin, 1978.

Whigs and Hunters: The Origin of the Black Act. London: Allen Lane, 1975.

Thompson, Helen. 'Betsy Thoughtless and the Persistence of Coquettish Volition'. *Journal for Early Modern Cultural Studies* 4, no. 1 (2004): 102–26.

Ingenuous Subjection: Compliance and Power in the Eighteenth-Century Domestic Novel. Philadelphia: University of Pennsylvania Press, 2005.

Trefman, Simon. *Sam. Foote, Comedian 1720–1777*. New York: New York University Press, 1971.

Uglow, Jenny. 'Fielding, Grub Street, and Canary Wharf'. In *Grub Street and the Ivory Tower: Literary Journalism and Literary Scholarship from Fielding to the Internet*. Edited by Jeremy Treglown and Bridget Bennett, 1–21. Oxford: Clarendon, 1998.

Virgin, Paul. *The Church in an Age of Negligence*. Cambridge: Cambridge University Press, 1991.

Vranjes, Vlasta. 'Jane Austen, Lord Hardwicke's Marriage Act, and the National Courtship Plot'. *CLIO* 43, no. 2 (2014): 197–223.

Walker, Eric C. *Marriage, Writing, and Romanticism: Wordsworth and Austen after War*. Stanford: Stanford University Press, 2009.

Warner, Jessica. *Craze: Gin and Debauchery in the Age of Reason*. London: Random House, 2002.

Warner, William Beatty. *Licensing Entertainment: The Elevation of Novel Reading in Britain, 1684–1750*. Berkeley: University of California Press, 1998.

Watt, Ian. *The Rise of the Novel: Studies in Defoe, Richardson and Fielding*. Berkeley: University of California Press, 1957.

Weinreb, Ben and Christopher Hibbert. *The London Encyclopaedia*. London: Macmillan, 1983.

White, Gabrielle D. V. *Jane Austen in the Context of Abolition: 'A Fling at the Slave Trade'*. New York: Palgrave Macmillan, 2006.

White, Laura Mooneyham. 'Jane Austen and the Marriage Plot: Questions of Persistence'. In *Jane Austen and the Discourses of Feminism*. Edited by Devoney Looser, 71–86. New York: St. Martin's, 1995.

Jane Austen's Anglicanism. Farnham: Ashgate, 2011.

Williams, Murial Brittain. *Marriage: Fielding's Mirror of Morality*. Tuscaloosa: University of Alabama Press, 1973.

Witte, John, Jr. 'Church, State and Marriage: Four Early Modern Protestant Models'. *Oxford Journal of Law and Religion* 1, no. 1 (2012): 1–18.

From Sacrament to Contract: Marriage, Religion, and Law in the Western Tradition. Louisville, KY: Westminster John Knox Press, 1997.

Wolff, Cynthia Griffin. *Samuel Richardson and the Eighteenth-Century Puritan Character*. Hamden, CT: Shoe String Press, 1972.

Yates, Mary V. 'The Christian Rake in *Sir Charles Grandison*'. *SEL* 24, no. 3 (1984): 545–61.

Yeazell, Ruth Bernard. *Fictions of Modesty: Women and Courtship in the English Novel*. Chicago: University of Chicago Press, 1991.

Young, B. W. *Religion and Enlightenment in Eighteenth-Century England: Theological Debate from Locke to Burke*. Oxford: Clarendon, 1998.

Zomchick, John P. *Family and the Law in Eighteenth-Century Fiction: The Public Conscience in the Private Sphere*. Cambridge: Cambridge University Press, 1993.

Index